The Cambridge Companion to Twentieth-Century Opera

This Companion celebrates the extraordinary riches of the twentieth-century operatic repertoire in a collection of specially commissioned essays written by a distinguished team of academics, critics and practitioners. Beginning with a discussion of the century's vital inheritance from late-romantic operatic traditions in Germany and Italy, the wide-ranging text embraces fresh investigations into various aspects of the genre in the modern age, with a comprehensive coverage of the work of individual composers from Debussy and Schoenberg to John Adams and Harrison Birtwistle. Traditional stylistic categorizations (including symbolism, expressionism, neo-classicism and minimalism) are reassessed from new critical perspectives, and the distinctive operatic traditions of Continental and Eastern Europe, Russia and the Soviet Union, the United Kingdom and United States are subjected to fresh scrutiny. The volume includes essays devoted to avant-garde music theatre, operettas and musicals, and filmed opera, and ends with a provocative discussion of the position of the genre in today's cultural marketplace.

The Cambridge Companion to

TWENTIETH-
CENTURY OPERA

EDITED BY

Mervyn Cooke

Professor of Music
University of Nottingham

 CAMBRIDGE
UNIVERSITY PRESS

CAMBRIDGE UNIVERSITY PRESS
Cambridge, New York, Melbourne, Madrid, Cape Town, Singapore, São Paulo

CAMBRIDGE UNIVERSITY PRESS
The Edinburgh Building, Cambridge CB2 2RU, UK

Published in the United States of America by Cambridge University Press, New York

www.cambridge.org
Information on this title: www.cambridge.org/9780521783934

First published 2005

Printed in the United Kingdom at the University Press, Cambridge

A catalogue record for this book is available from the British Library

ISBN-13 978-0-521-78009-4 hardback
ISBN-10 0-521-78009-8 hardback
ISBN-13 978-0-521-78393-4 paperback
ISBN-10 0-521-78393-3 paperback

In memory of
Anthony Pople
1955–2003

Contents

Illustrations

Notes on the contributors

Robert Adlington is Senior Lecturer in Music at the University of Nottingham. He has written widely on twentieth-century music, with a particular focus on recent British and Dutch music. His monograph *The Music of Harrison Birtwistle* was published by Cambridge University Press in 2000, and he has written articles on Birtwistle, Rebecca Saunders and the Australian Fluxus revivalists 'SLAVE PIANOS'. He has published a book on Louis Andriessen's *De Staat* (Ashgate, 2004) and is currently preparing further publications on musical life in Amsterdam in the late 1960s.

Arved Ashby is Associate Professor of Musicology at the Ohio State University. Much of his work has centered on Alban Berg and the historiography of twelve-tone music, and in 1996 he received the Alfred Einstein Award from the American Musicological Society for an article involving these subjects. He designed, edited and contributed to the recent collection *The Pleasure of Modernist Music: Listening, Meaning, Intention, Ideology* (University of Rochester Press, 2004). In addition to interests in modernism and popular culture, he has also explored the phenomenological, McCluhanesque correlations between Western concert music and the mass media. To this end, he is now working on a book entitled *Absolute Music in the Age of Mechanical Reproduction*. He wrote criticism for the *American Record Guide* from 1987 to 2001, and now contributes regularly to *Gramophone*. He also composes.

Stephen Banfield is Stanley Hugh Badock Professor of Music at the University of Bristol, having previously been Elgar Professor of Music at the University of Birmingham and, before that, lecturer, then senior lecturer in music at Keele University. He is the author of *Sensibility and English Song* (1985), *Sondheim's Broadway Musicals* (1993) and *Gerald Finzi* (1997), and editor of Volume VI of *The Blackwell History of Music in Britain* (1995). His current projects include a study of Jerome Kern, an edition of Weill's musical *Love Life* for the Kurt Weill Edition, and a history of music in the British Empire.

Rachel Beckles Willson is Senior Lecturer in Music at Royal Holloway, University of London. Her research has focused primarily on the analysis, history and performance of music in Hungary, and her work has been published in *Music Analysis*, *Music & Letters*, *Contemporary Music Review*, *Central Europe* and *Slavonica*. Her books include *Perspectives on Kurtág* (with Alan E. Williams; Guildford, 2001) and *György Kurtág's* The Sayings of Péter Bornemisza *opus 7* (Aldershot, 2003). She is currently completing *Ligeti, Kurtág and Hungarian Music during the Cold War* for Cambridge University Press.

Virgilio Bernardoni is Associate Professor of Musical Dramaturgy and of the History of Modern and Contemporary Music at the University of Bergamo, and a member of the Scientific Committee of the Centro Studi Giacomo Puccini, Lucca, for whom he edits the journal *Studi Pucciniani*. He is the author of numerous articles and essays on Italian opera, and on musical theory and pedagogy in the nineteenth and twentieth centuries. He has written and edited a number of volumes on the subject of *fin de siècle* and early twentieth-century opera in Italy: *La maschera e la favola nell'opera italiana del primo Novecento* (1986), *Puccini* (1996), *Suono, parola, scena. Studi e testi sulla musica italiana nel Novecento* (with Giorgio Pestelli, 2003), and *«L'insolita forma»: strutture e processi analitici per l'opera italiana nell'epoca di Puccini* (with Michele Girardi and Arthur Groos; special issue of *Studi Pucciniani*, 3, 2004).

Mervyn Cooke is Professor of Music at the University of Nottingham. He studied at the Royal Academy of Music and at King's College, Cambridge, and was for six years Research Fellow and Director of Music at Fitzwilliam College, Cambridge. His books include studies of Britten's *Billy Budd* and *War Requiem* (Cambridge University Press), a monograph *Britten and the Far East* (The Boydell Press), *Jazz* (World of Art) and *The Chronicle of Jazz* (both Thames & Hudson); he has also edited *The Cambridge Companion to Benjamin Britten* and (with David Horn) *The Cambridge Companion to Jazz*. He is currently writing a history of film music for Cambridge University Press, and (with Donald Mitchell and Philip Reed) is co-editor of the ongoing edition of Britten's correspondence published by Faber and Faber. He is also active as a pianist and composer, his compositions having been broadcast on BBC Radio 3 and Radio France and performed at London's South Bank and St John's Smith Square.

John Deathridge is the King Edward Professor of Music at King's College London. He was formerly Reader in Music at Cambridge University, where he was a Fellow of King's College from 1983 to 1996. His main interests are social theory, theories of the avant-garde, and German music in the nineteenth and twentieth centuries. He has published widely on Wagner in particular and is also a regular broadcaster and performer.

Marina Frolova-Walker is a lecturer in the Faculty of Music at the University of Cambridge and a Fellow of Clare College, Cambridge. She studied musicology at the Moscow Conservatoire, receiving her doctorate in 1994, and subsequently taught at the Moscow Conservatoire College, the University of Ulster, Goldsmiths' College, London and the University of Southampton. Her principal fields of research are Russian and Soviet music and nationalism in music. She has published articles in *Cambridge Opera Journal*, *Journal of the American Musicological Society* and the revised edition of *New Grove*. She is currently writing *Russia: Music and Nation* for Yale University Press.

Caroline Harvey completed a PhD on Benjamin Britten at the University of Leeds, working jointly in English and Music to explore literary, political and cultural aspects of the composer's vocal and operatic output. She has lectured on Britten's *A Midsummer Night's Dream* at the Britten–Pears School for Advanced Musical Studies, concentrating on the literary and theatrical history of the play as a background to Britten's desire to create an authentically Shakespearean libretto for his opera. She has also written on Britten's musical settings of T. S. Eliot in the Canticles and on Eliot's ambivalent views of poetry set to music, work that was published as 'Benjamin Britten and T. S. Eliot *Entre Deux Guerres* and After' in *T. S. Eliot's Orchestra*, ed. John Xiros Cooper (Garland, 2000). She lives and works in Toronto, Canada.

Guido Heldt is a lecturer in the Department of Music at the University of Bristol. He studied musicology, art history and philosophy at the University of Münster and, as a visiting student, at King's College London and Oxford University. His doctoral thesis at Münster was a study of English tone poems of the early twentieth century and competing ideas of a national music in England. He has taught at the Music Department of the Free University Berlin (1997–2003) and as a visiting professor at the History Department of Wilfrid Laurier University (2003), teaching cultural history. He is currently working on film-music analysis and narrative theory, composer biopics in German and American cinema, musical films in Nazi Germany and American popular music in German post-war film.

Elise K. Kirk is an author, lecturer and musicologist who specializes in the fields of opera and American cultural history. She is founding editor of the award-winning *Dallas Opera Magazine* and her articles have appeared in *Opera News*, *Kennedy Center Stagebill*, *The New Grove Dictionary of Opera*, *White House History* and numerous other publications. Her books include *Opera and Vivaldi*, *Musical Highlights from the White House* and *Music at the White House: A History of the American Spirit*, which won the distinguished ASCAP award from the American Society of Composers, Authors and Publishers. This book also became the subject of a documentary film aired on American public television in 2003. Her most recent book, *American Opera* (2001), is a comprehensive study of opera by American composers from 1757 to the explosion of eclectic forms that characterize the nation's opera in modern times.

Christopher Mark is Head of the Department of Music and Sound Recording at the University of Surrey. The author of *Early Benjamin Britten: A Study of Technical and Stylistic Evolution* (Garland), he has contributed chapters to *The Cambridge Companion to Benjamin Britten*, *The Cambridge Companion to Elgar* and *Tippett Studies* (also published by Cambridge University Press). He is currently completing a monograph on the music of the Anglo-Australian composer Roger Smalley, and is planning an extended study of melancholy in twentieth-century English music. In 1999 he organized the inaugural Biennial International Conference on Twentieth-Century Music, held at the University of Surrey, and is Editor-in-Chief of the journal *twentieth-century music.*

Nicholas Payne became Director of Opera Europa in 2003, since when he has concentrated on building both the membership and the services offered by this organization for professional opera companies and opera festivals throughout Europe. He joined the staff at the Royal Opera House, Covent Garden, in 1968 for the final two years of the David Webster/Georg Solti era. After a spell at the Arts Council of Great Britain during the early 1970s, he worked for four different UK opera companies over 27 consecutive years. He has been Financial Controller of Welsh National Opera, General Administrator of Leeds-based Opera North, Director of the Royal Opera Covent Garden, and General Director of English National Opera

Nigel Simeone is Professor of Historical Musicology at the University of Sheffield. He has written extensively on French music of the twentieth century and his books include *Paris: A Musical Gazetteer* (Yale University Press, 2000) and the first systematic catalogue of the music of Olivier Messiaen (Hans Schneider, 1998). He has also edited and translated correspondence by Messiaen, Poulenc and Tournemire. His articles include several on the musical life of Paris, including studies of music at the 1937 Paris Exposition, and of concert giving and music publishing under the German Occupation. He has recently completed *Messiaen* (with Peter Hill; Yale University Press, 2005), a biography which includes the first publication of diaries, letters, documents and photographs from the composer's private archives.

Alan Street is a lecturer in Music at the University of Exeter. Formerly a member of the teaching staff at the University of Keele, he has also held research posts at Clare College, Cambridge, and Yale University (where he worked with Allen Forte). A member of the Editorial Board of the journal *Music Analysis* since 1994, he became its Editor in 2005. In 1999, he was invited to become a member of the Advisory Board for the 'Composers of the Twentieth Century' series published by Yale University Press. The author of numerous articles on aspects of musical and critical theory, his most recent published work includes a contribution to *L'orizzonte filosofico del comporre nel ventesimo secolo* (Venice: Mulino, 2003), edited by Gianmario Borio.

Tom Sutcliffe is the author of *Believing in Opera* (Faber and Faber, 1996) and editor of *The Faber Book of Opera* (2000); he has contributed articles and reviews to the *Guardian*, *London Evening Standard*, *Musical Times*, *Spectator*, *Opera Now*, *Opera News*, *Opern Welt* and *Vogue*, and also edited *Music and Musicians* magazine. He chairs the music section of the Critics' Circle and has broadcast extensively. As a countertenor he has performed with Nikolaus Harnoncourt, Denis Stevens, Musica Reservata and Pro Cantione Antiqua. Since 1998 he has been working as a dramaturg for Keith Warner on opera productions in Brussels and Vienna. He has twice been awarded Leverhulme Research Fellowships, and is married to the playwright and librettist Meredith Oakes.

Chris Walton studied music at Cambridge, Oxford and Zurich universities. He spent 1989–90 at Munich University as a Research Fellow of the Alexander von Humboldt Foundation, and was from 1990 to 2001 Head of Music Division at the Zurich Central Library. He also lectured in music history at the Swiss Federal Technical University and worked as a freelance repetiteur. While in Switzerland, he chaired numerous societies and foundations, including the Allgemeine Musikgesellschaft Zurich, the world's oldest music society, of which he was made an honorary member in 2001. He has published widely on topics ranging from Swiss Renaissance music to contemporary South African composers. His current research centres on Richard Wagner and the Wesendoncks. He was appointed Professor and Head of Music Department at Pretoria University in 2001, and is currently Chairman of the African branch of RILM.

Philip Weller is a lecturer in Music at the University of Nottingham, having previously lectured at the University of Liverpool. He studied at the Universities of Cambridge, Heidelberg, Paris and London, and held a Frances A. Yates Fellowship at the Warburg Institute. His musical and research interests have centred on music in France during the Enlightenment and the first half of the twentieth century, and on the poetics of opera. He also has a continuing passion for historiographical topics, for Beethoven, and for the relationship of music to language and the theatre. His study of Segalen and Debussy appeared in *Reading Diversity*, published by Glasgow University Press in 2000, and he is currently completing critical essays on the Messiaen song cycles and the poetry of Cécile Sauvage.

Arnold Whittall is Professor Emeritus of Music Theory and Analysis at King's College London, and consultant editor for the Cambridge

University Press series 'Music in the Twentieth Century'. His writings include two substantial studies of twentieth-century music – *Musical Composition in the Twentieth Century* (Oxford University Press, 1999) and *Exploring Twentieth-Century Music: Tradition and Innovation* (Cambridge University Press, 2003) – and many articles focusing on composers of opera ranging from Wagner, Strauss, Britten and Tippett to Birtwistle and Adams. He wrote the section on the twentieth century for the article on 'Opera' in *The New Grove Dictionary of Music and Musicians*, second edition (Macmillan, 2001).

Acknowledgements

My principal debt of thanks is to Vicki Cooper – kindest and most encouraging of commissioning editors – and her staff at Cambridge University Press, without whose constant support and patience this volume could never have materialized. Special thanks are due to Becky Jones and Clive Unger-Hamilton for helping with the finishing touches and steering the book efficiently into production. Valuable advice on various aspects of the text along the way has been received from Patrick Carnegy, Eoin Coleman, Fiona Ford and Aine Sheil.

To work with such a varied and distinguished team of contributors has been a constant pleasure, and several have provided input to the project that has affected the book well beyond the confines of their individual textual contributions. In particular I am grateful to Nigel Simeone and Philip Weller, not only for their expertise and efficiency in compiling the Chronology and translating Chapter 3 respectively, but also for their characteristic blend of acumen, enthusiasm and friendship that has made our many discussions and exchanges of correspondence on all aspects of twentieth-century opera so memorable. Tom Sutcliffe has given generously of his time in helping me with various matters, and in kindly making available several of the book's illustrations. Arved Ashby deserves particular gratitude for having taken on Chapter 15 at short notice.

Thanks are due to the following for their help in sourcing illustrations, and for granting the necessary permissions for their reproduction: Daniel Cande, Wilfried Hösl, Susanne Lutz (Pressebüro, Bayerische Staatsoper), Hendrikje Mautner (Oper Frankfurt) and Professor Günther Kieser; Gisela Prossnitz, Monika Rittershaus and Ruth Walz; Dr Christopher Grogan and Dr Nick Clark (Britten–Pears Library, Aldeburgh); Deen van Meer and Lizet Kraal (GKf Amsterdam); Richard Jeffery and David Knight (BBC); Gerard Mortier, Stéphane Löber and Pierrette Chastel (Opéra Bastille); Rachel Beckles Willson and Annegret Strehle (Schott); and Margaret Williams and Michael Burt (MJW Productions).

Most importantly of all, it is a pleasure to recall the enthusiasm for the project shown by Anthony Pople, who died after he had already started work on a chapter devoted to minimalist opera that was to have formed an essential part of this collection of essays. Whilst Anthony would be endearingly intolerant of anyone who (as he would view it) wasted energy on feeling melancholy about his untimely passing, this book is affectionately dedicated to his memory with a mixed sense of both celebrating his astonishingly productive life and career – and his phenomenally indomitable high spirits, even in times of acute personal crisis – and a very real sadness that we have lost such an infectiously energetic and pleasant friend and colleague.

M. C.

A chronology of twentieth-century operatic premieres

NIGEL SIMEONE

This chronology is necessarily selective, but I have tried to include as many major operatic works as possible, especially those with any hold on the repertoire, as well as lesser-known operas which have particular national or other significance (Catalan, Finnish, Flemish, Greek, Latvian, Lithuanian, Portuguese, Romanian and Slovak operas, for instance). Some composers have established themselves firmly in the opera-going public's estimation as great exponents of the genre (notably Strauss, Puccini, Janáček, Berg, Weill and Britten), while others have written outstanding operas which are only rarely performed (Hindemith and Roussel, for example). Since the 1960s, the works of Birtwistle and Maxwell Davies, then Casken, Turnage, Macmillan, Adès and others have demonstrated that new opera in Britain is flourishing; and the same can be said of Adams and Glass in the United States, of Rihm in Germany, and so on. Earlier in the century, composers whose work is rarely seen in theatres today enjoyed immense success: the likes of Braunfels, Bruneau, Klenau, Korngold, Schreker and Wolf-Ferrari were performed widely, but of these only Korngold and Schreker are staged at all regularly now – and only then after decades of neglect.

A few works are listed here because of their originality, or their oddness: Zillig's *Das Opfer* (about Scott of the Antarctic) is written in a rigorously serial language but features a dance chorus of penguins; Pratella's *L'aviatore Dro* is a rare example of an Italian Futurist opera; Redolfi's *Crysallis* is the first sub-aquatic opera (for soprano and amphibious percussion); Blomdahl's *Aniara* is innovative – as the first 'space opera' – but it is also a work of lasting quality. Two operas have been listed because of their connections with much more famous works by Strauss: Gnecchi's *Cassandra* (1905) was at the centre of a scandal in 1909 when the Italian critic Giovanni Tebaldini drew attention to the striking similarities between Gnecchi's work and Strauss's *Elektra*, which was composed in 1906–8, after the premiere of *Cassandra*. Another work with a Strauss connection is Mariotte's *Salomé* (1908), which set the original French text of Wilde's play and was composed before Strauss's work even though it was first performed three years later. Monleone's *Cavalleria rusticana* brought about a lawsuit, since Mascagni was worried that another opera of the same name might damage the earning potential of his own *Cav* (1890). Opera is full of such strange coincidences and odd quirks of history: two operas called *Fedra* performed in Italy within a fortnight of each other in 1915, and the famous case of the two *Wozzecks*: Berg's in 1925 and Gurlitt's the following year. What became of Gurlitt? He was a pupil of Humperdinck's who settled in Japan in 1939, where he spent the rest of his life promoting German opera.

Compiling a list of this kind is a curiously fascinating activity, since the same year, or even the same month, could produce such a bewildering diversity of styles. Taking an example more or less at random, 1920 included *Der Schatzgräber*, one of Schreker's biggest successes at the time; Janáček's *The Excursions of Mr Brouček*, a stunningly original work, but one which took its composer the best part of a decade to finish; the first successful Latvian opera (*Banuta*); an Italian Futurist opera (*L'aviatore Dro*); the veteran Bruneau's *Le Roi Candaule*; and *Die tote Stadt* by Korngold. While he was still only in his early twenties, Korngold already had two significant operatic successes behind him, and *Die tote Stadt* was to be performed all over Europe and in New York within less than a decade of its simultaneous premieres in Hamburg and Cologne.

1900

14 Jan., Rome	Puccini: *Tosca*
22 Jan., Vienna	Zemlinsky: *Es war einmal*
2 Feb., Paris	Charpentier: *Louise*
22 Feb., Venice	Wolf-Ferrari: *Cenerentola*
27 Aug., Béziers	Fauré: *Prométhée*
24 Oct., Barcelona	Vives: *Euda d'Uriach*
3 Nov., Moscow	Rimsky-Korsakov: *The Tale of Tsar Saltan*
10 Nov., Milan	Leoncavallo: *Zazà*
14 Nov., Bucharest	Caudella: *Petru Rares*

1901

15 Feb., Paris	Leroux: *Astarté*
31 March, Prague	Dvořák: *Rusalka*
29 April, Paris	Bruneau: *L'Ouragon*
29 May, Dresden	Paderewski: *Manru*
9 Nov., Elberfeld	Pfitzner: *Die Rose vom Liebesgarten*
20 Nov., Paris	Massenet: *Grisélidis*
21 Nov., Dresden	Strauss: *Feuersnot*

1902

15 Feb., Leipzig	Weingartner: *Orestes*
18 Feb., Paris	Massenet: *Le Jongleur de Notre-Dame*
2 April, London	German: *Merrie England*
30 April, Paris	Debussy: *Pelléas et Mélisande*
6 Nov., Milan	Cilea: *Adriana Lecouvreur*
28 Nov., Copenhagen	Nielsen: *Saul og David*
9 Dec., St Petersburg	Nápravník: *Francesca da Rimini*
25 Dec., Moscow	Rimsky-Korsakov: *Kaschey The Immortal*

1903

7 Jan., Brussels	D'Indy: *L'Etranger*
9 Feb., Nice	Massenet: *Marie-Magdeleine*
1 Oct., Dresden	Blech: *Alpenkönig und Menschenfreund*
10 Oct., Antwerp	Gilson: *Prinses Zonnenschijn*
15 Nov., Prague	D'Albert: *Tiefland*
27 Nov., Munich	Wolf-Ferrari: *Le donne curiose*
30 Nov., Brussels	Chausson: *Le Roi Arthus*
3 Dec., Barcelona	Mánen: *Acté*
19 Dec., Milan	Giordano: *Siberia*
23 Dec., Paris	Leroux: *La Reine Fiammette*

1904

21 Jan., Brno	Janáček: *Jenůfa*
29 Jan., Hamburg	S. Wagner: *Der Kobold*
17 Feb., Milan	Puccini: *Madama Butterfly*
18 Feb., Monte Carlo	Saint-Saëns: *Hélène*
25 March, Prague	Dvořák: *Armida*
30 March, Elberfeld	Delius: *Koanga*
16 Oct., St Petersburg	Rimsky-Korsakov: *Pan Voyevoda*
30 Nov., Turin	Alfano: *Risurrezione*

1905

14 Feb., Monte Carlo	Massenet: *Chérubin*
3 March, Paris	Bruneau: *L'Enfant Roi*

16 March, Monte Carlo	Mascagni: *Amica*
14 April, Berlin	Humperdinck: *Die Heirat wider Willen*
16 April, Prague	Foerster: *Jessika*
5 Dec., Bologna	Gnecchi: *Cassandra*
9 Dec., Dresden	Strauss: *Salome*
26 Dec., Paris	Widor: *Les Pêcheurs de Saint-Jean*
30 Dec., Vienna	Lehár: *Die lustige Witwe*

1906

24 Jan., Moscow	Rakhmaninov: *The Miserly Knight* and *Francesca da Rimini*
31 Jan., Boston	Converse: *The Pipe of Desire*
19 March, Munich	Wolf-Ferrari: *I Quattro Rusteghi*
27 March, Paris	C. Erlanger: *Aphrodite*
31 Oct., Paris	Massenet: *Ariane*
11 Nov., Leipzig	Smyth: *The Wreckers*
11 Nov., Copenhagen	Nielsen: *Maskerade*

1907

2 Feb., Paris	Bruneau: *Naïs Micoulin*
5 Feb., Amsterdam	Monleone: *Cavalleria rusticana*
7 Feb., Monte Carlo	Massenet: *Thérèse*
20 Feb., St Petersburg	Rimsky-Korsakov: *The Legend of the Invisible City of Kitezh*
21 Feb., Berlin	Delius: *A Village Romeo and Juliet*
10 May, Paris	Dukas: *Ariane et Barbe-bleue*
5 June, Paris	Messager: *Fortunio*
2 Nov., Vienna	Fall: *Die Dollarprinzessin*
6 Nov., Paris	Leroux: *Le Chemineau*

1908

2 Jan., Vienna	Goldmark: *Ein Wintermärchen*
18 June, Viipuri	Merikanto: *Pohjan Neito*
30 Oct., Lyon	Mariotte: *Salomé*
4 Nov., Hamburg	Blech: *Versiegelt*
14 Nov., Vienna	O. Straus: *Der tapfere Soldat*

1909

10 Jan., Paris	H. Février: *Monna Vanna*
25 Jan., Dresden	Strauss: *Elektra*
9 Feb., Nice	Nougès: *Quo Vadis*
25 March, Stuttgart	Braunfels: *Prinzessin Brambilla*
7 Oct., Moscow	Rimsky-Korsakov: *The Golden Cockerel*
4 Dec., Munich	Wolf-Ferrari: *Il segreto di Susanna*
8 Dec., Paris	Séverac: *Le Coeur du moulin*

1910

23 Jan., Karlsruhe	S. Wagner: *Banadietrich*
19 Feb., Monte Carlo	Massenet: *Don Quichotte*
12 April, Vienna	Bittner: *Der Musikant*
17 Nov., Helsinki	Merikanto: *Elinan Surma*
30 Nov., Paris	Bloch: *Macbeth*
2 Dec., Vienna	Zemlinsky: *Kleider machen Leute*
10 Dec., New York	Puccini: *La fanciulla del West*
28 Dec., New York	Humperdinck: *Königskinder*

1911

26 Jan., Dresden	Strauss: *Der Rosenkavalier*
3 March, Boston	Converse: *The Sacrifice*
19 May, Paris	Ravel: *L'Heure espagnole*
2 June, Buenos Aires	Mascagni: *Isabeau*
14 Oct., Milan	Zandonai: *Conchita*
9 Nov., Vienna	Bittner: *Der Bergsee*
23 Nov., Vienna	Kienzl: *Der Kuhreigen*
15 Dec., Paris	Magnard: *Bérénice*
23 Dec., Berlin	Wolf-Ferrari: *I gioielli della Madonna*

1912

18 Jan., Frankfurt	Waltershausen: *Oberst Chabert*
1 Feb., Nancy	Ropartz: *Le Pays*
7 Feb., Paris	Lazzari: *La Lépreuse*

17 Feb., Monte Carlo	Massenet: *Roma*
14 March, New York	Parker: *Mona*
13 April, Hamburg	Busoni: *Die Brautwahl*
15 June, London	Holbrooke: *The Children on Don*
18 Aug., Frankfurt	Schreker: *Der ferne Klang*
16 Sept., London	Leoncavallo: *Zingari*
25 Oct., Stuttgart	Strauss: *Ariadne auf Naxos* (first version)

1913

22 Jan., Dresden	Dohnányi: *Tante Simona*
4 March, Monte Carlo	Fauré: *Pénélope*
15 March, Vienna	Schreker: *Das Spielwerk und die Prinzessin*
1 April, Nice	Falla: *La vida breve*
10 April, Milan	Montemezzi: *L'amore di tre Re*
4 June, Paris	Charpentier: *Julien ou La Vie du Poète*
5 June, Paris	Mussorgsky: *Khovanschina* (rev. Stravinsky and Ravel)
4 Dec., Dresden	Wolf-Ferrari: *L'amore medico*
15 Dec., Milan	Mascagni: *Parisina*

1914

10 Feb., Milan	Smareglia: *L'abisso*
19 Feb., Turin	Zandonai: *Francesca da Rimini*
1 April, Vienna	Schmidt: *Notre Dame*
19 April, Dessau	Sinding: *Der heilige Berg*
15 May, Paris	Rabaud: *Mârouf, Savetier du Caire*
17 May, Darmstadt	Weingartner: *Kain und Abel*
26 May, Paris	Stravinsky: *Le Rossignol*
11 June, Leipzig	Graener: *Don Juans letztes Abenteuer*
4 July, London	Holbrooke: *Dylan, Son of the Wave*
26 Aug., Glastonbury	Boughton: *The Immortal Hour*

1915

20 March, Milan	Pizzetti: *Fedra*
3 April, Rome	Romani: *Fedra*

1 July, Los Angeles	Parker: *Fairyland*
26 Sept., Stuttgart	Schillings: *Mona Lisa*
10 Oct., Prague	Novák: *The Imp of Zvíkov*

1916

14 Jan., London	Stanford: *The Critic or An Opera Rehearsed*
28 Jan., London	Smyth: *The Boatswain's Mate*
28 Jan., New York	Granados: *Goyescas*
23 Feb., Darmstadt	Weingartner: *Dame Kobold*
5 March, Dresden	D'Albert: *Die toten Augen*
11 March, Athens	Kalomiris: *The Master Builder*
28 March, Munich	Korngold: *Violanta* and *Der Ring des Polykrates*
4 Oct., Vienna	Strauss: *Ariadne auf Naxos* (revised version)
15 Oct., Darmstadt	Bittner: *Das höllisch Gold*
18 Nov., Prague	Novák: *Karlstejn*
5 Dec., London	Holst: *Sāvitri*
6 Dec., Vienna	Kienzl: *Das Testament*
25 Dec., Paris	Bruneau: *Les Quatre journées*

1917

20 Jan., Vienna	Oberleithner: *Der eiserne Heiland*
30 Jan., Stuttgart	Zemlinsky: *Eine florentinische Tragödie*
8 March, New York	De Koven: *The Canterbury Pilgrims*
27 March, Monte Carlo	Puccini: *La rondine*
30 April, Rome	Mascagni: *Lodoletta*
11 May, Zurich	Busoni: *Turandot* and *Arlecchino*
12 June, Munich	Pfitzner: *Palestrina*
8 Dec., Athens	Kalomiris: *The Mother's Ring*
11 Dec., Dresden	Pfitzner: *Das Christelflein*

1918

25 April, Frankfurt	Schreker: *Die Gezeichneten*
24 May, Budapest	Bartók: *Bluebeard's Castle*
28 Sept., Lausanne	Stravinsky: *L'Histoire du Soldat*

5 Nov., Karlsruhe	S. Wagner: *Schwarzschwanenreich*
11 Dec., Berne	Wehrli: *Das heisse Eisen*
14 Dec., New York	Puccini: *Il tabarro*, *Suor Angelica* and *Gianni Schicchi* ('Il Trittico')

1919

7 April, Birmingham	Messager: *Monsieur Beaucaire*
16 April, Zurich	Schoeck: *Don Ranudo*
10 Oct., Vienna	Strauss: *Die Frau ohne Schatten*
21 Oct., Frankfurt	Delius: *Fennimore and Gerda*

1920

2 Jan., New York	De Koven: *Rip van Winkle*
21 Jan., Frankfurt	Schreker: *Der Schatzgräber*
29 Jan., Darmstadt	Reznicek: *Ritter Blaubart*
30 Jan., Helsinki	Merikanto: *Regina von Emmeritz*
23 April, Prague	Janáček: *The Excursions of Mr Brouček*
13 May, Vienna	Weingartner: *Die Dorfschule* and *Meister Andrea*
29 May, Riga	Kalnins: *Banuta*
1 July, Frankfurt	R. Stephan: *Die ersten Menschen*
10 July, Paris	Malipiero: *Sette canzoni*
4 Sept., Lugo di Romagna	Pratella: *L'aviatore Dro*
1 Dec., Paris	Bruneau: *Le Roi Candaule*
4 Dec., Cologne and Hamburg	Korngold: *Die tote Stadt* (simultaneous premieres)
4 Dec., Munich	Braunfels: *Die Vögel*
9 Dec., London	Somerville: *David Garrick*

1921

16 Feb., Kaunas	Petrauskas: *Birute*
14 March, Paris	Dupont: *Antar*
15 May, Hanover	Wellesz: *Die Prinzessin Girnara*

4 June, Stuttgart	Hindemith: *Mörder, Hoffnung der Frauen* and *Das Nusch-Nuschi*
11 June, Mézières	Honegger: *Le Roi David*
23 Nov., Brno	Janáček: *Kát'a Kabanová*
10 Dec., Bologna	Alfano: *La leggenda di Sakuntala*
30 Dec., Chicago	Prokofiev: *The Love for Three Oranges*

1922

14 Feb., Rome	Zandonai: *Giulietta e Romeo*
26 March, Frankfurt	Hindemith: *Sancta Susanna*
10 May, Zurich	Schoeck: *Venus*
13 May, Warsaw	Szymanowski: *Hagith*
18 May, Paris	Stravinsky: *Renard*
28 May, Cologne	Zemlinsky: *Der Zwerg*
3 June, Paris	Stravinsky: *Mavra* (stage premiere)
11 June, London	Vaughan Williams: *The Shepherds of the Delectable Mountains*
16 Dec., Milan	Pizzetti: *Dèbora e Jaéle*
19 Dec., Berlin	Schmidt: *Fredigundis*
29 Dec., Paris	Cras: *Polyphème*

1923

23 March, Seville	Falla: *El retablo de Maese Pedro* (concert performance)
26 April, Milan	Respighi: *Belfagor*
29 April, Düsseldorf	Gál: *Die heilige Ente*
13 May, Prague	Novák: *Lucerna*
14 May, London	Holst: *The Perfect Fool*
1 June, Paris	Roussel: *Padmâvatî*
4 June, Birmingham	Smyth: *Fête galante*
25 June, Paris	Falla: *El retablo de Maese Pedro* (private stage premiere)
27 Oct., Berlin	Reznicek: *Holofernes*
10 Nov., Budapest	Hubay: *Anna Karenina*
15 Nov., Prague	Foerster: *The Heart*
8 Dec., Paris	Milhaud: *La Brebis égarée*

1924

19 March, Paris	Tournemire: *Les Dieux sont morts*
20 March, Mannheim	Wellesz: *Alkestis*
27 March, Cologne	Schreker: *Irrelohe*
24 April, Paris	Berners: *Le Carosse du Saint-Sacrement*
1 May, Milan	Boito: *Nerone*
6 June, Prague	Schoenberg: *Erwartung*
9 June, Frankfurt	Křenek: *Der Sprung über den Schatten*
4 July, London	Vaughan Williams: *Hugh the Drover*
21 Aug., Glastonbury	Boughton: *The Queen of Cornwall*
27 Sept., Birmingham	Bantock: *The Seal Woman*
14 Oct., Vienna	Schoenberg: *Die glückliche Hand*
21 Oct., Berlin	Křenek: *Zwingburg*
25 Oct., Helsinki	Madetoja: *Pohjalaisia*
4 Nov., Dresden	Strauss: *Intermezzo*
6 Nov., Brno	Janáček: *The Cunning Little Vixen*

1925

23 Jan., Stockholm	Atterberg: *Bäckahästen*
19 Feb., Venice	Wolf-Ferrari: *Gli amanti sposi*
7 March, Milan	Zandonai: *I cavalieri di Ekebù*
21 March, Monte Carlo	Ravel: *L'Enfant et les sortilèges*
3 April, Manchester	Holst: *At the Boar's Head*
21 May, Dresden	Busoni: *Doktor Faust*
1 June, Paris	Roussel: *La Naissance de la lyre*
30 Oct., Düsseldorf	Malipiero: *L'Orfeide*
11 Nov., Brno	Janáček: *Sarka*
14 Dec., Berlin	Berg: *Wozzeck*

1926

13 Feb., Monte Carlo	Honegger: *Judith*
27 March, Dresden	Weill: *Der Protagonist*
22 April, Bremen	Gurlitt: *Wozzeck*
25 April, Milan	Puccini: *Turandot*
4 May, Venice	Castelnuovo-Tedesco: *La Mandragola*
7 May, Brussels	Milhaud: *Les Malheurs d'Orphée*
19 June, Warsaw	Szymanowski: *King Roger*

16 Oct., Budapest	Kodály: *Háry János*
9 Nov., Dresden	Hindemith: *Cardillac*
14 Nov., Frankfurt	D'Albert: *Der Golem*
27 Nov., Kassel	Křenek: *Orpheus und Eurydike*
18 Dec., Brno	Janáček: *The Makropulos Affair*

1927

8 Jan., Dresden	Schoeck: *Penthesilea*
28 Jan., Paris	Ibert: *Angélique*
10 Feb., Leipzig	Křenek: *Jonny spielt auf*
17 Feb., Dresden and Breslau	Graener: *Hanneles Himmelfahrt* (simultaneous premieres)
17 Feb., New York	D. Taylor: *The King's Henchman*
2 March, Berlin	Weill: *Royal Palace*
17 March, Baku	Glière: *Shakh-Senem*
7 April, Paris	Gaubert: *Naïla*
27 April, Prague	Weinberger: *Schwanda the Bagpiper*
5 May, Turin	Alfano: *Madonna Imperia*
30 May, Paris	Stravinsky: *Oedipus Rex* (concert performance)
17 July, Baden-Baden	Milhaud: *L'Enlèvement d'Europe*
	Toch: *Die Prinzessin auf der Erbse*
	Hindemith: *Hin und zurück*
18 July, Berlin	Weill: *Mahagonny-Songspiel*
7 Oct., Hamburg	Korngold: *Das Wunder der Heliane*
18 Nov., Hamburg	Respighi: *La campana sommersa*
5 Dec., Paris	Samuel-Rousseau: *Le Bon Roi Dagobert*
16 Dec., Paris	Milhaud: *Le Pauvre matelot*
28 Dec., Brussels	Honegger: *Antigone*
29 Dec., Milan	Wolf-Ferrari: *Sly*

1928

16 Jan., Paris (Opéra)	Lazzari: *La Tour de feu*
16 Jan., Paris (Opéra-Comique)	Bruneau: *Angelo, Tyran de Padoue*
31 Jan., Weimar	A. Tcherepnin: *Ol-Ol*
18 Feb., Leipzig	Weill: *Der Zar lässt sich photographieren*
23 Feb., Vienna	Stravinsky: *Oedipus Rex* (stage premiere)
8 March, Mainz	Malipiero: *Il finto Arlecchino*

24 March, Antwerp	Lilien: *Beatrix*
31 March, Prague	Malipiero: *Filomela e l'Infatuato*
20 April, Wiesbaden	Milhaud: *L'Abandon d'Ariane* and *La Délivrance de Thésée*
5 May, Brno	Martinů: *The Soldier and the Dancer*
6 May, Wiesbaden	Křenek: *Schwergewicht*, *Der Diktator* and *Das geheime Königreich*
15 May, Bucharest	Dragoi: *Napasta*
16 May, Milan	Pizzetti: *Fra Gherardo*
6 June, Dresden	Strauss: *Die ägyptische Helena*
9 June, Lisbon	Coelho: *Belkiss*
28 July, Baden-Baden	Hindemith: *Lehrstück*
31 Aug., Berlin	Weill: *Die Dreigroschenoper*
8 Oct., Prague	Jeremias: *The Brothers Karamazov*
27 Oct., Barcelona	Toldrá: *El Giravolt de Maig*
1 Dec., Leipzig	D'Albert: *Die schwarze Orchidee*
19 Dec., Copenhagen	Høffding: *The Emperor's New Clothes*

1929

1 Feb., Huddersfield	Holbrooke: *Bronwen*
9 Feb., Budapest	Dohnányi: *The Tenor*
21 March, London	Vaughan Williams: *Sir John in Love*
3 April, Paris	Canteloube: *Le Mas*
13 April, Duisburg	Brand: *Maschinist Hopkins*
23 April, Edinburgh	Tovey: *The Bride of Dionysus*
29 April, Brussels	Prokofiev: *The Gambler*
7 May, Ljubljana	Kogoj: *Black Masks*
8 June, Berlin	Hindemith: *Neues vom Tage*
25 June, London	Goossens: *Judith*
2 Sept., Berlin	Weill: *Happy End*
27 Nov., Brno	Křička: *Bílý Pán*

1930

15 Jan., Paris	Ibert: *Le Roi d'Yvetot*
18 Jan., Leningrad	Shostakovich: *The Nose*
19 Jan., Leipzig	Křenek: *Leben des Orest*
1 Feb., Frankfurt	Schoenberg: *Von heute auf morgen*
9 March, Leipzig	Weill: *Aufstieg und Fall der Stadt Mahagonny*

12 April, Brno	Janáček: *From the House of the Dead*
19 April, Naples	Alfano: *L'ultimo Lord*
29 April, Rome	Pizzetti: *Lo straniero*
5 May, Berlin	Milhaud: *Christophe Colomb*
24 May, Gera	Zádor: *X-mal Rembrandt*
25 May, Frankfurt	Antheil: *Transatlantic*
2 June, Paris	Delannoy: *Le Fou de la Dame*
	Rosenthal: *Rayons de Soieries*
8 June, Königsberg	Toch: *Des Fächer*
21 June, Berlin	Hindemith: *Wir bauen eine Stadt*
23 June, Berlin Radio	Weill: *Der Jasager*
3 Oct., Dresden	Schoeck: *Vom Fischer un syner Fru*
11 Nov., Dresden	Reznicek: *Spiel oder Ernst?*
	Lothar: *Lord Spleen*
29 Nov., Brno	Gotovac: *Morana*
10 Dec., Berlin	Rathaus: *Fremde Erde*
10 Dec., Chicago	Forest: *Camille*
12 Dec., Paris	Honegger: *Les Aventures du Roi Pausole*

1931

7 Jan., Paris	Bruneau: *Virginie*
26 Feb., Budapest	Hubay: *The Mask*
28 Feb., Munich	Weinberger: *Die geliebte Stimme*
4 March, Liège	Ysaÿe: *Piér le Houïeu*
5 March, Rome	Wolf-Ferrari: *La vedova scaltra*
17 May, Munich	Hába: *The Mother*
20 June, Vienna	Wellesz: *Die Bakchantinnen*
23 June, Paris	Honegger: *Amphion*
12 Nov., Berlin and Munich	Pfitzner: *Das Herz* (simultaneous premieres)
13 Nov., Schwerin	Graener: *Friedmann Bach*
19 Nov., New York	Gruenberg: *Jack and the Beanstalk*

1932

5 Jan., Paris	Milhaud: *Maximilien*
27 Jan., Brno	Schulhoff: *Flames*
14 Feb., Mannheim	Goldschmidt: *Der gewaltige Hahnrei*

10 March, Berlin	Weill: *Die Bürgschaft*
17 March, Rome	Casella: *La donna serpente*
8 April, Munich	Heger: *Der Bettler Namenlos*
24 April, Budapest	Kodály: *The Spinning Room*
6 Sept., Venice	Casella: *La favola d'Orfeo*
29 Sept., Dresden	D'Albert: *Mister Wu*
29 Oct., Berlin	Schreker: *Der Schmied von Gent*

1933

7 Jan., New York	Gruenberg: *Emperor Jones*
16 Feb., Kaunas	Karnavicius: *Grazina*
18 Feb., Leipzig, Magdeburg, Erfurt	Weill: *Der Silbersee* (simultaneous premieres)
17 March, Vienna	A. Tcherepnin: *Die Hochzeit der Sobeide*
13 June, Amsterdam	Pijper: *Halewijn*
26 June, Paris	Canteloube: *Vercingétorix*
1 July, Dresden	Strauss: *Arabella*
9 Sept., Riga	Kalnins: *The Country's Awakening*
14 Oct., Zurich	Zemlinsky: *Der Kreidekreis*
4 Nov., Stuttgart	Klenau: *Michael Kohlhaas*

1934

13 Jan., Braunschweig	Malipiero: *La favola del figlio cambiato*
22 Jan., Leningrad	Shostakovich: *Lady Macbeth of Mtsensk*
23 Jan., Rome	Respighi: *La fiamma*
27 Jan., Stockholm	Atterberg: *Fanal*
8 Feb., Hartford, Conn.	Thomson: *Four Saints in Three Acts* (New York premiere 20 Feb.)
10 Feb., New York	Hanson: *Merry Mount*
28 Feb., New York	Antheil: *Helen Retires*
13 March, Brno Radio	Janáček: *Fate*
30 April, Paris	Stravinsky: *Perséphone*

1935

16 Jan., Milan	Mascagni: *Nerone*
17 Feb., Helsinki	Madetoja: *Juha*

20 Feb., Dresden	Wagner-Régeny: *Der Günstling*
23 Feb., Brno	Martinů: *Plays about Mary*
21 March, Paris	Hahn: *Le Marchand de Venise*
22 May, Frankfurt	Egk: *Die Zaubergeige*
24 June, Dresden	Strauss: *Die schweigsame Frau*
28 June, London	Weill: *A Kingdom for a Cow*
30 Sept., Boston	Gershwin: *Porgy and Bess* (New York premiere 10 Oct.)
22 Oct., Leningrad	Dzerzhinsky: *Quiet Flows the Don*

1936

22 Jan., Rome	Alfano: *Cyrano de Bergerac*
8 Feb., Genoa	Malipiero: *Giulio Cesare*
12 Feb., Milan	Wolf-Ferrari: *Il campiello*
10 March, Paris	Enesco: *Oedipe*
18 May, London	Vaughan Williams: *The Poisoned Kiss*
26 May, Frankfurt	Reutter: *Doktor Johannes Faust*
15 Oct., Berne Radio	Sutermeister: *Die schwarze Spinne*
14 Nov., Olomouc	Roussel: *Le Testament de la Tante Caroline*
19 Nov., New York	Weill: *Johnny Johnson*

1937

4 Jan., New York	Weill: *The Eternal Road*
23 Jan., Berlin	Klenau: *Rembrandt van Rijn*
24 Feb., Milan	Respighi: *Lucrezia*
2 March, Dresden	Schoeck: *Massimilla Doni*
10 March, Monte Carlo	Honegger and Ibert: *L'Aiglon*
18 March, Prague Radio	Martinů: *Comedy on the Bridge*
1 April, Philadelphia	Menotti: *Amelia goes to the Ball* (New York premiere 11 April)
21 April, New York	Copland: *The Second Hurricane*
24 April, Rome	Ghislanzoni: *Re Lear*
19 May, Florence	Casella: *Il deserto tentato*
2 June, Zurich	Berg: *Lulu*
8 June, Frankfurt	Orff: *Carmina Burana*
16 June, New York	Blitzstein: *The Cradle will Rock*
24 June, London	Goossens: *Don Juan de Mañara*

12 Nov., Hamburg	Zillig: *Das Opfer*
18 Nov., Vienna	Weinberger: *Wallenstein*
24 Nov., Kassel	J. Haas: *Tobias Wunderlich*
1 Dec., London	Vaughan Williams: *Riders to the Sea*

1938

1 Feb., Paris	Milhaud: *Esther de Carpentras* (stage premiere)
13 Feb., Paris	Honegger and Ibert: *Les Petites Cardinal*
21 Feb., London	Holst: *The Wandering Scholar*
22 Feb., Leningrad	Kabalevsky: *Colas Breugnon*
16 March, Prague	Martinů: *Julietta*
2 April, Brno	P. Haas: *The Charlatan*
28 May, Zurich	Hindemith: *Mathis der Maler*
15 June, Prague	Křenek: *Karl V.*
24 July, Munich	Strauss: *Friedenstag*
15 Oct., Dresden	Strauss: *Daphne*
24 Nov., Berlin	Egk: *Peer Gynt*

1939

28 Jan., Berlin	Wagner-Régeny: *Die Bürger von Calais*
1 Feb., Milan	Wolf-Ferrari: *La dama boba*
5 Feb., Munich	Orff: *Der Mond*
16 March, Paris	Sauguet: *La Chartreuse de Parme*
29 March, Berlin	Klenau: *Elisabeth von England*
22 April, NBC Radio	Menotti: *The Old Maid and the Thief*
18 May, New York	Moore: *The Devil and Daniel Webster*
7 Oct., Antwerp	Milhaud: *Médée*
7 Oct., Stockholm	Korngold: *Die Kathrin*
9 Dec., Bologna	Pratella: *La leggenda di San Fabiano*

1940

6 April, Rio de Janeiro	Villa-Lobos: *Izaht* (concert performance)
13 April, Dresden	Sutermeister: *Romeo und Julia*

18 May, Florence	Dallapiccola: *Volo di notte*
23 June, Moscow	Prokofiev: *Semyon Kotko*

1941

5 Feb., Wuppertal	Blacher: *Fürstin Tarakanowa*
4 April, Vienna	Wagner-Régeny: *Johanna Balk*
5 May, New York	Britten: *Paul Bunyan*

1942

28 March, Zurich	Martin: *Le Vin herbé* (concert performance)
15 April, Strasbourg	Bresgen: *Dornröschen*
30 April, Dresden	Sutermeister: *Die Zauberinsel*
25 July, Paris	Delannoy: *Ginevra*
7 Oct., Frankfurt	Reutter: *Odysseus*
28 Oct., Munich	Strauss: *Capriccio*
18 Nov., Parma	Rota: *Ariodante*

1943

31 Jan., Göttingen	Bresgen: *Das Urteil des Paris*
20 Feb., Frankfurt	Orff: *Die Kluge*
23 Sept., Theresienstadt	Krása: *Brundibár*
6 Nov., Leipzig	Orff: *Catulli Carmina*

1944

2 July, Dresden	J. Haas: *Die Hochzeit des Jobs*
4 July, Paris	Sauguet: *La Gageure imprévue*
16 Oct., Moscow	Prokofiev: *War and Peace* (concert performance)

1945

7 June, London	Britten: *Peter Grimes*
8 Sept., Prague	I. Krejčí: *Scandal in Ephesus*
18 Dec., Athens	Kalomiris: *Anatoli*

1946

5 May, Prague	Prokofiev: *The Betrothal in a Monastery*
8 May, New York	Menotti: *The Medium*
12 July, Glyndebourne	Britten: *The Rape of Lucretia*
16 Dec., Philadelphia	Weill: *Street Scene* (New York premiere 9 Jan. 1947)

1947

2 Jan., Milan	Pizzetti: *L'Orò*
18 Feb., New York	Menotti: *The Telephone*
7 May, New York	Thomson: *The Mother of Us All*
3 June, Paris	Poulenc: *Les Mamelles de Tirésias*
15 June, Stuttgart	Orff: *Die Bernauerin*
20 June, Glyndebourne	Britten: *Albert Herring*
6 Aug., Salzburg	Einem: *Dantons Tod*
2 Nov., Moscow	Kabalevsky: *Taras and His Family*

1948

25 Jan., Göttingen	Reutter: *Der Weg nach Freudenstadt*
24 May, Cambridge	Gay arr. Britten: *The Beggar's Opera*
15 July, Bloomington, Indiana	Weill: *Down in the Valley*
26 July, Los Angeles	Villa-Lobos: *Magdalena*
15 Aug., Salzburg	Martin: *Le Vin herbé* (stage premiere)
14 Oct., Stockholm	Sutermeister: *Raskolnikoff*
3 Dec., Leningrad	Prokofiev: *The Story of a Real Man* (private performance)
18 Dec., Berlin	Egk: *Circe*

1949

29 Jan., Strasbourg	Delannoy: *Puck*
23 Feb., BBC Radio	Gerhard: *The Duenna* (concert performance)
14 June, Aldeburgh	Britten: *The Little Sweep*
9 Aug., Salzburg	Orff: *Antigonae*
29 Sept., London	Bliss: *The Olympians*

30 Oct., New York	Weill: *Lost in the Stars*
31 Oct., New York	Blitzstein: *Regina*
1 Dec., RAI broadcast	Dallapiccola: *Il prigioniero*
10 Dec., Bratislava	Suchoň: *The Whirlpool*

1950

29 Jan., Strasbourg	Arrieu: *Noé*
1 March, Philadelphia	Menotti: *The Consul* (New York premiere 15 March)
12 May, Paris	Milhaud: *Bolivar*
20 May, Florence	Dallapiccola: *Il prigioniero* (stage premiere)
9 Aug., Salzburg	Blacher: *Romeo und Julia* (stage premiere)
30 Oct., Rome	Dallapiccola: *Job*

1951

9 March, Paris	Tailleferre: *Il était un petit navire*
11 April, Monte Carlo	Tailleferre: *Parfums*
26 April, London	Vaughan Williams: *The Pilgrim's Progress*
1 June, Paris	Bondeville: *Madame Bovary*
11 Sept., Venice	Stravinsky: *The Rake's Progress*
22 Nov., Stockholm	Sutermeister: *Der rote Stiefel*
1 Dec., London	Britten: *Billy Budd*
24 Dec., NBC TV	Menotti: *Amahl and the Night Visitors*

1952

17 Feb., Hanover	Henze: *Boulevard Solitude*
26 March, Basle	Liebermann: *Leonore 40/45*
12 June, Waltham, Mass.	Bernstein: *Trouble in Tahiti*
14 Aug., Salzburg	Strauss: *Die Liebe der Danae* (original premiere cancelled in 1944)

1953

13 Feb., Milan	Orff: *Trionfo di Afrodite*
8 June, London	Britten: *Gloriana*
28 June, Frankfurt Radio	Blacher: *Abstrakte Oper No. 1*

1954

1 April, New York	Copland: *The Tender Land*
1 June, Jerusalem	Milhaud: *David*
17 June, Aldeburgh	Berkeley: *A Dinner Engagement*
20 June, Frankfurt	Reutter: *Die Brücke von San Luis Rey*
17 Aug., Salzburg	Liebermann: *Penelope*
14 Sept., Venice	Britten: *The Turn of the Screw*
22 Sept., London	Berkeley: *Nelson*
3 Dec., London	Walton: *Troilus and Cressida*
27 Dec., New York	Menotti: *The Saint of Bleecker Street*

1955

27 Jan., London	Tippett: *The Midsummer Marriage*
11 March, Brussels	Tansman: *Le Serment*
21 April, Palermo	Rota: *Il cappello di paglia di Firenze*
17 Aug., Salzburg	Egk: *Irische Legende*
14 Sept., Venice	Prokofiev: *The Fiery Angel* (first complete staged performance)
17 Oct., Hamburg	Křenek: *Pallas Athene weint*
26 Nov., Moscow	Kabalevsky: *Nikita Vershinin*
3 Dec., Louisville	Liebermann: *The School for Wives*

1956

1 Feb., Nancy	Landowski: *Le Fou*
24 Feb., Tallahassee	Floyd: *Susannah*
17 June, Vienna	Martin: *Der Sturm*
23 Sept., Berlin	Henze: *König Hirsch*
2 Oct., London	Berkeley: *Ruth*
29 Oct., Boston	Bernstein: *Candide* (New York premiere 1 Dec.)

1957

26 Jan., Milan	Poulenc: *Dialogues des Carmélites* (in Italian; French premiere Paris, 21 June)
9 May, Schwetzingen	Egk: *Der Revisor*

6 June, Zurich	Schoenberg: *Moses und Aron*
8 June, Cologne	Fortner: *Bluthochzeit*
11 Aug., Munich	Hindemith: *Die Harmonie der Welt*

1958

15 Jan., New York	Barber: *Vanessa*
1 March, Milan	Pizzetti: *Assassinio nella cattedrale*
18 June, Aldeburgh	Britten: *Noye's Fludde*
3 Oct., Berlin	Milhaud: *Fiesta*
13 Dec., Rio de Janeiro	Villa-Lobos: *Izaht* (stage premiere)

1959

24 Jan., Moscow	Shostakovich: *Moscow, Cheryomushki*
6 Feb., Paris	Poulenc: *La Voix humaine*
9 March, New York	Blitzstein: *Juno*
31 May, Stockholm	Blomdahl: *Aniara*
10 June, Swiss Television	Sutermeister: *Seraphine*
17 June, Spoleto	Barber: *A Hand of Bridge*
11 Dec., Stuttgart	Orff: *Oedipus der Tyrann*
15 Dec., Moscow	Prokofiev: *War and Peace* (first staged performance in relatively complete form)

1960

10 March, Bratislava	Suchoň: *Svätopluk*
22 May, Hamburg	Henze: *Der Prinz von Homburg*
11 June, Aldeburgh	Britten: *A Midsummer Night's Dream*
15 Aug., Salzburg	Martin: *Le Mystère de la Nativité*
30 Sept., Paris RFT broadcast	Tailleferre: *La Petite sirène*
13 Nov., BBC Radio	Britten: *Billy Budd* (premiere of revised version in two acts)

1961

25 Feb., Bielefeld	Mihalovici: *Krapp ou La dernière bande*
3 March, Paris	Tansman: *Sabbataï Zévi*

9 June, Zurich	Martinů: *The Greek Passion*
17 Dec., Mannheim	Hindemith: *The Long Christmas Dinner*

1962

29 May, Coventry	Tippett: *King Priam*
14 June, CBS (TV broadcast)	Stravinsky: *The Flood*
18 June, Milan	Falla: *Atálantida* (stage premiere)

1963

23 April, Geneva	Martin: *Monsieur de Pourceaugnac*
6 May, Milan	Berio: *Passaggio*
2 July, London	Williamson: *Our Man in Havana*

1964

11 June, Aldeburgh	Williamson: *English Eccentrics*
12 June, Orford	Britten: *Curlew River*
24 July, Buenos Aires	Ginastera: *Don Rodrigo*
6 Sept., ZDF (TV broadcast)	Sutermeister: *Das Gespenst von Canterville*
17 Sept., Hamburg	Einem: *Der Zerrissene*
12 Nov., London	Maw: *One Man Show*

1965

15 Feb., Cologne	Zimmermann: *Die Soldaten*
24 Feb., London	R. R. Bennett: *The Mines of Sulphur*
7 April, Berlin	Henze: *Der junge Lord*
11 April, New York	Rorem: *Miss Julie*
22 May, Farnham	Williamson: *The Happy Prince*
22 July, Nice	Tansman: *L'Usignolo di Boboli*

1966

4 Feb., Hamburg	Blacher: *Zwischenfälle bei einer Notlandung*
9 June, Orford	Britten: *The Burning Fiery Furnace*

13 June, Geneva	Milhaud: *La Mère coupable*
7 July, Cheltenham	Crosse: *Purgatory*
6 Aug., Salzburg	Henze: *The Bassarids*
16 Sept., New York	Barber: *Antony and Cleopatra*
8 Oct., Berlin	Haubenstock-Ramati: *Amerika*
15 Nov., Berlin	Dessau: *Puntila*
29 Nov., London	Williamson: *The Violins of Saint-Jacques*

1967

5 March, Hamburg	Goehr: *Arden muss sterben*
19 May, Washington	Ginastera: *Bomarzo*
26 May, Zurich	Sutermeister: *Madame Bovary*
3 June, Aldeburgh	Walton: *The Bear*
	Berkeley: *Castaway*
31 Oct., London	R. R. Bennett: *A Penny for a Song*
30 Nov., London	Musgrave: *The Decision*

1968

14 Jan., Naples	Rota: *Aladino e la lampada magica*
5 Feb., Paris	Ohana: *Syllabaire pour Phèdre*
4 March, Hamburg	Searle: *Hamlet*
8 June, Aldeburgh	Birtwistle: *Punch and Judy*
10 June, Orford	Britten: *The Prodigal Son*
29 Sept., Berlin	Dallapiccola: *Ulisse*
21 Dec., Hamburg	Menotti: *Help, Help, The Globolinks!*

1969

15 Jan., Milan	Pousseur: *Votre Faust*
24 Jan., Marseille	Daniel-Lesur: *Andrea del Sarto*
28 March, Coventry	R. R. Bennett: *All The King's Men*
8 May, Brighton	Birtwistle: *Down by the Greenwood Side*
7 June, Aldeburgh	Crosse: *The Grace of Todd*
20 June, Hamburg	Penderecki: *The Devils of Loudun*
18 Dec., London	Williamson: *Lucky Peter's Journey*

1970

16 Jan., Marseille	Saguer: *Mariana Pinéda*
22 Jan., Seattle	Floyd: *Of Mice and Men*
13 April, London	R. R. Bennett: *Victory*
19 July, Glyndebourne	Maw: *The Rising of the Moon*
12 Aug., Santa Fe	Berio: *Opera*
2 Dec., London	Tippett: *The Knot Garden*

1971

28 Jan., London	Brian: *Agamemnon*
25 April, Hamburg	Kagel: *Staatstheater*
16 May, BBC (TV broadcast)	Britten: *Owen Wingrave*
29 April, Schwetzingen	Reimann: *Melusine*
23 May, Vienna	Einem: *Der Besuch der alten Dame*
16 June, Brno	Martinů: *Three Wishes*
20 June, Kiel	Yun: *Geisterliebe*
12 Aug., Santa Fe	Villa-Lobos: *Yerma*
10 Sept., Washington	Ginastera: *Beatrix Cenci*

1972

12 July, London	Maxwell Davies: *Taverner*
23 Oct., Berlin	Fortner: *Elisabeth Tudor*

1973

7 Feb., Brussels	Nabokov: *Love's Labour's Lost*
16 June, Snape	Britten: *Death in Venice*
20 Aug., Salzburg	Orff: *De temporum fine comedia*

1974

13 March, London	Crosse: *The Story of Vasco*
16 March, Stirling	Hamilton: *The Cataline Conspiracy*
11 June, Snape	Musgrave: *The Voice of Ariadne*
25 July, Sarlat-le-Canéda	Tansman: *Georges Dandin*

1975

4 Aug., Avignon	Jolas: *Le Pavillon au bord de la rivière*
16 Dec., Amsterdam	Ullmann: *Der Kaiser von Atlantis* (composed 1943, Theresienstadt)

1976

12 July, London	Henze: *We Come to the River*
25 July, Avignon	Glass: *Einstein on the Beach*

1977

2 Feb., London	Hamilton: *The Royal Hunt of the Sun*
29 April, Mannheim	Rihm: *Faust und Yorick*
6 June, Bath	Tavener: *A Gentle Spirit*
7 June, Moscow	Schedrin: *Dead Souls*
18 June, Kirkwall	Maxwell Davies: *The Martyrdom of St Magnus*
22 June, Spoleto	Rota: *Napoli milionaria*
7 July, London	Tippett: *The Ice Break*
16 July, BBC Radio	Alwyn: *Miss Julie*
6 Sept., Edinburgh	Musgrave: *Mary Queen of Scots*
29 Sept., London	Blake: *Toussaint*

1978

12 April, Stockholm	Ligeti: *Le Grand Macabre*
9 July, Munich	Reimann: *Lear*
29 Nov., Chicago	Penderecki: *Paradise Lost*

1979

24 Feb., Paris	Berg: *Lulu* (three-act version completed by Čerha)
8 March, Hamburg	Rihm: *Jakob Lenz*
1 Oct., London	Tavener: *Thérèse*

1980

2 Sept., Edinburgh	Maxwell Davies: *The Lighthouse*
5 Sept., Rotterdam	Glass: *Satyagraha*
28 Nov., Brussels	Knussen: *Where the Wild Things Are* (first version; premiere of definitive version 9 Jan. 1984, London)
6 Dec., Hamburg	Reutter: *Hamlet*

1981

3 April, Milan	Stockhausen: *Donnerstag aus Licht*
7 May, London	Hamilton: *Anna Karenina*

1982

9 March, Milan	Berio: *La vera storia*
30 May, Amsterdam	Glass: *The Photographer*
14 Sept., BBC Radio	Musgrave: *An Occurrence at Owl Creek Bridge*

1983

2 June, Stuttgart	Henze: *The English Cat*
17 June, Houston	Bernstein: *A Quiet Place*
28 Nov., Paris	Messiaen: *Saint-François d'Assise*

1984

24 March, Stuttgart	Glass: *Akhnaten*
25 May, Milan	Stockhausen: *Samstag aus Licht*
7 Aug., Salzburg	Berio: *Un re in ascolto*
13 Oct., Glyndebourne	Knussen: *Higgelty Piggelty Pop!* (incomplete; premiere of definitive version 5 June 1990, Los Angeles)

1985

1 Feb., Toulouse	Landowski: *Montségur*
16 Feb., Milan	Donatoni: *Atem*
22 July, Munich	Sutermeister: *Le Roi Bérenger*
6 Dec., Cambridge, Mass.	Glass: *The Juniper Tree*

1986

6 Jan., London	Osborne: *Hell's Angels*
1 March, Adelaide	Meale: *Voss*
15 March, Paris	Denisov: *L'Ecume des jours*
21 May, London	Birtwistle: *The Mask of Orpheus*
27 July, Avignon	Jolas: *Le Cyclope*
15 Aug., Salzburg	Penderecki: *Die schwarze Maske*
11 Nov., Washington	Menotti: *Goya*

1987

25 March, Mannheim	Rihm: *Die Hamletmaschine*
8 July, Cheltenham	Weir: *A Night at the Chinese Opera*
21 Aug., Gibellina, Sicily	Xenakis: *Oresteia* (stage premiere)
4 Oct., Berlin	Rihm: *Oedipus*
5 Oct., Glyndebourne	Osborne: *The Electrification of the Soviet Union*
22 Oct., Houston	Adams: *Nixon in China*

1988

7 May, Milan	Stockhausen: *Montag aus Licht*
18 May, Cambridge, Mass.	Glass: *The Fall of the House of Usher*
17 June, Munich	Turnage: *Greek*
8 July, Houston	Glass: *The Making of the Representative for Planet 8*
15 July, Vienna (Airport)	Glass: *1000 Airplanes on the Roof*
16 Sept., Seoul	Menotti: *The Wedding*
18 Sept., Darmstadt	Maxwell Davies: *Resurrection*

1989

20 May, Paris	Höller: *Der Meister und Margarita*
25 May, London	Blake: *The Plumber's Gift*
28 June, London	Casken: *Golem*
27 Oct., Houston	Tippett: *New Year*

1990

5 May, Berlin	Henze: *Das verratene Meer*
18 May, London	Holloway: *Clarissa*
7 Oct., Glasgow	Weir: *The Vanishing Bridegroom*
30 Oct., Vienna	Einem: *Tulifant*

1991

19 March, Brussels	Adams: *The Death of Klinghoffer*
30 May, London	Birtwistle: *Gawain*
6 July, Munich	Penderecki: *Ubu Rex*

1992

9 Feb., Hamburg	Rihm: *Die Eroberung von Mexico*
13 April, Amsterdam	Schnittke: *Life with an Idiot*
19 June, Aldeburgh	Tavener: *Mary of Egypt*
2 Sept., Berlin	Reimann: *Das Schloss*
12 Oct., New York	Glass: *The Voyage*
4 Dec., Grenoble	Redolfi: *Crysallis: opéra subaquatique*

1993

| 28 May, Leipzig | Stockhausen: *Dienstag aus Licht* (stage premiere) |

1994

| 20 April, London | Weir: *Blond Ekbert* |
| 8 July, London | Firsova: *The Nightingale and the Rose* |

10 Sept., Magdeburg	Goldschmidt: *Beatrice Cenci* (composed 1949–50)
24 Oct., Glyndebourne	Birtwistle: *The Second Mrs Kong*
14 Dec., Stockholm	Schedrin: *Lolita*

1995

20 Jan., Norfolk, Va.	Musgrave: *Simón Bolívar*
26 May, Vienna	Schnittke: *Gesualdo*
22 June, Hamburg	Schnittke: *Historia von D. Johann Fausten*
1 July, Cheltenham	Adès: *Powder Her Face*
15 Sept., London	Goehr: *Arianna*

1996

17 March, Lyon	Landowski: *Galina*
20 July, Llandudno	Maxwell Davies: *The Doctor of Myddfai*
23 Aug., Edinburgh	Macmillan: *Ines de Castro*
12 Sept., Leipzig	Stockhausen: *Freitag aus Licht*
2 Nov., Milan	Berio: *Outis*

1997

11 Jan., Munich	Henze: *Venus and Adonis*
10 May, Heidelberg	Glass: *Marriages between Zones 3, 4 and 5*
15 Oct., Norwich	Alwyn: *Miss Julie* (stage premiere)
8 Nov., New York	Tan Dun: *Marco Polo*
12 Dec., London	Brian: *The Cenci* (concert performance)

1998

7 March, Kansas City	Mollicone: *Coyote Tales*
13 March, Houston	Adamo: *Little Women*
15 June, London	Bryars: *Dr Ox's Experiment*

1999

24 July, Salzburg	Berio: *Cronaca del luogo*
16 Sept., Berlin	Carter: *What Next?*
1 Dec., Amsterdam	Andriessen: *Writing to Vermeer*
20 Dec., New York	Harbison: *The Great Gatsby*

2000

16 Feb., London	Turnage: *The Silver Tassie*
23 Feb., Madrid	C. Halffter: *Don Quijote*
6 March, Copenhagen	Ruders: *The Handmaid's Tale*
18 April, Berlin	Birtwistle: *The Last Supper*
15 Aug., Salzburg	Saariaho: *L'Amour de loin*
15 Sept., Helsinki	Sallinen: *King Lear*
17 Sept., Seattle	Glass: *In the Penal Colony*
20 Nov., Brussels	Casken: *God's Liar*
15 Dec., Paris	Adams: *El Niño*

PART ONE

Legacies

1 Opera in transition

ARNOLD WHITTALL

I

'More books on Wagner! Yes, the cry is still they come.' Since the first two sentences of a review article in the *Musical Times* for November 1899 (volume 40, 744) would not seem out of place in a similar context more than a century later, the reader of this introductory chapter might anticipate a sermon on the text 'plus ça change, plus c'est la même chose'. Even allowing for the fact that opera-goers in 1899 were not able to bolster their 'live' listening with a wide choice of performances on CD and DVD, and were not yet travelling to opera houses by private car in casual clothes, still less jetting off to Adelaide or Santa Fe to catch a rarity or a special, star-studded production of a classic, it might still be reassuring to emphasize elements of cultural common ground between then and now: and a description of the world of opera at the end of the nineteenth century which underlines its tradition-establishing role for the new century becomes even more plausible when the topic of repertory is considered.

During the 1899 Covent Garden season, which ran from early April to late July, there were 69 performances, all of operas which were composed during the nineteenth century, with the sole exception of Mozart's *Don Giovanni*, heard three times. The programme extended from Beethoven's *Fidelio* (performed only once) through Bellini's *Norma*, Donizetti's *Lucia di Lammermoor*, Meyerbeer's *Les Huguenots*, Wagner's *Der fliegende Holländer*, *Tannhäuser* and *Lohengrin*, Verdi's *Rigoletto* and *Aida*, Leoncavallo's *Pagliacci*, Mascagni's *Cavalleria rusticana*, Wagner's *Die Walküre*, *Tristan* and *Die Meistersinger*, as well as Gounod's *Faust*, Berlioz's *Roméo et Juliette* and Bizet's *Carmen* – with, as novelties, Mancinelli's *Ero e Leandro*, de Lara's *Messaline*, Adam's *Le Chalet* and Puccini's *La Bohème* (*Musical Times*, 1899, 536).

A year later, in 1900, the season came even closer to a present-day equivalent: *Don Giovanni*, Wagner's *Ring*, *Tannhäuser*, *Lohengrin* and *Die Meistersinger*, Rossini's *The Barber of Seville*, *Lucia di Lammermoor*, *Rigoletto* and *Aida*, *Les Huguenots*, *Roméo et Juliette*, *Faust*, *Carmen*, *La Bohème*, 'Cav.' and 'Pag.': the only novelty was Puccini's brand-new *Tosca*. (The *Musical Times* reviewer responded quite positively to this work, praising 'the sense of impulsive passionate life it conveys; the chief defects are lack of strong, broad melody and of anything like development, and of crudity in the obtaining of effects': see volume 41 (1900), 536.) Not one of those operas in the 1900 programme has completely disappeared from the repertory a century later: and while a slightly different situation obtained in countries (Germany, in particular) where a greater number of companies were promoting a wider range of contemporary composers, it is clear the core operatic repertory at the start of the new century was not so much 'in transition' – poised to change considerably and constantly in the years ahead – as establishing a kind of steady state which would be inflected to varying degrees during the twentieth century itself, but not drastically altered.

II

Other constants involved matters of finance and patronage. Whether the location was Berlin, where the Kaiser and members of his entourage were actively involved in the running of the Court Opera, or Chicago, where opera meant 'commercial theatre, mounted by an impresario with the expectation of making a profit' (Marsh 1992, 841), it was already a topic of considerable controversy when taxes collected from the expanding and increasingly affluent bourgeoisie were used to fund such an elitist form of entertainment. As a result, opera companies experienced as much administrative and artistic instability as many state-funded enterprises continue to do, a century later.

The intensely hierarchical, international star system was also already in place: for example, at New York's Metropolitan Opera, 'each of the seven highest-priced singers were paid more than the entire conducting staff' and 'the audience at the popular-priced Saturday nights did not get to hear either De Reszke, even once' (Meyer 1983, 75, 73) – the De Reszke brothers being among the most highly regarded, and expensive, singers of the time.

In 1890s New York, *fin de siècle* gaiety 'had a frenetic quality; the rich felt beleaguered on all sides' (Meyer 1983, 67): and this spirit, a heady mixture of excitement and anxiety, was common in other centres of civilization as the old century came to an end. It is therefore no surprise to find that opera companies did not react to this spirit of intense cultural self-examination with a sense of 'out with the old, in with the new', tending rather to take pride in the positive, commercially successful balance between old and new which had already been achieved. As the twentieth century proceded, it added Monteverdi, Handel, Rameau, and more Mozart to the mainstream repertory, as well as operas by Strauss,

Janáček, Britten and a few other twentieth-century composers. It extended the historical span of the repertory, while gradually turning away from the near-contemporary emphasis of those 1899 and 1900 seasons. London cannot exactly be deemed typical, lacking the well-established civic and court theatres prominent elsewhere in Europe, but the thinking behind the repertory reflected that found in other major centres – understandably, since the opera manager in London between 1897 and 1900, Maurice Grau, fulfilled the same function at the Metropolitan Opera in New York.

It is therefore tempting to develop the argument that not only the operatic repertory, but also the institutional structures that brought that repertory to life in the theatre, were less explicitly dedicated to the pursuit of change and even transformation, than those forces in society and culture which might be thought to impinge profoundly – if indirectly – on any major artistic genre. Obviously enough, operatic composition from around the year 1909 did not suddenly and irreversibly attempt to match the degree of innovation evident in Schoenberg's *Erwartung*. (In any case, *Erwartung* was not staged until 1924.) When matters of scale and style are concerned, those operas composed in the twentieth century which have been most often performed, from *Tosca* and Janáček's *Kat'a Kabanová* to Britten's *Peter Grimes* and Stravinsky's *The Rake's Progress*, have mediated to varying degrees between nineteenth-century modes of expression and musical styles tending to challenge or even reject such modes of expression. After all, even *Erwartung*, or Stravinsky's *Oedipus Rex*, while inconceivable in a nineteenth-century context, cannot seriously be considered 'anti-operas'. Only with much later works like Mauricio Kagel's *Staatstheater* (1967–70) and John Cage's *Europeras* (1987–91) is the genre itself approached in a deconstructive spirit. And such works are in turn inconceivable without a continuing, flourishing tradition of 'conventional' opera to be placed against them.

III

That flourishing tradition, as a cultural as well as a creative phenomenon, was a product of the nineteenth century. Even a cursory glance at the reports of opera performances in Europe and America in the 1890s indicates just how well established the genre was as a form of cultured entertainment. Yet it was still barely seventy years since 'modern music theater began, in Paris, around 1830' (Gerhard 1998, 40). What also began then was the process Anselm Gerhard calls '*Verstädterung*', or 'urbanization', with French '*grand opéra*' aimed at a bourgeois rather than aristocratic audience. An art-form which had begun with adapting myth and legend for the enlightenment of the few moved in the direction of a style of mass entertainment appropriate for a culture whose primary values were those of capitalism, and which therefore reflected in its subject-matter the profound changes in social, political and economic life after 1789.

There are indeed enormous differences between an early seventeenth-century opera such as Monteverdi's *Orfeo*, and a late nineteenth-century one such as Puccini's *La Bohème*. Yet there are fundamental musical values shared, to do with matters of melodic shaping, rhythmic structuring and harmonic organization, which some twentieth-century opera composers challenged but did not destroy: and it is the persistence of these values which has helped to ensure that opera and mass entertainment have remained distinct cultural categories. Even if the need for mass entertainment since the middle of the nineteenth century had not been channelled into music hall, cinema and pop concert, it is very unlikely that operas with any recognizable relationship to Humperdinck's *Hänsel und Gretel*, *La Bohème*, or any other product of the 1890s, would have permanently colonized this area of cultural practice. Musical comedy in its various manifestations was never robust enough to gain mass appeal, and while those through-composed musicals beloved of the later twentieth-century might reflect certain aspects of 'veristic' operas by Mascagni, Leoncavallo and others, in one fundamental respect – the kind of singing required – there remains a clear dividing line between 'serious' and 'popular' musical theatre.

IV

General historians, like musicologists, deal in constant, complex transitions. For Eric Hobsbawm, the period from 1870 to 1914 was not only one in which 'bourgeois society' passed through 'an identity crisis', but also an 'era when both the creative arts and the public for them lost their bearings' (1994, 219). It is by no means inherently paradoxical that the accelerating popularization that went with 'urbanization' – 'the number of theatres in Germany tripled between 1870 and 1896, from two hundred to six hundred' (221) – was paralleled by the emergence of a small but potent avant-garde, dedicated to challenging the complacency and conservatism on which popularization was believed to depend. While there was no doubt that 'the public for the arts, richer, more cultured and more democratized, was enthusiastic and receptive' (222), and that 'culture in the accepted elite sense was also notably internationalized by the sheer ease of personal movement within a broad cultural zone' (223), it was never likely that opera, with its elaborate requirements for collective performance and relatively formal institutional context, would give a higher priority to the progressively experimental, in matters of musical language and dramatic content, over the well tried.

Yet despite the evident fact that 'the crux of the crisis of the arts lay in the growing divergence between what was contemporary and what was "modern"' (226), we should not forget that the situation around 1900 was the result of a quite striking degree of absorption of the new over the preceding three or four decades. As Hobsbawm sees it, 'the fortress of the established bourgeois public, grand opera, which had been shocked by the populism of Bizet's *Carmen* in 1875, had by the early 1900s accepted not only Wagner, but the curious combination of arias and social realism (*verismo*) about the lower orders (Mascagni's *Cavalleria rusticana*, 1890; Charpentier's *Louise*, 1900)' (227). By 1900, clearly, the opera-going public had managed to regain its bearings. It was only later – in 1907 or thereabouts – that a 'visible break between the *fin de siècle* and the twentieth-century *avant gardes* occurred', and by then 'the innovators of the last quarter of the nineteenth century had already become part of the cultural baggage of the educated middle classes' (235–6).

V

We still lack a wide-ranging study of the relations, across Europe and America, between opera composers and operatic institutions during the *fin de siècle*. But it is clear enough that many composers were as closely involved in conducting operas, and, like Richard Strauss, in being part of the institution's management structure, as in writing operas. Half-hearted commitment to the operatic culture was not a serious option.

Strauss's career began when he was appointed third conductor at the Munich Hofoper at the age of 22, in 1886. In 1889 he moved to Weimar as Kapellmeister (as such, subordinate to the Hofkapellmeister), then back to Munich (1894–8) before becoming joint Hofkapellmeister to the Prussian Court in Berlin in 1898. With the help of the German railway system, Strauss was constantly on the move during these years, conducting programmes in theatres and concert halls which reflected his concern to promote the newer music – by Wagner, Liszt and himself, in particular (see Schuh 1982). That someone so closely involved in the day-to-day rough-and-tumble of opera-house politics should wish to compose opera himself was by no means a foregone conclusion – after all, Mahler did not do so – and the relative failure of Strauss's first two efforts, *Guntram*

(1894) and *Feuersnot* (1901), offers salutary proof that even the most expert interpreter of Mozart and Wagner might find it quite difficult to emulate their operatic achievements. Nevertheless, a late-century culture committed to the new made it possible for those early failures to be forgotten and superseded, and this in a national context where composers could succeed with operas as different as Humperdinck's fairy-tale *Hänsel und Gretel* (1893) and Eugen d'Albert's veristic *Tiefland* (1903).

It was Siegfried Wagner, no less, who declared in 1894 that *Hänsel und Gretel* was 'the most important opera since *Parsifal*', thereby provoking Hanslick's tetchy rejoinder: 'the best in a full twelve years? An irritating pronouncement, and the worst of it is – that it is true'. The by-then aged Viennese critic also noted that Humperdinck's opera skilfully matched the spirit of the time: 'The public desires new themes and yet adheres to Wagnerism. Humperdinck satisfied both requirements' (Hanslick 1951, 321). For all the stylistic affinities, Humperdinck most certainly did not 'adhere to Wagner' when it came to the choice of subject-matter, but his skill in keeping afloat in the immediate aftermath of the Wagnerian hurricane without abandoning all possible points of contact with the Master's work points to the larger paradox of the *fin de siècle* on the German front expounded by Carl Dahlhaus: 'legitimate Wagnerianism lay in departing from mythological tragedy, in avoiding the overwhelming presence of Wagner's legacy by seeking refuge in musicotheatrical genres considered peripheral by Wagner himself' (1989, 341). As a fairy-tale opera, *Hänsel und Gretel* is linked by Dahlhaus with Pfitzner's early *Der arme Heinrich* (1893) and Wolf's *Der Corregidor* (1896) as moving significantly into those 'peripheral' areas: and Siegfried Wagner's own operas, beginning with *Der Bärenhäuter* (1898), continued this trend. Despite evidence of a certain dependency on Richard Wagner's musico-dramatic style, these works are most successful when seeking to recreate the pre-1850 world of the romantic opera. Nevertheless, this does not mean that the 'transition' apparent in German opera in the 1890s was wholly retrogressive. No composer was more aware than Humperdinck of the challenges facing contemporary composers, and his prescription for the future involved moving more firmly away from Wagnerian precedent, and from symphonic, musical continuity, in the interests of supporting the currently fashionable search for realism.

In 1898, Humperdinck argued that 'modern opera is moving along a road which must lead to melodrama. With the endeavour to get reality on to the stage which is endemic to our time, a form must surely be found which will answer this call of the times, and in my opinion that form is melodrama' (Dahlhaus 1985, 100). It is difficult to conceive of anything more peripheral to the Wagnerian heritage than this idea. A more realistic operatic advance into non-Wagnerian territory lies in the view of the medium, attached especially to Pfitzner by Dahlhaus, that 'saw language rather than stage configurations, as the primary medium for communicating [the] "poetic idea" '. As Dahlhaus observes, this is the aesthetic of a *Lieder* composer rather than of a Wagner, for whom action on stage, or 'pantomime', was 'the main complement to music in musical drama' (1985, 100). As such, it was well suited to an operatic culture in which conservative and more radical impulses were often fiercely at odds.

This tension was not the result of German operatic culture in the 1890s being wholly dependent on connections between its institutions and royal or aristocratic patrons – Hamburg was one example of a free city whose opera house flourished, if turbulently, with Mahler as chief conductor (1891–7). Nevertheless, in Hamburg the influence of the reigning Intendant, Bernhard Baruch Pollini, might well have been even more significant than that of the chief conductor. Pollini was 'a skilled manager and talent-scout who had a shrewd, well-developed sense of what the public wanted and who might therefore be regarded as more representative of the tastes and prejudices of the time than Mahler himself' (Whittall 1991, 346).

The importance of such managers in the determining of artistic policy and in influencing repertory and personnel should not be underestimated, even though other areas of commercial activity were becoming increasingly important – like that of the music publisher, who was often a closer ally of the composer, and the composer-conductor, than were his institutional colleagues and superiors. And not the least of the general manager's problems were the result of finding himself caught between idealistic musicians on the one hand, and hard-headed providers of financial support on the other.

The fact that, to prosper, opera companies needed a combination of artistic vision and practical competence, is well illustrated in Vienna. From the mid-1850s it had been accepted that the general director or chief administrator of the Hofoper might be a musician, and from 1881 to 1897 the post was held by Wilhelm Jahn – a far less familiar name than that of Hans Richter, the principal conductor. Jahn was nevertheless

> an extremely able conductor who specialized in Italian and French opera, while Richter excelled in the German repertory. The two men were also complementary in temperament and, aided by the general prosperity of the Habsburg monarchy in the 1880s, they made the Vienna Hofoper one of the foremost musical institutions in Europe; the works of Wagner and Verdi were actively promoted; Mascagni came to conduct his *Cavalleria rusticana* (1891); Massenet's *Manon* and *Werther* (1892) were produced, the latter a world première, as well as Smetana's *Bartered Bride* (1896) and *Dalibor* (1897).
> (Carner and Klein 1992, 996–7)

Under Jahn, the Hofoper was the very model of an enlightened international house, strongly committed to contemporary music and well able to
capitalize on the fact that this music did not challenge the general public
to the extent that the soon-to-emerge avant-garde, in Vienna and elsewhere, would aim to do. As a multitude of cultural historians have
argued, such avant-garde initiatives emerged at precisely the time when
the Austro-Hungarian Empire began to lose its confidence and virtually,
it seems with hindsight, to will its own disintegration. Thus Mahler's
fabled period as Jahn's successor in Vienna (1897–1907) enriched the
repertory, and advanced performance standards in the direction of those
that prevail today, at precisely the time when the institution, and the kind
of music drama it supported, were in increasing danger of seeming
irrelevant to authentically twentieth-century modes of thought. That
the triumphant survival of opera in Vienna between 1900 and 1914 can
be seen as setting the pattern for comparable survivals throughout the
world of high culture for the rest of the century should not be allowed to
conceal the extent to which this survival was achieved at the cost of
constant struggles at every level, both within the institution itself and
between it and the civic and social authorities on which it depended for its
day-to-day existence.

VI

In late nineteenth-century Italy, too, civic priorities would often conflict
with artistic imperatives:

> With the extension of suffrage and the coming of democratic politics,
> municipalities were less willing to spend local tax revenue on subsidizing
> the pleasures of the rich. In 1897, a mere four years after the première of
> Verdi's last opera *Falstaff* there, the Milan city council refused, though only
> temporarily, to pay anything towards the La Scala season. There followed a
> long period of wrangles and attempted compromises.   (Rosselli 1991, 148)

This, it should be noted, was at a time when, in Italy, 'impresarios went
into eclipse; . . . their role was taken over by the publishers, who . . .
exercised increasing control over the material of opera and could even
cripple a composer's career' (Dean 1999, 129). In such circumstances it
was the composer able to balance the public's interest in a medium still
dominated by the new – if not the 'modern' – and the commercial criteria
of this new breed of managers who was most likely to succeed.

The wrangling between opera-house managements and civic fund-
holders would nevertheless hardly have happened at all had opera not

continued to be valued by enough citizens able to make their voices heard, and even to argue that opera was evolving in ways that showed some sense of civic concerns. What else was 'realism' (*verismo*) but an attempt to bring musical drama closer to the real world of contemporary society? As John Rosselli noted, few of the operas written according to these new desiderata have survived, not least because composers like Leoncavallo, Giordano and Cilea were far less adept than Strauss or Debussy at transcending the sordid or bizarre aspects of their subjects with music of genuine substance. What they excelled at was 'using music for theatrical effect; they knew ... how long an episode should last or where a high note should be placed for maximum applause. Their music tended to work best when it was most utilitarian and was advancing the action and to sound tawdry or empty when striving for beauty or significance' (Rosselli 1991, 140). There also seems reasonably solid agreement among musicologists and music lovers alike that Puccini was able to provide sufficient 'genuine substance' in his music to achieve a no less genuine beauty and significance, and place his work on a different level from that of his Italian veristic contemporaries.

Comparing Charpentier's *Louise* with *La Bohème*, Dahlhaus contrasted the French composer's 'deficient sense of form' with Puccini's ability to develop and control his diverse materials 'according to the strictures of motivic-harmonic logic' (1989, 355). If this does indeed go to the heart of Puccini's special achievement, as well as explaining his survival, it is the more remarkable given an autograph manuscript which is a 'patchwork quilt of experiments, rejections, additions and refinements' (Groos and Parker 1986, 114). This document gives 'an overriding impression of the enormous difficulty of *fin de siècle* opera composition' (54), a claim which fits well with Mosco Carner's argument that Puccini must be placed against a fully-detailed picture of *fin de siècle* culture 'if his artistic personality, with its inner contradictions and morbid traits, is to be fully comprehended' (1992, 299).

VII

The leading proponents of French *fin de siècle* operatic culture, challenged as severely as the Italian by tensions between commercial imperatives and artistic perceptions, benefit no less from such contextualized consideration. The principal opera house in Paris, the Théâtre National de l'Opéra, had opened in 1875, and the first director 'profited from public interest in the novelty of the building but made few significant musical inaugurations, and during ten years of directing operas produced not one foreign work'. Perhaps for that very reason, box-office receipts during the later 1870s were so healthy that the director 'was called before members of the grant-awarding national assembly to discuss reduction of their support. However, after he underlined the precariousness of the political future and the sudden downturn in attendances that might easily befall the opera house, the level of subsidy was sustained' (Langham Smith 1992b, 875). By the 1890s foreign operas – Wagner and the later Verdi along with revivals of Rossini – were to be heard more often than formerly, but the emphasis remained on French works. Among the most notable were Saint-Saëns's *Samson et Dalila* (1893) and Alfred Bruneau's *Messidor* (1897), this last a 'half-fantastic, half-*vériste*' extravaganza 'marking a substantial departure from the Opéra's conservative policy with regard to subject-matter in an era when the librettist's name almost always preceded that of the composer' (876–7). The veristic aspect is no surprise, since the libretto of *Messidor* was by none other than Emile Zola, and the work was first heard 'at the height of the Dreyfus affair, in which Bruneau actively followed Zola's support of Dreyfus'. As an indication of how directly matters musical could be affected by wider social and political contexts, Bruneau's pro-Dreyfus stance led to 'a marked fall in his popularity and for some years his works were less than welcome in Paris' (Langham Smith 1992a, 620).

It was nevertheless not the Théâtre National but the Opéra-Comique which cultivated a series of 'staged works in the naturalist tradition of Zola' (Langham Smith 1992b, 878), culminating in Charpentier's *Louise* in 1900. It also mounted no fewer than five Massenet premieres during the 1890s, and can generally be seen as a more enterprising institution than its grander rival: Verdi's *Falstaff* in 1894 and Puccini's *La Bohème* in 1898 had their first French airings there. Yet the Opéra-Comique's main claim to twentieth-century fame remains its staging of Debussy's *Pelléas et Mélisande* in 1902. Even though Debussy's symbolist aesthetic did not instantly eliminate all the alternatives on offer, it provided new perspectives on other, earlier styles of French opera which have remained relevant ever since.

St Petersburg was another major operatic centre in which, during the 1890s, the new and local were able to co-exist with the more longstanding foreign repertory. As a result of the relatively stable period of government under Tsar Alexander II, 'an indigenous classical repertory began to accumulate. It was largely the work of a new generation of professionally skilled composers', pre-eminently Tchaikovsky and Rimsky-Korsakov who, as early as the end of the 1870s, had 'laid the cornerstone of an enduring – and exportable – repertory'. Indeed, 'by 1890 the indigenous repertory [centering on the operas of Rimsky-Korsakov] had achieved incontestable dominance at the Mariinsky and had been expanded to include works of Musorgsky and Borodin made performable by Rimsky-Korsakov' (Taruskin 1992b, 133). It was Savva Ivanovich Mamentov's opera company in Moscow which 'became the main outlet for Rimsky-Korsakov's voluminous late operatic production, from *Sadko* (1897)' (Taruskin 1992a, 477): but even before the new century had begun, Rimsky's influence and achievement were sufficient to ensure that those composers who came after him would have to contend with his example, even as they determined (not always successfully) to escape it.

VIII

As this brief survey has shown, that stage in the Age of Empire represented by the 1890s was far from exclusively backward-looking or decadent. There was much more to contemporary opera than the treatment of sordid subjects in the most easily accessible manner, and there were already plentiful hints of that Age of Extremes which, after 1914, would replace the Age of Empire in Hobsbawm's grand chronological (and ideological) scheme. The well-rehearsed contrasts between 'number' and 'symphonic' opera, and between relatively epic or relatively realistic subjects, so significant before 1900 (though never absolute), would remain matters of debate, and of inspiration, right through the twentieth century itself. So much so, indeed, that it might plausibly be claimed that opera as both genre and institution survived into the twenty-first century at least in part because it did not abandon the most fundamental qualities which made contemporary opera in the later nineteenth century so successful.

2 Wagner and beyond

JOHN DEATHRIDGE

Wagner was not the only one to change the course of opera's history in the nineteenth century and into the twentieth. And indeed only his most fanatic admirers have ever thought otherwise. It is hard nonetheless not to think of him as someone who left an indelible stamp on twentieth-century opera. Every figure of importance is said to have reacted to him positively or negatively, and rarely indifferently. The possibility exists that this is just another part of the Wagnerian myth that has spread itself like a vulture over Western music since the end of high romanticism, in spite of formidable opposition. The great conductor Hans von Bülow insisted with his usual caustic wit that Richard Strauss should be called Richard III in the dynasty of German music as a Richard II after Wagner was inconceivable (Kennedy 1995, 9). W. H. Auden ventured to suggest that Wagner had no real successors at all, calling him 'a giant without issue' (cited in V. Stravinsky and Craft 1978, 400). Not everyone needed to take an interest in him after all, while some of those who did paid him the briefest of respects and quickly went their own way. Igor Stravinsky tells a nice story of how he was persuaded by Diaghilev to go with him at short notice to Bayreuth in 1912 to see *Parsifal*, even though it meant interrupting work on *Le Sacre du printemps* (Stravinsky 1936, 67–8). With dismay he noted the mausoleum-like interior of the festival theatre, deplored the cult-like performance, lambasted the Wagner faithful for putting up with it – and simply fled. He did admire 'the web-like blending of the orchestra from under the stage', which meant that *Parsifal* might have been a headache, but at least 'a headache with aspirin' (Stravinsky and Craft 1966, 189).

But the driest of statistics can still hint at the scale of Wagner's presence in the twentieth century, including some of its contradictions. The well-known distaste for him among the modernists of the Weimar Republic shrinks not a little in significance when set against the cold facts of operatic life at the time. Performances of Wagner's operas in German-speaking theatres in 1926–7 amounted to 13.9 percent of the total, easily beating Verdi into second place at 11.3 percent, Puccini into third at 7.8 percent and Mozart into fourth at 6.6 percent. In contrast, the number of performances of *all* new operas amounted to a mere 4.5 percent (Köhler 1968). In the 1920s and 1930s, Wagner was excoriated by progressive thinkers and linked musically by scurrilously minded theatre composers to perilous subjects. When Paul

Hindemith cited King Marke's music from *Tristan und Isolde* in the castration scene in his one-act opera *Das Nusch-Nuschi* (1921) his morally hidebound audience (predictably) prompted a scandal. And among other memorable Wagner-deflating moments is the line 'cash makes you randy' in Bertolt Brecht's and Hanns Eisler's *Die Rundköpfe und die Spitzköpfe* (composed 1934–6), sung by a bawdy procuress to the opening of *Tristan* with obvious relish. Avant-garde antics like these, however, only served to enhance the popularity of Wagner's works, which continued to dominate the operatic stage with ease.

Except for the unwary, the precise nature of Wagner's influence will probably always be elusive. Part of the problem is Wagner himself, or rather the way circumstances led him to present his work to the world. The simple fact is that the daring project about opera and drama he launched in literary form in Swiss exile soon after the Dresden uprising of 1849 unleashed a war of words on an international level which, as the reaction of the influential French critic François-Joseph Fétis shows, set the tone of the debate about his fight for the soul of opera before a note of the major works on which his reputation now rests had been composed, let alone heard. (Fétis attempted to disavow Wagner's writings on the future of opera and drama in a seven-instalment philippic in the Paris periodical press in 1852, followed by another three polemical articles a year later, despite the fact that he still knew practically nothing of Wagner's music except the overture to *Tannhäuser*: see K. Ellis 1999.) Indeed, by the end of the 1850s the battle and its terms of engagement – 'Total Work of Art' (*Gesamtkunstwerk*), 'Music of the Future' (*Zukunftsmusik*), 'Unending Melody' (*unendliche Melodie*) are just a few of the slogans Wagner bandied about – were already notorious among cognoscenti and to some extent the public at large, even though there had been virtually no exposure to the music to which they actually related. In its edition of 20 November 1858, the satirical London weekly *Punch* – to cite just one example – referred disparagingly to Wagner and 'other crotchet-mongers of the *Music of the Future*'. How that squared with the best-known of Wagner's pieces in London at the time, the *Tannhäuser* Overture and the Wedding March from *Lohengrin*, both of which were extremely popular precisely because they looked back to Mendelssohn rather than to a brave new operatic world in the future, is anyone's guess.

If the controversy about Wagner began to rage in Europe while *Der Ring des Nibelungen* (composed 1848–74) and *Tristan und Isolde* (composed 1856–9) were still incomplete and unperformed, it is hardly surprising that similar splits between theory and practice in the debate about his influence exist to this day. Certainly it was unhelpful that theory and practice initially appeared largely in reverse order. When Wagner's ideas about opera were discussed with such harsh polemics in the early 1850s, the chances were strong even then that certain slogans would stick no matter what the reality of the works to which they related turned out to be. These same slogans, plus a few ingrained habits arising from them such as the Great Leitmotiv Hunt or the chase for the proverbial *Gesamtkunstwerk* in which all the arts are supposed to find themselves miraculously on an equal footing, inevitably spilt over with disconcerting regularity into accounts of operas by other composers where they were used – and often still are – like Rorschach tests to diagnose 'Wagnerian' tendencies.

In fact not a single stage work by Wagner uses so-called leitmotives in the same way as the next. Quite apart from the obvious point that composers after him often used recurring motifs in a manner derived from other, usually non-German, sources, or from the relatively primitive use of motifs in Wagner's early operas while also alluding (confusingly for some historians) to his later music dramas in terms of harmony and melody (see, for example, Huebner 1993), it seems pointless to take the existence of motifs as a hard-and-fast rule for detecting his influence without first defining more closely the different ways he used such a technique himself.

Nor is all the talk about a supposed synthesis of the arts in most cases much more than shallow high-mindedness. The claim that Wagner wanted to put his music on the same level as the other arts is to confuse an argument about particularism (he took the fairly standard left-Hegelian line that the separation of the arts reflected the deleterious fragmentation of modern industrial society and the resulting alienation of the individual) with a bland notion of equality. Admittedly, misunderstanding of the issue in Wagner's so-called Zürich writings (1849–51) has arisen in part because of his love affair at the time with left-Hegelian dialectics, which to the uninitiated can appear mainly inscrutable. At the root of the confusion is his quasi-Hegelian argument for music involving both its subservience to the other arts and, precisely because of that subservience, its ultimate redemptive power. Thus we read in the essay 'The Art-Work of the Future' of 'the power [of music] to deny itself in order to hold out its redeeming hand to its sister arts' and in 'Judaism in Music' (which despite its revolting racism is in Wagner's terms actually a seminal essay about music) that 'music can articulate the most sublime of truths through renewed interaction with the other arts.' (See R. Wagner 1911/1914, volume 3, 96–7, and volume 5, 74. For a different interpretation, which to a large extent reflects the standard view in Wagner scholarship, see Nattiez 1993, 128–38.) In other words, well before 1854 when he first read Schopenhauer, who famously placed music at the centre of his philosophical ideas, Wagner was already making it clear that music is the crown-jewel of the arts – not the classical music of old, to be sure, but a different kind of music which needed the other arts more than it had ever needed them before. It must interact with them, derive its power from them, let them act as catalysts in allowing it to grow up, to come of age.

Despite all the impressive talk of *Wagnérisme* – fundamentally a literary concept – or 'the birth of film out of the spirit of [Wagner's] music' (Adorno 1981, 107), there is no getting away from music as the *fons et origo* of the entire Wagnerian project. Given the huge cultural responsibility Wagner wanted music to bear, this by no means excludes politics, and it is true even when the emphasis is placed on words, despite serious misapprehensions about this issue in particular. There is some truth to the idea that the strange alliterative language Wagner first used in the opening work in the *Ring* cycle, *Das Rheingold*, which has the effect of everyday speech rather than verse, and the first successful setting of a libretto in actual prose, the tavern scene in Musorgsky's *Boris Godunov* (written 1868–9; revised 1871–2), both antici- pate a later fashion for the operatic 'bleeding slice of life', as Tonio expresses it in the Prologue of Leoncavallo's *Pagliacci* (1892). And indeed realistic operas with prose libretti like Charpentier's *Louise* (1900) became immensely popular in Europe around the turn of the century. But *Das Rheingold* is far from being 'the musical equivalent of prose drama' accounting for the 'inspirational limitedness' of its music (Magee 2000, 130), or an instance where 'word and tone, each contributing to its share of the synthesis, are blended inseparably into a single unit' (Stein 1960, 85). If a work so obviously dominated by rich musical invention can be misjudged this badly (Wagner was so proud of it he sent a copy to Brahms in 1875 with a note pointing out its prodigious number of themes and the ingenious ways he had managed to vary and develop them: see Kloss 1909, 570), it is hardly a surprise that the fabled *Gesamtkunstwerk*, still rising to the surface of the Wagner literature and its vast oceans, has yielded scant insight into his historical role.

Wagner's Ten Commandments

If we abandon the Great Leitmotiv Hunt and the chase for the *Ge- samtkunstwerk*, what do we have left? Carl Dahlhaus has already said in an important essay on Wagner's influence that no historian in their right mind would ever claim that the composer's theory contains the only valid criteria with which to judge his successors (Müller and Wapnewski 1992, 547). Nor, it should be added, are the claims set out in Wagner's prose works the only means of measuring his own achievements, except perhaps for the most dogmatic of his admirers (and enemies). Nonetheless it makes sense to look at the bold and intimidating attack he launched against 'opera' and his insistence on the rise of what he liked to call 'drama' over its ashes, if only to understand the enormous impact his work made on other composers, and why even the strongest of them seem to have reacted with surprising reticence, much as an attentive schoolchild might to a stern and charismatic teacher in the presence of whom even the mere thought of a spirited riposte can feel less than wise. Edward Lockspeiser once remarked that the almost brutal finality of Wagner's idea of drama was in itself an aggressive obstacle for anyone brave enough to want to contribute meaningfully to the operatic stage after his death. And Lockspeiser rightly compared the historical stop-sign that his work seemed to present with Claude Debussy's reluctance to complete certain of his most cherished projects for the stage which he expressed in a letter to Pierre Louÿs in 1895, and which remained with him for the rest of his life (Lockspeiser 1978, volume 2, 215). The dream-like incompleteness of Debussy's work does indeed make a striking comparison with Wagner's goal-directed obsessiveness – 'Bayreuth or bust', as Stravinsky once succinctly put it (Stravinsky and Craft 1966, 139).

Moreover, it is easy now to underestimate Wagner's powerful presence on the musical scene in Europe during the final decade of his life, let alone that of his second wife Cosima, who after his death dominated his heirs and other keepers of the Bayreuthian flame sometimes with brutal language reminiscent of a military campaign. In a letter to Strauss dated 7 January 1890, for example, she speaks of 'purging' the Rhineland and the area around the River Main and 'occupying' it with her favourite Bayreuth luminaries who with her formidable influence held, or were about to hold, important theatrical posts in that part of Germany (C. Wagner 1980, 204). Indeed, apart from Humperdinck's *Hänsel und Gretel* (1893) – an exception that proves the rule – the impressive number of operas listed near the start of Dahlhaus's essay that were written with obvious allegiances to Wagner – Ernest Reyer's *Sigurd* (1884), Edouard Lalo's *Le Roi d'Ys* (1888), Strauss's *Guntram* (1894), Hans Pfitzner's *Der arme Heinrich* (1895), Vincent d'Indy's *L'Etranger* (1903), August Bungert's *Homerische Welt* (1896–1903), and to which many more can be added, including Felix Weingartner's *Genesius* (1892) – owe their place in the admittedly capacious graveyard of past operatic disasters not only to inferior talent, but also to a puritanical party-line emanating from Bayreuth that simply inhibited the progressively minded operatic composers of the day. Certainly it may not be a coincidence that strong works with clear links to Wagner such as Debussy's *Pelléas et Mélisande* (1902) and Strauss's *Salome* (1905) only really began to emerge in the first decade of the twentieth century when the influence of the Bayreuthians was already in sharp decline and copyright restrictions imposed on Wagner's works for 30 years after his death were rapidly nearing their end.

Still, Wagner was always more than happy to explain his mission to anyone willing to listen. And against expectations he usually did so with exceptional clarity and succinctness. On 17 January 1873 in Berlin he read the libretto of *Götterdämmerung*, the fourth part of his *Ring* cycle, to an invited audience and prefaced the reading with an exposition of his entire programme for the future of 'drama' (R. Wagner 1911/1914, volume 9, 308–10; for an idiosyncratic English translation, see W. A. Ellis 1892–9, volume 5, 305–6). It reads today like a manifesto – one of the clearest and shortest he ever wrote – and like all good manifestos it is pithy and shrewdly polemical. It needs to be emphasized perhaps that Wagner, who on this occasion was in distinguished company including Prince George of Prussia and the Crown Prince of Württemberg, almost certainly did not intend to unfurl his project to his exalted listeners like holy commandments thundering down from Mount Sinai. But one wonders nevertheless whether the ten points he made in his talk came across like that to some. A composer who believes in true drama, he said in so many words, shall:

1. write no more operas;
2. attend to the dramatic dialogue, the focus of the music;
3. not covet the lyrical in opera;
4. regard German music as victorious over all its rivals;
5. marry music and drama in a way that appeals not to abstract reflection, but to feeling;
6. allow music to reveal the most intimate motifs of the drama in all their ramifications;
7. regard the modern orchestra as the greatest achievement of the modern age;
8. allow the modern orchestra to combine the archetypal *moments* provided by music in ancient tragedy with the action of the *entire* drama (Wagner's emphasis);
9. extend the dramatic dialogue over the entire drama like a spoken play, but articulate it solely in music;
10. create a new kind of drama that appeals not to opera-lovers but to truly educated persons concerned with the cultivation of a genuine German culture (*eine originale Kultur des deutschen Geistes*).

The supposed demise of opera

It is true, as scholars always insist, that Wagner was not the sole destroyer of the so-called number opera inherited from the seventeenth and eighteenth centuries. Greater continuity and flexibility in adapting dramatic moments into wider musical expanses without the stop-go character of older opera divided into recitatives, arias, choruses and ensembles is also noticeable in the most interesting French and Italian works for the musical stage in the nineteenth century. That Wagner himself learnt a thing or two from these non-German sources, in particular the operas of Scribe and Meyerbeer, is indeed one of the great unstated facts in his public pronouncements about his own project, though in private he tended to be more frank about it. It is difficult to deny, however, that the widening of tonality and thematic continuity in his mature works, and their vast tracts of music with swift changes in stylistic level and syntax, together constitute a bold adventure in harmony and large-scale structure that left an indelible mark on opera and the history of music in general.

Coupled with the (now underestimated) literary impact of Wagner's manifestos against opera, which codified its demise not only with polemical brevity but also with eye-crossing tedium in longer theoretical treatises that nonetheless seem to have impressed influential figures in the later part of the nineteenth century like Nietzsche and Strauss (see editor's postscript to R. Wagner 1984, 525, 531–2), his music dramas were undoubtedly one of the main reasons for the declining status of 'opera' in the nineteenth century – opera, that is, as a series of items performed exquisitely by renowned singers for the sake of sheer enjoyment and in which meaningful drama (at least according to Wagner) had only peripheral status. Theodor Adorno was not being entirely perverse when he pointed out that the revival of the number convention in Stravinsky's *The Rake's Progress* (1951) – an opera which at first sight seems about as far from Wagnerian drama as can be imagined – was only possible as ironic stylization because the damning verdict which Wagner as theorist and as artist had long since delivered on the enclosed forms Stravinsky sought lovingly to resuscitate still retained its validity (Adorno 1978b, 'Wagners Aktualität', 548–9).

It is even likely that Wagner's own works would have stood little chance of survival had they not paid more than just a few respects to the opera industry they were supposed to be undermining. Beloved moments like Siegmund's 'Spring Song' in *Die Walküre* (1870) or the famous Quintet in *Die Meistersinger von Nürnberg* (1868) have served the popularity of his music well. Nor is it exactly a secret that the Wagner repertoire has had more than its fair share of formidable singer cults, even if they have become increasingly eccentric and isolated over the years. (The rarity value of first-rate Wagner singers in the twenty-first century has practically turned them into the equivalent of the northern right whales of the Western Atlantic whose pending extinction is always woefully – and not unjustly – predicted by small groups of dedicated activists.)

The war against opera and its supposed vices was therefore never completely unsympathetic to composers who continued to believe in the object at which Wagner's intellectual aggression was directed. Puccini, for one, was always willing to learn from *Tristan und Isolde* (1865) and *Parsifal* (1882) in particular. And exactly for this reason German critics felt compelled at once to appropriate his first substantial European triumph *Manon Lescaut* (1893) as part of the Wagnerian legacy. A typical example is Alfred Kühn, who wrote enthusiastically of Puccini that 'no one has ever understood so well how to make such beautiful *music* out of Wagner's *musical initiatives*' (1894, 64). Given Wagner's and Puccini's almost antithetical use of music for dramatic purposes (as we shall see), the author's emphases could hardly be more misleading.

The real cause of the pre-emptive critical strike was that along with Mascagni's hugely successful *Cavalleria rusticana* (1890) Puccini's opera actually posed a threat, showing modern international audiences that an entirely different kind of operatic dramaturgy was still possible. Vivid characters, believable situations, scenery without heavy mythological detail, shameless coveting of the lyrical, fast-moving dialogue and the very roots of drama itself were brought back to real life, as it were, well beyond the reach of the internalized subjectivity of Wagner's phantasmagorias. Indeed, no one was clearer about this than Puccini himself, who said in an interview with a German journalist defending the right of the Wagner family to restrict performances of *Parsifal* to Bayreuth after its copyright ran out in 1913:

> I am not a Wagnerian; my musical education was in the Italian school. Even though I have been influenced by Wagner like every other modern musician in the way I use the orchestra for illustration and in the thematic characterisation of persons and situations, as a composer I have always remained, and still remain, Italian. My music is rooted in the peculiarity of my native country. (Reported in *Neue Zeitschrift für Musik*, 79 (1912), 241)

Puccini was being ingenuous, perhaps, in insisting on a counterweight to Wagner's fourth and tenth commandments demanding the cultivation by educated persons of a genuine German culture. An Italian school of opera seemed to be still alive and kicking, and moreover for some high-minded intellectual elites it was proving to be disconcertingly popular, and with little sign of fatigue. But in view of the increasingly cosmopolitan strategies of opera composers around the turn of the century (to which ironically the overtly nationalist stance of Wagner and Puccini had contributed), Puccini's point about his supposed Italian roots is surely less significant than his fundamental difference of opinion with Wagner about the nature of opera – a difference which on a broader level was to have palpable consequences for the whole future of the genre.

Wagner's new drama and its challengers

Like Puccini and many other composers of opera around the turn of the century (Debussy and Strauss immediately spring to mind), Wagner had all his life been interested in the spoken theatre. And the fundamental question he kept asking himself was: what precisely is the difference between a drama that relies on words and one whose *raison d'être* is music? His response is embedded in his eighth commandment (with rallying support from the second, fifth and sixth) which advocates a link through music between the individual moments of a drama and its entire action. What he meant was that in musical drama it was possible to create a logical chain of structured presence infinitely greater in depth and power than it ever could be in a spoken play precisely because it was always musically bonded with other moments both future and past inside the same dramatic structure. Admittedly the idea was not without its rhetorical baggage, including a specious comparison with music in ancient Greek tragedy and his much-trumpeted intention to revive the spirit of Aeschylean drama in a modern guise using newly invented myths of his own based on sources from the Middle Ages.

A more accurate and insightful account of what he actually achieved, however, comes not from Wagner, but from one of his most imaginative interpreters. In 1895, at one of the most significant moments in the history of Wagnerism, 300 copies of Adolphe Appia's *La Mise en scène du drame wagnérien* were printed in Paris and rapidly devoured by small groups of symbolist poets, anti-realists, producers, composers – anyone interested in the artistic avant-garde of the day. And in this ground-breaking document they found a definition of Wagnerian drama that comes extremely close to its oneiric world and internally prescribed sense of time that in literature and music were already turning out to be the most durable aspects of Wagner's legacy:

> What characterizes Wagnerian drama and constitutes its high value is the power it possesses, by music, to *express* the interior drama, whereas spoken drama can merely *signify* it. As music is *Time*, it gives to the interior drama a duration that must correspond to the length of the performance itself ... Therefore, given the special nature of music, the interior drama cannot possibly find a satisfactory model for its development in the time-frame provided for spoken drama by life itself.
> (Appia 1982, 41–2; original French text in Appia 1983, volume 1, 261–83)

The musical realists of the 1890s, taking their cue from Bizet's *Carmen* (1875), had already thrown down the gauntlet to music's supposedly exclusive right to create 'interior drama' by inventing a new kind of opera where music, and not just the spoken word, had the right to an exterior temporality – or at least an illusion of it – driven by 'life itself'. The idea of fast and furious events conditioning internal emotional states within a dramaturgy taking leanness and concision to a radical extreme was of course the prerogative of Verdi. But with the huge success of Wagner's example to contend with, Verdi's successors were all the more determined to put 'life' to the fore with realistic action with which any audience could immediately identify, as opposed to the internal states of mind in Wagnerian drama that claimed to exist outside real time.

These starkly opposed views of operatic dramaturgy were highly influential in the twentieth century. And some of the most interesting operas took a radical stance on either side. Schoenberg's one-act opera *Erwartung* (composed in 1909) is frequently cited as a daring experiment in atonality with a lineage that can clearly be traced back to some of the bolder moments in Wagner's harmony which stretch tonality to its limits. But what is really Wagnerian about it is its almost self-consciously interior sound-world that continuously threatens to engulf its neurasthenic protagonist (a woman searching frantically for her dead lover) and its references to the language of dreams inside a dramatic space 'on the border of a forest' – the opening stage direction – which is essentially without concrete social identity. True, accepting Wagner's premise unconditionally, as Pfitzner did in *Palestrina* (1917), could also bring with it a sense of high-minded didacticism and belatedness. *Palestrina* looks at first sight as though it should be a historical drama about a sixteenth-century Italian composer. In fact, using Wagner's *Die Meistersinger* as a model, it is an allegory with considerable ahistorical pretensions about the superiority of German music which Pfitzner himself described as 'autumnal' – a melancholic farewell to the Wagnerian ideal.

Jettisoning Wagnerian interiority altogether on the other hand, or half-parodying it as in Jim's defiant aria to the coming of day in Brecht's and Weill's *Aufstieg und Fall der Stadt Mahagonny* (1930), only served to expose the hollow ambitions of full-scale works that had nothing really significant in the long term to put in its place. The outstanding exceptions are nearly all the mature operas of Leoš Janáček. Indeed there could hardly be anything less like Wagner's lengthy psychological explorations of character entwined in labyrinthine musical structures. Janáček's best works for the stage are justly admired for their concision, raw emotion, sinewy harmony, bare textures, direct expression and a dramatic immediacy that goes directly to the heart of the listener. Even some of his subjects are simply inconceivable in the context of Wagner's concept of temporality where real historical time can never exist, even in its most grotesque forms – the journey of the philistine Prague landlord Brouček to the moon and the fifteenth century in *The Excursions of Mr Brouček* (1920), for instance, or the heroine Emilia Marty in *The Makropulos Affair* (1926) who can live for 300 years.

Apart from Janáček, most valiant efforts to recapture or to reject Wagner's idea of drama pale before the achievement of Alban Berg's *Wozzeck* (1925), one of the undisputed masterpieces of modern opera. Berg had to twist the knife twice: besides turning Wagner's concept psychologically on its head, he also set it on a dangerous collision course with its challengers. In his 1929 lecture on *Wozzeck*, Berg himself formally eschewed 'the Wagnerian recipe of "through-composing" ' (Redlich 1957, 261–85; 267), and famously relied on traditional forms like the passacaglia and sonata to ensure musical cohesion. Indeed, to describe *Wozzeck* without careful qualification as a post-Wagnerian opera at all can be seriously misleading. On one level it is a realistic melodrama on a par with Puccini's *Tosca* (1900) in which its protagonist also suffers appalling abuse. (Not insignificantly both operas take their time-frame of 'life itself' from spoken plays.) But on another its fifteen scenes are highly subjective musical journeys into deracinated states of mind closer to the central idea behind Wagnerian drama, from which, as we have seen, Puccini explicity distanced himself. The complex orchestral environment each time envelops the characters, not to explore rich Wagnerian lives to be sure, but human existences that have been devastated and emptied out by modern social conditions. Berg's compassionate spirit, which owes not a little to a profoundly ironic adaptation of Wagner's idea of interior drama on an ambitious musical scale, is never more in evidence than it is in this astonishing work.

For composers working in a post-Wagnerian environment, negotiating between Wagner's example and a radical rejection of it was often more important than adhering rigorously to the one or the other. Not that this guaranteed unalloyed triumph. Franz Schreker's *Der ferne Klang* (1912) and Ernst Křenek's *Jonny spielt auf* (1927) veer awkwardly between idealized musical spaces and realistic scenes of petty bourgeois life (e.g. the bizarre scene in Křenek's opera in which the hero Max shares his sorrows with a singing glacier outside his hotel in the Alps) and it is doubtless this uncertainty of dramatic aim that has helped to consign these works, and others of the same ilk, to the limbo of Fascinating Operas of the Past (FOPS) – occasionally revived, but stubbornly grounded on the remoter borders of the repertoire.

Admiring historical studies of FOPS from the 1920s and 1930s will probably never be in short supply. What is sorely missing is a sober critical investigation into the reasons for their initial success and long-term failure which takes a hard look at their Wagnerian and anti-Wagnerian pedigree. *Jonny spielt auf* – probably the most famous example – was taken up after its premiere by over 30 stages in German-speaking countries during its first season and around 20 foreign theatres during the next two years, making it one of the greatest operatic hits of all time. But history has been less than kind to it and it is simply no good blaming its subsequent lacklustre fame solely on the influence of Goebbel's Nazi propaganda machine, which notoriously excoriated the work, among other reasons because the character Jonny is a negro jazz-band musician who first enters carrying a golden saxophone – a sexually uninhibited image that could hardly be more removed visually and musically from the interior spaces of Wagner's music dramas. Indeed, the resolute refusal of Wagnerian drama to move outside the subjective musical worlds of its characters, thus measuring itself idealistically against the 'impurities' of real life, was shamelessly exploited by Hitler, whom Goebbels described as listening to Wagner as if 'the drama were in artistic unison with his political being' (1936, 67). It was only logical, therefore, that the image of Jonny should be emblazoned over the brochure of the Nazis' notorious 1938 Düsseldorf exhibition *Entartete Musik* ('Degenerate Music') as a telling symbol of everything opposed to the racist musical ideals of the Third Reich.

But public demand for performances of Křenek's opera had already begun to wane before the Nazis assumed power in 1933. Unsettling though the political upheavals surrounding the so-called *Zeitopern* of the 1920s and early 1930s were, their deliberately ephemeral topicality is not quite enough to explain their weaknessess. Alone the label *Zeitoper* (opera of the times) marks the opposition of these works to the Wagnerian ideal of an operatic dramaturgy beyond history, including Hindemith's *Neues vom Tage* (1929) and Caspar Neher's and Weill's *Die Bürgschaft* (1932). A more fruitful line of critical enquiry could well lie in a closer scrutiny of the role of music in relation to the perception of dramatic time about which composers were often confused, or which they simply miscalculated – a sympathetic failing perhaps in view of the social pressure that was increasingly being brought to bear on opera, especially after the First World War. If reflection on Wagner's influence can teach us anything, it is that he raised the stakes of opera to such a pitch that it proved extremely difficult for those after him to choose convincing forms of musical dramaturgy in a spectrum of possibilities which in no small measure due to his own example had become much broader, and to reconcile that choice with the heavy demands placed on works of art in the modern era. In the case of opera, that included a growing sense of unease about its validity which, from the middle of the nineteenth century onwards, Wagner himself had already forcefully expressed.

3 Puccini and the dissolution of the Italian tradition

VIRGILIO BERNARDONI

Examining the debate which developed in Italy during the early years of the twentieth century around the concept of romanticism is a useful and effective way of charting the relationship of intellectual and critical ideas to the realities of the national operatic tradition. The common ground of the discussion was to locate the idea of the romantic tradition in a synthesis of various historical, aesthetic and ethical characteristics, and to identify it with the period of the *melodramma*, a genre which brought with it notions of humanity and moral character, of stylistic features (sentimentalism, expression of the passions, primacy of melody), and of formal and linguistic conventions, which, taken together, go to make up the received view of Italian musicality. From the varied pronouncements and points of view expressed within this complex of ideas and character-istics, an ideological divide seems clear between those musicians who remained loyal to the melodramatic tradition (essentially, those born around 1860 and who first came to prominence around 1890, such as Francesco Cilea, Umberto Giordano, Ruggero Leoncavallo, Pietro Mascagni and Giacomo Puccini) and those who, being more sharply critical of this tradition, inclined towards a radical re-evaluation both of dramaturgical categories and also of the musical language itself within a modernist perspective (those musicians who were born around 1880 and came to prominence around 1910, such as Alfredo Casella, Gian Francesco Malipiero and Ildebrando Pizzetti).

In this context, the voice of Fausto Torrefranca stands out as that of a strong and intransigent critic of the most recent tendencies of the Italian tradition. Viewing music history primarily as the development of genres, he went so far as to deny romanticism all historiographical validity, to the extent that it was identified with the era of the *melodramma* (which 'never was the ideal of our national musical culture'). In opposition to it he placed the symphony, a genre which he saw as embodying the most authentic Italian tradition (albeit an interrupted one), and whose artistic renewal by means of new creative impulses he regarded as essential. The inevitable consequence of this was the establishment of a clear distinction between the categories of 'musician' and 'opera composer', two types of activity which could no longer be simply assumed to be the same, not least since the second was in the process of exhausting itself in the febrile pursuit of passion and dramaticism in the manner typical of operatic *verismo*. This was, he considered, a state of decadence of which the operas of Puccini offered a clear example: female characters who had inherited from the Verdi of *La traviata* 'the ethereal spirit of sentimentality and unhappiness' while exuding poignantly an aura of 'humanity and sincerity'; typically melodramatic situations (as in *La Bohème*: 'the poet's sudden realization [of his love], his lover's consumption, and the simple goodness of all the girls fallen on hard times'), balanced only by the 'lacrimose idealization' of musical pathos; and at times an excess of realism (as, for example, in *Tosca*) which seemed to be unaware that the essence of romanticism lay, precisely, in a combination of qualities which joins the trivial with the ideal, and finds a balance between the realism of the plot and the idealizing representation of the action through the expressive means of music (Torrefranca 1912, 30, 51, 54).

Among musicians of a modernist persuasion, on the one hand we find Malipiero invoking an absolute creative freedom from received operatic conventions (in the first place from operatic vocality and the 'petulance of singers and their vocal organs') and from the obligatory requirements of stage spectacle, in the name of a more fully integrated balance between music and poetry (Malipiero 1913, 1); while, on the other, Casella went as far as refusing to recognize any reasons at all for the survival of the *melodramma*, which he saw as having been henceforth assimilated into the modern tradition of instrumental music in its primary and most characteristic dimension, namely, a dramatic sense. From here, the future of musical theatre is foreseen precisely as 'the union of the medium of sound with a certain quasi-sculptural vision: forms, colours, gestures', and in terms of the need to combine the idioms of the Italian comic tradition with those of contemporary ballet in a new form of 'figural comedy in which gesture will substitute for text, and out of which will re-emerge the wonderful energy and comic verve of eighteenth-century Neapolitan comedy' (1919, 2, and 1921). Of its nineteenth-century roots, Casella therefore allowed to modern Italian music only the rather minor and certainly intermittent current of nineteenth-century operatic comedy: from *Il barbiere* (1816), the most successful of all Rossini's operas, to Verdi's *Falstaff* (1893).

Nevertheless, other musical figures of the early twentieth century took up less radical positions. Pizzetti, for example, convinced of the irreplaceable and indeed exemplary theatrical quality of Bellini and middle-period Verdi, set out to demonstrate that his idea of a 'Latin musical drama' – basically an Italianate version of modern, that is, post-Wagnerian music drama, which Pizzetti described as 'an opera of poetry and music combined' – stood in a relationship of continuity-within-diversity to the traditional *melodramma*. Both of these two genres were after all 'battle-fields of human feelings and passions [set] in conflict', with 'characters whose actions are motivated by these feelings and passions' (1945, 53–4). The essence of any form of operatic theatre consisted more in this intrinsically dramatic duality than in any external musical or scenic factors. But the attachment to tradition was fundamental above all for the cluster of more reactionary tendencies which were embodied in the *Manifesto di musicisti italiani per la tradizione dell'arte romantica dell'800* ('Manifesto by Italian musicians in favour of the romantic artistic tradition of the nineteenth century'), printed on 17 December 1932 in two leading national newspapers, the *Corriere della sera* and *La Stampa*, and signed by, among others, prominent composers such as Pizzetti, Ottorino Respighi and Riccardo Zandonai.

Presenting a selection of the most reactionary objectives favoured by the more backward-looking wing of fascist musical culture, this *Manifesto* sought to reaffirm the legitimacy of the 'free expansion of lyricism', as also of 'the vehemence and intensity of dramatic expression', giving preference to 'the rhetoric . . . of feeling over [that of] culture'. It declared itself against the kind of art that 'has no human content' and is nothing but a 'mechanical play, a cerebral juggling', in favour of the 'romanticism of yesteryear, which . . . is life in action, in joy and sorrow'. By affirming the primacy of the romantic tradition over more recent developments (described as 'mere atonal and polytonal trumpetings', and criticized for their 'objectivism' and 'expressionism'), the *Manifesto* gave voice to those aspirations towards a restoration of certain key aspects of the old order which were active during the 1930s. So much so that, in this general climate directed towards the explicit denial of modernist aspirations, even a musician who can hardly be suspected of conservatism such as Mario Labroca nevertheless pointed to the fundamental need for a recovery of the lyric and operatic forms of the romantic era. For him, the supreme model is still given by the operas of Verdi, which embody the 'romantic spirit' to the extent that they represent the 'making explicit of feeling', while yet setting this expression within a 'rigidly classical' musical form, directly descended from the intrumental forms of the seventeenth and eighteenth centuries. And so from here, there is a clear invitation to confront the entirety of the Italian musical tradition – an invitation which, within the context of the age-old polarity between musical drama and symphony, seems to announce a brilliant, and potentially reconciling, compromise solution (Labroca 1934).

In fact, more than with the dramatic subjects, the plots, and the particular qualities of the *dramatis personae* of the *melodramma*, which had all declined in the general taste, the modernists felt called to measure themselves against the overall efficiency and effectiveness of the forms and dramaturgical conventions of the genre – conventions which were fully in the contemporary consciousness thanks to the overwhelming presence of such repertory pieces in the programmes of the opera houses. In their (never slavishly imitative) confrontation with nineteenth-century models of the lyric number, negotiating between the negation, elaboration and restitution of older vocal models, is to be found one of the most productive (rather than ideological) factors of the romantic inheritance within Italian twentieth-century dramatic and operatic music. The critic Guido M. Gatti had already realized this when, implicitly criticizing the anti-melodramatic position taken by Casella, he found himself unable to deny the links that still bound contemporary Italian opera to its nineteenth-century roots. And this even led him to see in the rise of neo-classicism the emergence of a kind of musical neo-romanticism, guaranteed by what seemed likely to be the secure future of opera as a genre (which was by then judged to be on the point of ceding its position to the pre-eminence of ballet), by the renewed vitality of its closed forms, and by the tenacious resistance of melody to the new types of prosodical and text-based vocal writing (Gatti 1925, 18–19). This amounted to a recognition of the existence of certain constants within the genre of Italian opera: the primacy of singing, by means of which the human characters individualize themselves; the importance assigned to balance and equilibrium within the musical forms, grounded in the metrical structures and general layout of the dramatic text.

The legacy of the *fin de siècle*

Once *verismo* had run its course, which in the case of Mascagni stretched from *Cavalleria rusticana* (1890) to the less extreme versions of the style found in *L'amico Fritz* (1891), *Silvano* (1895) and *Zanetto* (1896), and taking in along the way such works as *Tilda* by Cilea, *Mala vita* by Giordano, and *Pagliacci* by Leoncavallo (all dating from 1892), the composers of the 1860 generation began to show signs of anxiety in the face of this tradition. And so they began to move in directions which would subsequently bring good fortune and success: towards a confrontation with broader European tendencies (at that time bound up with the whole process of the internationalization of Italian culture in its 'Scapigliatura/ Decadent' phase, a process by which important elements of *verismo* had already found their way into a variety of non-Italian (chiefly French) contexts, from the elegant and affecting lyricism of Gounod, Massenet and Ambroise Thomas, to the realism of Bizet's *Carmen* (1875); and towards the recovery and assimilation of musical and dramaturgical solutions to the problem of musical theatre from further afield.

In the meantime, and in a climate in which echoes of the polemical debate around opera and musical drama were still strong, the musicians of the 1860 generation faced in definitive fashion the question of Wagnerian music drama, and – while still maintaining a certain distance from the sheer complexity of thought such an enterprise would have entailed – drew certain inspirations from it. Among these were: a degree of nationalistic defiance on behalf of the Latin-Mediterranean epic, read in a primarily historical light, as an alternative to Nordic-Germanic epic, of predominantly mythological character; a series of harmonic innovations, but only so far as they offered musical materials which could function effectively together with other materials, and would fit with a variety of contexts; the challenge of reshaping motivic contours and of increasing the symphonic contribution, but within an operatic system which nevertheless refused to embrace the whole network of leitmotivic elaboration and which presented itself instead as a renewal and further development of the Italian method of using reminiscence motifs. Leoncavallo, with his opera *I Medici* (1893, set in Renaissance Florence at the time of the Pazzi Conspiracy), explored the project of creating a truly Italian form of operatic epic, 'animated by a high philosophical and patriotic content, yet drawn from and grounded in reality' (Leoncavallo, *Appunti*, 24).

Puccini, after having completed his 'revision' of *Die Meistersinger* (the usual kind of cutting meted out to Wagnerian music dramas when given in Italian translation), just as he was beginning on the composition of *Manon Lescaut* (1893), made use of the '*Tristan* chord' as well as of reminiscences of Wagnerian situations to express the true love of the two young lovers (the whole of the duet between Manon and Des Grieux in Act II, for example, recalls that of Tristan and Isolde), in opposition to the Arcadian and eighteenth-century colour of the ridiculous passion of the aged Geronte. Similarly, in Leoncavallo's *La Bohème* (1897) the various harmonies and motifs of Tristanesque inspiration take on something of the expressive colouring of solitude, of illness and death. But this is so only in contrast to the youthfulness of the bohemians, the musical expression of which includes quotations from Meyerbeer's *Les Huguenots* (1836) – at that time performed quite frequently in Italian theatres – and even embraces the Rossinian pastiche of Schaunard's 'cantata'. In this way, once the initial score had been settled with the problem of Wagnerian reception (seen at its high point in the dense leitmotivic working found in the operas of Antonio Smareglia) in the years around the turn of the century, there was a move to confront the impressionist challenge of Debussy (*Pelléas et Mélisande* was first given at La Scala, Milan, in 1908) and the proto-expressionism of Richard Strauss, while also embracing – in this case, too, via Paris – a rather late encounter with the tradition of Russian grand opera (*Boris Godunov* was given at La Scala in 1909).

On the other hand, at the *fin de siècle* we see the appearance of retrospective currents, and a movement towards explicitly old-fashioned types of opera. Alberto Franchetti, for example, conceived his *Cristoforo Colombo* (1892) as an 'opera-ballet' *all'italiana*, but using a historical subject in the manner of early nineteenth-century Parisian grand opera. And in the wake of Verdi's *Falstaff* (1893), there was a flowering of operatic comedy, a foretaste of the later fashion for comic 'revivalism' and the return to the *buffo* genre on the eighteenth-century model. Act II of Puccini's *La Bohème* (1896), for example, is a famous instance of brilliant comic dynamism. Mascagni and the librettist Luigi Illica, in their collaboration on *Le maschere* (1901), set out on an ambitious, even audacious project (which in the event was not a great artistic success): to present the *commedia dell'arte* as nothing less than the archetype of an Italian form of dramatic art that was 'true and human'. And the character role of Michonnet in Cilea's *Adriana Lecouvreur* (1902) quite literally takes its cue from the protagonist of Rossini's *Barbiere*, deriving from it its most amusing characteristics and comic traits.

At the same time, the Italian tradition was in the process of beginning to free itself from the well-worn cliché of its 'national operatic product' in order to move outwards into the more cosmopolitan world of the new international operatic market, run on commercial lines by the powerful Milanese publishing houses (Ricordi and Sonzogno), and also into a new cosmopolitanism of operatic subjects, times, places and climates, all to be represented with realistic precision and plausibility. For Puccini, for example, the translation of ambience into musical atmosphere is always a preliminary creative operation of fundamental importance, but it takes on a special intensity in operas on exotic subjects, in which the relationship of the music to setting and ambience acts either as a function of local colour (in *Madama Butterfly* the Japanese melodies, which are contrasted with the hymn of the American Navy; in *La fanciulla del West* the Indian Zuni melodies; and in *Turandot* the 'original' Chinese music), or else as an active principle of modernization within the musical language itself, favouring the use of long pedals, unresolved dissonances, harmonic ostinatos of 'primitive' character, and of bitonal passages, which all conflict in various ways with the fundamentally Italian character of the Puccinian style, as expressed in its essential diatonicism, in the stability of its tonal centres, and through the primacy of melody.

With its assertion of such thematic and stylistic ideas as the comic, the antique and the exotic, late nineteenth-century opera entered into a dynamic relationship with tradition, thereby opening the way to a kind of dialectic between, on the one hand, opera as the possession and indeed the satisfaction of norms held in common by composers, interpreters and public alike; and, on the other, opera as a project of research, as an individual intellectual adventure, yearning for and struggling towards renewal. In general terms, in trying to evaluate the gains and losses, it is above all the metric and lyric schemes, the melodic and dramatic periods of the nineteenth-century tradition which tend to disappear, to make way for a musical syntax that is no longer periodic but rather is more often grounded in the idea of the lyric fragment or moment. In this perspective, it is the Verdi–Boito line of development (the lyric use of the classic Italian *endecasillabo* (11-syllable line) in *Aida*, for example, or of the pervasive experimentation with metrical and poetic forms in *Falstaff*) which served as a model, even more than Strauss's *Salome* (performed for the first time in Italy in 1906, in Italian translation), and which was able to develop and establish new prosodical standards. Mascagni's *Guglielmo Ratcliff* (completed in 1895), based on Alessandro Maffei's version of Heine, offers an early example of *Literaturoper*, having been composed on a text written originally as a piece of literary rather than staged theatre, and may be seen as anti-operatic in its narrative approach and in its use of unrhymed *endecasillabi* in the libretto.

Puccini himself, from the period of even his most popular and successful operas, never concealed his preference for using a wide variety of metres (unrhymed *endecasillabi* and *settenari*, for instance, which once were reserved for recitative); and he also showed a certain indifference to lyric verse-types with their rhymed, closed forms. In the second place, and on a more general level, even the dynamic process of both satisfying and playing on the public's expectations enters once more into a phase of relatively greater equilibrium. Overturning the formal and expressive balance of the traditional *melodramma*, the taste for complex and intricately worked plots placed the music in a somewhat secondary position relative to the presentation of the action, and favoured the adoption within the operatic sphere of procedures indebted to literary or bourgeois-theatrical models, with a marked preference for types of plot based on the narrative conventions of the popular novel (typical cases of this would be *Andrea Chenier*, *Adriana Lecouvreur* and *Siberia*) or of more complex theatrical plays (such as *Fedora* and *La Tosca*, by Victorien Sardou). In Puccini's *Tosca* (1900), from the standpoint of sheer theatricality, we find an extraordinarily impressive combination of elements: extremes of passion, a dramatic escape, 'theatre within the theatre', torture, an attempted rape and subsequent murder, an onstage execution by firing squad, the heroine's suicide; and, on top of all this, the powerful element of ceremony and spectacle of baroque Rome, and the evocation of a pastoral dawn at the beginning of Act III, echoing with rustic voices. It is Puccini's great merit to have treated his subject in such variety and yet with such skill and tact as to make of it a coherent dramatic whole, seeking deep within his characters in order to bring out the turbulent erotic feeling of Tosca and Cavaradossi, and the monstrous inhumanity of Scarpia, whom the series of three striking chords heard at the very opening of the opera (the 'Scarpia motif') immediately characterizes, with no need for further elaboration, as a sadistic demon.

Gabriele D'Annunzio and the temptations of decadence

A new repertory of shared musical and stylistic features, which lend a semblance of mutual familiarity to many operas of the early years of the century, is confirmed by the extensive use of subjects which continue to draw on the attractions and aestheticizing tendencies of *fin de siècle* decadence: archaisms, folkloric allusions, instrumental writing with hints of a late nineteenth-century polyphonic character, sinuous chromaticisms and touches of modality, decorative harmonic sequences lacking an essential functional context, polytonal allusions and the pervasive use of free declamatory writing, thereby favouring a rapid pacing of the text. Mascagni's *Iris* (1898) and *Isabeau* (1912), although arising out of the somewhat homespun reception and assimilation of decadent themes on the part of Luigi Illica, offered Mascagni concrete opportunities to extract himself from the familiar subjects of *verismo*. In *Iris* it is the floridly decorative nature of the exotic material which weaves around the usual erotic events of the action a precious halo of symbols (as, for example, in the little theatre of the three 'Egoisms' in Act III); while in *Isabeau* it is the sheer brilliance and splendour of an aestheticizing medievalism and the associated cult of beauty which lead quite naturally to certain stylistic archaisms (parallel triads, effects of 'primitive' polyphony) and to a sense of pure scenic contemplation. The librettist Silvio Benco created a series of dramatic scenarios for Smareglia (*La falena*, 1897; *Oceana*, 1902; *Abisso*, 1913) and for the young Malipiero (*Elen e Fuldano*, 1907; *Canossa*, 1911–12) which are set against a symbolist background, and tend also to reposition the usual atmosphere of quasi-medieval or Nordic aestheticism within a dreamlike dimension, as opposed to a realistic one, operating more by suggestion than by action and leaving ample space for the free play of the irrational forces of the unconscious. Franco Alfano in *La leggenda di Sakuntala* (begun in 1914, premiered in 1921), skilfully fashioned a dramaturgy that proceeds more by allusion than by representation and emerges from a clearly impressionist stylistic matrix. All these are dramatic and aesthetic themes that, in exalted form, flow directly into the D'Annunzian phase of musical drama.

The development of the musical interests of the towering literary figure of D'Annunzio unfolded over a broad span of genres – from the novel to the drama, and from drama to the opera libretto. And the transfer from the one to the other of the same freedom of subject matter, of the same sensuality in the dramatic figures, of the same sophisticated and *recherché* quality of the sensations, functioned for the composers who set his texts as the catalyst of a process of change which was pursued, at the musical level, through the enrichment of the harmonic language and of the orchestral palette. In truth, D'Annunzio's contribution to opera may be thought of as a somewhat audience-directed operation, offering spectators the sheer immediacy and impact of a grandiose approach, with a certain standardization (and indeed repetition) of dramatic themes and motifs, with a superabundance of Gothic and medieval theatrical settings, great battle scenes, suicides, motifs of incest and adultery, erotic encounters inspired by passages of romance, scenes of love and death, and so on. In the libretto of *Parisina* – the only one of his texts conceived expressly for operatic setting – the delirium of the protagonist recalls the fantasies of Francesca and of Isolde, while the eroticism of the great scene in which Ugo and Parisina find passion, and also meet their deaths, makes explicit what in Wagner's *Tristan* remains at the level of suggestion. This kind of Tristaneque atmosphere is evident also in the verse written for the love duet added to the libretto reworking of *Francesca da Rimini* (1914): 'As an enemy I saw the light, – As a friend I found the night' ('Nemica ebbi la luce, – Amica ebbi la notte', Act III). These words were destined to furnish what would become the best-known passage of Zandonai's opera.

From the collaborations with more traditional composers, which the poet pursued in a rather distant and aloof way, usually with his own commercial interests at heart, remote from the project and most often delegating the work to others through the intermediary of his publisher Tito Ricordi, came diverse results. Mascagni interpreted the drama of *Parisina* (1913) with an incomparable modernist tension that has scarcely an equal in the Italian works of its time. And yet, notwithstanding the cuts made to D'Annunzio's prolix text, it tends to lose itself in the intricate spider's web of pastiche *strambotti* and medieval litanies, while still managing to present itself to best advantage in the musical continuity of a noble declamation, supported by a mobile and remarkably intense symphonic texture in the orchestra. In his setting of *Francesca* (1914),

Zandonai moves skilfully within a versatile linguistic and stylistic range. There are archaisms in the popular songs, written in period style (complete with lutes, 'pifferi' wind-players, 'viole pompose', and plagal cadences!); passages of chromaticism as a symbol standing both for intoxication and for magic; and harmonic colourings of impressionist derivation for the moments of coastal or seascape atmosphere. Italo Montemezzi first passed through a phase of D'Annunzianism at second hand, in the dark and turbulent idiom of *L'amore dei tre Re* (1913), composed to a libretto by Sem Benelli. Then, when approaching the composition of *La Nave* (1918), Montemezzi sought to intensify and enhance the asymmetrical phrasing and impact of his declamatory writing through the use of a chromaticism of broadly Straussian character.

Undoubtedly the most significant results were obtained by Pizzetti, the only composer to whom D'Annunzio ever paid sustained attention. From the *Musiche per "La nave"* (1908), developing through the incidental music to *La Pisanella* (1912–13) and carried through into the opera *Fedra* (1915), Pizzetti developed a new ideal of drama based, precisely, on the assumption of an archaizing fiction. The recovery and appropriation, within an avowedly modern style, of past idioms – of ancient modality, of Palestrina's polyphony, of madrigalian techniques, and, above all, of a pervasive use of syllabic declamation, even in the music for the chorus, which borrowed from plainchant its preference for movement by small intervals and for a vocal ambitus confined within the mid-range – bespeaks a musical dramaturgy that has remained largely immune both from the influence of Wagnerian reception, and from any kind of *verismo* survival.

D'Annunzio's libretti imposed on all these musicians an effort of acculturation and forced them to confront two major questions, both of which obliged them to loosen somewhat their ties to the received tradition. On the one hand, D'Annunzio's dramas tend to suppress or at least play down the conflict of psychologically plausible emotions, which had been essential to the very substance and character of the genre of Italian opera throughout its history. And on the other, faced with a level of verbal poetry which itself aspired towards the condition of music, they were led into a radical reconsideration of the relations between words and music – and not always to the advantage of the singing line, which generally remained in a state of subordination to the elevated tone of the words, and for which the composer was therefore forced either to find alternative vocal solutions, or else to channel the vocal element into the broader continuity of a sustained declamation.

The first case is well illustrated by the traditional lyric-operatic structures of Alberto Franchetti's *La figlia di Iorio* (1906). For example, in the great duet between Aligi and Mila which opens Act II (this is the episode during which the passion between the two is consummated), the popular song sung by Mila which opens the scene and the archaic-religious tone of the chorus of pilgrims in the middle of the scene (which connote, respectively, local colour and the age-old, ancestral religiosity of D'Annunzian tragedy) are not enough to hide the extreme formal conventionality of the whole piece, which, in line with tradition, presents an opening *tempo d'attacco* ('Se vuol sangue') followed by a *cantabile* ('Rinverdisca per noi'), and then by a finale ('Aligi fratel mio!') which engages in a crescendo of animation, not without a clear memory of the traditional *cabaletta* in the unison high notes which the two singers share at the end. At the opposing end of the spectrum stands the 'musical prose' of Pizzetti's *Fedra*, modelled directly on the word- and phrase-rhythms of D'Annunzio's verse and anchored to the scenic movement of the stage action, as projected through the motivic texture of the orchestra operating now in the dimension of memory and reminiscence, now in that of foreknowledge and intimation.

Perhaps as a result of D'Annunzio's tendency to withdraw from any kind of effective or practical interaction with his composers, for most of them their collaborations with him were to remain unique occurrences. Franchetti, after a long silence, teamed up with Giovacchino Forzano (later the librettist of two thirds of Puccini's *Trittico*) who led him first to the mythologizing archaisms of *Notte di leggenda* (1915) and then to the graceful 'superhuman' mythological fable of *Glauco* (1922); Mascagni tempered the emphatic and vehement style typical of the decadent aesthetic in his virtuoso idyll *Lodoletta* (1917); and Zandonai, beginning an artistic relationship of several years with the librettist Giuseppe Adami, turned towards an essentially rather lightweight revitalization of Italian comedy (*La via della finestra*, 1919). Only Pizzetti, who became his own librettist, confirmed and developed the linguistic and dramatic codes established in his *Fedra* through a series of works produced in response to varied poetic ideas and scenarios: the biblical dramas *Dèbora e Jaéle* (1922) and *Lo straniero* (1930), and a *Fra Gherardo* (1928) inspired by the vivid *Chronicle* of the thirteenth-century Franciscan writer Fra Salimbene de Adam.

By way of contrast, a wide range of composers showed themselves ready to make use of themes and formulae of D'Annunzian inspiration. Umberto Giordano in *La cena delle beffe* (1924), based on the neo-Gothic romantic-novelistic approach of Sem Benelli, displays, in the opera's expansive approach to lyric expression and its symphonic flights, a clear relationship to his own most conventional *verismo* manner. Respighi and Claudio Guastalla in *La campana sommersa* (1929) – a rather strange mixture of the human and the fantastic – set out to aestheticize the legend, arriving at their most interesting and involving results in those passages drenched in a magical sensuality, as for example in the duets sung by the two protagonists, Enrico and Rautendelein. Then, in *La fiamma* (1934), they buried the modernist aspirations of the most evolved D'Annunzian aesthetic in what is in effect a true and traditional *melodramma*, in which the Byzantine frame of the dramatic action (which takes place in seventh-century Ravenna – a local and historical colour evoked musically in the presentation of oriental scalic and melodic patterns) becomes the setting for the unfolding of the individual dramas of three tragic figures: Basilio, victim of an old man's love for a young woman, Silvana; Silvana herself, attracted by the young man, her stepson Donello, and burning with an ambiguous disquiet as she recognises herself to be a witch; and the aged mother Eudossia, implacable in her hostility towards her young rival). The unfolding of these personal human fates is articulated through the familiar dramatic and musical form of a number opera, with arias, duets, and elaborated finales to the acts.

Tradition in crisis

Puccini meanwhile maintained a guarded position in relation to D'Annunzio, and an aristocratic distance from the temptations of the decadent aesthetic. The long-drawn-out problem of the various attempts at a collaboration with D'Annunzio – first of all in 1906–7, then again in 1912 – demonstrates very well their inability to find a mid-point of stylistic contact, in which 'the painful experience of life and love ... might logically live and palpitate in a cloud of living poetry, rather than in a dream-world' (Gara 1958, 328). The result was a very particular approach to dramaturgy which perceived clearly the need for renewal, and also began to move towards the revitalization of the musical language, recalling in certain points the neurotic anxiety of the crisis through which operatic music was passing, while still preserving a solid foundation and never abandoning its polemical stance *vis à vis* the modernist current of the early years of the century, judged guilty of a certain corruption of the taste and technique that went into the making of opera in the true sense.

From *La fanciulla del West* to *Turandot*, Puccini showed a special awareness of – and sensitivity to – the crisis of nineteenth-century melodrama, displaying in these later operas an increasing refinement of musical means and a diversification and enrichment of his dramatic subjects. His approach to vocal writing went far beyond the received patterns of

Italian *bel canto*, and was generally reduced to a series of skilfully frag-mented melodic ideas: this approach is fundamental to both *La fanciulla del West* (1910) and *Il tabarro* (1918), two operas which display a marked openness to declamatory singing, with a corresponding shift of interest at times onto the distinctive use of timbre and sonority in the 'symphonic' orchestral material, at other times onto the rich and suggestive quality of the harmony. The operetta-like approach of *La rondine* (1917) includes, among other things, a reflection on the use of functional types of music (e.g. dance-types, including waltzes). But by the following year it is a fully retrospective view, looking back to genres by now firmly historicized, that stands at the basis of *Il trittico* (1918), a three-in-one work which might almost be described as a mannerist compendium of the dramatic tenden-cies of the preceding twenty years: from the Grand Guignol-style realism of *Il tabarro* (a revisiting of the typical *verismo* subjects of the 1890s), to the sentimental exploration of the tragic situation of the central heroine in *Suor Angelica* (a perfect example of the 'Puccinian manner'), to the recovery and revitalization of the comic in *Gianni Schicchi* (which, unlike other contemporary revivals of the eighteenth-century *buffo* manner, offers a kind of comedy that is anything but 'reconstructed', being grounded in a perceptibly modern idiom in respect both of the musical language and of the scenic approach). And finally *Turandot* (1926) opens up the possibility of the renewal of opera by means of a return to mythic and legendary subjects.

Puccini explored a range of strategies as he confronted modern com-posers and styles. *Il tabarro* contains Debussyan orchestral traits (and indeed a stream-like musical flow that is also somewhat Debussyan), touches of dissonance redolent of Strauss (in the tense scene of the lighted match), and even citations of Stravinsky (the waltz of the little out-of-tune barrel-organ). *Suor Angelica* displays archaizing traits (allusions to organum, the sonority of *a cappella* choral singing, modal inflections), which are bound up with the religious and liturgical setting of the action. *Turandot* reviews and reworks the formal schemes of the nineteenth-century *melodramma* (the conventional types of arias and duets) with a kind of studied meticulousness in the recovery of remote and old-fashioned procedures; while, at the same time, it presents an unusual stylistic fragmentation, proceeding by means of 'blocks' conceived either on the basis of exoticism, as an element capable of revitalizing the forms and structures of Western traditions, or, at other times, on that of the free use of dissonant intervals and harmonic agglomerations; or, again, on the sentimental and pathos-driven form of melody that is so deeply charac-teristic of Puccini's normal style. By these musical means, the contrasts and oppositions of the protagonist's gradual process of humanization are rendered in a directly scenic way: the warm glow of the golden reflections and the cool brilliance of the silver reflections, the sun and the moon, the sunset and the dawn, the cruelty of Turandot and the sacrifice of Liù, the failure of the Prince of Persia and the success of the Unknown Prince, the frozen body of the princess illuminated by the cutting light of the moon, and the 'burning hands' with which Calaf clasps her in the moment of their embrace, death and love.

Thus within the Puccinian theatre we can observe the gradual appearance of fissures in the logic of psychological 'identification', a phenomenon which is fundamental to a kind of dramaturgy which – in the romantic manner – continued to present itself as the confessional disclosure and evocation of a certain kind of realistic psychology. And on the other hand, we also see the emergence of a clear emotional distance on the composer's part from the events and situations of the action, even to the extent of a certain lack of sympathy for his characters, anticipated in the almost documentary-like dispassion first shown in *Il tabarro* and then, fully fledged, in the vocal part given to the princess Turandot – abstract, cold, impersonal – for the entire first act. Here she seems a distinctly unusual Puccinian protagonist in her state of human incommunicativeness.

Turandot is the last Italian opera to have gained a foothold in the international repertoire. It is a work that stands at the very limits of the grand tradition of opera in Italy (which was henceforth dead as a compositional phenomenon, while still continuing to live magnificently for the musical public in the form of an operatic repertory), and of the genre of opera as a broader category (which managed to survive, while remaining an object of indifference to the vast majority of the general public, more and more cut off from an appreciation of the more novel realizations of the genre). The establishment of the Maggio Musicale at Florence in 1931 – in the full flush of the Italian rediscovery of the romantic operas of Verdi, which was in turn the point of departure for the more extensive reappropriation of the nineteenth-century repertory in general – was intended to satisfy the demand for operas of the past, offering them to the public in lavish and prestigious stagings, given by celebrated conductors and singers, and often produced by directors and designers borrowed for the occasion from the figurative arts (among others, Sironi, Casorati, De Chirico), with the intention of achieving a more even overall balance by giving the scenic function (usually held to be secondary) a weight and prominence equal to that of the other elements of the dramatic spectacle.

Meanwhile, other types of spectacle were exercising a varied influence on the paths and approaches musicians were taking. Pizzetti (*Sinfonia del fuoco* for *Cabiria*, 1914) and Mascagni (*Rapsodia satanica*, 1915) were both attracted by the beginnings of cinematography, which in its turn drew on situations which were markedly melodramatic. And the ballet became a viable alternative to opera both for Malipiero, who in his 'symphonic drama' *Pantea* (completed in 1919) gave active expression to his polemic against the predominance of the singer-actor, and for Casella, who with *La giara* (1924, from the novella of the same title by Luigi Pirandello) attempted a distinctively Italian contribution to the international world of modern European ballet music.

Within this context, the crisis of tradition touched upon the very substance of the categories which lay at the root of *melodramma* as a genre, bringing into question the normative power of the relevant conventions, the temporal structures and the narrative categories, of operatic theatre. Malipiero – who also became his own librettist – elaborated his own version of an anti-theatrical dramaturgy. The libretto, once the recitatives had been excised, became an assemblage of poetic texts taken from the medieval and Renaissance eras. The relativization of the idea of a coherent narrative sequence, implicit in the whole dramatic layout, adapts itself to the paradoxical and at times grotesque character of the episodes, and to the interweaving of distanced and stylized figures (masks, allegories, marionettes, character-types) and of sentiments, of scenic plans and settings. The opera presents itself as a sequence of unrelated episodes, linked by instrumental interludes and culminating in closed song-forms: the 'lyric piece' is thus entirely parenthetic to the action, which is represented by means of pantomimic gestures during the symphonic instrumental sections. This model, invented for the *Sette canzoni* (1920, a sequence of 'seven dramatic expressions' which were then placed at the centre of the triptych *L'Orfeide* of 1925), could be easily applied to works that were similarly structured, such as the diptych *Filomela e l'Infatuato* (1928) and *Merlino mastro d'organi* (1934, an allegorical self-representation of music itself), or the trilogy entitled *Mistero di Venezia* (*Il finto Arlecchino*, 1928; *Le aquile di Aquileia* and *I corvi di San Marco*, 1932). But it was also applied to works such as the *Tre commedie goldoniane* (1926), which sought to reinstate a new solution to the problem of operatic dialogue, while transforming several of the most distinctive figures of Goldonian theatre into character-types lacking any human or psychological density, reduced instead to the status of masks of grotesque or tragic character, and suffused with a sense of ironic nostalgia.

Malipiero's theatrical utopia reaches its high point in *Torneo notturno* (1931), in which the composer achieves a new balance between a discontinuous approach to dramatic structure and the narrative continuity of the action, a solution which is sketched out in the dialectical relationship between the two characters: the Despairing Man ('Il Disperato') who is drowning in his own anguish and anxiety, and the Thoughtless Man ('Lo Spensierato'), who is impudent and unscrupulous. The centrepiece of the opera is the 'Canzone del Tempo': 'Chi ha tempo e tempo aspetta, il tempo perde' ('Whoever has time, and waits for time, loses time'), the text of which is formed of a chain of *strambotti* attributed to Serafino dall'Aquila (1466–1500). It is sung by the Thoughtless Man in the first Nocturne and then repeated – in whole or in part – in the six which follow. It thus stands at the very centre of the opera and becomes its dramatic core, both for its warning about the transitory nature of human existence, and for the way it alludes to the irreconcilable dualism between time, which disperses everything, and the ultimately hopeless determination to grasp and embrace life fully. It is also a distinctive example of Malipiero's highly characteristic approach to vocality: in setting the Renaissance texts he loved with an appropriately direct and elemental scansion, he deliberately alienated the musical from the verbal accent in his out-of-phase treatment of the textual and poetic stresses relative to the beats of the bar, thereby relegating the word to the status of a purely rhythmic pattern, geared solely towards prosody and largely indifferent to the communicative and expressive aspirations of music.

But already his next opera, *La favola del figlio cambiato* (1932–3), composed to a text by Pirandello (traces of Pirandellism can also be found in the typecasting of his characters from as early as the *Sette canzoni*), marked the composer's return to a unified action and plot, to a libretto with dialogue, and, as a consequence, to the extensive use of sung recitative. Malipiero thus stakes his claim for the recovery of a 'lyric conception' of opera, a conception which pervades the works of the 1930s, and is inspired by a classicizing ideal (*Giulio Cesare*, 1936; *Antonio e Cleopatra*, 1938) – albeit one by no means wholly devoid of encomiastic intentions *vis à vis* the Fascist regime.

Archaism, neo-classicism and the renewal of comedy

The importance Malipiero accorded to medieval and Renaissance traditions of Italian poetry lent his approach to drama an archaizing character which, as an expression both of a certain cult of the antique and of a fastidious love for rare and beautiful objects, was closely bound up with the tenets of D'Annunzian aestheticism. (Malipiero lived out in sentimental fashion the duality between classic and romantic, viewing the beauty of Venice through its portrayal in the novels of D'Annunzio, and attending with antiquarian passion to his edition of the works of Monteverdi, thereby facilitating the composer's rebirth in Italy – so that in all this he is, of the musical generation of 1880, the one most intimately compromised by his involvement with D'Annunzian aesthetic ideas.) Among his dramatic works the 'mystery' *San Francesco d'Assisi* (1922), inspired by the *Fioretti* (the 'Little Flowers of St Francis') and by the poetry of Jacopone da Todi, lays claim to an original and distinctive position within a clearly medievalizing aesthetic. In the four tableaux into which this one-act drama is divided, Malipiero emphasizes an almost anti-theatrical orientation, achieved by means of a process of distillation, almost of 'drying out' – of the words, of the characters (which are denuded of any kind of emotional or psychological individuation), of the vocalism (aiming at a pseudo-Gregorian purity, and, in the choruses, at a kind of writing which recalls the simplicity of the polyphonic lauda), of instrumental timbre and sonority, and finally of the scenic and theatrical apparatus. The result is a prototype of chamber opera, born out of a radical archaism in its dramatic approach, which enjoyed a certain successs in the 1920s and 1930s.

In similar vein, Pizzetti twice worked with the fifteenth-century miracle play entitled *La sacra rappresentazione di Abram e d'Isaac* by Feo Belcari, the first time by composing incidental music for a stage production (1926), then following this with a fully sung version (1937). Respighi, too, explored this aesthetic with his *Lauda per la natività del Signore* (1930) and the 'concert-opera' *Maria Egiziaca* (1932), which finds its expressive high points in the vocal intensity of the protagonist's mystical exaltation, and in the poetic quotation borrowed from St Francis which provides the text of the final chorus: 'Laudato sii, Signore'. In *Maria d'Alessandria* (1937) by Giorgio Federico Ghedini, the composer's approach emphasizes the work's oratorio-like characteristics.

Mystery-play, dramatic lauda, *sacra rappresentazione* – all these genres stand within the framework of a broader and more general expression of antiquarian taste, which also embraces the intellectualizing reinvention of mythological opera (for example in *La favola d'Orfeo* of Casella, based on Poliziano in the version by Corrado Pavolini, 1932) and revivalist reworkings in modern style of the early 'proto-melodramas'. Indeed, Monteverdi's *L'Orfeo* became a veritable stadium for often naïve pseudo-philological exertions: in 1928 it was performed at Leningrad in Malipiero's version; in 1934 it was given in two further versions, one at Perugia (by Giacomo Orefice) and the other at Rome (by Giacomo Benvenuti); and in 1935 it finally arrived at La Scala in the 'free interpretation' by Respighi and Guastalla. All these versions are in reality adaptations: they cut whatever in the general layout and conception seemed redundant; they 'complete' the harmonic syntax wherever it was felt to be insufficent, even primitive; and they 'reconstruct' with modern instruments whatever of the early approach to timbre and sonority was judged inadequate to be presented to contemporary ears.

During the first decades of the century, however, neo-classicism came to the fore and expressed itself above all in the recovery and revitalization of eighteenth-century comedy, a development which favoured the reinstatement of the structural properties and other features of *opera buffa*, and also leaned (somewhat ambitiously) in the direction of the absolute Mozartian ideal. Ermanno Wolf-Ferrari made of this idealizing approach the very cornerstone of his operatic work, producing a series of pieces characterized by a somewhat melancholy and well-mannered type of comedy, inspired by Goldoni (*Le donne curiose, I quattro rusteghi, Gli amanti sposi, La vedova scaltra, Il campiello*, works composed between 1903 and 1936) and also by Molière (*L'amore medico*, 1913). Alongside this series of works we find the varied post-D'Annunzian approaches of Zandonai, of Adriano Lualdi (*Il diavolo nel campanile, Le furie di Arlecchino*, 1925), of Felice Lattuada (*Le preziose ridicole*, 1929), of Luigi Ferrari-Trecate (*Ciottolino, La bella e il mostro, Le astuzie di Bertoldo*, works composed between 1922 and 1934), and of Ghedini with his Boccaccio-inspired 'divertissement' entitled *La pulce d'oro* (1940).

Respighi (*Belfagor*, 1923) and Casella (*La Donna serpente*, 1932) treated the subject matter of legend and fable by means of a notably eclectic approach, and with a quick-witted sense of the comic. *Belfagor*, based on the comedy by Ercole Luigi Morselli, sets the decidedly anti-heroic episode of a devil-turned-man who is scorned and shamed by the human beings in the story ('a devil who gets married, falls in love, and is ridiculed'). The work plays on the multiple levels of style suggested by the grotesque, free-and-easy character of the protagonist, by the vein of sentimentality appropriate to the young lovers, and by the strong presence of Rossinian vivacity (as in the protagonist's comic rigmarole of self-presentation, 'Sono un grosso mercante ritirato') which replays similar hints present in the ballet of a few years before, *La boutique fantasque* (1918). Casella stays close to the magic of Carlo Gozzi's tale, to the freshness and ingenuity of its fantasy and invention, and to the complications of a plot that is elaborated to the very limits of comprehensibility (embracing as it does a whole series of metamorphoses, apparitions and sudden changes of scene and locality), while also bringing to it all the bubbling vitality, the optimism, the comedic energy and the colourful irony that had matured in his instrumental music.

By these means *La Donna serpente* became an opera in complete contradiction to the norms of the melodramatic model. It is a work in which the text and the other dramatic elements (including the vocal writing) are subordinated to the musical invention and to the refined play of stylistic registers, including a range of well-judged references to stylistic features of the music of the past. The comic element (above all, the use of masks) is taken as an unending source of rhythmic vitality and dynamism, and possesses a clear Rossinian character and edge. And then into the various incarnations of the chorus is distilled the whole imaginative repertoire of the nineteenth century – the chorus is called upon to impersonate figures which are at times fantastic (fairies, gnomes, spirit-lovers), and at others sacred and ritualistic in character (priests, warriors). For the rest, the score abounds in ariosos, in Handelian arias, in *concertato* writing in the typical eighteenth-century manner, in duets and terzettos, all connected together according to a very immediate and graphic dramatic process which assigns to music the role of an abstract scenic flow, one which pursues its course more or less oblivious to the blandishments of sentiment.

In the aftermath of the Second World War, it was precisely the eclectic spirit of operatic comedy which offered the final opportunity of resistance to the received melodramatic tradition. Italian opera survived the apocalypse, firstly by lightening its burden of dramatic themes, which were orientated now for the most part towards the use of the grotesque, of the fabulous and legendary, and of the comic – this, then, was one of the fruits of the lesson pioneered by Casella in favour of a 'delightful and entertaining' theatre, and against a theatre 'of preaching and moralism, of pseudo-religion, of stasis and contemplation' (1932); and secondly by emphasizing a craftsmanlike concept of operatic composition, entirely remote from the intellectualizing and ideological agenda of the theatrical preoccupations favoured by the avant-garde.

Translated from the Italian by Philip Weller.

PART TWO

Trends

4 Words and actions

CAROLINE HARVEY

Subject-matter in twentieth-century opera has been shaped by influences as divergent as psychoanalysis, the cinema and television, the preference of many composers for chamber opera, the abandonment of verse or rhymed texts as the standard libretto, and an ironic scrutiny of the form of opera itself. 'Can I find [an ending] that is not trivial?', the Countess asks at the close of Strauss's last opera, *Capriccio* (1942). The problem of triviality confronted many composers after Wagner, whose music-dramas appeared as the pinnacle of operatic development. In the new century it was questionable whether opera as a viable art-form had not been consumed alongside Tristan and Isolde in the passion of the 'Liebestod', or the Teutonic gods in the fiery collapse of *Der Ring des Nibelungen*.

One solution was to make triviality itself into an operatic subject, as Křenek so successfully did with his *Zeitoper*, *Jonny spielt auf* (1927), which closes with the image of the black jazz violinist Jonny fiddling astride the globe. Another was to absorb Wagner's musical techniques and dramatic ideals into nationally inflected works: Debussy's *Pelléas et Mélisande* (1902) owes much to Wagner, but its speech-melody closely resembles the contours of spoken French. A letter Debussy wrote to Ernest Chausson on 2 October 1893 shows how concerned he was to discover a Wagnerian element 'appearing in the corner of a bar' (Lesure and Nichols 1987, 54). One of the major props in his endeavour to avoid such Wagnerisms was Maeterlinck's symbolic text. Its verbal indirection allowed Debussy to set a *Tristan*-like plot as a story of alienation and incompleteness, not passion (Holloway 1979, 61, 68–9). The same evasiveness, it could be argued, helped distinguish Debussy's opera from *Parsifal*, not in terms of the opera's sound-world but because it avoids the Christian allegory of Wagner's last work. Dvořák's fairy opera *Rusalka* (1901), too, absorbed and transformed Wagnerian techniques. It tells the European legend of Undine or Melusine, but borrows characters from Czech legend and introduces folk-like elements into parts of the through-composed score. A third solution to Wagner was to ignore his music-dramas and the idea of the *Gesamtkunstwerk*, and to rely instead on the alternative tradition of Verdi and number opera. *Verismo* opera first presented itself in Italy as a new direction, but was quickly taken up elsewhere, for example in France with Charpentier's *Louise* (1900) and in Bohemia amongst the younger generation of composers (Tyrrell 1988, 123).

In understanding the influences shaping opera and operatic subjects in the 1890s and the early decades of the twentieth century, it is important to look beyond developments in music to other artistic forms. Literary and dramatic schools of thought, as well as new styles in painting and architecture, were important sources of change. Naturalism, a major contributor to *verismo*, was literary in origin; symbolism, which enters operatic history through works like *Pelléas* and Dukas' *Ariane et Barbe-bleue* (1907), was also first literary and dramatic. Working in opposition to the naturalism of Zola and the descriptive tendency of the Parnassian poets, the symbolists transformed Wagner's ideal of the organic art-work into a vehicle for poetic suggestiveness. The evasive, half-spoken quality in Maeterlinck's play *Pelléas et Mélisande* (1892) was precisely what attracted Debussy, as he explained in 1902 in his article 'Pourquoi j'ai écrit "Pelléas"' (Debussy 1987, 62–4). Expressionism was another reaction against naturalism that began in literature and painting around the turn of the century and would likewise significantly shape twentieth-century opera. By the 1920s, expressionism's distorted, highly coloured depictions of human experience and perception had reached the operatic stage in the early works of Hindemith and Weill, as well as Berg's *Wozzeck*. The same decade saw a number of other solutions to the problems Wagner still presented. With Stravinsky's *Mavra* (1922) and Hindemith's *Cardillac* (1926), neo-classicism deliberately turned back to operatic techniques pre-dating Wagner, while the short-lived but influential *Zeitopern* of Křenek, Hindemith and Weill eschewed mythology for contemporary life: gramo-phones, telephones, cameras, even trains appeared in the stage action, accompanied by jazz tunes and dances reflecting the current craze for American music and culture.

Operatic subject-matter was further transformed from the turn of the century onwards by the new science of psychoanalysis. At times the influence was direct: Hugo von Hofmannsthal was reading Freud and Breuer's *Studies on Hysteria* when he wrote his play *Elektra*, the basis for Strauss's opera of 1909. More importantly, Freud's work became a pervasive influence on how the individual subject could be understood. Not only did inner psychological 'action' become a viable operatic subject, as in Bartók's only opera *Duke Bluebeard's Castle* (first performed in 1918), but the reality of human experience had profoundly shifted away from psychological unity towards fragmentation, conflict and the emergence of the unconscious drives from repression. Works like Schoenberg's *Erwartung* (1909) and *Die glückliche Hand* (1910–13) – both given their first performances in 1924 – as well as his unfinished *Moses und Aron* (1930–32), Berg's *Wozzeck* (1925) and *Lulu* (1928–35, first performed incomplete in 1937), and Britten's *Peter Grimes* (1945) and *Death in Venice* (1973) all suggest that the divided individual represented reality.

Nevertheless, Wagner remained a potent presence, a predecessor who demanded at least acknowledgement if not obeisance. This was nowhere clearer than in the career of Richard Strauss, Germany's most prominent opera composer up to the middle of the century. Stefan Zweig, one of Strauss's librettists in the 1930s, reports the composer as saying, 'with a broad, Bavarian grin', that he had made a detour around Wagner rather than try to climb higher (1943, 279). But Strauss had in fact tried the Wagnerian route, in *Salome* (1905) and *Elektra* (1909) as well as the early failure *Guntram* (1894), for which, in direct emulation of Wagner, he wrote his own libretto. *Der Rosenkavalier* (1911) represents the beginning of the Straussian detour. A comedy drawing on the format of number opera to represent the pathos and the farce of love and sexual desire, Strauss's and Hofmannsthal's Viennese period-piece is a deliberate step backwards, or sideways, from Wagner. The Strauss–Hofmannsthal works of the 1910s present a variety of solutions to the serious mythologizing of the legendary founder of the Bayreuth Festival. *Ariadne auf Naxos*, first performed in 1912 as the third act to Molière's *Le bourgeois gentilhomme* and later revised to be an independent piece, offers a delightfully ironic treatment of myth through the eruptions of *commedia dell'arte* characters into the tragedy of Ariadne, abandoned on Naxos by Theseus. In strong contrast to this deliberate trivialization of a legendary subject, *Die Frau ohne Schatten* (1919) presents an invented mythological world in which the empress must find a shadow in order to bear children, the only action that will prevent the emperor from turning to stone. Bizarre, densely symbolic, and at times inscrutable, Hofmannsthal's libretto is made credible by a score that provides motivic links between characters, symbols and scenes, and ultimately succeeds in humanizing the spirit empress. Later Strauss operas reproduce the themes of the earlier works: domestic and sentimental love in *Intermezzo* (1924), *Arabella* (1933) and the comedy *Die schweigsame Frau* (1935), and a series of reworked classical myths in *Die ägyptische Helena* (1928), *Daphne* (1938) and *Die Liebe der Danae* (1938–40, first performed in 1952). The 'conversation-piece with music', *Capriccio* (1942), refines the pathos and farce of *Der Rosenkavalier* into a work of sustained musical and verbal wit, leaving the question of trivial endings unanswered.

Sexuality

What is not reproduced in Strauss's operas after 1911 is the grotesque sexuality of *Salome* and *Elektra*. The subject-matter (if not the scores) of this pair of operas shares with the late nineteenth century a fascination with the figure of the castrating woman, as well as growing interest in sexual complexes and neuroses (see Kramer 1990 and Tambling 1996, 161–85). However, Salome's kissing the head of Jochanaan and Elektra's invoking the name of Agamemnon in an incestuous obsession with the father also initiate a characteristically twentieth-century fascination with sexuality, both in its sordid and its redemptive aspects. Sexual jealousy disfigures the lives of the characters in Janáček's *Jenůfa* (1904), both literally (Laca's slashing Jenůfa's face in Act I) and metaphorically, when the Kostelnička drowns Jenůfa's illegitimate child, an act for which she later forfeits her own freedom and subsequently her life. Such jealousy also emerges in murderous form in the prisoners' narratives in Janáček's last opera, *From the House of the Dead* (1927–8, first performed in 1930). Sexual desire and brutality are also closely linked in the work of Puccini's that comes closest to the conventions of *verismo: Tosca* (1900). Sexual promiscuity plays a role in almost all of Puccini's works, from the buying of a Japanese wife in *Madama Butterfly* (1904, revised in 1906), to the demands of Jack Rance for Minnie's favours in *La fanciulla del West* (1910), and to Magda's reluctance to leave the demi-monde for a settled, but tedious, domesticity in *La rondine* (1917). In *Turandot* (1926), the opera in which Puccini finally turned his back on *verismo* for a fantastic orientalist fable, sexuality ironically plays a role by its very absence from the icy Chinese princess.

Selfless love or willing sacrifice of the kind Puccini popularized in the characters of Mimì, Cio-Cio-San, Liù and others was always in tension, however, with the early Straussian heroines, the forebears of some important evocations of femininity as inherently sexual. The title role in Berg's *Lulu* embodies an endlessly enticing but elusive, even empty, femininity that is finally brought to ground by Jack the Ripper. Her changeability is signalled by the many names men give her: Eve, Nelly, Mignon, Lulu. The only character to love Lulu, rather than wish to possess her, is the Countess Geschwitz, the first portrayal of lesbianism on the operatic stage. Homosexual desire was later explored more fully by Britten, covertly in *Peter Grimes* (1945), *Billy Budd* (1951) and *The Turn of the Screw* (1954), and more openly in *Death in Venice* (1973). Taken together, these operas present a 'homosexual vision' that is largely negative in some readings, but does contain redemptive moments (Brett 1983, 192). This pattern was picked up by Tippett in *The Knot Garden* (1970), where both gay and straight relationships become tangled in psychological destruction before provisional solutions are reached. Tippett's earlier opera, *The Midsummer Marriage* (1955), recounts the quest for sexual and spiritual wholeness with less hesitation, borrowing from Jungian psychology to do so.

Less than a decade later, the Argentinian composer Alberto Ginastera produced the first of three operas that treat sexuality as a central, and violent, aspect of legend and history. *Don Rodrigo* (1964) tells the legend of the eighth-century King of Spain whose rape of his ward Florinda leads to his downfall and the country's invasion by the Moors, while *Beatrix Cenci* (1971) stages the sexual excesses of the Count whose rape of his daughter leads to his murder and the family's torture and execution. Ginastera's second opera, *Bomarzo* (1967), is based on a fictional account of the sixteenth-century nobleman Pier Francesco Orsini, whose sexual neuroses and fantasies are replayed through flashbacks. The opera's subjects – 'sex, violence and hallucination', as the composer described them – led to a municipal decree prohibiting performance in Buenos Aires, but the work proved highly successful at its Washington premiere (see *Neue Zeitschrift für Musik* 7–8 (1967), 293, and Urtubey 1968, 21). Sexual subject-matter caused a more prolonged controversy in Austria in 1980 when Gottfried von Einem's opera *Jesu Hochzeit* was due to be premiered in Orford Church in a double-bill with Britten's *The Prodigal Son* (1968). Einem's inclusion of a scene in which Christ has an erotic encounter with a female, Death, prevented performance in an ecclesiastical setting, and demonstrations came close to preventing the work's production at the Theater an der Wien. Clearly, then, sexuality remained a provocative topic throughout the century, simultaneously able to draw large audiences (as both *Salome* and *Elektra* did) and to engender controversy and occasionally censorship.

Mythology and neo-classicism

The attempt to control the body and bodily pleasures forms the subject of Hans Werner Henze's *The Bassarids* (1966), with a libretto by W. H. Auden and Chester Kallman. Adapting the story of Pentheus and his attempt to control the new cult of Dionysus from Euripides' tragedy *The Bacchae*, the opera shows how classical mythology continued to provide pertinent subjects for the modern age. Although early mythological operas like Ernest Chausson's *Le roi Arthus* (1903) inevitably owe a debt to Wagner, younger composers were able to distance themselves from his example. Stravinsky's 1928 opera-oratorio *Oedipus Rex*, based on Sophocles, became an important model for a less fervent treatment of myth or legend. Jean Cocteau's French libretto was translated into Latin, a 'dead' language, in order to underscore the monumental nature of the drama. The interventions of the Speaker, who recounts the well-known story in the vernacular, create a further barrier between the action and the audience's emotional response. Stravinsky's statuesque work was followed in later decades by Carl Orff's series of classical operas, *Antigonae* (1949), *Oedipus der Tyrann* (1959) and *Prometheus* (1968), the last using the original Greek of Aeschylus. The story of Antigone had earlier been set by Honegger, a year before Stravinsky's influential work, and also with a libretto by Cocteau. George Enescu, too, had considered dramatizing the Oedipus story as early as 1910: his four-act lyrical tragedy, *Oedipe*, was composed over the course of the 1920s and premiered in Paris in 1936.

The fascination in the interwar years with Greek stories in which the individual is pitted against the gods may derive from a modernist rejection of the recent past in favour of an older tradition, which offered an apparent sense of timelessness. Paradoxically, the problem for many modern artists was an acute awareness of history that prevented any sense of working within a living tradition. Nowhere was the irony of modernism more consciously articulated than in the works of Stravinsky after *Pulcinella* (1920), the piece that ushered in his long neo-classical period. The culmination of this body of works was *The Rake's Progress* (1951), the century's greatest neo-classical stage-work (see Chapter 7). Based on William Hogarth's series of eight paintings (1733–35) – housed in the Sir John Soane Museum in London – and with a libretto by Auden and Kallman, the opera presents its tale of moral failings and redemption through a sustained pastiche of both eighteenth-century verse (see Mendelson 1993, 606, 615) and Mozartian musical forms. The type of story itself – a morality – along with period touches like the mock pastoral of the opening scenes, further 'dates' the opera to Hogarth's time. This thorough stylization in the artistic and aesthetic dress of another age might well have prevented *The Rake* from entering the repertoire, were it not for the equally emphatic twentieth-century elements. First, the irony (if not the wit) of the enterprise is wholly un-Mozartian, underlining the 'neo' of the work's classicism. In the second place, many aspects of the drama have a contemporary resonance. Nick Shadow's false-bottomed machine for turning stones into bread satirizes modern enterprise and commercial know-how, while Sellem's auction provides a sharply funny commentary on greed and complacency, the very things that have led Tom Rakewell into his devilish predicament in the first place. Even the ambiguous sexuality of Baba the Turk marks the opera as belonging to Auden's, not Hogarth's, time. Finally, and most importantly, the theme of redemption through love might be seen as a response, though not a solution, to twentieth-century suffering. 'We must love one another or die', Auden wrote in his poem 'September 1, 1939' in New York on the eve of the Second World War. Later, he revised the line to read 'and die': so Tom/Adonis, having gained his Anne/Venus and lost his wits, loves and dies. Although the Bedlam scene is one of the few retained from Hogarth, Tom's madness strikes a distinctly contemporary note: in the modern economy of the emotions, love always comes at a price.

Nationalism and politics

The Rake's Progress is a decisively international work: premiered at La Fenice in Venice, with a Mozartian score by a Russian who had been naturalized first in France then in the USA, and a book devised by another naturalized American, the opera rejects in every possible way the nationalism of Stravinsky's great *bête noire*, Wagner. Yet nationalist topics did not cease to interest composers after 1900. Stravinsky's teacher in the early years of the century, Rimsky-Korsakov, produced the culmination of a long line of folkloric and nationalistic operas in his *The Legend of the Invisible City of Kitezh and the Maiden Fevroniya* (1907). Arguably a more representative opera than Rimsky's *The Golden Cockerel* (1909), the love of Fevroniya and Vsevolod is depicted in spiritual and symbolic action influenced by Christian mysticism, pantheism and Russian folklore, and incorporating the history of the Mongol invasion of Russia in the thirteenth century. Prokofiev's epic *War and Peace* (1941–52) gives a more overtly patriotic account of nineteenth-century Russian history, especially in the second ('war') section. His adaptation of Tolstoy is the most important, and certainly the most extended, historical operatic project of the century. Far removed from the witty modernism of the same composer's *The Love for Three Oranges* (1921) or the dark sexual theme of *The Fiery Angel* (1919–27), *War and Peace* engages the listener on a number of levels, pyschological and historical, private and patriotic.

The fact that two of the century's more overtly nationalist operas are Russian raises the issue of how to define 'national' opera, a title often reserved for works composed and produced on the fringes of Western Europe (Russia, Bohemia) or in the New World. Ethan Mordden's definition of a 'national opera' as one that 'aims at a celebration of cultural ambitions' (1978, 167) provokes a re-evaluation: in this sense, not just works like Pfitzner's *Palestrina* (1917) or Virgil Thomson's *The Mother of Us All* (1947) qualify as national operas, but also the works of Strauss, Puccini, Janáček, Britten and Menotti, along with those of Rimsky-Korsakov and Prokofiev.

A similar difficulty accrues to the definition of political opera. In recent years, the term 'political' has shifted its meaning to include any work that is ideologically motivated, a definition that in its loosest interpretation might include all opera. For the purposes of this chapter, it is more helpful to restrict 'political' subject-matter either to themes drawn from historical rebellion, revolution or unrest; or to works that have deliberate designs on the listener, aiming to influence his or her values and beliefs. Examples of the second type can be found in a number of avant-garde works from the postwar period, especially in Italy. Giacomo Manzoni's *La sentenza* (1960) mixes musical and political radicalism, and was followed five years later by *Atomtod*, a work that provoked interventions from political and ecclesiastical authorities. Luigi Nono's *Intolleranza 1960*, as the title suggests, explored questions of political and social conscience through a collage of texts and images; his later *Al gran sole carico d'amore* (1975) was produced in collaboration with the Moscow theatre director Yuri Lyubimov, and incorporated material concerning the Paris Commune of 1871 and industrial unrest in 1950s Turin. Luigi Dallapiccola's *Il prigioniero*, first broadcast in 1949 and staged a year later, offers a symbolic – and pessimistic – treatment of liberty. Just before the Second World War in the United States, political and proletarian themes began to occupy Marc Blitzstein, in *The Cradle Will Rock* (1937) and *No For an Answer* (1936–40, first performed in 1941). In the late 1930s, Strauss also produced his only overtly political work, the pacifist opera *Friedenstag* which, ironically enough, was first endorsed by the Nazis as an embodiment of their principles before falling into disfavour. Ten years earlier, Brecht's and Weill's *Die Dreigroschenoper* had subjected bourgeois values to a remorseless irony, while less than a year after the Wall Street Crash their *Aufstieg und Fall der Stadt Mahagonny* criticized capitalism and greed through the techniques of Brechtian epic theatre.

More recently, Britten's television opera *Owen Wingrave* (1971) set out its composer's strongest dramatic statement of his pacifist convictions; six years later, David Blake's *Toussaint* adopted Brecht's *Verfremdungseffekt* (alienation technique) to depict events in Haiti during the independence movement led by the former black slave, Toussaint l'Ouverture (1746–1803). Alan Bush's *Wat Tyler* (1953), significantly staged in the newly formed German Democratic Republic rather than Britain, similarly turned to historical rebellion to make a political point. In a related vein, Rimsky's *The Golden Cockerel* and Boris Blacher's *Preussisches Märchen* (1949) both satirize militarism, a recurrent twentieth-century reality. The same issue was taken up with greater seriousness, but only partial success, in Henze's *We Come to the River* (1976), with a libretto by the left-wing playwright Edward Bond. 'Political' operas that are historical rather than ideological have also occupied a number of composers. They include Gottfried von Einem, whose *Dantons Tod* (1947) condenses the play by Georg Büchner (1813–37) into a compact drama on the French Revolution that also reflected the condition of post-war Europe; and John Adams, who has turned to contemporary political history and conflict in *Nixon in China* (1987) and *The Death of Klinghoffer* (1991). Philip Glass's *Satyagraha* (1980) draws on the history of Gandhi's peaceful protests in South Africa early in the century to explore the 'truth-force' of the opera's title in past, present and future.

Portraits

Satyagraha was the second of three stage works that Glass calls 'portrait operas'; it was followed by his portrayal of the Egyptian king Amenhotep IV in *Akhnaten* (1984), and preceded by *Einstein on the Beach* (1976), a seminal work in the American minimalist school. The historical figure of Albert Einstein is not portrayed in naturalistic action, but through a series of verbal signs and visual images representing his ideas and influence: chanted numbers and sol-fa syllables, trains and space-ships. Glass's collaboration with the experimental theatre director Robert Wilson thus pushes the idea of historical portraiture into new dramaturgical territory.

Earlier 'portrait operas' by Pfitzner and Hindemith were more conventional in their dramaturgy and, in the case of *Palestrina*, markedly more conservative. Pfitzner's reactionary opera dramatizes the life of the sixteenth-century Italian composer and his conflict with the Council of Trent in order to comment indirectly on musical modernism and political liberalism. Hindemith's ideological leanings are worked out in a more complex and compelling form in *Mathis der Maler*, composed in the early 1930s when Hitler came to power and produced – in neutral Zurich – in 1938. Based on the life of the painter Matthias Grünewald (?1480–1528) and his great Isenheim altarpiece (housed in the museum at Colmar, France), the opera explores the rôle of the artist in times of political turmoil. Hindemith's painter, who embodies the composer's own predicament as a German artist in the 1930s, first involves himself directly in the Peasant Revolt of 1525, but later comes to see that his art is a more appropriate response to human suffering.

An opera that takes legend rather than history as its starting-point also deserves mention under the heading of 'portrait operas': Ferruccio Busoni's *Doktor Faust* (1916–24, completed by Philipp Jarnach in 1925). Another exiled artist-figure, Faust discovers that when his magical powers are paid for with his soul, the marker of humanity, they ultimately prove as illusory as Helen of Troy. Yet the work ends, like Stravinsky's *Rake*, with the possibility of redemption: at Faust's demise, his dead child is reborn as a youth, and Mephistopheles gains Faust but not his aspirations: 'Was ich versäumte, / schöpfe du nach' ('What I neglected, you shall achieve', final scene).

Literature and librettists

Busoni's source for *Doktor Faust* was, interestingly, not Goethe's tragedy but the puppet-play tradition dating back to the sixteenth century. *Literaturoper* ('literary opera'), however, forms an important category in twentieth-century opera, alongside historical and political, national, neo-classical, sexual and psychological concerns. The richness of works that adapt 'classic' texts without departing too far from the spirit or letter of the original can be seen in operas as different as Berg's *Wozzeck* (1925) and Britten's *A Midsummer Night's Dream* (1960), both of which feature libretti prepared by the composers themselves.

Berg's opera is closely derived from Büchner's fragmentary drama *Woyzeck* (1837). Joseph Kerman has argued that the libretto for *Wozzeck*, like those for *Pelléas*, *Tosca* and *Der Rosenkavalier*, allowed the composer to set dialogue that was comparatively 'ordinary', closer to real speech than the conventionalized verse libretti of the eighteenth and nineteenth centuries (1989, 179). While this is true, Büchner's text has an intensity that does not sound like naturalistic writing. The complex interplay of images of fire, knives, blood, stillness and movement combines to produce a dense poetic text, the starting-point for one of the most carefully structured operatic scores of the century. The close matching of mood, image and tone in the opera suggests that Berg's imagination was stimulated as much by the verbal textures of Büchner's play as by its enigmatic conversations or its quasi-cinematic cross-cutting.

The 'madness' of Britten's *Dream* is of a different order, but the opera is similarly enriched by Shakespeare's words, which were carefully retained by the composer and his co-librettist Peter Pears (see Cooke 1993). Although the number of lines is reduced by half, often by the loss of purely 'poetic' rather than narrative elements, the libretto retains the magical qualities of the moonlit 'nightrule' presided over by Oberon. Indeed, the only significant interpretative decision taken by Britten and Pears was to remove the Athenian first act and to open the opera with the quarrel of the fairy king and queen. The result is a stage-work in which the daylight 'reality' of Athens is framed by, suspended within, the world of dreams, night and fairyland. The common-sense interpretation advocated in the play by Theseus in his speech on lunatics, lovers and poets is not allowed to colour the opera's dramatic and musical world. The large-scale structural change does not prevent the opera from being recognisably the same drama, however.

Britten's insistence on fidelity to Shakespeare in the *Dream* is in contrast to Luciano Berio's *Un re in ascolto* (1984), an examination of the nature of perception and artistic creation. Here, the impresario Prospero (borrowed from *The Tempest* and various adaptations or commentaries on that play) is 'condemned to listen, waiting in the midst of some vast web of noises whose meaning must be grasped and interpreted' (Vogt 1990, 174). Shakespeare provides the point of departure for an opera whose metaphysical dimensions reflect postmodern concerns with communication and interpretation. Earlier in the century, Ralph Vaughan Williams's *Sir John in Love* (1929) might also be seen as a vehicle for the exploration of contemporary currents of thought. An adaptation of *The Merry Wives of Windsor*, a play that casts a satirical London eye on rural life, Vaughan Williams's lush opera instead reflects the composer's 'anti-urban, anti-industrial-age bias' (Schmidgall 1990, 326). Nevertheless, the composer's decision to interpolate contemporary lyrics (from other Shakespeare plays, as well as Jonson, Campion and Sidney) is 'thoroughly Shakespearean' (327).

Swiss composer Frank Martin deserves mention for his *Der Sturm* (1956), an operatic setting of A. W. von Schlegel's translation of *The Tempest*. Schlegel's early nineteenth-century translations of Shakespeare are themselves German literary classics, and Martin's libretto follows Schlegel/Shakespeare closely with only minor abridgement. The opera presents a convincing musical portrait of the magical island, its creatures and the magus himself, both irascible and forgiving, full of an elegiac sense of loss over his magical powers but finally redeemed by his restoration to ordinary humanity. Many other composers throughout the century also turned to Shakespeare as a source for operatic material, including Bloch (*Macbeth*, 1910), Holst (*At the Boar's Head*, 1925), Wolf-Ferrari (*Sly*, 1927), Boris Blacher (*Romeo und Julia*, 1947), Marcel Delannoy (*Puck*, 1949), Samuel Barber (*Antony and Cleopatra*, 1966), Stephen Oliver (*Timon of Athens*, 1991) and Henze (*Venus and Adonis*, 1997). While Shakespeare has remained an important source of dramatic material since the operas of Verdi, even where the operas are adaptations rather than complete settings of the plays, other literary classics have likewise offered operatic material to twentieth-century composers. Manuel de Falla turned to Cervantes for a single episode from *Don Quixote* in *El retablo de Maese Pedro* (1923), Prokofiev to Dostoyevsky's novella *The Gambler* for an opera of the same name (1929) and Leonard Bernstein to Voltaire's satirical short story of 1759 for his musical *Candide* (1956), while Walton drew on Chaucer and Boccaccio for *Troilus and Cressida* (1954), Dallapiccola on Homer for *Ulisse* (1968) and Bruno Maderna on the Roman satire by Petronius for *Satyricon* (1973). (For further discussion of literary adaptations in the Soviet Union and United States, see Chapters 11 and 12 respectively.)

But the most thorough exploration of opera's capacity to transform literary texts into musico-dramatic works remains Britten's operatic oeuvre. From the sympathetic interpretation of the solitary fisherman Peter Grimes in George Crabbe's *The Borough* (1810) and the moral questioning onboard *The Indomitable* (renamed from the original *Bellipotent*) in the floating world of Melville's *Billy Budd* (1891, published 1924), to the unnerving Jamesian ghosts of *The Turn of the Screw* (published 1898) and finally to the encounter with beauty-mortality in Thomas Mann's *Death in Venice* (published 1912), Britten simultaneously offered homage to literary figures and ushered their works into the rich fabric of a new form.

Britten worked with a number of librettists throughout his career, including Auden, E. M. Forster, Ronald Duncan, Montagu Slater, Eric Crozier, Myfanwy Piper and William Plomer. Many of them were writers in their own right, sometimes with strong dramatic ideas of their own; it may have been partly for this reason that Britten did not establish long working relationships with any of his librettists until later in his career. By contrast, Strauss established a fruitful relationship early on, one that produced some of his best-known works (*Der Rosenkavalier*, *Elektra*, *Arabella*) as well as more enigmatic operas like *Die Frau ohne Schatten*. The long working relationship between Strauss and Hugo von Hofmannsthal remained the century's most important collaboration between a composer and writer. As Strauss discovered, Hofmannsthal needed careful handling, but his preference for solitude means that we are fortunate in having a large body of correspondence, at times written almost daily, charting the details of their collaborations from *Elektra* to *Arabella*, the libretto for which Hofmannsthal was drafting when he died in 1929. The letters offer a fascinating insight not just into two contrasting characters – Strauss good-humoured, even bluff, Hofmannsthal precise and cautious – but into the nature of operatic collaboration itself. 'Discussions of this sort, which show how each of us visualizes the joint work, are indispensable', Hofmannsthal writes on 25 May 1911 in reply to Strauss's detailed ideas for *Ariadne*: 'This is the only way to collaborate ... We must not merely work together, but actually *into each other's hands*' (Hammelmann and Osers 1961, 83; emphasis in original).

'Working into each other's hands' meant that Strauss took the final decisions on dramatic and stylistic matters, as well as initiating many of the changes during the process of drafting a libretto. But it also meant that Hofmannsthal had an unusually high degree of influence, not just over stylistic details, but dramatic structure and even the choice of subjects. It is striking that from the early days, the writer felt free to judge Strauss's enthusiasms and to veto any he found either boring or vulgar, as his letter of 1 October 1906 makes clear: 'I should like ... to explain to you my notions (fairly liberal as they are) of what I consider possible opera subjects and what, on the other hand, I consider absolutely out of the question nowadays' (9). Strauss's hopes of a 'Semiramis' opera based on Calderón came to nothing, though he was still putting the idea forward to his librettists in the 1930s, as did his enthusiasm in 1916 for either a realistic domestic comedy (which found fulfilment, without a Hofmannsthal text, in *Intermezzo*) or a spy intrigue set in Vienna during the Congress of 1814–15. Instead, he set *Ariadne* and *Die Frau ohne Schatten*, both ideas that originated with the writer.

Thus from *Der Rosenkavalier* and *Ariadne* to the symbolism of *Die Frau ohne Schatten* and finally the more sentimental *Arabella*, Hofmannsthal played a major role in shaping the types of opera Strauss produced. The librettist's choice of subjects, like his concern with their right interpretation (e.g. 'Even the musical, conceptual unity of the whole opera would suffer if the personality of the Marschallin were to be deprived of her full stature', 12 July 1910; 61) helped to shape what was in effect a nationwide operatic project in Germany during the first three decades of the century. Without Hofmannsthal, Strauss's joking threat to become 'the Offenbach of the 20th century' (5 June 1916; 250), a sentimental purveyor of operetta or Bavarian kitsch (see his letter to Stefan Zweig dated 21 January 1934 in Schuh 1957, 55), might have come more nearly into existence, in place of the fascinating and at times problematic series of mythological, sentimental and parodic operas we have. Strauss's need for the support Hofmannsthal gave him cannot be better gauged, finally, than by reading the composer's frustrated attempts to get Joseph Gregor to write workable librettos in the mid-1930s: 'Handlung und Rollen! Keine Gedanken! Keine Dichtung! Theater!' ('Action and character! No ideas! No poetry! Theatre!' (Tenschert 1955, 30)). At one time or another, Hofmannsthal had met these requirements.

Strauss's explosive prescription can stand for twentieth-century operatic texts as a whole. The words librettists have provided for composers to set, whatever their subject or their starting-point, whatever their tradition or their influences, can be judged successful only if they can be transformed into dramatic, and musical, action.

5 Symbolist opera: trials, triumphs, tributaries

PHILIP WELLER

[Winter, 1914:] The coal merchant had a pretty wife who was also an excellent musician,
and she gave [Debussy] some [coal] in return for an inscription on her copy of
Pelléas ... GABRIEL ASTRUC (1929)

The idea that so aesthetically rarefied a work as *Pelléas* might have been
the occasion of a request (in wartime, too) for a quick autograph from
Debussy by a local tradesman's wife with a passionate interest in music
reminds us just how widely known and well loved the opera had become
in France after the polemics of the work's initial reception had died down.
It further helps us to understand why nearly 30 years later, after a fairly
dismal decade for the opera during the 1930s, the wartime performances
given in 1942 at the Opéra-Comique under Roger Désormière were to be
such an important manifestation of national identity and 'cultural resistance' during the Nazi Occupation, and also how they managed to exert
such a powerful fascination at the collective psychological level, as well as
bringing about a certain reinvigoration of the work itself as a musical and
dramatic entity (Nichols and Langham Smith 1989, 156–9).

This in turn provides a context – to an extent backward looking and
more than a little nostalgic, yet honest and deeply felt – for the renewed
passion with which the piece now came to be viewed, both in itself and as
an embodiment of French taste and identity; and also for the sense of
shock that greeted the groundbreaking, in every sense iconoclastic postwar production by Valentine Hugo, also given at the 'temple' of the
Opéra-Comique, in 1947. The décor of Hugo's production, in line with
the radicalism of her general concept of the work, went very much further
than did the thoughtfully simplified, slightly modernized designs of
Valdo-Barbey for the 1930 revival (Valdo-Barbey 1926). That the 1947
staging was felt to be so shocking can be easily documented, but is made
even more obvious by the almost immediate return to a 'revivalist' mode
of production for the 1952 staging, which deliberately aimed at what
would probably be thought of today as a historical reconstruction in the
realist French Gothic spirit of the original 1902 stage sets by Jusseaume
and Ronsin (Nichols and Langham Smith, 1989, 159–61; see illustrations
in Lesure 1980, 85–91).

But the mould had been broken. The task of preserving an original
production at all costs as a would-be permanent link with the past, as a

Figure 5.1 Debussy's *Pelléas et Mélisande*, directed by Peter Sellars with set designs by George Tsypin (Netherlands Opera, 1993). *Left to right*: Arkel (Robert Lloyd), Golaud (Willard White) and Mélisande (Elise Ross). Photo: Deen van Meer.

kind of talisman even, could now be seen and understood more clearly for what it was – a fantasy that carried with it a strong dose of fetishism and which, beneath a veil of fidelity, in fact showed little confidence in the opera's inner strength and complexity as a vehicle for new interpretative work. Moreover, there are signs that by 1914 Debussy himself may have been growing tired of the constraining literalism of the 1902 sets and longing for something new (Nichols and Langham Smith 1989, 154), even if his expressive vision for the music – both in his imagination and as realized through Messager's expert conducting at the premiere – seems to have remained fairly consistent over the years. The 1947 Hugo production (seen also at Covent Garden in 1949) had done its work, however. Not only was the way now open for other more experimental productions to take place across Europe, even little by little in France (though significantly not in Paris, at least not until the 1970s); but the first steps had been taken, in the realm of staging and design, towards the more thorough-going musical and interpretative revaluation of the work that was to occur under the impetus of Pierre Boulez in 1969 (at Covent Garden) and again in 1992 (in the staging for Welsh National Opera, produced by the charismatic German theatre director Peter Stein).

The exploration of new, more or less radical styles of operatic production was a widespread postwar phenomenon, the most famous – and most obviously institutionalized – instance of which was the remaking of the Bayreuth tradition during the 1950s and 1960s. Partly because of the great scale of the undertaking and the wide diffusion of knowledge about

Bayreuth, partly because of the simple fact of Wieland Wagner's uniquely powerful vision and the sheer energy and practical genius with which he set about realizing it, this radical shift in stagecraft – which itself owed much to the physical simplicity and extreme concentration on lighting effects that had emerged from symbolist thinking about the nature and workings of the theatre, as well as to the seminal ideas of such prewar figures as Adolphe Appia and Gordon Craig and their disciples in Germany – quickly set up what was to become something close to a distinctive postwar ideal: a new anti-realist orthodoxy with a strongly abstract and symbolic bias. The over-riding need for a fearlessly radical intepretative approach to production had been the difficult, yet in the end revelatory, conclusion to which Wieland Wagner gradually came during his months of intensive study and reflexion in the immediate aftermath of 1945 (Spotts 1994, 208–11).

Symbolist opera, during its brief but intensive historical moment in the years preceding the First World War, had also reacted against the pre-vailing bourgeois and conventional view of theatre and musical drama. It stood against what it saw as the false grandiloquence of grand opera and the romantic melodrama, the exaggeration and sentimentality of *verismo*, and the banality of naturalism and the realist theatre. (To Debussy's annoyance the star of Gustave Charpentier's hugely popular *Louise* was indisputably in the ascendant following its premiere in 1900; even during the *Pelléas* rehearsals in early 1902, Mary Garden was still busy singing Charpentier's title role.) Symbolist opera took its cue from Wagner, as poets and writers and artists had done, and as we can conveniently observe in the socio-cultural phenomenon 'wagnérisme' and the brief existence of the Parisian *Revue wagnérienne* (1885–8). Yet it was a pro-foundly altered version of the Wagnerian ideal which was its point of departure – the transformative product (so to speak) of the symbolists' reading of Wagner, allied with a radical compositional rethinking of how this kind of drama could best be embodied musically.

Above all, there was a strong antipathy and resistance to external realism, especially in its most literalistic guise. Human content, so the argument went, could be conveyed more directly and authentically, with greater subtlety and complexity, by ignoring the lure of realism and illusionism and concentrating instead on finding a language of atmo-sphere and evocation (this was one of the key tenets of symbolism as it was manifested in every medium and genre). The poetic descent of the movement took Baudelaire and Mallarmé as its patrilineal creators; but the transference of symbolist ideas on to the stage in live theatre became an issue of real aesthetic and cultural importance only with the rise to public prominence in Paris of Maurice Maeterlinck around 1890 (McGuinness 2000).

Stories and scenarios: Maeterlinck and beyond

Both Maeterlinck's dramatic experimentation and the various operatic responses to it involved a radical rethinking of what a theatrical scenario could consist of, and what kinds of psychological and expressive results might then be drawn from it. Maeterlinck's exploration of the possibilities of static theatre, his extreme reduction of external action, his exploitation of silence not just as a dramatic effect but as a surrounding medium for language and gesture, and his concentration on evocation and atmosphere, as well as an idiosyncratic approach to stage rhetoric (which in most respects is in fact anti-rhetorical), all pointed in one general direction: the creation of a sense of mystery and depth.

It is noteworthy that Debussy should first have expressed his need for a novel and 'original' operatic subject in terms not of plot or action but of dramatic atmosphere, and that he seems already to have heard his musical sound-world inwardly *before* finding a subject that was appropriate to it. All this is most strikingly expressed – as early as 1889–90 – in the conversations he had with his former teacher Ernest Guiraud. Having returned from the revelatory journeys to Bayreuth he made in 1888 and 1889 when he saw Wagner's *Parsifal, Die Meistersinger* and *Tristan,* Debussy's ideas were now heading in an entirely new and anti-Wagnerian direction. He described his search for

> [a] kind of poet . . . who only hints at what is to be said. The ideal would be two associated dreams [i.e. that of the poet and that of the musician]. No place, nor time. No big scene. No compulsion on the musician, who must complete and give body to the work of the poet . . . My idea is of a short libretto with mobile scenes . . . No discussion or arguments between the characters, whom I see at the mercy of life or destiny.
>
> (Lockspeiser 1978, 205, translating the recollections of Maurice Emmanuel)

That his practical needs – as well as his dreams – were answered by the appearance of Maeterlinck's *Pelléas et Mélisande* both in book form (Maeterlinck 1892) and in the theatre (at the Bouffes Parisiens in 1893, directed by Lugné-Poë) is the key historical conjunction through which symbolist opera was able to come into being as it did (though prior to this he seems briefly to have considered setting Maeterlinck's earlier play *La Princesse Maleine* of 1889). Debussy attended the single staged performance given on 17 May 1893 by the Théâtre de l'Oeuvre, having previously bought himself a copy of the printed text (Lesure 2003, 140–41). From this point on he devoted, with significant intervals, fully ten years of his life to the creation of the opera he had already intuited, as if from a mysterious distance, inside his head. The vicissitudes of the '*Pelléas* years' are a vital and enthralling story in their own right (Grayson 1986; Lesure 1991). And after the long years spent imagining the action as a totality while working on the score, Debussy spent hundreds of hours in rehearsal at the Opéra-Comique during the weeks and months leading up to the now-legendary dress rehearsal, followed by the premiere on 30 April 1902 (chronology, based on the unpublished diary of Henri Büsser and other sources, in Lesure 2003, 219–22). At this point the man whose aesthetic ideal was one of fantasy and infinitely extensible imagination was finally brought face to face with all the mundane practicalities of the cumbersome theatrical machine. Yet although, as we can read in his correspondence, he often expressed anger and frustration at all the various practical difficulties associated with the theatre, he seems never to have lost faith in the immediacy and power of the experience that could be conveyed through the medium of dramatic music, rightly understood and entered into.

Maeterlinck's libretto *Ariane et Barbe-Bleue*, written in the first place as a vehicle for his mistress, the soprano Georgette Leblanc (whom Debussy had refused to cast as the first Mélisande), might have been set to music by Grieg. But it was Paul Dukas who, around 1899–1900, began work intensively on his setting of the text, and the finished opera was given at the Opéra-Comique on 10 May 1907, with Leblanc in the title role and with set designs again by Jusseaume. This opera, too, was a sustained labour of love by a relatively young and idealistic composer, just as *Pelléas* had been. Debussy and Dukas were close and artistically intimate friends during these years, who shared many of their views about literature and the arts; and although little direct evidence survives, there can be no doubt that they would have discussed Maeterlinck and his ideas as well as those of such key poetic figures as Baudelaire and Mallarmé (Lesure 2003, 94). Dukas, moreover, was one of the very few privileged interlocutors with whom Debussy shared the whole story, the trials and tribulations as well as the triumphs, of the ten-year gestation of *Pelléas*.

The fact that later generations have treated *Ariane* so neglectfully by comparison with *Pelléas* should not blind us to Dukas's importance within the historical moment of symbolist opera and its immediate aftermath. There may or may not be good reasons why *Ariane* is often thought to be theatrically unviable – the extreme prominence (and vocal demands) of the role of Ariane, for instance; the extreme paucity of that of Bluebeard; and the particular kind of monumental stasis which the opera as a whole is seen as embodying (not unlike the equally controversial case of Messiaen's *Saint-François d'Assise* of 1983). But it made a great impact in the early years of its life and was staged internationally more quickly than *Pelléas* was. Within six years of the premiere, it had been seen and heard at Vienna (1908), Brussels (1909), New York and Milan (1911), Buenos Aires (1912) and Madrid (1913). By comparison, *Pelléas* was not staged abroad until 1907, when it was given in Brussels, though its international productions in the years 1907–11 were numerous and were spread far and wide, on both sides of the Atlantic – this was a period which set it firmly on the path to worldwide fame.

Of the early stagings of *Ariane*, by far the most significant, historically speaking, was that given in Vienna at the Volksoper (2 April 1908) where the work's reception was ennobled not just by the presence and the admiration of Schoenberg, Berg and Webern, but even more by the eloquent and impassioned advocacy of its conductor, Zemlinsky (Beaumont 2000, 161–2), who conducted it again at the Prague convention of the International Society for Contemporary Music in 1925, in a beautifully crafted and distinctly modern production by the great tenor-turned-director Louis Laber (220–21, 332–5). In Paris, the work continued to be given with success during the inter-war years, and Messiaen's revelatory experience when he first heard the work at the Opéra in January 1935 – the first time it had been given a Parisian performance away from the Opéra-Comique – was acknowledged in a rapturous letter to Dukas himself, who had been his revered teacher. The impression was so strong that he was moved to write a review which became one of his most elaborated, and most moving, critical essays when it was published in the commemorative issue of *La Revue musicale* the following year (Messiaen 1935 and 1936).

But – at the risk of stating the obvious – *Ariane* sounds nothing like *Pelléas*. And it is clear that the hyper-refined style of the latter never was the only possible sound-world for Maeterlinck's subtle verbal play and inconclusive action. Dukas has a sheer sonorous and orchestral power that Debussy reserves for brief moments (Golaud's murder of Pelléas at the very end of Act IV, for example); and both his textures and his paragraphing are more conventionally sustained and long-breathed – though his sensitivity to the rise and fall of the dialogue and to the psychological force-field is as acute as Debussy's, if less neurotically fine-grained and intense. Perhaps most importantly, they share a fundamental approach that is grounded in a prosodical conception of opera, and which, giving primacy to the pacing of the text as much as to that of the action, seeks above all a method of word setting that is true to the accentual and declamatory qualities of the French language, while also maximizing and intensifying whatever incipiently musical value these speech patterns may possess.

If Maeterlinck worked by a kind of controlled ambiguity, writing in a suspended and elusive verbal style that withholds as much as it gives, then much of his expressive 'message' consisted not in presence but in absence – what was implied but not stated, and what was called forth through the gaps in the dialogue and the action. He used intentionally simple verbal formulations, making them mysterious by means of frequent ellipses and non sequiturs, and by a refusal to explain potential ambiguities. Moreover the sense of time too was often blurred, both within the overall distribution and sequencing of the action, and in terms of the dramatic setting and its location. These devices were employed because Maeterlinck was primarily interested in evoking deep-seated emotions and psychological states, which he was convinced could not be directly expressed through a traditional, cumulative rhetoric or through the complications of external action, however striking and carefully constructed. This poetic ambiguity found in music an ideal means of 'prolongation' (as Debussy called it) of its latent emotional and psychological content. Not only esoteric symbolist ideas about musical essences (reflected, at a distance, in Pater's famous dictum that all art aspires to the condition of music), but also the more concrete principles of music drama, in which much of the expressive and communicative burden is displaced from the audience's direct intelligence of the text and its vocal projection on to their imaginative response to the musical continuity, could be fused together to give a new and highly effective vehicle for the realization of Maeterlinck's aims in the theatre. Indeed it might be argued that his attempt to achieve an atmosphere of openness and ambiguity by purely verbal means actually needed the support of music, as a parallel medium unfettered by the constraints of language, in order to work to best advantage. Music took over where verbal techniques of suggestion left off, and had the incalculable virtue of providing expressive continuity and richness of texture and nuance, where the poet could provide only ellipses and non sequiturs. Music also worked to intensify the unspoken emotions which lay beneath and behind the surface of the text. Thus Debussy's music in a sense restored to *Pelléas* a necessary darkness and depth which it otherwise lacked. And yet it is one of the ironies of operatic history that the full scale and significance of this 'restoration' did not become fully clear until a later stage of the performance tradition, when the opera had been partly stripped of its envelope of 'sensitivity' and was shown with its nerve-endings more fully exposed than before – though without endangering the miraculous beauty of its vocal and orchestral sound-world.

One of the many remarkable things about *Pelléas* at the craftsmanlike and technical level is how closely, despite the necessary cuts, it engaged with the substance and the letter of the playtext – though Debussy's skilful changes and reorderings are subtler and more far-reaching in effect than might appear at first sight, especially in the way they serve to manipulate the sense of time and accentuate the idea of circularity and cyclicity, thereby gaining additional space within the action for music to operate as the main expressive and dramatic agent (Grayson 1997). Nevertheless, Debussy's scenario stays relatively close to Maeterlinck's, and realizes its dramatic potential in a musical style that deepens and enriches the life of the play, transforming it without doing violence to its basic structure. To this extent it stands as a shining example of *Literaturoper*. Dukas similarly took over the main substance of *Ariane* from Maeterlinck fully intact, and stayed even closer than Debussy had done to the letter of the text, which he set more or less verbatim. Béla Balázs did no such thing with *Duke Bluebeard's Castle*, however. Whereas in Dukas the Bluebeard story is a fully fledged three-act drama of liberation, both spiritual and physical, involving the peasants of the estate and Ariane's nurse as well as the protagonist herself (Maeterlinck 1901; Dukas 1936), in Balázs the totality of the action consists in the arrival of Judith with Bluebeard, followed by the opening of the seven doors – an episode which in Dukas is confined to the second half of Act I, and occurs as part of a much larger scenario. Bartók, building on the compactness of Balázs's initial vision, achieves a spiritual concentration and a sheer psychological force that Dukas, for all the power and sweep of his music, can never quite match.

At a formal and textual level Dukas works within the parameters set by Maeterlinck, breaking through them only by the sheer scale and intensity of his musical thought, by the pacing and the sense of power and depth he brings to the action. The opera is composed, orchestrally and vocally, on a heroic scale, and describes a broad cyclic arc which is musically enacted by the return of the opening orchestral material in the final scene. As in Bartók (surely coincidentally), this material is centred on F sharp, and in both cases the cyclicity represents the female protagonist's failure to transform the situation in which she has found herself. But here the similarity ends, for the two conclusions are in all other respects very different. In *Bluebeard's Castle*, Judith finally joins the three other wives beyond the seventh door, while Bluebeard is left isolated in spiritual and emotional darkness, whereas in *Ariane* the heroine leaves the stage (in company with her faithful nurse) at the end of the opera, having tried in vain to persuade the other wives to assert their freedom and leave with her. In *Ariane* the wives sing; in *Bluebeard* they do not. More surprisingly, perhaps, Dukas's Bluebeard sings very little. His presence is felt through the general situation and the control he exercises over it; but it is not a physically immediate, vocal and psychological presence, except at two important moments (he intervenes at the opening of the seventh door, and is brought in as a silent captive in the final scene). Nor are these major divergences in scale and scope the only differences between the two scenarios. Whereas in Dukas, following Maeterlinck, the first six doors each reveal a torrent of different jewels (brilliantly depicted with a different timbral and tonal approach in the orchestra), Balázs describes a series of imagined pictures which give Judith – and the audience too – what is in effect a 'symbolist portrait' of Bluebeard's persona, in both its outer and its inner dimensions. His use of the scenic device of the doors acts both as a convenient framework for the action and as a means of access to the synaesthetic and spiritual vision which lies at the heart of his conception, in which the transporting power of music, in carrying us beyond the immediate reality of the scenario into a mythic fantasy-dimension beyond the scenic, is crucial. The opening of the doors is thus part of the psychological grammar of the work, as well as a brilliant piece of stage mechanics, which contrives to give a sense of imaginative breadth and diversity to the action while keeping it compact and outwardly static.

In selecting the episode of the doors as the near-totality of his scenario, Balázs has deliberately jettisoned the greater part of the (external) action laid down for *Ariane*. He in fact moves so far beyond Maeterlinck, in both a craftsmanlike and a dramaturgical way, that he brings about a fundamental alteration in the inner dynamic of the piece. His text, though obviously built upon the Bluebeard material, can scarcely be called a mere version – as opposed to a complete reworking – of Maeterlinck's libretto. He was undoubtedly familiar, as Dukas had been, with the original fairytale (Perrault 1697), and also used a range of Maeterlinckian motifs and insights. But he builds his own dramatic concept with a staggering sureness of touch that perhaps owes something to other Maeterlinck dramas (Leafstedt 1999, 37–44), yet impresses above all by its sheer unexampled originality – including not least the brilliant use of the regular folk-ballad metre for the dialogue (which is all cast in eight-syllable lines). It was surely this skilful adaptation of the 'universal' character of the symbolist aesthetic to a specifically Hungarian context, as well as the latent Wagnerianism of the underlying dramatic idea (the anguished male protagonist faced with the possibility of redemption by the female), which must have attracted Bartók to this text in the first place. Indeed, it was precisely their shared interest in the marriage of a decisively nationalist-Hungarian stance with an uncompromising international-modernist concern for cultural renewal that joined Bartók to Balázs at this period, and united them both in this project and in *The Wooden Prince* (Frigyesi 1998).

When the text of *Duke Bluebeard's Castle* was first published in a Budapest theatre periodical in 1910, it was described as a 'mystery play' (Balázs 1910). But though there is indeed a (somewhat generalized) Gothic atmosphere in the visual description and presentation of the

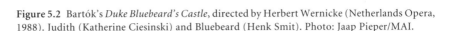

Figure 5.2 Bartók's *Duke Bluebeard's Castle*, directed by Herbert Wernicke (Netherlands Opera, 1988). Judith (Katherine Ciesinski) and Bluebeard (Henk Smit). Photo: Jaap Pieper/MAI.

castle, the sense in which the drama is a 'mystery' is not so much medieval as mythic. Far more even than in Maeterlinck and Dukas, it carries a distinctively modern, and potently symbolic, charge. To begin with, the castle itself seems animate. It appears to mourn and suffer, it weeps, sighs, bleeds, and languishes in oppressive darkness. Even as the physical qualities of the setting are conveyed to us in graphic detail through Judith's discovery and growing awareness of her surroundings, there is a strong sense in which – as hinted at in the spoken Prologue – the entire scenario stands as a grand metaphor for Bluebeard's psyche, and Judith's confrontation with it. To this extent the drama as a whole may be read as a journey of two souls towards one another, in the hope of union and liberation, but which ultimately fails when Judith the bringer of light and love fails to overcome the darkness of her husband's soul. All the detailed physical qualities – evident both in the general aspect of the castle, and in the particular scenes it reveals as the doors are opened one by one – stand in relation to the large-scale opposition of light and dark which governs the symbolism of the entire drama. And it is in Bartók's tireless efforts to find a compositional equivalent for this process (i.e. of the interaction and contrast between types of light and types of dark, encompassing too the infinitely nuanced range which extends between the two) that the music takes on its profound and haunting dramatic quality. This is a quality not of discursiveness, not of structural functions or thematic working, nor even of musical event and gesture (though there is plenty of the latter in the score), but of what has been memorably called, in connection with Debussy's *Pelléas*, 'tonalities of light and dark' (Nichols and Langham Smith 1989, 107ff.).

The communicative power of the Bluebeard story as presented by Balázs and Bartók lies in the tension between the intensely graphic quality of its imagery and the inexpressible 'beyondness' of its ideas and content. As with *Pelléas*, it is surely wrong to see just the immaterial, spiritual message as constituting the essence of the drama. Rather, it is familiar things and everyday perceptions which take on an intensified aura within this 'visionary' framework. The combined effect of the stage setting and the suggestive power of music transforms the imagined scenes 'revealed' by the opening of the doors into true visions. There is a process of stylization and defamiliarization, but its purpose is to achieve not so much strangeness *per se* as an intensification of 'the real'. In symbolist art, the physical characteristics of what is represented are often *more* graphic for the spectator than in realist art – because they are treated selectively and in greater isolation than they would be within a fuller, and inevitably more cluttered, realist context. There is an intensity of focus on the important images that creates a sense of heightened perception and psychological response, without obliterating the manifest external qualities that have triggered them. The possibility of achieving such effects is one of the great strengths of the theatre as a medium, and its potential is realized through the expressive tension between the theatrical framework and the musical-verbal language which is deployed within it. This, too, is a phenomenon which unites the realm of stagecraft, in its physical and visual aspect, with that of music and the evocative power of the word.

And so the 'mystery' into which Judith is initiated is not an evasive Gothic dream, but the unseen realities of her husband's soul. The drama is a journey of discovery, and of realization – a realization, in the end, of the depths of Bluebeard's despair and inner darkness. It is a journey which, through the agency of Bartók's music and the singing presences we see and hear on stage (or, indeed, inside our own minds), we too are enabled to make, vicariously and sympathetically. There is an overall movement from initial darkness (their arrival in the great hall, followed by the torture chamber and armoury: Doors 1–2), through the visions of beauty and radiance (treasury, garden, kingdom: Doors 3–5), back to an even more sinister darkness, enlivened only by a baleful glimmer (the lake of tears: Door 6). This is then followed by the bittersweet spectacle of the three bejewelled wives (Door 7), in which there is a truly heartrending mixture of the light and the dark: a return to the initial Stygian gloom, but coloured by onstage light from various sources, including a narrow beam of moonlight and the brightness of the women's apparel.

The opera as a whole thus describes the opening and closing off of hope: darkness (initially centred on F sharp), followed by an influx of light through the three central doors (including the glory of Bluebeard's kingdom, centred on C), which is then closed off more fully and more poignantly than before. This dramatic outline reinforces the sense of ultimate despair and gives us the full measure of Bluebeard's tragedy when he sings, at the very end: 'And now, forever, all shall be night... night... night...' (*éjjel... éjjel... éjjel...*). Musically, this final closing of the door of hope is expressed through the return of the pentatonically organized music, again centred on F sharp, from the beginning of the opera, but now cast in a more dissonant and anguished form. Significantly, it took Bartók a long while to arrive at this conclusion in its final shape. He first wrote a simpler, more translucent ending (1911), seemingly modelled on the closing section of *Pelléas*, before deciding to make the final stages blacker and more painful. In 1911–12 Bluebeard's final line (quoted above) was added, other dialogue deleted, and various musical alterations made. Then in 1917–18 the music was worked over once more (in preparation for the belated premiere on 24 May 1918), and its sound-world made more dissonant, reflecting general changes in Bartók's compositional language in the intervening years, but also his by now darker conception of the ending of the drama (Leafstedt 1999, 142–4 and 153–8).

Sound-worlds: musical dramaturgy and the poetics of opera

In working towards a distinctively symbolist version of musical drama, the question of the action and subject matter was, as we have already begun to see, only half the problem. The ability to reinvent the operatic scenario, and to envisage what kinds of expressive and psychological effects might be drawn from it, depended on a composer also being able to find an appropriate musical idiom within which to work. Expressive force of style was needed to sustain the dramatic vision convincingly; and only when music was fully integrated as the main vehicle of the action would the aspiration towards a form of total expression be fulfilled. As both Debussy and Dukas had done, Bartók took a deeply empirical approach to his compositional task and worked on his opera intermittently over several years, constantly refining various aspects of its style and sound-world, as close study of the surviving sources reveals (Kroó

1981 and 1993; Leafstedt 1999, 125–58). Like Debussy, he paid particular attention to the refinement of details in the rhythmic delineation and declamatory profile of the vocal parts – a procedure which is of special interest in regard to the broader aesthetic concerns of the symbolist operatic project. Similarly to Debussy and Dukas, he envisaged a fundamentally syllabic declamation, grounded in the speech patterns of the language (Hungarian in his case, French in theirs), and seeking to give an audibly 'national' character to the vocal lines.

This approach to word setting was characteristically radical, but not by any means unique. Composers as diverse as Strauss and Puccini had been moving towards the use of a freer, more flexible kind of vocal line, at least in certain areas of their operas – a vocal line built up from small rhythmic and melodic shapes which corresponded in some degree to the accentual patterns of the words, rather than arbitrarily seeking to fit the text beneath broader, independently conceived melodic spans. And a radical individualist such as Janáček, in moving through the various phases of revision of *Jenůfa* (1903–4, 1906, 1907–8) and on towards the composition of his later operas, came more and more to see in 'speech melodies' (*nápěvky*) the main source of his melodic ideas within the vocal line. As in the case of Debussy and Bartók, it would be wrong to see in these melodic shapes a direct transcription of linguistic accentuation in any very literal sense. As with other aspects of opera, there is a strong element of stylization and 'idiomatic translation' involved, and the resultant melodic style in the end stands or falls by its own merits. The idea of faithful accentuation ultimately remains an aspiration rather than an objective technique, its goal being obviously as much rhetorical as strictly phonetic. Many operas written with the sounds and articulation of the spoken language uppermost in the composer's mind still survive linguistic translation triumphantly (*Jenůfa* initially made its way on the international stage in German, with great success, beginning with the important productions given at Vienna and Cologne in 1918 and Berlin and New York in 1924), even if few would deny that the original language, when well declaimed, brings with it a dimension of colour and expressive idiom that is ultimately irreplaceable.

Nevertheless, for all these common developments across Europe, a passionate concern with prosody was one of the major compositional preoccupations to which the symbolist aesthetic gave rise. For Debussy, it was not just a question of the *génie de la langue* (a feeling for the distinctive qualities of French declamation which was one of the things he most admired, for example, in Rameau), but also one of psychology and dramaturgy in a broader sense. In the first place, following Maeterlinck, he was aiming at a clear evocation of humanity and human emotion, in as simple and direct a form as possible, despite the apparent stylization and ambiguity of the dialogue forms in the playtext/ libretto. And this need for clear declamation was combined – at least in his own mind – with what he saw as the distilled, limpid quality of expression, full of nuance but never obscure, at which he was aiming:

> It is important to insist on the simplicity [to be found] in *Pelléas*: I spent twelve [*recte* ten] years striving to remove from it everything superfluous that had somehow slipped in unawares – but I never set out to revolutionize anything at all. . . . I merely tried to show how people who were singing [in a drama] could at the same time remain human and natural, without needing to become like madmen or ciphers.
>
> (Debussy, in Lesure 1993, 247)

His technique of word setting – one that, as studies of the sketches and drafts have shown, was a constant, almost obsessive preoccupation during the long years of writing the opera – seems to have grown more decisive and more refined as he went along. Such flexible declamation, in which the kind and degree of emotion a character might be feeling at any given moment could in theory be mirrored in the vocal line, and in the way this line was amplified and intensified by the orchestra, was closely related to Debussy's general views on dramatic expression, which embraced not just prosody but also the broader musical life of the piece as a representation of the inner life of the characters:

> It is quite wrong to think that a fixed melodic line (*une ligne mélodique arrêtée*) can be made to contain all the infinite nuances through which a character passes [during the course of a drama]: that's not just an error of taste but a fundamental error (*une faute de "quantité"*). So that, if there's little or no trace of . . . a symphonic thread in *Pelléas*, this is in reaction to the nefarious neo-Wagnerian aesthetic which claims to be able to render, simultaneously, the emotion expressed by a character and the inner reflections which cause him [or her] to act as they do. In my opinion these are two contradictory operations, from an operatic point of view, which in combination can only serve to weaken or undermine one another. It's surely far better that music should attempt by simple means – a chord? a curve? – to represent the [various] ambient and psychological states as they follow one another (*les états d'ambiance ou d'âme successifs*), without forcing them to awkwardly follow the pattern of a preordained symphonic development, which is *always arbitrary* . . .   (246)

Here we see that, however separate the spheres of declamation and of the orchestral continuity might appear to be at a technical level, in Debussy's thinking they are very much two aspects of a greater whole. And it is this extreme degree of linkage between the various musical and scenic elements – or dimensions – of the score that characterizes the approach of all three composers. Yet again, this preoccupation stems ultimately from Wagner. But the symbolist ethos is perhaps even more radically synaesthetic, at least in aspiration – and so the way the orchestra was made to relate to what was happening in the vocal line at any given moment was crucial for each of them in different ways. Bartók's extensive revisions to the details of the declamation in *Bluebeard* show this preoccupation just as clearly as do Debussy's. And despite the greater breadth and solidity of the orchestral writing in *Ariane* by comparison with *Pelléas*, a stylistic feature which Dukas counterbalanced by consciously making space for the voice where necessary, he too was fundamentally concerned with speech values, drawing in part no doubt on the example set by Debussy. Writing in 1927 to Guy-Ropartz about a forthcoming concert performance of *Ariane*, Dukas emphasized the fully integrated relationship of the musical fabric as a whole to the rhythms and pacing of the vocal declamation, advising him that

> as a general rule, [you should] beat time [*conduire* = 'set a tempo'] at the speed of spoken theatrical diction. This is essential for the first chorus as it is [also] for the *soli*. As soon as the voices enter the tempo must be based on the rate of delivery of stage declamation. And your four main beats should give, with the appropriate subdivisions, a resolute *allegro*.
>
> (Dukas, in Favre 1971, 160)

All these observations serve to emphasize the centrality of the voice – a centrality which brings with it the corollary of an orchestral continuity that is able to endow the words with a rich unspoken hinterland of complex, nuanced emotion, without ever threatening to overwhelm or undermine them.

Schoenberg, too, saw the importance of giving primacy to the voice, both for expressive reasons (the voice is the primary vehicle of human emotion in life, and *a fortiori* in opera), and also for clarity's sake (only with a fully resolved and articulate vocal part can the human situation be made intelligible). But typically for Schoenberg, he complicates this essentially simple observation, twisting it so as to give it a more theoretical slant. He asserts that, in consequence of this primacy of the voice, all the compositional material should in some way be encapsulated or 'embraced within' the vocal line (Schoenberg 1975, 106): the singing and declaiming voice is audibly to the fore, while the psychological background, with all its emotional ambience and implied undercurrents, is provided by the orchestral amplification of this 'basic line'. Like Debussy, though in far less polemical and censorious terms, Schoenberg claimed that Wagner, despite acting with excellent dramatic ideas and intentions, had nevertheless overloaded and at times over-structured his orchestral textures, with the result that the freedom of both the vocal line and the dramatic movement was compromised (105–6). Yet if he doubted the dramatic appropriateness of such an overly symphonic approach to thematic working and paragraphing within the orchestra, Schoenberg never doubted the viability of the general Wagnerian vision. It needed to be taken further, transcended even, but was groundbreaking in many of the right ways. He saw that Wagner had taken a bold and necessary path in seeking to reformulate the whole relationship between the sustained impact and mobility of the dramatic message and the continuous musical unfolding towards which he had been working for most of his career. Perhaps the crucial discovery he had made, along the way, was how to shape the orchestral continuity so as to render every change and every turn in the dramatic situation immediately clear to the audience. In through-composed opera the composer needed to be able to signpost the drama as far as possible at every level – scenic, atmospheric, psychological – with a real sureness of touch.

This sense of continuity, of the continuous unfolding of the orchestral materials, enabled a rapidity and a responsiveness to nuance in the psychological texture of the piece which stands at the heart of both the symbolist and the expressionist vision. This went hand in hand with the new general relationship of music to theatre, alluded to by Schoenberg, and also with the new approaches to prosody and vocal writing, and to the way orchestral textures were constructed, which we have already observed. For a strong tendency to downplay the sheer audibility and strong profiling of motives (as Wagner had understood them) is a key technical aspect of this approach to the handling of the orchestra in both *Pelléas* and *Erwartung*. If the sheer fluid beauty of Debussy's sense of form ultimately works against the creation of solid musical architecture, it nevertheless enables precisely this kind of subtle psychological play within the fabric of the drama. The technical means which make this possible consist in finding motivic shapes that can merge and combine with unselfconscious ease, by virtue of their shared intervallic elements:

> In *Pelléas* every motif shares the same intervals with every other: they can be fragmented into accompaniment or ostinato; every ostinato or accompaniment [figure] can emerge as a motif; and the harmony everywhere consists of these same intervals superimposed into chords ... The large-scale corollary of this is that there is no 'architecture' in *Pelléas* ... [whose] very special felicity ... [consists in] the way in which the turn of the speech, a passing reference, an underlying feeling or mood, immediately impresses itself upon the local expression. The music in *Pelléas* actually reacts to the words rather than, in Wagner, being the expression and embodiment of them.
>
> (Holloway 1979, 137)

If both Debussy's and Schoenberg's motivic technique and approach were ultimately derived from the Wagnerian model, they sought a version of it that was internalized and distilled into something less self-dramatizing and less strongly projected, and was subsumed within an overall texture whose primary purpose was psychological reaction and evocation.

Symbolism and expressionism

From its emergence in the 1890s symbolism rapidly grew into a European phenomenon, becoming rooted and acclimatized in Scandinavia, Russia, Germany and elsewhere in central Europe, including Hungary, as well as in its homeland in France and Belgium (Balakian 1982). There were productive ties to Germany in particular, not least because strong and influential artistic personalities came under the spell of symbolist ideas, both through their own visits to Paris and through the diffusion of Maeterlinckian and Mallarméan texts in printed form. The poet Stefan George, for example, was in Paris during 1889 and for a brief period had attended Mallarmé's Tuesday evening literary and intellectual gatherings (where Debussy was also a valued if somewhat sporadic guest). And in later years, after going back to Germany, he became a reference point for intellectual and artistic circles with symbolist leanings and aspirations, in Munich and elsewhere. Kandinsky also went for a time to Paris (1906–7) and, on his return to Germany, became closely involved with the Munich Artists' Theatre (Münchener Künstlertheater), a group with strong symbolist interests in the realm of dramatic spectacle and stage design (Weiss 1977 and 1979).

George was, of all contemporary writers, the preferred poet of the Schoenberg circle during the pre-First World War period; and the exchange of ideas between Schoenberg and Kandinsky was in many ways decisive for them both during the crucial years 1911–14. Moreover, the rapidity of their artistic sympathy when they first became acquainted in January 1911 can be accounted for by the fact that during the immediately preceding years – the years of *Erwartung* and free atonality, of the *Harmonielehre* and Kandinsky's epoch-making text *Concerning the Spiritual in Art*, which explicitly mentions Wagner, Maeterlinck and Debussy (Kandinsky 1965) – they had been working towards similar aesthetic goals in parallel, but independent ways. Moreover, they both held strong views on the aims and nature of dramatic representation which chimed in with the broadly anti-realist stance then current among the avant-garde in Austria and Germany:

> Kandinsky abstracts all unessential transitory characteristics in order to throw into relief the intrinsic, unchangeable shape of things, . . . [whereas] Schoenberg . . . is closer to Maeterlinck's de-individualized characters who

represent something beyond themselves ... They shared the
Expressionists' disgust with the theater of edification, with the socially
critical plays of Naturalism, and their mistrust of the word [and verbal
communication] in the established sense ... They also shared a ... belief
in ... showing the essence of things, only revealed to the artist in visionary
ecstasy, to other human beings as primordial truth ... Like most of the
Expressionst dramatists, [they] also wanted ... to reveal transcendental
forces and relationships, ... which no longer fit into a pattern of causality;
thus the stage is no longer a mirror of the realistic world, but one of 'true
being', beyond the seeming world of material things.

(Hahl-Koch 1984, 163–4)

No doubt this list of aspirations goes well beyond that of the symbolists,
certainly in tone and emphasis if not in ideas *per se*. Any French thinker
would probably have fought shy of the notion of visionary ecstasy or of
primordial truth, let alone that of 'true being', and would have been
content with a more circumspect, less prophetic, and perhaps more ironic
approach to such serious topics. And although the symbolist approach
certainly aimed to evoke interior realities and states of the soul, it is
difficult to imagine Debussy having much liking for the fervour of the
German expressionists' overtly spiritualist and philosophical rhetoric,
which he would surely have seen as needlessly grandiloquent and in
poor taste. Such points of contact and connection as there are do not in
themselves, even taken together, constitute a consciously linked aesthetic
or artistic programme. But they do help to bridge the cultural gap, at the
level of underlying and formative ideas, between the world of symbolism
and that of expressionism. Symbolist poetics had emerged partly out of
the intensive French response to Wagner in the 1880s and 1890s. And it
was the broader insights and aesthetic goals of symbolism that in turn
now re-entered the vast sea of late-romantic culture in Germany, and
especially the post-Wagnerian world of musical drama, as an invigorating
current that helped to bring about the cultural and artistic transformation
without which Wagner's legacy could scarcely have been turned into a
viable expressive vehicle for drama in the changed circumstances of
modern times.

   These observations help to sketch in a context which lends support to
the notion that *Erwartung* is at root a symbolist opera – one that is
conceived with a German psychological slant, and felt with an expressionistic intensity and edge, as well as being expressed in Schoenberg's free-
atonal style without reference to French stylistic models, but which still
shares important underlying principles with the Maeterlinckian vision
and its derivatives. In this sense, there is a strong kinship of aims and ideas
between symbolism and expressionism, even if they express themselves

very differently, and even if their cultural paths diverge more or less from the very beginning. The interpenetration of inner and outer worlds is similar, as is the expressive priority given to what might be called the 'psychic dimension' of the action. Certainly, whatever in Maeterlinck's aesthetic is couched in the language of ambiguity and evasion takes on a much sharper psychological edge in Schoenberg. Yet the Pappenheim libretto for *Erwartung* uses the imagery of nature with the same kind of selective intensity as Maeterlinck does – and the nocturnal phenomena of light (moon, shadows, appearances) and movement (breeze, branches, sounds) are lavishly provided within the text for Schoenberg to work his orchestral magic on. And so, with the combined suggestive force of voice and orchestra, they are simultaneously both a symbolic projection of the Woman's fears and anxieties, and a representation of the external perceptions that have triggered them.

The flexibility and multivalency of the orchestral continuity was another point they had in common. The orchestra may articulate physical move-ment, effects of atmosphere (the wind, the light, the play of natural forms), and other perceptual or ambient qualities. But above all it effortlessly bridges the gap between the fragile exterior world of human perception and the psychic world within. In their approach to instrumentation, they shared an approach which favoured the avoidance of mixed colours, or at least sought unprecedented orchestral combinations which allowed primary instrumen-tal colours to speak both pure, as clear individual 'voices' within a freely polyphonic texture, and as combined in new, often radically unconventional ways. Each of them had an ear for such sonorities, both in themselves, as effects of timbre and colour in their own right, and as expressive metonymies for states of mind or being. As Webern observed of *Erwartung* as early as 1912 (and here we may briefly note in passing just how well he and Berg obviously knew this score from its inception, despite its belated premiere at Prague, under Zemlinsky, on 6 June 1924):

> The score of this monodrama is an unprecedented event. All traditional formal principles have been severed; there is always something new, presented with the most rapidly shifting expression.
>
> This is also true of the orchestration: a continuous succession of sounds never heard before. There is no measure in the score that doesn't demonstrate a completely new sound pattern. The treatment of the instruments is entirely soloistic ... [Of the chordal voicing:] Each color derives from an entirely different timbral family. There is absolutely no blended sound [*Mischklang*] here; each color resounds soloistically, unbroken ...
>
> ... Thus this music flows by, tightly bound forms along with disinte-grating ones, breaking up recitative forms, giving expression to the most hidden and faintest stirrings of emotion.   (Webern 1912, 227–30)

Such obsessive concern with timbre and texture, at both the general and the more detailed, fine-grained level, illustrates very well the increasingly important role played by sheer sonority in modern opera, not just as an effect of colouristic originality, but as a means to creating a truly distinctive sound-world for the chosen subject matter. As generic traditions of opera began to lose their hold as a vehicle for new work within an increasingly fixed, historicized repertory, so the importance of the individual project, and the *ad hoc* working out of all the dramatic, musical and scenic parameters in relation to the character of the subject, increased. This again was grounded ultimately in the *Gesamtkunstwerk* idea, but went far beyond Wagner in a way he could scarcely have envisaged it being applied. This too is a sphere of operatic development, whether viewed in a broadly cultural or in a more closely technical sense, that confirms the underground affinities between the symbolist and expressionist approaches, quite apart from the question of possible historical continuities and moments of demonstrable influence.

One final aspect of the handling of orchestral texture which links Schoenberg to symbolist practice is its aspiration towards an aesthetic of sustained eloquence, transforming the moment-to-moment unfolding of the psychological action into free musical form. In a 1912 diary entry Schoenberg considered the – fundamentally paradoxical – linkage of the concept of the obbligato line with the non-repeating spontaneity of recitative, and brought this combined idea into relation with the idea of *unendliche Melodie*. This strongly suggests that, like Debussy, he was attempting to break down the powerful musical constructs of the Wagnerian imagination and distil away what he felt to be its excessive orchestral substance, in order to arrive at an expressive essence of it couched in a quite different musical and textural style. In this, the brilliantly anti-constructive phase of Schoenbergian atonality, which was reacting with every fibre of its being against the equally brilliant constructedness of Wagner, we are confronted by the paradox that *Erwartung*, with its aesthetic of non-repetition, free unfolding, athematic variation, pervasive asymmetry and radical atonality, was none the less, despite these divergences, a profoundly Wagnerian work at a strongly sublimated remote or background level (Dahlhaus 1987, 145).

The quality of 'endlessness' in *unendliche Melodie* was in this sense a dramatic and epistemological ideal, rather than anything more literalistic having to do with the melodic character of themes and textural combinations of such themes. It is thus at root a psychological and rhetorical quality more than it is a stylistic one in the narrower, technical sense. If, according to Wagner, 'a musical structure is "melodic" to the extent that it is eloquent' (146), then asymmetrical, athematic, non-repeating 'free flow' or 'perpetual variation' in the orchestra not only is no bar to lucid expression, but may, in extreme human states, be the only true and adequate expressive means. It is by this measure that *Erwartung* is 'case study and construction in one, [in which] the seismographic registration of traumatic shock becomes, at the same time, the structural law of the music' (146 and 149, citing Theodor W. Adorno). This aesthetic of direct 'idiomatic translation' from the psychological and the atmospheric to the musical is the point of contact at which the symbolist and expressionist operatic worlds touch.

The literary and aesthetic as well as the more centrally dramatic concerns of symbolism may thus be seen to have influenced the expressionist approach to opera at a deeply implicit, formative level. But there are other connections, too, of a more immediate and concrete kind. We have already observed how Berg, in the company of Schoenberg and Webern, attended the Viennese production of *Ariane* conducted by Zemlinsky in 1908. And although, over the longer term, the operatic models of both Dukas and Debussy were equally important to him – surely more as an approach and an aspiration, than at a stylistic or constructional level – Berg was obviously immediately enthralled by *Ariane*. During the summer of 1909, in the year following the performances at the Volksoper, he even suggested to his future wife Helene that he might play through *Ariane* to her at the piano, in company with such other luminary scores as *Parsifal* and *Elektra* (Grun 1971, 89). And he later admitted to Ernest Ansermet that the example of *Pelléas* had inspired him to use orchestral interludes as an integral part of the drama in *Wozzeck*, and that the way Debussy had invested each scene of his opera with a distinctive, localized expressive character had given him the idea of using a varied sequence of abstract instrumental forms as an underlying constructive and dramaturgical device (Carner 1983, 178).

Here, then, is a thought-provoking link between the symbolist works and Berg's operatic practice: a way of writing in a continuously unfolding and sustained manner, yet with maximum differentiation from scene to scene, so that the phases of the drama may be clearly and audibly characterized. Such considerations are less of a problem in *Erwartung*, where the piece as a whole is short and condensed, and the totality of the action is constituted by the expansion of a brief moment of highest psychic intensity and complexity ('In *Erwartung* the aim is to represent *in slow motion* everything that occurs during a single second of maximum spiritual excitement, stretching it out to half an hour'; Schoenberg 1975, 105). But if a composer wished to adopt the idea of the orchestral continuity as the foundation of a drama with a cast of characters and a sequential action, and in doing so give voice not only to the psychological 'atmosphere' in which they are all enveloped, but also, just as importantly, to an articulate series of situations, then some effective means of contrast and internal sectionalization was essential. And it was equally essential to achieve this sense of ongoing contrast without recourse to over-specific motivic design, or to an overtly discursive or developmental orchestral approach. Berg himself did of course use a closely woven inner tissue of thematic ideas; but, as with his underlying constructive forms, this dimension of his scores is in fact handled very fluidly, and is to a considerable extent subsumed within the expressive 'scenic and psychological flow' of the music as a whole. Here, too, there is an implied affinity with the 'tonalities of light and dark' theory – the composer's interpretative grasp of the expressive ambience of every situation (potentially of every moment), with all its simultaneous physical and psychic impulses, would govern the course of his musical invention and formal sense, as he sought to invest each scene with its appropriate sonic character.

Legacy: later perspectives

My argument has been that symbolist opera in the strict sense was a relatively contained, short-lived phenomenon, just as Maeterlinck's period of intense theatrical activity in the 1890s had been short-lived, but that it had long-range consequences which went well beyond the confines of its own historical moment. Both these cultural manifestations of symbolist ideas – the theatrical and the operatic – were powerful and ultimately long-lasting, not merely in what they aspired to but in what they actually managed to achieve in so short a space of time. If symbolism's aims and ideals were in part absorbed into the expressionist project, then it is chiefly in this guise that they lived on. It was the range of sound-worlds conjured up by (largely Austro-German) expressionism which were to be one of the decisive aural influences on the modernist avant-garde, in both its free-atonal and its serial manifestation; so that the renewed pursuit of hyperexpressive opera in the 1960s and 1970s, in taking its cue from *Wozzeck* and *Erwartung*, and increasingly from Berg's *Lulu* as well, was invisibly connected to earlier symbolist ideas by this means. And the idea of an expressive 'scenic and psychological flow' as the *raison d'être* of the orchestral continuity, liberated from the symphonic paragraphing and dense leitmotivic networks of Wagner, was exemplified and further developed primarily through the ongoing reception of Berg and Schoenberg. So that, even if acoustically and stylistically there is no audible link between, say, Debussy's 1904 incidental music commissioned for André Antoine's production of *Le Roi Lear* (though the composer admittedly never showed any sign of wanting to treat the subject operatically) and Aribert Reimann's shatteringly powerful *Lear*

(1978), the latter could scarcely have come to be as it was without the mediating histories of symbolist and expressionist opera which had first internalized and tamed the Wagnerian legacy, before transforming it and extending it in new directions, in a cumulative process which inevitably lost all contact with its own origins.

If the Wagnerian vision remained a strong one, still fascinating and capable of further evolution, the methods and the aesthetic as well as the stories and scenarios had had to change, and indeed go on changing. Wagner's heroic championing of an extended operatic language (of tonality, of the contrapuntal combination of themes, of the stretching of the principle of theatrical gesture and the expressive moment to encompass a musical process of vast symphonic breadth) was positioned at a historical crux, and had to be diverted – by the sheer force of a strong, though not necessarily revolutionary, musical personality – into something else. This is surely the sense in which Debussy referred to Wagner as a sunset rather than a dawn, and sought a way of internalizing and sublimating what he continued to love and admire, while simultaneously feeling the necessity of denial and confrontation, and finally of transcendence (Holloway 1979; Abbate 1981).

It was not until the greater diffusion of the Berg operas in the theatre after World War Two, as well as the rejuvenation of *Pelléas* and its recasting in the role of a 'universal' rather than a more narrowly focused 'national' opera (as gradually happened also with Janáček), that these dramaturgical questions could be more fully and more deeply explored, both in terms of stage production and at the critical and psychological level. To consider briefly a contrasting example will serve to broaden and also reflect back on the scope of this latter stage of the argument, in both a historical and an aesthetic perspective. For one can hear the apparently direct – yet from the vantage point of the later twentieth century 'retrospective' and *post hoc* – influence of Wagner on the centrally modernist, and still broadly expressionist, idiom of a work such as Harrison Birtwistle's *Gawain* (1991, revised 1994). This three-act opera on the grand scale, having taken its mythic subject matter and atmosphere from Arthurian legend as a dramatic starting point, triumphantly dares to bring back an audibly Wagnerian dimension of sound and gesture and graft it on to an idiom that, like Reimann's, has come straight out of something much more recent, and without obvious surface connections either to Wagner or to symbolism.

Both Reimann and Birtwistle stand, independently of one other and of late twentieth-century operatic culture in general, as heroic reaffirmations of a large-scale approach to opera which seeks to harness all the power and reach of mythic narrative and bring it together with a musical idiom that allows no compromises or half-measures. The resulting works, when experienced as live theatre, both lay claim to something almost cosmic, as well as numinous and potentially tragic – though the magical quest-element of *Gawain* diverts this tragic potential into an atmosphere of gritty heroic determination in the protagonist's struggle for self-realization in the face of far greater forces than just his series of one-to-one encounters along the way. *Lear* responds to the enormity of the Shakespearean subject and its dramatic themes with music of an extremity which is commensurate with the terrible human conflicts and realizations which stand at the heart of the story. Yet the very massiveness and at times violence of its sound-world take us beyond the individual human plight, however heartrending, and into something bigger – a larger dimension which lies beyond the scenic and beyond the physical *tout court*, beyond even the pathos of shared human emotion. We are moved into a ritualized tragic world against which the protagonist and the audience are both powerless. And this miraculous (if supremely painful and despairing) shift is fundamentally brought about by Reimann's deployment of his vast orchestra, or rather, by the orchestra in its relation to the voices and to the physical presences on stage. As in *Gawain*, the orchestral conception is central. It is the force-field generated by the tension between the immensely varied vocal writing and the – at times massively subdivided, often clustered – instrumental textures which surround the voices, that gives the work its unique visceral impact in the theatre.

Certain dramaturgical features ultimately traceable back to symbolist practice are still profoundly there in Reimann: the lack of regularly paragraphed musical forms and thematic profiles; the adoption of a musical continuity which renders the moment-to-moment flux of the dramatic situation while at the same time saturating it with an often almost unbearably intense level of expressivity that at times approaches the cataclysmic; the exploitation of physical extremes of sound (an extension of the principle of 'tonalities of light and dark' used in *Pelléas* or *Ariane* or *Bluebeard*) to give a powerful sense of dramatic differentiation and contrast without becoming symphonic or discursive; the use of the orchestra not just to give dramatic ambience to the scenes and to support the voices, but to propel and animate the forces of nature which approximate, in this epic tragedy, to those of destiny; and the pervasive use of free vocal writing, ranging outwards from middle-range syllabic declamation to more sustained if still angular lyric lines, explosive vocal gestures, hysterical coloratura and tense parlando. Reimann had clearly taken these stylistic procedures from sources many times removed from Debussy or Bartók, though strong traces of *Erwartung* and more importantly of Berg (both *Wozzeck* and *Lulu*) can be heard in this as in many other neo-expressionist operas of the 1960s and 1970s – most strikingly of all, perhaps, in Zimmermann's *Die Soldaten* of 1965. But the immense distance travelled since the pre-1914 world serves to emphasize once again what the real necessity had been of remaking the Wagnerian legacy at an absolutely fundamental level, yet without suppressing its most vital and powerful expressive impulses.

Debussy himself saw very clearly that it is, finally, its capacity for profound psychological and situational expression within the context of a sensitively drawn human drama which gives any opera its lasting power and relevance, and that refinements of style and atmosphere or new features of construction and invention are finally subordinate to the projection of this human content. As if in premonition of what would happen during later years, he had insisted already in 1902 that

> the drama of *Pelléas*, ... despite its dreamlike atmosphere, [in fact] contains far more of humanity than do the so-called 'documents of real life' (*les soi-disant «documents sur la vie»*) ... There is in it a language of evocation, the sensibility [and emotion] of which [I judged] suitable to be prolonged in music and in the 'orchestral décor' ... I do not claim to have discovered everything in *Pelléas*. But I have tried to forge a path which others will be able to follow, extending and enriching it with personal discoveries which perhaps will be able to deliver dramatic music from the heavy constraints which have burdened it for so long.   (Debussy, in Lesure 1987, 63–4)

Along with the many explicit references to his struggle to absorb and transform Wagner, this comes as close as any of his observations to identifying the essential, yet also the most difficult and elusive of tasks facing any operatic composer working in the twentieth century – that of finding an approach to musical form, in the realm both of vocal writing and of the orchestral continuity, that is aesthetically persuasive and consistent, yet at the same time fully transparent to the human values and the moment-to-moment life of the unfolding drama which it embodies.

6 Expression and construction: the stage works of Schoenberg and Berg

ALAN STREET

To attempt to site the stage works of the Second Viennese School in relation to more encompassing artistic tendencies within opera since 1900 is to come face to face with a number of apparent incongruities. For example, of the six scores which reached a definitive form, only two or three of them – Alban Berg's *Wozzeck* and *Lulu*, and perhaps Arnold Schoenberg's *Moses und Aron* – could be said to have achieved a secure place in the international repertory. Furthermore, if totalitarian censorship, much less perceived considerations of linguistic complexity, has failed to exert any lastingly adverse affect on the canonical status of these compositions, then the further critical veneration of Schoenberg's *Erwartung*, reverently anticipated by Anton von Webern over a decade before the work's delayed first performance in 1924 (see Webern 1912), does not alter the fact that they remain the legacy of Schoenberg and Berg only. While Berg's 1929 lecture on *Wozzeck* identified the work as the first full-scale opera to have emerged from 'the movement that people quite wrongly called atonality' (Jarman 1989a, 154), it could hardly have been expected to predict two further historical outcomes: that of the two major stage works of the 1930s, one (*Moses*) would remain a two-act fragment, while the other (*Lulu*), requiring partial completion of just 87 bars, would have to wait more that four decades for its intended three-act performance. Thus what began when Schoenberg composed *Erwartung* in an intense phase of inspiration over three weeks in the late summer of 1909 subsequently imposed an interpretative chronology that was only free to proceed with real conviction almost 70 years later following the Parisian premiere of the complete *Lulu* (in the realization by Friedrich Čerha) on 24 February 1979.

Lulu, in particular, has been responsible for encouraging a thoroughgoing reappraisal of Berg's approach to matters of compositional practice. Yet if evidence of systematic organization is held to have strengthened his reputation among the post-1945 generations of high-modernist composers and analytically inclined music theorists, then perhaps this seemingly blanket belief too now stands in some need of reappraisal. In sum, present-day attunement to a postmodern sensibility has been increasingly responsible for refocusing critical perceptions in favour of an irreducible plurality of values and affinities. Thus advocating the impression of artistic renewal founded on a monolithic programme of action risks forcing a common stock of received wisdom onto a historical reality that in its time was infinitely more fluid and contingent in nature. Similarly, for a group of composers compelled, like so many of their creative contemporaries, to withdraw from the commitment to a consensual form of expression, linguistic reinvention of the medium was never allowed to become the abstract end in itself that subsequent theoretical codification might suppose it to have been. Hence, just as Schoenberg, writing to Rudolf Kolisch shortly after the completion of the second act of *Moses und Aron*, thought to reinforce the point that the aesthetic qualities of his serial pieces lay in the fact that they were 'twelve-note *compositions*, not *twelve-note* compositions' (1964, 164–5; emphases in original), so his lecture written on the occasion of the 1928 Breslau production of *Die glückliche Hand* sought to convey a continuing incomprehension as to why its modes of representation might ever have 'been called expressionist' (1928b, 105).

True, the sense of distortion or exaggeration placed in the service of subjective emotion is a substantive characteristic to a greater or lesser degree of each of the works under consideration here. And, just as importantly, the rarefied spiritual content of Schoenberg's art around 1911–12 was sufficient not only for several of his paintings to have formed part of the first exhibition of the Munich-based *Blaue Reiter* group, but also for examples of compositions by himself, Berg and Webern to have appeared in the group's first (and only) published almanac (Kandinsky and Marc 1912). Nonetheless, any impression of a concerted conviction in the ideals of a distinctive musical expressionism would seem to have arisen, as Jost Hermand has suggested (1979), very much after the fact. Moreover, that these same works should share even less common ground with the Russian abstract geometric movement known as Constructivism, founded in 1914 by Vladimir Tatlin, would seem to remove any firm historical, or at least thematic foundation from the present chapter. However, to combine the terms expression and construction within an implied binary opposition is also to recall the important role such complementary concepts have played in respect of certain longstanding interpretative traditions – in particular, with regard to the nineteenth-century critical conflict fought out on the terrain of opera between (loosely speaking) Wagnerian symbolists and Hanslickian formalists (summarized in Abbate 1992), or in relation to the Germanic history of dialectical philosophy variously represented by Immanuel Kant, Georg Wilhelm Friedrich Hegel and Theodor Adorno (surveyed in Roberts 1988).

Indeed, while both of these perspectives at least partially inform the circumstances of production and reception through which these works came collectively into existence and continue to be known, they also help to define the overall continuum of reflective and affective significance against which each composition must individually be measured.

Genre

A thicker contextualization of this repertoire is certainly obliged first of all to acknowledge its emergence from a diverse historical field within Austro-Germany. Apart from the dominant figure of Richard Strauss, Franz Schreker (*Der ferne Klang*, premiered in 1912), Hans Pfitzner (*Palestrina*, premiered in 1917), Erich Wolfgang Korngold (*Violanta* and *Die tote Stadt*, premiered in 1916 and 1920) and Alexander Zemlinsky (*Ein florentinische Tragödie* and *Der Zwerg*, premiered in 1917 and 1922) each enjoyed a degree of theatrical success that was only later matched by the first performance of *Wozzeck*. For the young Schoenberg, and for his pupils Berg and Webern, Wagnerian music drama represented the pinnacle of operatic ambition. Yet as Gustav Mahler's decade-long tenure as Director of the Viennese Hofoper (1897–1907) would have symbolically confirmed, the strength of Viennese music, in particular during the nineteenth century, lay not in the field of opera, but in the tradition of instrumental composition extending from Beethoven to Brahms.

In view of this, it is understandable that progressive *fin de siècle* aspirations should have sought to establish a distinctive creative identity by aiming to reconfigure the further musical and extra-musical potential of the symphonic music drama in an alternative domain – that of instrumental programme music. Strauss's reinvention of the symphonic poem as a multi-dimensional meta-genre capable of unfolding a vivid sequence of affects within an overarching single-movement cyclic design was subsequently taken over in ever more complex ways in Schoenberg's compositions from *Verklärte Nacht* (1899) to the First Chamber Symphony (1906). Reflecting on what made such procedures possible in a number of essays written from the 1920s onwards, Schoenberg noted that 'a subconsciously functioning *sense of form*' based on orthodox harmonic relationships became increasingly taxed by another impulse, 'the tendency towards "music as expression"' (1941, 218 (emphasis in original); 1926, 260). Following the emancipation of the dissonance, however, the pursuit of aphoristic precision in pieces of extreme brevity – still impelled by what Schoenberg termed 'very powerful expressive forces' (1926, 262) – was due to consequences both positive and negative: on the one hand an intuitive recognition of the need 'to counterbalance extreme emotionality with extraordinary shortness' (1941, 217) and, on the other, a growing awareness that modes of formal articulation comparable to those provided by tonality had not yet become apparent.

What therefore provided the most cohesive structural possibility in the composition of operas, songs and symphonic poems for the generation after Wagner lay not in the realm of musical substance *per se*, but rather in the wide-ranging formal and pictorial implications which could be derived from a verbal text. Already the symphonic poems of Liszt and, to a lesser extent, Strauss had tended to represent their programmatic sources in a non-narrative fashion, allowing an imagistic sequence of differently characterized segments to approximate to the impression of a wordless song-cycle (Daverio 1993, 215–8). Hence for Schoenberg to have negotiated the transition to atonality, as Reinhold Brinkmann has written (1992), by employing the *Lied* form and instrumental character piece as generic paradigms was in turn a logical historical extension of this development. The Stefan George settings of the Second String Quartet, the Two Songs, Op. 14, and *Das Buch der hängenden Gärten*, along with the Three Piano Pieces, Op. 11, appear to make the transitional process transparent, as does the reference to the mirroring of textual form and changes in semantic 'character and mood' that emerged somewhat later in the course of Schoenberg's essay 'Composition with Twelve Tones (1)' (1941, 217). Nevertheless, reading more closely through Schoenberg's attempts at discursive rationalization, and particularly those written in closer historical proximity to the works they seek to describe, reveals a number of possible anomalies – comments aimed not merely at excusing an occasional disregard for 'the continuation ... of poetic events' (1912, 144), but also at defending an evident 'turn away from expressive music' very soon after the first steps in a new territory where the composer 'had still been using expression to the fullest' (1926, 260).

From *Erwartung* to *Wozzeck*

The reason for Schoenberg's seeming ambivalence – and its definitive connection with *Erwartung* and *Die glückliche Hand* – is partly to be explained by his appeal to 'the ecstasy of composing' which appears in the essay 'The Relationship to the Text' that was also included for publication in the *Blaue Reiter Almanac* in 1912. Additional references to the 'capacity of pure perception' and a language 'which the reason does not understand' (1912, 144, 142; emphasis in original) are among the first of many allusions that the composer was later to make to 'the miraculous contributions of the subconscious' (1949, 85). While his explicit analysis of the creative relationship between the rational and emotive faculties, 'Heart and Brain in Music' (1946), argues for the essential inseparability of the two, neither can accomplish anything of worth, the composer goes on to suggest, without the benefit of inspiration. Commenting some 30 years later with the benefit of hindsight, then, Schoenberg was at pains to emphasize the impossibility of distinguishing between artistic acts of spontaneous expression and deliberate construction. At the point when *Erwartung* came into being, however, his aesthetic credo was altogether more polarized: dedicated to nothing less, in fact, than the complete 'elimination of the conscious will in art' (Hahl-Koch 1984, 23). An extreme formulation of a late-bourgeois commitment to the ideals of romantic individualism, this remark of Schoenberg's to Wassily Kandinsky in 1911 effectively conveys his absolute belief in the capacity of genius to be self-determining. In so far as it might retain any valid link to consciousness, creation had become a truly ecstatic experience. Yet the impression of intuitive immediacy that also made rapid execution a creative imperative was itself reinforced by a thorough distrust of purposive intervention, as the following statement from the composer's letter to Ferruccio Busoni dated 24 August 1909 (at around the time *Erwartung* was written) makes plain:

My only intention is
          to have *no* intentions!
    No formal, architectural or other intentions (except perhaps of
capturing the mood of a poem), no aesthetic intentions – none of any
kind; at most this:
        to place nothing in the stream of my unconscious sensations. But
    to allow anything to infiltrate which may be invoked either by
intelligence or consciousness.   (Busoni 1987, 396)

The composer's own description of *Erwartung* as depicting 'a single second of maximum spiritual excitement' (c. 1930, 105) would consequently seem to mark it as a uniquely creative epiphany; by comparison, his further mention of a slow-motion time-scale intended to convey a nightmarish vision over approximately half an hour characterizes the work dramatically, as Peter Franklin observes, less as a Freudian case study than the 'frozen illustration of a terrifying idea' (1985, 95). Technically speaking, it is the apparent liquidation of all recognizable resources of motivic-thematic form building that most vividly conveys the effect of compositional encephalography. In view of the fact that Schoenberg may have felt able to draw on a range of precedents for the work's expressive idiolect (for instance, the nineteenth-century tradition of operatic mad scenes, or more particularly the music given to Kundry in Act II of Wagner's *Parsifal*, or the central monologue Strauss composed for Klytämnestra in *Elektra*), this departure has rightly been viewed as *Erwartung*'s most radical feature – though Karl H. Wörner (1970) has revealed a striking degree of commonality with Georg Benda's melo-drama *Ariadne auf Naxos* of 1775. Even if Schoenberg's score cannot be regarded as the authentic transcription of a purely improvised perform-ance, the dating of the completed short score between 27 August and 12 September 1909 is proof that the composer had very little time in which to plan and execute his response to Marie Pappenheim's text.

Pappenheim, a former medical student and amateur poet, produced her 'lyric poem' over a similar time-scale in response to a rather vague request from Schoenberg for a libretto (Simms 2000, 91). The sole character, an unnamed Woman, recounts her experience disjointedly, as if in a dream state, across four scenes in which a road, a deserted house, a forest and a clearing are the barely intelligible signs of physical orientation. The dramatic crux, which emerges in the final and longest scene, and the evident focus of her predominantly erotic reminiscences, is an encounter with the corpse of the lover for whom she has been search-ing. At first acquaintance, the impression of a fully synthesized musico-textual stream-of-consciousness might appear to resist any further attempt to categorize the composer's technical approach. However, as Robert Falck has shown (1992), a reading of the text in line with Carl Dahlhaus's notion of (contracted) Wagnerian poetic-musical periods permits the score to be understood as an extended autologue or interior monologue sequence expanded through a series of memory episodes and a significant phase of spectral dialogue addressed to the deceased figure.

Like Franklin, Falck too questions the potential for any literal Freudian reading of *Erwartung*. (As Bryan Simms has indicated (1997, 104–5), the few excisions which Schoenberg did make to the text effec-tively cancel the elements of reportage and underlying sexual causation Pappenheim intended – the original version of her libretto clearly identi-fied the Woman as having shot her lover – in order to register the maximal effect of psychic profusion.) Nevertheless, the memory episodes themselves remain highly suggestive of a more elusive layer of meaning – and all the more so when considered in the context of the other remark-able feature of *Erwartung*, its intertextual relationship with the composer's own set of Eight Songs, Op. 6. The inclusion of a passage, beginning at bar 401, from the sixth song, 'Am Wegrand', while recognized some time ago by Adorno (1973, 46–7), would seem to gain in importance from the possible reference to at least one other setting from the collection, that of the first song, 'Traumleben', in bars 328–32. And if aspects of the libretto would in turn appear to be illuminated through comparison with the very first psychoanalytic case study conducted by Freud and Josef Breuer, that of Anna O, then the Dora case history, with its intimation of past events either reproduced or revised within the present instance, might appear to reveal the composer as indulging, consciously or otherwise, in a process of creative free association (see Street 2000, 120–27).

Because of the ambiguous nature of its intertextual connections, *Erwartung* can be thought to retain an irreducibly enigmatic quality. That such correspondences may still invite an autobiographical, even psychobiographical decoding is nonetheless due to the manner in which extra-musical investments of this kind, rather than remaining isolated instances of affective association, represent a consistent feature of Second Viennese custom. While *Erwartung* succeeds in sublimating this predilection, however, *Die glückliche Hand* renders its personal motivations peculiarly apparent. Admittedly the two scores considered as a complementary pairing symbolically reproduce the tragic triangulation linking love, nature and art long since established as a preoccupation of the romantic tradition: the composer himself regarded them in this way, a preference subsequently realized in staged form at the Kroll Oper in Berlin on 7 June 1930. Yet by emphasizing the effects of male jealousy, in particular, as a consequence of amatory betrayal in the later work, Schoenberg, himself the recently aggrieved victim of marital infidelity (see Kallir 1984, 23–8), comes close to abandoning a desire for thematic generalization in favour of the literal depiction of personal biography.

Like *Erwartung*, *Die glückliche Hand* has four scenes inhabited by an unnamed single (here male) figure. In the composer's own retrospective opinion, the two pieces were altogether different in their manipulation of temporal experience, *Die glückliche Hand* representing less the sense of overall expansion than the compression of a 'major drama' into a span of approximately 20 minutes' duration (Schoenberg c. 1930, 105). No doubt Schoenberg's conviction was determined by his unswerving commitment to the authenticity of the work's aesthetic ambition: a conception involving not merely the self-authorship of the libretto and an expansion of forces to include a 12-voice mixed chorus and two mimes, but also the integration of specific visual resources, including the production of illustrations for set designs and the precise orchestration of stage lighting. (For Schoenberg's ambitious plans to make a film of the work, see Chapter 16.)

Despite the multi-dimensional character of *Die glückliche Hand*, Schoenberg himself supposed that its various facets should be comprehended as nothing more than 'that which is usually symbolized by tones' (1928b, 107). And, true to the integrity of the composer's intuitive aesthetic, the communication of '*inner processes*' (105; emphasis in original) was held to rely on the same subconscious feeling for form through which *Erwartung* apparently came into being. At this point, however, the historical evidence which Schoenberg's 1928 lecture neglects to mention can be thought to reassert itself. Indeed, the ironic disjunction which ostensibly separates the title from its subject matter and on which Schoenberg did equivocally pass comment points to a tension between expression and construction that had begun to jar all too insistently. As Joseph Auner has so clearly demonstrated (1989; 1997), the protracted completion of *Die glückliche Hand* over a four-year period shows it to have been the product of a rather different and unmistakably crisis-bound phase of Schoenberg's development, one during which the doctrine of spontaneous creation began to grow progressively more restrictive and inhibiting. Thus the existence of detailed sketch materials, just as much as the eventual incorporation of thematic recall, contrapuntal working and explicit formal articulation, categorize the score, unlike *Erwartung*, as one of the composer's 'worked' rather than 'purely impressionistic' pieces (Auner 1989, 123; for a detailed analytical interpretation of the structural planning involved in *Die glückliche Hand*, see Auner 1996).

The sense of conflict is itself encapsulated as the climactic point of the third scene of *Die glückliche Hand*, where the male protagonist incites the hostility of the watching artisans by fashioning a jewelled diadem at a single stroke. Although unflinching in his readiness to provoke the bourgeois subject from a state of materialist conformity, the artist-martyr must forever be prepared to endure the burden of the fabulous monster that sits on his back in Scenes 1 and 4, a figure which might well be thought to emblematize the discontinuities of self, elusiveness of reality and prevailing impossibility of human freedom that will attend the failure of his universally redemptive aspirations.

That Schoenberg eventually felt bound to distance himself somewhat from the unfulfilled Utopian artistic quest that had been apparent in his work from at least the Op. 6 songs onwards was made plain by the ironic character of *Pierrot lunaire*, the piece he composed while still completing *Die glückliche Hand*. However, in so far as *Erwartung* permits its female protagonist to reiterate this same questing spirit through her closing words ('I was searching . . .') and *Die glückliche Hand* enshrines its self-sacrificing intent in the reinterpreted form of the Wagnerian *Gesamtkunstwerk*, the composer also gestures towards a more contemporary thematic significance underlying both works – namely, the presence of emancipatory gender politics on the one hand, and the repressive effects of ethnic persecution on the other. As indifferent to the former message, or as incapable of responding directly to the latter sense of cultural oppression as he may have been, the oblique agonistic fashionings of identity are, as Elizabeth L. Keathley (2000) and Julie Brown (1994) have shown, an undeniable factor bearing on Schoenberg's aesthetic choices in the first decade of the twentieth century. Consequently, the aspects of feminist *Bildungsroman* encoded in Pappenheim's text for *Erwartung*, like the composer's wish to conceive the emancipation of the dissonance as a response to Wagnerite diatribes against the enjewishment of Germanic musical language, speak as forcefully through these works as any abstract articulation of the relationship between logic and liberation. Furthermore, the recognition that the composer's later dramatic scores represent an attempt to find more binding forms of resolution for these same concerns also re-emphasizes the way in which stage composition retained its primacy for Schoenberg as a vehicle for creative inquiry.

In the months between completing *Erwartung* and beginning work on *Die glückliche Hand*, Schoenberg wrote to the managing director of Universal Edition, Emil Hertzka, in order to protest against the institutional disregard habitually paid to his status as a teacher in Vienna. Raising the case of the 24-year-old Berg, Schoenberg drew specific attention to his alleged early limitations as a pupil: a gifted composer to be sure, but at first 'absolutely incapable of writing an instrumental movement or inventing an instrumental theme' (1964, 23). While Berg's youthful penchant for *Lieder* composition should not perhaps have been so readily dismissed as a defect in light of the formative role then being played by lyric forms in the exploration of atonality, the second and more telling irony to be drawn from his teacher's corrective assessment – in respect of the brilliant amalgam of vocal and instrumental models that so memorably characterizes *Wozzeck* – would only become clear through hindsight a decade and a half later.

Although a great deal has rightly been said about the distinctive profile of Berg's score, its generic and technical indebtedness can be readily conceded. First and foremost, what Joseph Kerman deems the consummation of the Germanic desire 'to organize opera as a grandiose symphonic unity' (1989, 182) effectively maximizes the hybridity of *fin de siècle* instrumental composition by unfolding the dramatic design through a multi-dimensional sequence of absolute musical forms. In this regard, the examples of Strauss and Schoenberg seem to be developed into a conspectus of the various formal types in historical play at the beginning of the last century, whether revived (character piece, Act I) maintained and extended (symphony, Act II) or newly realized (invention, Act III). With so broad an array of organizational resources in evidence, however, the potential for creating confusion rather than clarity would have been far from negligible. Consequently a meticulously assembled vocabulary of leitmotives was made to function not only in the service of character delineation, but also as the basis for an elaborate web of thematic interrelation after the manner of Schoenberg's own developing variation technique.

If Berg's apprentice efforts at composition had shown him to be lacking in certain aspects of musical craftsmanship, the same could not be said of his literary facility. The early sophistication of the composer's poetic sensibility manifested in his choice of song texts clearly prepared him for the challenge he would later set for himself in electing to rework Georg Büchner's play *Woyzeck* as a libretto. Having chosen to run musical and dramatic organization so closely together, the composer denied that his intention was ever to achieve a radical reform of the genre (Berg 1927, 152). And in the sense that the dynamics of musical form had consciously been used to propel the demands of stage action since at least the time of Mozart, Berg's intended synthesis, despite its thoroughgoing nature, is unquestionably the product of established tradition. In this regard, while *Wozzeck* represents a further instance of the post-Wagnerian preference for literary-operatic inspiration exhibited by Debussy, Strauss and Zemlinsky, the libretto's repeated reference to the cosmically misaligned condition of the natural world invokes a mythic quality that is ultimately closer in spirit to the Wagnerian apotheosis of romanticism than the aesthetic innovations of modernity. Similarly, the central placement of its Act II symphonic drama within a plot curve drawn between culmination and catharsis ultimately underscores the work's proximity to the prevailing Germanic model of the late nineteenth century.

While Berg's reshaping of Büchner's dramatic mobile into a three-act design, each of five scenes, has generally been celebrated as a perfect alignment of form and function, the impression of 'a slightly haphazard quality', to quote Derrick Puffett (1989, 182), is still apparent. Moreover, although the foreshortened structure of each scene is handled through an instinct for musical pacing that seems capable of accommodating the dual influences of literary epic and Straussian opera within a syntax whose flexibility is all but cinematic, the tendency for the contrasting characters of the musical surface to act as the primary source of coherence – even to the degree that, as Kerman argues (1989, 182), the relationship between stage and score approximates to that which exists between film image and film soundtrack – is itself surprisingly strong.

However, if the examples set by both preceding and contemporary generations account for the work's historical grounding, they do not provide an explanation for what Douglas Jarman describes as 'the seemingly paradoxical fusion of technical calculation and emotional spontaneity that gives Berg's music its peculiar fascination' (1989a, 21). Put simply, resolving this paradox has come to seem synonymous with decoding the composer's autobiographical intentions – in effect, by uncovering the apparently extraordinary lengths to which Berg was prepared to go in order to ensure a complete correlation between the representation of personal experience and the constructive mechanisms of architectural design. As Jarman has also noted (1997, 175–6), *Wozzeck* is the pivotal instance in the equation of Berg's own personal relations with the possibilities of musical form. Hence the composer's identification with Wozzeck as soldier and father of an illegitimate child by a woman named Marie is supported structurally by the self-quotations from attempted early piano sonatas that separately convey the vulnerability of each figure during the course of Act III. Moreover, whether the D minor interlude self-reference that forms the composer's requiem for his central character achieves either a passion-like pathos or instead marks a slide into sentimental self-pity as has variously been argued – compare the favourable view of Adorno (1929, 624–5) with the more ambivalent judgement of Kerman (1989, 188–9) – the further impression of a personal testament to the creative association sustained between pupil and teacher is itself made altogether more highly charged, as Anthony Pople observed (1997b, 151–2), by the fact that the supposed homage to Schoenberg's First Chamber Symphony which forms the basis of Act II scene 3 occurs in connection with sordid dramatic circumstances that in outline evidently resemble those surrounding Schoenberg's earlier marital crisis.

The nature of Berg's attitude towards his teacher was undoubtedly complex and multifaceted. Having expressed repeated opposition to an operatic treatment of *Woyzeck*, Schoenberg's eventual enthusiasm for the work, expressed to Hertzka in late 1921 (Jarman 1989a, 22), may well have been sufficiently nuanced as to appreciate at least some of the allusions composed into the score. So, for instance, the first statement of what is perhaps the most important motive in the whole opera, the 'Wir arme Leut!' ('Poor folk like us!') figure, begins a reordered but complete version of the musically appropriate letters of Schoenberg's name (in German notation: S – H – E – G – A – B – D – C) in bars 136–7 of Act I scene 1. This sequence also includes the musically appropriate letters of Berg's name as its central segment, confined to the line sung by the composer's alter ego Wozzeck, and is linked to the lack of one particular material necessity, namely money, which would seem to identify it as a gesture of genuine, if ironic, collegiality. However, the fact that this same passage is sung in response to the taunts of the Captain, a figure satirized, like Dr Schön in *Lulu*, on account of his obsession with bourgeois respectability, perhaps indicates a more ambivalent attitude. As Jarman observes (1997, 178–9), the similarity of certain names and situations in *Lulu* may well have played a decisive role in persuading Berg to set Wedekind's plays. Consequently the use of the Gavotte and Musette as antiquated dance forms to signify Schön's (and thus Schoenberg's) respect for social convention in Act I scene 2 seems retrospectively to confirm a similar role and association for the dance suite which characterizes the Captain (and hence Schoenberg) in the first scene of *Wozzeck*.

However, the relationship between sensuous and cerebral impulses embodied in *Wozzeck* concerns not just the communication of private circumstances, but rather an emblematic illustration of their intimate connection with public existence. For Berg, appreciating one's situated condition entailed reaffirming the inextricable bond between self and milieu. And in the case of this 'provincial Viennese, reluctant intellectual and naïve worshipper of idols', to quote Arved Ashby (2002, 409), a Wozzeck-like fear of the natural sublime meant that the desired sense of self could only be acquired and maintained through the cultural, and specifically the aesthetic, sphere. Consequently the fashioning of esoteric formal templates also came to act as an enabling illusion; less a symbol of subjective confinement for the composer than the kind of recurrent pattern-ing that could confirm a stability of fit between art and life through its apparently predetermined nature. In part, it was the adoption of Schoenbergian principles of musical autonomy which ensured that the dual dimensions of structure and selfhood would achieve a coherent synthesis. Yet as Christopher Hailey has indicated (1989), the belief by which Berg felt able to speak directly to a native audience through *Wozzeck* became plausible because the extremes he elected to mediate between were themselves so intrinsically Viennese. Wagner and Schoenberg apart, it is the logic of Beethoven or Brahms and the lyricism of Schubert or Johann Strauss that are made to coalesce so powerfully in the musical language of the opera. Moreover, its staged dynamics too, aside from exemplifying any supposed lexicon of expressionist dramaturgy, are every-where shot through with the complementary impulses of instinct and discipline, a confluence of competing tensions which the D minor interlude in Act III ultimately resolves on a musical, and specifically Mahlerian, plane.

From *Von Heute auf Morgen* to *Lulu*

A product largely of the postwar years, *Wozzeck* can be said to exhibit a number of characteristic historical markers. Chief among them is the generic reorientation towards more accessible forms of expression, a strategy that, as Christopher Butler has remarked (1994, 257–8), might be taken as inevitable if modernism were to survive beyond its initial shock impact. Even so, it is a shared identity as explicit structures of feeling which, if anything, can be said to demarcate *Erwartung*, *Die glückliche Hand* and *Wozzeck* from the second phase of stage composition undertaken by both Schoenberg and Berg. That any rationale in support of historical periodization for these works remains somewhat artificial, however, is proven at least in part by the chronology of their first performances, which effectively compressed a thirteen-year creative gestation into a span of eighteen months between June 1924 and December 1925. Nonetheless, an engrained critical belief in the linguistic difference in kind separating free atonality from serially ordered twelve-note composition still tends to suggest that *Von Heute auf Morgen*, *Moses und Aron* and *Lulu* belong to a new and different stage of musical development.

While Schoenberg's initial and somewhat chauvinistic declaration predicting serialism's hundred-year longevity – 'Today [i.e. in c. 1921] I have discovered something which will assure the supremacy of German music for the next hundred years' (quoted in Haimo 1990, 1) – appeared to convey a new mood of confidence, his plotting of a gradual course through its substantive implications proved altogether more circumspect. Once again, as Brinkmann observes (1997, 208–9), the stage works of the 1920s and 1930s, like those preceding the First World War, represent the culmination of progressive formal expansion in both instrumental and vocal terms. In spite of such technical innovation, however, Schoenberg was obliged to acknowledge a temporary waning of his influence over the younger generation. In particular, the rapidly changing adherences to *Neue Sachlichkeit* or *Gebrauchsmusik* principles, for example, that he mentions in the essay 'How One Becomes Lonely' (1937, 52) were no longer the outcome of reverence for past achievements, so much as the expression of a constantly self-renewing value, namely topicality.

The one-act *opera buffa* conception of *Von Heute auf Morgen*, composed between October 1928 and January 1929 to a libretto by the composer's second wife Gertrud, was Schoenberg's attempt to address this foregrounding of contemporary trends through the most up to date of dramatic genres, the *Zeitoper*. Ostensibly detached from the purely aesthetic preoccupations of expression and construction, the work sought the fulfilment of 'one aim: genuine musical theatre' (Schoenberg c. 1930, 105). In formal terms, *Von Heute auf Morgen* continues the process of reorientation evident in *Die glückliche Hand*; thus large-scale instances of sectional recall linked to parallel dramatic events are embedded, as

Stephen Davison relates (2000), in a through-composed sequence which subsumes aria, arietta and recitative passages alongside occasional parodies of popular music. In addition, although the musical language is consistently based on the combinatorial hexachordal relationship between complementary prime and inverted forms of the series, the composer also thought to render its effects more lyrical by introducing a reordered scalic variant of the basic set for the purposes of vocal characterization. (An interesting analytical comparison of the approaches of Schoenberg and Berg to this aspect of serial practice is given in Ayrey 1996: see especially 13–21.)

In view of his readiness to make such apparently practical concessions, Schoenberg's contemporary censure of Ernst Křenek and Paul Hindemith for their lack of technical curiosity and even musical conscience in the essay 'Linear Counterpoint' might seem inappropriately harsh (1931, 294). But in fact the true purpose of *Von Heute auf Morgen* was not to celebrate postwar developments over and above their antecedents, but rather to critique them from within. Far from seeking to deflect from, much less satirize, the plot curve traced through *Erwartung* and *Die glückliche Hand*, the composer's figuring of desire among a quartet of domestic characters was aimed directly at the facile wish to live only in the present. Holding up a mirror to society was therefore Schoenberg's attempt to translate his central creative dichotomy into a popular parable contrasting the value of authentic feeling over thoughtless materialism. In this respect, the composer never envisaged the work merely as a way of accommodating his principles to those of the marketplace. Indeed, from this point they would come to acquire a far more austere quality, a formulation of the essential contradiction between style and idea entirely other in relation to the pluralistic competitive spirit of commerce.

Altogether, the disparity between the domestic struggle with material historical circumstance depicted in *Von Heute auf Morgen* and the theological conflict enacted in *Moses und Aron* is far less acute than might initially be supposed. Hence the fact that Schoenberg interrupted work on the latter to compose the former, along with the likelihood that the pair were meant to illustrate complementary female and male perspectives after the pattern set by his first two stage works, perhaps indicates that *Von Heute auf Morgen* represented a necessary clearing of creative space in order for the later opera to proceed. The composer's subsequent reconversion to Judaism in 1933 would ultimately confirm a sense of ethnic identity that had begun to strengthen once again around 1921 after the Schoenberg family had fallen victim to anti-Semitic prejudice during a vacation in Mattsee, near Salzburg. However, if the opera purportedly examines the theme of spiritual revelation, then it plainly does so through an uncompromising analysis of worldly motivation. In this respect, as Alexander Ringer explains, Schoenberg's *Hauptwerk* draws together the multiple strands of his aesthetic theology wherein fear, alienation and materialism are overcome through courageous self-denial, a state of being finally at home in that desert 'where pure ideas eternally prevail' (1980, 98).

The only one of the composer's dramatic works to feature named characters therefore relies primarily on allegorical rather than dramaturgical principles for its emblematization of his uncompromising aesthetic stance. Correspondingly, the prohibition against the making of graven images that forms the second commandment of the Decalogue is rewritten as a metaphysical conflict aimed at signifying the antinomy by which inspiration as a prompting of the spirit can never be given adequate concrete form. In Schoenberg's opera, Moses is forced to speak – his part is notably composed almost entirely as *Sprechgesang* – in defence of the absolute difference of the divine Word, a truth which Aron's sung fluency can only convey as sacrilege even as he strives to mediate on behalf of God's chosen people. Equally significant, however, as Bluma Goldstein observes (2000), is the fact that the Lutheran translation of the Bible which the composer most likely chose to form the basis of his libretto is adapted in ways which both displace and dehistoricize the nature of the covenant struck between God and Israel. In virtually all respects, then, the work is characterized by the turning away from expressive convention that was anticipated at the time of his earliest steps into the wilderness of atonality. Hence the unmistakable tendency of the score to question even its fundamental generic premise by seeking to place the post-Wagnerian legacy of musico-dramatic illusion in direct opposition to the distanced narrative effects of oratorio.

The linguistic exodus that commenced with the emancipation of the dissonance consequently finds its ascetic validation in the music's serial integrity. While underpinned once more by the principle of combinatoriality, Schoenberg's manipulations of the basic set for dramatic purposes are, as David Lewin was able to demonstrate over 30 years ago (1968), remarkably subtle. Thus in Act I scene 1, contrasting harmonic areas defined by hexachordal pitch-class content and differing modes of segmental partitioning serve to articulate the four stages through which Moses is called and persuaded to prophecy by God. That Moses is limited to hexachordal formations for his most complete utterances throughout this exchange, whereas the series in its entirety is first sung by Aron in Act I scene 2, exemplifies the manner in which medium and message are intricately, yet irreconcilably conjoined. Correspondingly the existence of the work as an unfinished fragment also conveys the impossibility of its complete realization; as Paul Griffiths observes, insofar as 'it exists at all, the opera is an expression of Schoenberg–Aron the teacher and composer', whereas the fact that it is broken off ensures that it remains the authentic utterance 'of Schoenberg–Moses the rigorous thinker' (1996, 201). Understood in relation to the tradition of nineteenth-century compositional metaphysics, therefore, Act III of *Moses und Aron* assumes the status of an unfinished tenth symphony. Interpreted as a manifestation of the twentieth century's loss of faith in the transformative power of art, however, it perhaps becomes, as Franklin supposes (1985, 111), another testament to the fate of a musical modernism ultimately overburdened by ideas. Yet to apprehend the work in a purely aesthetic sense is also to overlook its most crisis-ridden vein of contradiction: namely, as Goldstein suggests (2000, 186–8), that which separates the work from being read as the implacable condemnation of a Nazi *Führer-Volk* ideology obsessed with images and symbols on the one hand, or an absolutist vision of the covenant between artist and society that would seek to affirm its own comparably authoritarian ideals on the other.

In sum, it might be concluded that Schoenberg's four stage works present equally untheatrical manifestations of the dichotomy between expression and construction. Thus, by comparison with his pupil, Schoenberg stands revealed as 'a composer who wrote operas' (Hailey 1989, 228), while Berg was quintessentially an operatic composer. As debatable as any capsule judgement may be, the choice of a subject for a second opera saw Berg once more confirm his literary-dramatic disposition by settling on the two *Lulu* plays by the German author, Frank Wedekind. Again acting as his own librettist, the composer chose to set the text in the form of a number opera. Like *Von Heute auf Morgen*, therefore, *Lulu* represented an attempt to realize the idea of opera through an approach that was as much pre- as post-Wagnerian. Significantly, though, any likelihood that a more episodic mode of composition might have been preferred to the model adopted in *Wozzeck* was dispelled not only on the grounds that Berg chose to begin work on the opera with his formal design in place from the first, but also that the multi-levelled aspect of the earlier score was redefined in such a way that each of the three acts would be dominated by a distinct formal principle (Act I sonata, Act II rondo and Act III variations). In one respect, this complex schema does depart from that of *Wozzeck* inasmuch as musical and dramatic subdivisions are not always co-extensive. However, the introduction of doubled character roles and a centrally placed palindromic film sequence arguably increase the impression of meticulous patterning, creating a density of meaning which, as Jarman remarks (1991, 76), is further intensified by the fact that seemingly every aspect of the music is accorded a leitmotivic function.

Figure 6.1 Berg's *Lulu*, directed by Patrice Chéreau (first production of the three-act version completed by Friedrich Čerha; Paris Opéra, 1979): Yvonne Minton as Countess Geschwitz in Act III scene 2. Photo: Daniel Cande.

The extended array of harmonic resources Berg employed in the work, arrived at by a process of derivation and accumulation which started with the chart of serial permutations and initial sketches he committed to manuscript in July 1927, has become a particular focus for commentators aiming to celebrate the fertility, if not also the cerebral finesse of his compositional technique. In this respect, as George Perle has suggested (1985, 86, 205), although the basic set remained less of a guarantee of structural integrity than it was to prove for either Schoenberg or Webern, Berg's practice, far from being deficient in serial terms, was arguably more progressive in its grasp of the implications of combinatoriality than that of either his teacher or fellow pupil. Even so, while the various series, tropes and basic cells employed in *Lulu* combine to produce a music of extraordinary flexibility, the techniques of rotation, segmentation and extrapolation which the composer applied in order to control these elements can once again be thought to equate to a more or less systematized form of Schoenbergian developing variation.

Rhythm, metre and tempo can all be shown to play a comparably far-reaching role in the delineation of character type and plot correspondence. Of primary importance, however, is the way in which such elements contribute to a general perception of time itself being regulated and even reversed. The composer's habitual eschewal of retrograde and retrograde-inverted forms of the series in favour of larger-scale palindromic musical units consequently finds a visual analogue in the representation of Lulu's imprisonment and escape that becomes the narrative purpose of the opera's core film interlude. Hence the audience is increasingly made aware of multi-media resources coalescing into an overall mode of practice which seems committed to undermining collective belief in the logical association of cause and effect. As all-embracing as Berg's conception may appear on one level, though, and as salacious as the opera's subject matter may still seem on another, the work stays true to its Viennese, if not also Wagnerian theme – in short, the vicissitudes engendered by the life-enhancing and fateful consequences of erotic love. (As Nicholas Baragwanath has shown (1999), the expressive impulses of desire and deferral, along with their structural articulation through the conflicting implications of tonal hierarchy and symmetry, appear to form a direct parallel with themes and techniques established in *Tristan und Isolde* and *Der Ring des Nibelungen*. Thus the final 'Liebestod' sung by Countess Geschwitz at the end of *Lulu* achieves its special pathos through the thwarted belief in *Liebeserlösung*, an effect articulated through precise pitch axes allied to *Tristan* and *Götterdämmerung*.) But if sensuality is once again acknowledged as the essence of human identity, even to the extent that the composer writes himself into the opera in the guise of Alwa, one among many suitor-victims to Lulu, then the contradictory force field of horrific and farcical circumstances that also pervade *Wozzeck* would seem to function still more corrosively as social satire within *Lulu* on account of the recognizably bourgeois setting within which they are placed.

Altogether, Berg's deliberate disruption of emotive identification and stylized extension of conventional generic codes might seem to stamp *Lulu* as a work somewhat ahead of its time. In other words, clearly perceptible aspects of audible and visible stylistic flux appear to redefine the opposing forces of expression and construction as an aesthetic duality caught part way between the polarized dispositions of modernism and the self-referential surface effects of postmodernity. Indeed, pressed further, the same assumption could be felt to reveal the composer as questioning the underlying validity of his cultural existence: thus the profound immediacy of a supposed musical expressionism begins to dissect itself dramatically as a purely contingent mode of creative self-fashioning. Yet, as Jarman has observed (1991, 54–5), interpreters of all kinds do well to examine their ideological motives when aiming to categorize *Lulu*. For the possessive forms of manipulation that furnish the thematic substance of the opera have also seemingly served to blind both critics and directors to the fact that they too might fall prey to an appropriative strategy of representation.

A more historically informed reading would instead place *Lulu* in the context of epic theatre, the composer having gained first-hand acquaintance of the work of Brecht and Weill through his attendance at rehearsals of *Aufstieg und Fall der Stadt Mahagonny* in Vienna during 1932. Rather than conceiving *Lulu* in equivalent terms, however, Jarman argues (1991, 98) that Berg went on to achieve a rather more individual and unsettling form of theatrical amalgam that cuts across the epic/dramatic divide. Hence the characteristic alienation techniques which deflect from the plausible reality of the drama in order to clarify the distinction between observation and involvement are purposefully complicated by the seductive appeal of the composer's sensual investment. To respond fully to the disorienting effect of the opera is actually to appreciate a different kind of understanding – one both complicit with the dynamics of Berg's drama and altogether germane to the history of Second Viennese composition for the stage. Because by seeking to achieve a restorative confrontation with the instinctual drives that underpin social relations, the composer once again reanimates the impulse first given dramatic voice in *Erwartung*. Here, though, expression and construction form a more ambiguous and self-questioning association, still preserving a critical power for art even as they work to subvert the operatic genre from within.

Both *Moses und Aron* and *Lulu* represent definitive turning points in the working circumstances of their composers. That Berg never lived to complete *Lulu*, for example, was partly due to his need to compose a genre piece – the Violin Concerto – to commission. By comparison, Schoenberg, an exile in America from October 1933, maintained a steady production of genre works only to be denied the regular repertoire acceptance he recognized would be essential for economic survival. Market forces alone would almost certainly have condemned both pupil and teacher to be remembered as representatives of an isolated and obsolete Viennese sect. And yet, as Auner has remarked (1999, 15), the cultural significance of the Second Viennese School, at least creatively speaking, remains apparently self-renewing, with Webern and subsequently Berg attaining a perceived primacy across the decades since 1945.

Most recently, it is perhaps the complex examination of female sensuality and sexuality which unfolds in *Lulu* that has exerted the strongest hold on present-day sensibilities (see Lochhead 1997). By contrast, Schoenberg's cultural re-evaluation has been slower to gather momentum. However, this much said, the unison violin melody that accompanies Moses' despairing spoken phrase 'O Wort, du Wort das mir fehlt' ('Oh Word, that Word which fails me') at the end of Act II of *Moses und Aron*, 'the most expansive, most expressive melody Schoenberg ever wrote' (Brinkmann 1997, 211), would also seem to connect very forcefully with contemporary human concerns. In Brinkmann's view, the melody is answered not in the form of music for the stage, but in the Jewish 'Schema Israel' prayer that concludes *A Survivor from Warsaw* (1947).

Because through it, affirming the synonymity of his identity as an artist and a Jew, the composer was at last able to answer openly to the needs of the collective, transcending the bestiality of the Holocaust in a defiant gesture of political eschatology (212). What might seem to promise redemption from the experience of exile and the barbarism of ethnic annihilation nonetheless carries its own extremist shadow side. For in establishing his principles for a Jewish Unity party in 1933, the composer had previously insisted, as Goldstein relates, that it should be 'nationalchauvinist to the highest degree ... militant, aggressive, opposed to any pacifism, any internationalism' (2000, 188). In seeking to comprehend the significance of the relationship between expression and construction in the stage works of the Second Viennese School, therefore, perhaps the only conclusion which can safely be drawn is that no single interpretation should ever be thought definitive. Hence any belief that the territorial predispositions of the archaic world should have become the most prescient message of such fragile cultural forms by the beginning of the twenty-first century ought not to obscure their as yet unforeseen relevance for the civilization of tomorrow.

7 Neo-classical opera

CHRIS WALTON

'Back to Bach'; 'a call to order'; given the nature of the neo-classicists' own slogans, one can perhaps forgive their critics for portraying them as proponents of aesthetic regression. 'Stravinsky and Reaction' is in fact the very heading of the second half of Theodor Adorno's *Philosophy of the New Music*, written in the mid-1940s, in which the author uses all his formidable linguistic and philosophical powers to hold up Schoenberg as a paragon by at the same time stripping Stravinsky's works, in particular those of his neo-classical oeuvre, of any aesthetic justification: 'the *Soldier's Tale* turns psychotic behavioural patterns into musical configurations without any hesitation'; 'in purely musical terms, no difference can be perceived between his infantile and his neo-classical works' (Adorno 1978a, 160, 187). Pierre Boulez has been more succinct in his judgement of Stravinsky's neo-classicism: 'I really hate these works, I cannot stand them' (in Danuser 1997, 330).

The term 'neo-classicism' has been used both to castigate and to praise. It has generally been applied solely to that music written between c. 1920 and 1950 which – as in the case of Stravinsky – is essentially tonal and employs formal, harmonic or melodic elements (or any combination thereof) taken from the music of the eighteenth century, often to ironic effect – though the term 'neo-classicism' is somewhat misleading, in that the source of those forms and gestures was primarily the music of the baroque rather than of Viennese classicism. Taruskin has characterized the movement as possessing an 'aesthetic of abstraction' (1997, 466). However, 'neo-classical' has also been used to categorize just about all Western music composed during the period in question, on account of the antiquating tendencies so common at the time – for even Schoenberg and his followers, long regarded as an opposing pole to Stravinsky, utilized old forms and procedures. Neo-classicism of the Stravinskyan kind has been pilloried by left-wing critics on account of its popularity with the right-wing dictatorships of the 1930s and 1940s. However, other commentators, such as Elliott Carter, found neo-classicism attractive as a means of expressing an anti-German, anti-fascist aesthetic (Danuser 1997, 325). The term thus risks being used, in the words of Luciano Berio, as 'an empty container that can be filled with very different and contradictory elements' (326).

A 'return' to something that either existed or is at least thought to have existed – Richard Taruskin describes it as 'a tendentious journey back to where we had never been' (1993, 286) – suggests that there is something unpalatable in the present that one feels compelled to leave behind. And one does not have to be a Marxist historian to accept that artistic trends around 1920 and the years thereafter were influenced by a reaction against the chaos of four years of war, the ensuing influenza epidemic (whose death toll was even greater than that of the War), and the economic morass that followed both. Carter has written how he remembers his father taking him 'in about 1923 to see the French battlefield and to visit Germany during the million-or-more marks to the dollar period. So a retreat into a more ordered, more restrained style seemed a meaningful reaction' (Danuser 1997, 310).

This desire for a 'return to order' was in fact common to most of the leading composers in the years after the First World War. As Boulez has remarked of the Second Viennese School: '[Schoenberg's] *Erwartung, Die glückliche Hand*, even *Pierrot lunaire* ... are pieces where you are always on the verge of chaos ... you have no codified rules any more, no system of compositional regulations ... [Schoenberg and his followers] needed some kind of "Ordnung"' (322). Nor should it surprise one that, after such excesses of slaughter, the late-romantic and expressionist aesthetic excesses (real and perceived) of the prewar years should have seemed neither financially realizable nor even morally desirable. Neo-classicism certainly embraced a tendency to economy and restraint – say, at its most crass, the difference between the almost exactly contemporaneous *Frau ohne Schatten* by Strauss and Stravinsky's *Soldier's Tale* (first performed in 1919 and 1918 respectively), the former a vast opera on a quasi-mythical topic, given its premiere at the Viennese State Opera and demanding that venue's whole panoply of orchestral, vocal and theatrical forces, the latter a succinct retelling of a folk tale requiring three actors, a dancer and a band of seven players, and designed as a 'touring work' to be performed anywhere and everywhere. By 1916, even Strauss himself saw his *Frau ohne Schatten* as 'the last romantic opera' (Hammelmann and Osers 1961, 259), and pleaded with Hofmannsthal to turn with him to operetta, as 'tragedy in the theatre, after this war, strikes me at present as something rather idiotic and childish' (250).

The history of musical neo-classicism in the twentieth century is intricately involved with that of opera. To be sure, 'antiquating' tendencies have probably existed in music for almost as long as has music itself. The innovations of the Florentine Camerata and of Wagner – namely, the birth of opera and of music drama respectively – were both based upon a supposed 'return' to the practices of Classical Greek theatre. And, if one wanted, one could even place the birth of musical neo-classicism in

Wagner's own work, be it in the diatonic bombast of *Die Meistersinger* (1868) or the allusions to the music of the baroque in *Parsifal* (1882) – see, for example, the interlude in Act I during the walk to the Castle of the Grail, with its sequential harmony and dotted rhythms almost reminiscent of a French overture. A more convincing argument could be made for Strauss's *Rosenkavalier* (1911) or, more especially, *Ariadne auf Naxos* (1912–16) as the starting-point for neo-classicism, for they mark a step backwards (though the word is admittedly loaded) from the expressionism of *Salome* (1905) and *Elektra* (1909), and a conscious attempt to re-establish 'Mozartian' values. *Ariadne* was conceived by Strauss from the very start as a succession of closed musical numbers, with recitatives and arias modelled on Mozart, Bellini and Donizetti, and an orchestra of just fifteen to twenty players (though the forces needed were more than double that in the end). It even features characters taken from the Italian *commedia dell'arte* that were beloved of later, more overtly neo-classical music theatre – as in works by Busoni, Prokofiev and Stravinsky (see Strauss's letter to Hofmannsthal of 22 May 1911: 82). Contemporaneous with *Ariadne* was Pfitzner's *Palestrina* (1917), which takes the quasi-religious, antiquating element of *Parsifal* a few steps further through the incorporation of sections of Palestrina's *Missa Papae Marcelli* into its own musical fabric. However, apart from the fact that Pfitzner was working intentionally in the Wagnerian tradition, this is less a case of latent neo-classicism than of old music being utilized as local colour in a manner not too far removed from Puccini's *chinoiserie* (or, rather, *japonaiserie*) in *Madama Butterfly* (1904). An over-enthusiastic Englishman might even claim a fellow native as the creator of the first neo-classical opera: Ralph Vaughan Williams, in *Hugh the Drover*, completed in early 1914. An attempt to revive the English ballad opera, it uses recitative and, at least in part, a number format. Vaughan Williams's utilization of English folk song (both real and invented) is arguably not far removed from the neo-classicists' re-using of musical material taken from the eighteenth century – the proximity of the two ventures is underlined by the ease with which Vaughan Williams himself appropriated neo-classical gestures in his works of the 1920s such as the *Concerto Accademico* for violin and orchestra or the central section of the famous 'Greensleeves' interlude from his later opera *Sir John in Love* (1929), cast as a kind of invention for two flutes with string accompaniment. However, since Vaughan Williams had left neither tonality nor conventional musical form before *Hugh* and thus could not 'return' to it, and since his use of foreign melodic material is characterized by nostalgia instead of the neo-classicists' critical distance or ironic detachment, to add the prefix 'neo' to his 'classicality' would be stretching the term too far.

Busoni

If there is any single defining moment in neo-classical opera in all its guises, then it is a reaction against German music drama in general, and against Wagner in particular – a trend that had become clear even before the cataclysm of the First World War. Thomas Mann postulated in 1911 a 'new Classicality' that would be 'cooler, more refined, even of a healthier intellectuality' than Wagner (Erika Mann 1983, 28), though Ferruccio Busoni was the first composer to codify what this new aesthetic might entail, to give it a name and put it into practice. In the second edition of his *Sketch of a New Aesthetic of Music*, published in 1916, he wrote that 'I find qualified justification in the methods of old opera by which the atmosphere generated by the dramatic movement of a scene is concentrated in a single, closed piece (the aria)' (Busoni 1983, 58). This represented a definite break with the Wagnerian legacy, for Wagner himself over half a century earlier had declared the division of operatic music into recitative and aria to be *passé*. This declaration many, if not most, of his successors had long accepted as law. In 1913, Busoni wrote the libretto for his opera *Arlecchino* ('Harlequin', a figure taken from the *commedia dell'arte*). Its music was completed in 1916, and the work was first performed, in Zurich, on 11 May 1917. This opera is modelled on the number opera of the eighteenth century and includes ironic references to the musical styles and operatic situations of the late eighteenth and early nineteenth centuries, even featuring a parodistic duel. A further possible influence on Busoni was Ernst von Dohnányi's mime play *Der Schleier der Pierrette* (*The Veil of Pierrette*) after the play by Arthur Schnitzler, composed in 1908–9 and first performed in Dresden in 1910. Its characters include Pierrot, Pierrette and Arlechino (*sic*). In Busoni, Arlecchino is a non-singing role, though here, all the characters speak their parts. But while Dohnányi's score includes many dance numbers (mostly waltzes), the music is essentially late romantic, and the plot – a love triangle in which all three die of poison – is a far cry from either the *commedia dell'arte* or the ironic detachment of Busoni's *Arlecchino*. (Another, roughly contemporaneous, 'pantomime' using a character from the *commedia dell'arte* was Sibelius's *Scaramouche* to a text by Poul Knudsen and Mikael Trepka Bloch; again, its approach is far removed from Busoni's, and it was in any case not performed until 1922.)

The development of Busoni's aesthetic can be traced in his writings and correspondence of these years (see Busoni 1999). In 1919 he gave his ideas a collective name: 'Junge Klassizität' ('Young Classicality'). The phrase was first used in an unpublished article written in Zurich, 'Musikalischer Rückblick und Ausblick'; Busoni's famous open letter to

Figure 7.1 Busoni's *Arlecchino*: cover design to vocal score, 1917. (Via Chris Walton)

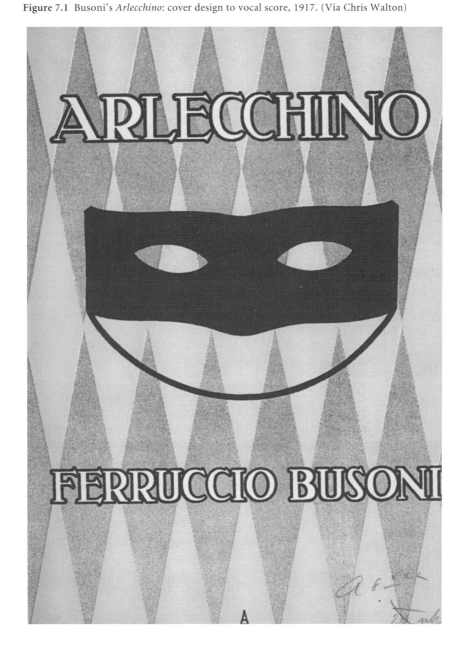

Paul Bekker, published in the *Frankfurter Zeitung* of 15/16 January 1920, contains his first published elucidation of the term (see also Messing 1988, 69–70). Busoni preferred it to 'new Classicality', as this smacked to him of merely imitating the past (he was also most probably aware of Mann's article of eight years earlier). Nevertheless, the term 'new Classicality' became increasingly associated with him. Busoni's ideas for opera were finally published in 1921 in an article entitled 'Über die

Möglichkeiten der Oper' ('On the possibilities of opera': Busoni 1983, 121–35). There, he held up the example of Mozart's *Magic Flute* as the operatic ideal, castigated the erotic and with it all excess of expression, called for love duets and everything that is purely illustrative to be abandoned, stressed the 'abstract' nature of music, and maintained that opera must comprise a series of short, closed numbers. Busoni may have codified what were to become the basic tenets of neo-classical opera, and first put them into practice in *Arlecchino*, but his oeuvre otherwise does display discrepancies between intention and effect. His friend, the Swiss composer Othmar Schoeck, once remarked that 'Busoni keeps coming with his Mozart scores, but when he writes something that works, it's always out of *Meistersinger*' (Walton 1994, 154) – a comment grounded in professional jealousy, perhaps, but uncomfortably close to the truth: there are passages in *Doktor Faust* in particular that suggest that Busoni aimed to create a 'new' German people's opera after the manner of *Die Meistersinger*.

Stravinsky in the 1920s

Stravinsky's first truly neo-classical stage work was *Pulcinella* (first performed in Paris in 1920), a ballet with songs in which he 're-composed' music by Pergolesi and his contemporaries, and in which the plot depicts the escapades of the title-hero, a figure taken – like Busoni's Harlequin – from the *commedia dell'arte*. This genre from the seventeenth and eighteenth centuries provided inspiration for numerous writers and composers in the early twentieth century, not just the 'Young' and 'Neo-' Classicists, and inspired several to experiment with mixtures of music and speech: besides the examples by Busoni, Dohnányi and Sibelius mentioned above, there is the obvious one of Schoenberg's *Pierrot lunaire*. Busoni's *Turandot*, first performed in a double bill with *Arlecchino* in Zurich in 1917, is based on the same fable by Carlo Gozzi (1720–1806) as is Puccini's opera of that name. However, unlike Puccini, Busoni retains Gozzi's *commedia dell'arte* figures Truffaldino and Pantalone, despite the Chinese setting. Gozzi was also the source for the plot of Prokofiev's *The Love for Three Oranges*, composed in 1919 and first performed in Chicago on 30 December 1921, and arguably the first full-scale opera to conform in large part to the neo-classical aesthetic. The plot tells of a hypochondriac prince in an imaginary kingdom who, through the machinations of various sorcerers, falls in love with three oranges, and in the end marries a princess who emerges from one of them (and with her, it is implied, lives happily ever after). The libretto, by Prokofiev himself, is a mixture of fairy tale, satire and slapstick; a prologue features an argument between 'Tragedians' and 'Ridiculous Ones', and the latter group reappears throughout the opera – even interfering in it to ensure the happy ending – thus providing an element of ironic detachment. Stylistically, the opera owes much to the neo-classical vein of the composer's *Classical Symphony* of 1916–17.

Stravinsky's first neo-classical opera – in which he follows Busoni's ideas implicitly, if not by intention – was *Mavra*, composed in 1921–2 and first performed in Paris on 3 June 1922. It is an *opera buffa* in one act of just 25 minutes, and is based on a story by Pushkin in which a girl disguises her lover as a (female) cook in order to inveigle him into her mother's house. A neighbour makes up the complement of four characters, and the whole is accompanied by a small orchestra dominated by wind instruments. The formal organization is that of a number opera with dialogue, while the music is decidedly tonal, largely periodic in structure, intentionally non-Wagnerian and occasionally even jazzy, with an emphasis on melody and accompaniment. Stravinsky's next opera (described by him as an 'opera-oratorio') is generally regarded as one of the seminal works of musical neo-classicism: *Oedipus Rex*, composed between January 1926 and May 1927. It is a setting of a Latin translation of Jean Cocteau's French version of the play by Sophocles, and is cast in two acts of just under half an hour each. Thebes is suffering from a plague, but the oracle says it can be saved if the murderer of its former king, Laius, can be found and punished. The current king, Oedipus, promises to do the deed and deliver his people, but when he discovers that he, unwittingly, is the murderer, that Laius was his father, and that the widowed queen he married is in fact his own mother, he gouges out his eyes and leaves the city.

According to Stravinsky himself, he had already made the decision to write an opera in a 'dead' language before he settled on the actual plot. Only at this point did he turn to his old friend Cocteau to provide the text; Cocteau's French was then translated into Latin by Abbé Jean Daniélou. The instrumental forces required by the work are greater than those of *Mavra*, but by no means excessive – triple woodwind, four each of trumpets and horns, three trombones, one tuba, percussion, harp, piano and strings. There are six solo roles – Oedipus (tenor), his wife Jocasta (mezzo-soprano), Créon (bass-baritone), Tirésias (bass), the Shepherd (tenor) and the Messenger (bass-baritone); a male chorus of only modest size is also required. The manner of staging was determined by Stravinsky himself: masks were to be worn, and there was to be next to no movement of the singers except of their arms, in order for them to appear as living statues. A narrator in evening dress relates the bare bones of the plot in the vernacular. Just as Stravinsky wanted a language that was 'turned to stone' for his text, so should the audience be alienated from the action itself. (While it is tempting to stress the undeniable parallels between the roughly contemporaneous alienating techniques in the dramatic work of Stravinsky and the playwright Bertolt Brecht, those of the former are a purely aesthetic device, while those of the latter were designed primarily as a means of raising the political consciousness of the audience.) The 'dead' language, combined with the use of masks and the altogether static nature of its production, also imparts to *Oedipus Rex* a certain ritual character that aligns it with other 'ritualistic' works in Stravinsky's oeuvre, such as *The Rite of Spring* (1913) and *Les Noces* (1923).

The music of *Oedipus* is decidedly tonal, its metres regular, its forms those of number opera, and there are no leitmotives or reminiscence motives, though a carefully devised key scheme helps to impart musical unity. The work's musical gestures (as Stravinsky once admitted) owe as much to Verdi and Italian opera of the nineteenth century as to the eighteenth century: Jocasta's aria 'Nonn'erubescite' is particularly and elaborately Italianate, and was a favourite of the young Benjamin Britten's. While an opera lasting less than an hour requiring modest forces (by comparison with pre-First World War conditions) might seem a typical example of the scaling-down of resources characteristic of the neo-classical period, one can however read *Oedipus* as having internalized those very late-romantic excesses that Stravinsky supposedly despised, their having been, as it were, subsumed into the very genesis of the work. For what could be more excessive than to take a Greek play, commission a French version of it and have this, in turn, translated into Latin, only to be explained anyway, in French, by a narrator? The whole paraphernalia of operatic production – costumes, sets, lighting – are channelled into a work where no one really does anything, nor does anything really happen, on stage. The details of the work's complex genesis were no secret, but became just as much a part of its mystique as (say) Berg's own analysis of his opera *Wozzeck* became an integral aspect of that work's reception history. *Oedipus Rex* was first performed as an oratorio by Diaghilev's Ballets Russes on 30 May 1927 in Paris, and as an opera on 23 February 1928 in Vienna. It was not an immediate success, but by the end of the decade it had been performed across Europe, and its influence was incalculable.

Stravinsky's neo-classical style, which drew not just on the music of the eighteenth and nineteenth centuries but also on jazz, had already left its mark on many of his contemporaries before *Oedipus*, and was to leave few untouched. In the works of the leading French composers of the

1920s, the influence of Stravinsky, of native *opéra bouffe* and of American popular music merged, often imperceptibly. There, as in Italy, the vestiges of the old number opera had not died, and now found new confirmation in the neo-classical aesthetic. Two years before the first performance of *Oedipus*, Ravel's *L'Enfant et les sortilèges* (1925) was given its world premiere in Monte Carlo; in this opera, the creatures and objects maltreated by a petulant child come to life to confront him. Although not neo-classical in intent, the influence of Stravinsky's music after 1918 is evident here, and Ravel follows Stravinsky's lead by including references to jazz (for a Wedgwood teapot that speaks English). The composers who made up 'Les Six' – Arthur Honegger, Francis Poulenc, Georges Auric, Germaine Tailleferre, Darius Milhaud and Louis Durey – were all influenced to a greater or lesser extent by the neo-classical Stravinsky, though Stravinskyan wit was transformed on occasion into Gallic absurdity. This was the case in Honegger's comic opera *Les Aventures du Roi Pausole*, first performed with much success at the Bouffes-Parisiens in 1930. Not only does this number oper(ett)a flirt brazenly with jazz, but its debt to Stravinsky is clear right from its opening bars, which contain an obvious, though possibly unintentional, reference to *Pulcinella*; as it happens, Honegger had as recently as 1925 spoken pejoratively about that same work (see Honegger 1925). *Pausole* found a worthy successor almost 20 years later in Poulenc's *Les Mamelles de Tirésias* (Paris, 1947), based on a surrealist comedy by Guillaume Apollinaire in which a man and his wife swap roles and sexes, and he bears thousands of children.

Stravinsky's modernist credentials enabled him to impart aesthetic validity to matters regarded by many as contrary to the modern – not just a return to tonality, but also to a number format in opera and to a heterogeneity of musical material that might now include everything down to the latest popular fashions, be these American jazz or local popular music. The boundaries between neo-classicism and existing traditions are in the case of some composers blurred; thus, Jaromir Weinberger's *Schwanda the Bagpiper* (Prague, 1927) is generally regarded as a Czech folk opera, though in its musical means it is not far from contemporaneous neo-classicism. Weinberger had studied with Max Reger, and besides its polkas and furiants, *Schwanda* displays its composer's delight and skill in writing fugues. The proximity of Vaughan Williams's neo-classicism of the 1920s to his folk-song inspired style has already been noted. The example of Stravinsky also had a liberating effect on the younger generation of American and English composers, ranging from Virgil Thomson with his starkly diatonic *Four Saints in Three Acts* (New York, 1934) to Britten, whose *Peter Grimes* (London, 1945) owes as much to Stravinsky as to Berg or Verdi. Even the very opening of the opera, with its dotted rhythms and bustling scale-patterns, is unmistakably neo-classical in origin.

Schoenberg and Berg

The neo-classical urge was by no means confined to Stravinsky and his fellow Parisians in the 1920s. It is, depending upon one's viewpoint, either a case of synchronicity or banal coincidence that in the same month that the epithet 'neo-classical' was publicly applied to Stravinsky's music for the first time, by Boris Schloezer in *La Revue contemporaine* on 1 February 1923, Schoenberg completed his Suite, Op. 25, and his *Klavierstücke*, Op. 23, in which works he first employed his newly invented 'technique of composing with twelve tones'. It was around the same time that he announced his discovery to his students (see Max Deutsch in Szmolyan 1971, 118). Given the fact that musical journalism had already, from 1920 onwards, defined Schoenberg and Stravinsky as musically and aesthetically opposing poles (the ideas behind Adorno's much later polemic had a long pedigree), it is not a little ironic that in his first works in the twelve-tone system, Schoenberg too utilized musical forms taken from the eighteenth century. Boulez has even maintained that 'Stravinsky's and Schoenberg's paths to neo-classicism differ basically only in one being diatonic and the other chromatic' (1977, 33–4). While this serves to blur considerable stylistic and aesthetic differences between the two men and their respective followers – for example, the elements of wit, of playfulness, distortion, even parody manifest in Stravinsky that are generally considered defining characteristics of neo-classicism are largely missing from Schoenberg – there are certain undoubted parallels. The very fact that Schoenberg found it necessary to pillory the 'neo-classicists' and 'pseudo-tonalists' in general, and Stravinsky in particular, in his own brief cantata *Der neue Klassizismus* (*The New Classicism*), Op. 28 no. 3 (1925), merely serves to underline the real similarities between the aesthetics of the two men. (Schoenberg's text mocks 'der kleine Modernsky' ('the little Modernsky'); Stravinsky referred to this 'very nasty verse about me (though I almost forgive him, for setting it to such a remarkable mirror canon)' in Stravinsky and Craft 1962a, 69.) For, as Adorno once commented of Schreker's influence on *Wozzeck*, 'one usually parodies that to which one is naturally drawn, even if one's feelings towards it are ambivalent' (1968, 26).

Schoenberg's one-act *Von Heute auf Morgen*, to a text by his wife, was the first twelve-tone opera, though it too uses set pieces and recitatives. First performed in Frankfurt in 1930, it was an attempt to ride the bandwagon of the *Zeitoper*: opera with a topical, often domestic theme. It depicts a simple marital squabble, not unlike that in Strauss's *Intermezzo* (1924) – the only opera by Strauss, apart from *Salome* and *Elektra*, that Schoenberg admitted to liking (Kennedy 1999, 33). But Schoenberg's humour (and that of his wife) is heavy-handed in a peculiarly Teutonic manner, while the dissonance level and complexity of the music stand in stark contrast to the triviality of the plot. The opera has the feel of unintentional parody (of 'something to which [Schoenberg] was naturally drawn') – as if what was supposed to be a fairy princess has turned out an ugly sister instead. An exactly contemporaneous, but more successful, operatic telling of a domestic squabble using neo-classical formal means is the one-act, 40-minute *Vom Fischer un syner Fru* (*Of the Fisherman and his Wife*; Dresden, 1930) by Othmar Schoeck. In his previous opera, *Penthesilea* (1923–5), Schoeck had ventured into expressionism and atonality, but *Vom Fischer*, based on the famous Grimm fairy tale, confirmed his return to tonality – though a tonality, as Derrick Puffett has written, 'after the Fall' (in Baumann 1982, 61). Here, the trajectory of the drama is perfectly matched by the musical form, that of a set of orchestral variations with concluding fugue after the manner of Brahms and of Schoeck's teacher, Reger.

Schoenberg's next, and final, opera was *Moses und Aron* (1930–32), which in its use of old forms such as canons and fugues is no less neo-classical than his other works of this period. Indeed, Boulez has described it, mockingly, as 'Schönberg as "Papa Bach" ', but has added that 'today *Moses und Aron* reminds me, in the best sense, of the Passions by Bach' (Danuser 1997, 331). The most influential example of eighteenth-century forms being used in an opera was undoubtedly *Wozzeck* by Schoenberg's former pupil, Alban Berg. It was composed between 1914 and 1922 and first performed under Erich Kleiber in Berlin in 1925. Berg's underpinning of the dramatic structure with instrumental forms from the baroque and classical periods (including a sonata movement, inventions, a pavane, a gigue, a gavotte with two doubles, etc.), and especially the highly stylized manner in which he does so, gives the work an undeniably neo-classical aspect. This is despite its dramatic immediacy, derived from Schoenbergian expressionism, and the fact that Berg's exploration of the sensual and erotic ran directly counter to Busoni's ideas for 'young Classical' opera: 'sensual or "sexual" music … has no place here', Busoni had written in 1921 (1983, 126). Berg's second opera, *Lulu*, also employs a host of old forms, from arietta and cavatina to rondo, embedded into an overall formal scheme even more constructivist in design than that of *Wozzeck*.

Hindemith, Orff and Weill

Stravinsky himself identified a further neo-classical 'school' besides his own and that of the Schoenbergians, namely that of Paul Hindemith. In his early twenties, Hindemith made a name for himself with three one-act operas in expressionist vein – *Mörder, Hoffnung der Frauen* (Stuttgart, 1921) to a text by Oskar Kokoschka, *Das Nusch-Nuschi* (Stuttgart, 1921), a setting of a marionette play by Franz Blei, and *Sancta Susanna* (Frankfurt am Main, 1922), to a libretto of nuns and sex by August Stramm. Hindemith's next opera, *Cardillac*, Op. 39, to a libretto in three acts by Ferdinand Lion after E. T. A. Hoffman's *Das Fräulein von Scuderi*, adopted the neo-classical 'aesthetic of abstraction' to remarkable dramatic effect. The work caused a sensation at its first performance in Dresden on 10 November 1927, and within months had been taken up by a score of other opera houses. The plot tells of a master goldsmith named Cardillac who cannot bear to be parted from his creations, and so kills those who acquire them in order to steal them back. The opera ends with his murder by a mob. In its consideration of the artist's place in society, *Cardillac* is in fact closely related to Pfitzner's *Palestrina*, though its aesthetic could hardly be further removed from that work. The immediacy of the drama contrasts starkly with its musical treatment; thus, to give one example, the love scene between the Young Cavalier and the Opera Singer in the first act is accompanied by a decidedly unpassionate, detached, mock-Bachian duet for two flutes. A moment of silence ensues, during which Cardillac bursts in, murders the Cavalier, and exits swiftly. Only then does the orchestra erupt. This opera is comprised of individual numbers; as in Berg's use of techniques taken from instrumental music in *Wozzeck*, Hindemith casts a large part of his final act as a passacaglia with 22 variations.

Hindemith's *Neues vom Tage* (1928–9; libretto by Marcellus Schiffer) was an essay in the *Zeitoper* genre then at the height of its popularity. This work, first performed in Berlin on 8 June 1929, had unforeseen consequences, for Adolf Hitler (who apparently never actually saw it) took exception to an aria in it that was sung in a bath. As a result, Hindemith's music was later banned in the Third Reich, and his opera *Mathis der Maler* (composed in 1934–5 to a libretto by Hindemith himself) had to be given its first performance outside Germany. The opera is set in Germany at the time of the Reformation and the ensuing religious wars. Its title figure is Matthias Grünewald, the painter of the famous Isenheim Altar. It, too, deals with the role of the artist in society, though here specifically with the ways in which Church and State impinge upon the artist and his work. The premiere of a symphony comprising music from this opera was planned by the Berlin Philharmonic under Wilhelm Furtwängler in 1934, and it was this that brought about that conductor's first open argument with the Nazi authorities, leading to his forced removal from his posts. This is not a little ironic, for *Mathis* represents yet another attempt to compose a new, German 'peoples' opera', and it is today common knowledge that Hindemith, although no supporter of Hitler, was in fact keen to find a *modus vivendi* with the Nazi regime in order to enable him to remain in the country. Grünewald was a painter beloved of Nazi art historians, and certain commentators see Mathis's acquiescence in the opera to the will of Cardinal Albrecht as symbolic of Hindemith's willingness to kowtow to the fascist state (Kater 1997). Others see Mathis's plight as representing the 'inner emigration' of non-Nazi composers who remained in Germany, while yet others see elements of anti-Nazi protest in the work (for example, Jackson 2004). What cannot be denied, however, is that the composer here aims at pleasing a wide audience, for long stretches of the opera represent the neo-classical Hindemith at his most accessible. A wide variety of musical sources is employed, from Catholic hymns and Protestant chorales to mock-modal Gregorian chant, while the overture (named the 'Engelkonzert' or 'Angels' Concert') – which opens demonstratively on a long G-major chord – even includes a chorale prelude on a German folk tune, with neo-baroque polyphonic figurations throughout. However, the Nazi authorities remained unbending, Hindemith exiled himself from his native land, and *Mathis* itself could not be performed on German soil. Like Berg's *Lulu* a year before it (and for similar reasons), it was given its world premiere in Zurich, in 1938. A final irony is the fact that the conductor of both premieres, the Swiss Robert Denzler, was found after the Second World War to have been a member of the German Nazi Party and was hounded out of his post at the Zurich City Theatre.

Hindemith's neo-classicism, which eschewed both Stravinskyan irony and the extremes of Schoenbergian dissonance, and managed to retain a populist aura, proved particularly influential in the 1930s and 1940s. This was especially the case in the German-speaking world, where the influence of Hindemith's style permeated much contemporary music. Whole schools of composers now indulged in pseudo-modal, motoric concerti grossi and organ toccatas and fugues in what became a kind of musical *lingua franca* (see, for example, the oeuvres of Hugo Distler, Ernst Pepping, Willy Burkhard, Adolf Brunner, Hans Schaeuble and many others). In German, Swiss and Austrian opera of this time, the neo-classical influence is obvious amongst the most diverse figures, from Alexander von Zemlinsky's *Der Kreidekreis* (Zurich, 1933), Werner Egk's *Die Zaubergeige* (Frankfurt am Main, 1935), Karl Amadeus Hartmann's *Des Simplicius Simplicissimus Jugend* (composed in 1934; first performed in Cologne, 1948), Heinrich Sutermeister's *Die schwarze Spinne* (first performed on Berne Radio in 1936) to Gottfried von Einem's *Dantons Tod* (Salzburg, 1947). It is just as evident in twelve-tone operas

Figure 7.2 Hindemith's *Mathis der Maler* (Zurich, 1938): costume design for Ursula by Jürg Stockar. (Via Chris Walton)

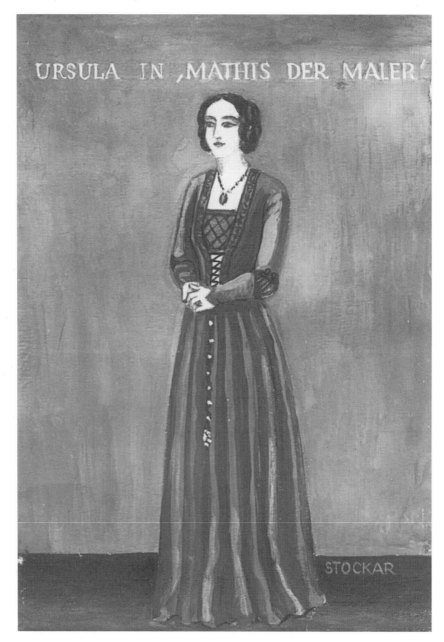

from the wider Schoenberg circle, such as *Das Opfer* by Winfried Zillig (Hamburg, 1937) – a work depicting the final days of Scott's Antarctic expedition, in which, however, the note of high tragedy is somewhat diminished by a singing and dancing chorus of malevolent penguins.

The combination of a Stravinskyan motoric drive, quasi-modal tonality and a talent for 'folksy' melodies provided a winning formula for Carl Orff. His earliest essay for the operatic stage had been a performing version of Monteverdi's *Orfeo* (Mannheim, 1925), which was, as it happens, almost exactly contemporaneous with Gian Francesco Malipiero's edition of the same work (published in London in 1923) – a reminder that the neo-classical movement coincided with, and fed off, the contemporary scholarly interest in pre-classical music, though in the case of Malipiero, that interest was not least a result of a flight from the present (Stenzl 1990, 110–11). The pomp and harmonic stasis of the prelude to *Orfeo* find echoes in Orff's scenic cantata *Carmina burana* (Frankfurt am Main, 1937), which the composer himself preferred in its stage version. Amongst the general public, this is probably the most popular piece of music written in the twentieth century, but it is also one of the most abhorred amongst the *cognoscenti* on account of its repetitive, primitivist (some have said: latently fascist) style. Nevertheless, Orff's operas, such as *Der Mond* (Munich, 1939), while not eschewing a saccharine-sweet sentimentality (that opera ends with a cooing child accompanied by the sounds of a Bavarian zither) demonstrate his considerable dramatic and melodic gifts and ability to speak directly to his (German) audience – something to which Schoenberg and Hindemith had vainly aspired. The stylistic plurality of *Der Mond* is not least a debt to the neo-classical Stravinsky: the work even has a narrator, like *Oedipus*, though his is here a singing part. In his later operas such as *Antigonae* (Salzburg, 1949) and *Oedipus der Tyrann* (Stuttgart, 1959), Orff carried on the peculiarly Germanic twentieth-century tradition of writing operas on Greek Classical themes, a tradition that had begun with Richard Strauss, but which also took new impetus from the example of the neo-classical Stravinsky.

Neo-classicism was taken into the realm of popular music theatre by Kurt Weill, a former student of Busoni's. For their *Dreigroschenoper* (Berlin, 1928), he and his librettist Brecht even took a specific eighteenth-century work as a model (John Gay's *Beggar's Opera*, which, incidentally, was also treated to a new version by Britten in 1948). Both the number format and the ironic use of popular music styles of the day place Weill's work in close proximity to Stravinsky's neo-classicism – a fact of which Stravinsky was himself aware (Craft 1982, 224).

The Rake's Progress

For what is generally accepted as the highpoint of neo-classicism in opera, we must turn once more to Stravinsky himself, who emigrated to the United States in 1939 and settled in California. The idea of composing an opera in English seems to have come to him soon afterwards. In 1947, he visited an exhibition in Chicago at which William Hogarth's series of paintings 'The Rake's Progress' was displayed. Stravinsky was struck by the operatic possibilities of the narrative they tell. At the suggestion of Aldous Huxley, W. H. Auden was engaged as librettist – soon to be joined by Auden's lover, Chester Kallman. Auden and Kallman brought elements of the Faust legend into the tale and constructed it around three wishes of the work's anti-hero – for money, happiness and the power to bring salvation to mankind – thereby imparting to this work, too, a certain ritual character.

Tom Rakewell comes into money, and forsakes his lover in the country, Anne Trulove, for the fleshly delights of London. He is accompanied all the while by his servant Nick Shadow who, as his name suggests, is the devil in disguise. Tom loses his fortune in a madcap scheme to turn stones into bread; Shadow claims his dues, and plays cards with Tom for the latter's soul. But Tom's faith in Love returns at the final moment, he gambles on the Queen of Hearts, and wins back his soul. As the vanquished Shadow descends into hell, his final act is to render Tom insane. The closing scene takes place in Bedlam, where Anne visits Tom one last time; he then dies, thinking himself Adonis to her Venus. The work ends with an epilogue in which the main characters offer an ironic commentary on the plot, after the example of Mozart's *Don Giovanni*.

This epilogue is but a final nod to Mozart in a work that takes his music as its prime inspiration. The music, which is decidedly tonal, is full of references to him, in particular to *Così fan tutte* (ostensibly just about the only music Stravinsky would listen to while writing his opera). After the world premiere in Venice on 11 September 1951, Robert Craft, Auden and the composer's wife even played 'a tune-detection game of citing resemblances to other operas' (Craft 1972, 29). The libretto, replete with references to English literary styles of the eighteenth century, has clear-cut numbers: arias, ensembles and choruses (generally written in rhyme), and recitatives (in prose). Stravinsky kept these divisions, following eighteenth-century musical conventions by setting most recitatives to just harpsichord accompaniment, even employing eighteenth-century cadential formulae to ironic effect. The orchestra is small, comprising double woodwind, timpani, strings and two each of trumpets and horns. *The Rake's Progress* has been criticized for Stravinsky's indisputably unidiomatic setting of the English language, though in fact this merely heightens the alienating effect of the linguistic and musical allusions to the eighteenth century, and in performance seems entirely appropriate. The *Rake*, not least because of its stylistic approachability, has become one of the most frequently performed operas from the postwar period. However, that same approachability has provoked the ire of composers and musicologists alike, in a manner exceeded perhaps only by the vitriol reserved for Orff. Boulez has written of the *Rake* that 'I find this kind of "pénible" imitation, also "trituration" of Mozart unbearable, simply unbearable. It is basically wrong, simply that. It is wrong because there is a composer who does not know what to do any more' (Danuser 1997, 331).

The *Rake* marks not just a culmination of Stravinsky's neo-classicism, but his farewell to it. While the Cantata and the Septet that he wrote immediately afterwards (in 1952–3) still retain obvious elements of neo-classicism in their melodic and harmonic gestures, these works already display a tendency to a serial treatment of his material. Stravinsky's first work based on a series, albeit only of five notes, was composed in 1954 (*In Memoriam Dylan Thomas*), his first twelve-note music just one year later (in the *Canticum sacrum*). The *Rake* also marks a caesura in the fortunes of the neo-classical movement as a whole. The various forms of neo-classicism had been the only 'modern' music favoured or allowed by the European fascist dictatorships, whereas the music of the Second Viennese School had been ignored or banned – in Italy, for example, the two leading exponents of musical neo-classicism, Malipiero and Alfredo Casella, had allied themselves closely with Mussolini's regime: Malipiero had even dedicated his opera *Giulio Cesare*, first performed in Genoa in 1936, to Italy's latter-day 'Caesar' (see Stenzl 1990, chapters 6 and 7). After the collapse of German and Italian fascism at the close of the Second World War, it was perhaps inevitable that neo-classicism should in certain circles seem tainted and 'regressive' (see the quotations from Adorno at the head of this chapter). The European avant-garde found its new heroes in the recently deceased Anton von Webern, whose Nazi sympathies were conveniently forgotten, and in the Darmstadt proponents of increasingly strict forms of serialism.

Nevertheless, the influence of neo-classicism – in particular, of Stravinsky – remained. It is well-nigh impossible to find an opera by any composer from the 1920s to the 1960s that does not bear some echo of the neo-classical aesthetic, down to Michael Tippett's *The Midsummer Marriage* (London, 1955) and Hans Werner Henze's *The Bassarids* (Salzburg, 1966). Even Carlo Gozzi, the source of inspiration for several of the early neo-classicists, continued to fascinate into the postwar years. He provided the substance of Heinz Kramer's libretto *König Hirsch* for Henze (composed from 1952 to 1955, and revised in 1962). Indeed, while it has been seen by many as an aberration, an artistic cul-de-sac diverting from the modernist path, the neo-classical movement can from today's perspective be interpreted, conversely, as linking up with postmodernism as part of a largely unbroken aesthetic continuum from around 1920 to the present day in which it is the serialist experiment that can appear the cul-de-sac. However, the dodecaphonic/serial and the neo-classical – the progressive and the 'traditional', if one will – are perhaps best understood as existing in a dialectical relationship in which the one acquires its meaning not least through the other, with the resultant creative tension informing much of the finest work of the adherents of both parties (even Adorno in his later years diluted his vitriol towards Stravinsky's neo-classicism; see 1978b, 382–409). The last word should perhaps be left to Henze, who has felt that tension keenly in his own work: 'enslaved by one, enthralled by the other, I have tried ever since to sustain a double life, a contradiction, a dualism within myself, and to draw the aesthetic consequences' (1996, 7).

PART THREE

Topographies

8 France and the Mediterranean

NIGEL SIMEONE

With Debussy's *Pelléas et Mélisande* and Dukas's *Ariane et Barbe-bleue*, French opera moved decisively beyond broadly imitative 'wagnérisme' to a more individual expressive language, and a far stronger sense of synthesizing Wagner's achievements rather than producing rather pale copies. But despite the innovations of Debussy and Dukas, the shadow of Wagner was to hang over a good deal of French opera for the first few decades of the twentieth century.

Gabriel Fauré – like Dukas – was among the many French pilgrims to Bayreuth in his youth, but his only completed opera came towards the end of his career. Already a successful composer of incidental music for plays – notably for Edmond Haraucourt's Shakespeare adaptation *Shylock* (1889) and Maeterlinck's *Pelléas et Mélisande* (1898) – Fauré began work in about 1907 on *Pénélope*, a 'drame lyrique' in three acts to a libretto by René Fauchois. The opera was complete in piano-vocal score by 1912 (when it was published by Heugel; a revised edition appeared in 1913). The orchestration, mostly by Fauré but partly by Fernand Pécoud, was completed early the next year in time for the premieres at Monte Carlo on 4 March 1913 and at the brand-new Théâtre des Champs-Elysées in Paris on 10 May 1913. *Pénélope* was a work which took Fauré considerably longer than any other and its attraction for him seems to have been as an affirmation of conjugal love (something Fauré himself only experienced intermittently); his son Philippe Fauré-Fremiet described it as 'a new *Bonne Chanson* on a mythic scale, sung by characters who are larger than life' (Fauré-Fremiet 1945, 17). This is a perceptive view of a work which, though organized on ostensibly Wagnerian principles, lacks something in dramatic coherence and, crucially, pace. But there is much to enjoy in Fauré's score, especially the many moments of intense lyricism; and while the opera avoids conventional arias, the music often blossoms into song-like writing which shows Fauré in his natural habitat.

The opening season of the Théâtre des Champs-Elysées in April, May and June 1913 – billed by Gabriel Astruc as the 'Grande Saison de Paris' – provides as good a place as any to see the cross-currents which were coursing through Parisian cultural life immediately before the outbreak of the First World War. Though this season has long acquired legendary status on account of the new ballets presented by Diaghilev's Ballets

Russes (Debussy's *Jeux* and Stravinsky's *Rite of Spring* within a fortnight of each other), opera also had a major part to play, not least with the first Paris performance of *Pénélope*. After an inaugural concert on 2 April (in which Saint-Saëns, Fauré, d'Indy, Debussy and Dukas all conducted their own works), the theatre began its life on 3 April with Berlioz's *Benvenuto Cellini*, conducted by Désiré-Emile Inghelbrecht; it was a long evening, since the opera was followed by a 'spectacle de danse' starring Anna Pavlova. *Benvenuto Cellini* was more of a novelty than might be imagined, as this was the first time it had been revived in Paris since its disastrous premiere at the Opéra in 1838. Also on the bill were two of Musorgsky's masterpieces, *Boris Godunov* and *Khovanschina*.

The influences of Russian music – especially Musorgsky – and of composers from Spain (several of them resident in Paris) were to have an important impact on French opera, not least as a counterpoise to Wagner; and in France, as elsewhere, composers were starting to experiment with the genre: in particular there was a move towards one-act operas. These were nothing new in themselves, but had been something of a Russian speciality in the later nineteenth century.

L'Heure espagnole

Ravel completed the piano-vocal score of his one-act opera *L'Heure espagnole* in October 1907, and it was published by Durand the following year. In 1909 Ravel finished the orchestration, but it was not until two years later that the work finally reached the stage, at the Opéra-Comique on 19 May 1911, partly because of some rather improbable scruples by the house's director, Albert Carré, over the delightfully saucy text. During 1910 extracts were given in concert and at least one unidentified critic asked the question which had been bothering Ravel for years: 'When will *L'heure espagnole* be performed at the Opéra-Comique?' (Orenstein 1975, 55). Two days before the long-delayed premiere, Ravel wrote a letter to *Le Figaro* explaining his aims in the opera:

> What have I attempted to do in writing *L'heure espagnole*? It is rather
> ambitious: to regenerate the Italian opera buffa – the principle only. This
> work is not conceived in traditional form. Like its ancestor, its only direct
> ancestor, Musorgsky's *Marriage*, which is a faithful interpretation of
> Gogol's play, *L'heure espagnole* is a *musical comedy*. Apart from a few cuts,
> I have not altered anything in Franc-Nohain's text. Only the concluding
> quintet, by its general layout, its vocalises and vocal effects, might recall the
> usual repertory ensembles. Except for this quintet, one finds mostly
> ordinary declamation rather than singing. The French language, like any

other, has its own accents and musical inflections, and I do not see why one should not take advantage of these qualities in order to arrive at correct prosody. The spirit of the work is frankly humoristic . . . I was thinking of a humorous musical work for some time, and the modern orchestra seemed perfectly adapted to underline and exaggerate comic effects. (55–6)

The 'ancestry' of Musorgsky's *The Marriage* is an intriguing reference, since Ravel could not apparently have known this work until its first publication in 1908: even Michel-Dimitri Calvocoressi – who introduced Ravel to much Russian music, was a fellow member of 'Les Apaches' and also a great authority on Musorgsky – had not come across it until then. The critical reaction to *L'Heure espagnole* was decidedly mixed: Gaston Carraud called the libretto a 'mildly pornographic vaudeville', while Emile Vuillermoz found the music immensely accomplished, but too clever by half and rather calculated: 'In the name of logic, Ravel removes from the musical language not only its internationalism and its universality, but its simple humanity' (57). One of the critics to praise the work was Ravel's former teacher Fauré, in his review for *Le Figaro* (20 May 1911). Fauré was impressed by Ravel's fidelity to Franc-Nohain and the care with which every nuance of the text seemed to be reflected in the score. He was also delighted by Ravel's brilliantly inventive sound-world: 'What harmonic and orchestral discoveries, what originality, what subtle ingenuity, and what gaiety of spirit!' (Fauré 1930, 116–7).

Louis Laloy was another enthusiast for the work, and in *La Grande Revue* (25 April 1911) he echoed some of Fauré's thoughts:

> Monsieur Ravel is such a pure musician that he never exceeds the limits of beauty; in his style, even when he disguises it intentionally, harmony is innate; and if we smile on hearing it, we are also moved by a tenderness whose object is none other than the music itself. Already the charm of the *Histoires naturelles* arose from this sweet soul which could be guessed at through the external irony. It is a much more significant work this time: never has the author shown himself to be more inventive, nor more the master of this genre which he has made his own. (Priest 1999, 259–60)

Ravel's only other completed opera, *L'Enfant et les sortilèges* (discussed below), was to be a work of even greater inventiveness, and one of astonishing, enchanting boldness.

The French had always been fascinated by Spain, and many French operas were based on Spanish themes. But what about a Spanish opera by a Spanish composer? In 1905, Falla's *La vida breve* won a competition organized by the Academia de Bellas Artes in Madrid for the best new one-act opera. Though a production was supposed to follow the award of the prize, nothing came of this. Falla moved to Paris in the summer of 1907, and that autumn he played the opera – which he considered his first fully mature work – to Dukas and

Albeniz; both admired it greatly (Pahissa 1954, 42–3). The work was first published in Paris, by the firm of Max Eschig, and the premiere eventually took place at the Municipal Casino in Nice on 1 April 1913, quickly followed by a first Paris performance at the Opéra-Comique on 30 December 1913. Pierre Lalo, often a hostile critic of Debussy and Ravel, reviewed the opera in *Le Temps*. It was the romantic love music that Lalo enjoyed least, finding it too reminiscent of the 'Italian influence which dominated Spanish music for so long'; but the picturesque qualities of the opera had, he thought,

> a particularly intense charm – no excess of colour, no deliberate searching for effect, but a subtle restraint, delicate and precise shading, discrimination and good taste. The most felicitous passage is that at the end of the first scene which describes twilight in Granada – a page of penetrating poetry which preserves in its sensitivity and melancholy accents, something intimate and concentrated.
>
> (Quoted in Pahissa 1954, 64)

While Lalo's comments are perceptive, it is amusing to note that at the time Falla wrote this music, he had never been to Granada, though he was to settle there permanently in 1920.

Before writing *La vida breve*, Falla had tried his hand at half a dozen zarzuelas, none of which had any success. But his enthusiastic interest in this popular theatrical form was to influence some of his subsequent stage works; so, too, was Falla's passion for the traditional music of his country, and Spanish music from the Renaissance and earlier. It was to be one of the great Spanish classics that provided the literary source for his most original operatic project. *El retablo de Maese Pedro* ('Master Peter's Puppet Show') was composed in 1919–22 as a 'puppet opera' in one act, with a libretto by Falla after Cervantes' *Don Quixote*. The work was a commission from the Princesse de Polignac, for a performance by puppets in her Paris home. In fact the first performance took place in Seville on 23 March 1923, and the Paris premiere was given to an invited audience in the Princess's salon at the Avenue Henri-Martin on the following 25 June. Wanda Landowska played the harpsichord part, while the puppet of Don Quixote was worked by Ricardo Viñes, assisted by his pupil Francis Poulenc. The more refined musical language of this work, drawing on many aspects of Spanish music as well as on trends in contemporary European musical thought, produced what Sylvia Kahan has described as 'something wholly original in all Spanish music' (2003, 236).

Le Rossignol

Diaghilev's Ballets Russes seasons in Paris were of an artistic significance that is now the stuff of legend. It should also be remembered that

Diaghilev introduced Parisian audiences to Russian opera, including Musorgsky's *Boris Godunov* and *Khovanschina*, Borodin's *Prince Igor* and at least one significant novelty, Stravinsky's *Le Rossignol*, a 'conte lyrique en trois actes' with a libretto by the composer and Stepan Mitusov based on the fairy tale by Hans Christian Andersen. Stravinsky began the work as early as 1908 – the ageing Rimsky-Korsakov reacted with approval when he was shown the sketches for Act I – but it was not completed until 1914 (in the interim Stravinsky was busy writing *The Firebird*, *Petrushka* and *The Rite of Spring*). The first performance of *Le Rossignol* was given at the Paris Opéra on 26 May 1914 and it revealed a work – lasting less than an hour – of slightly bewildering stylistic diversity (hardly surprising given what Stravinsky composed in between the first and second acts), which drew on both Russian and French predecessors, specifically Musorgsky and Debussy. A year earlier, Stravinsky talked of his unease with opera as a genre: in an interview with the *Daily Mail* (13 February 1913) he declared: 'I dislike opera. Music can be married to gesture or to words – not to both without bigamy. That is why the artistic basis of opera is wrong and why Wagner sounds best in the concert-room. In any case opera is a backwater. What operas have been written since *Parsifal*? Only two that count – [Strauss's] *Elektra* and Debussy's *Pelléas*' (quoted in White 1979, 225). So what of his own first effort in the genre? Though he quite enjoyed the hints of *Boris Godunov* in the Emperor's death-bed scene of *Le Rossignol*, Stravinsky's later judgement was chilly: 'Perhaps *The Nightingale* proves that I was right to compose ballets since I was not yet ready for an opera' (Stravinsky and Craft 1962b, 62 n. 2). The work was, however, a veritable feast for the eyes, and Stravinsky was generous with his praise of Benois: 'scenically, thanks to Alexandre Benois who designed the costumes and sets, it was the most beautiful of all my early Diaghilev works' (Stravinsky and Craft 1960, 132).

The influences on *Le Rossignol*, especially the earlier scenes, were almost as much French as they were Russian, and Stravinsky recalled this in describing the reaction to the first performance:

> The premiere was unsuccessful only in the sense that it failed to create a scandal ... As to its reception, the 'advanced' musicians were genuinely enthusiastic – or so I thought. That Ravel liked it, I am certain, but I am almost as convinced that Debussy did not, for I heard nothing from him about it. I remember this well, for I expected him to question me about the great difference between the music of Act I and the later acts, and though I knew he would have liked the Mussorgsky–Debussy beginning, he probably would have said about that, too, 'Young man, I do it better.' On my last trip to Russia I remember reading a remark in my diary – I kept a diary from 1906 to 1910 – written when I was composing the first act of *The*

Nightingale: 'Why should I be following Debussy so closely, when the real originator of this operatic style was Mussorgsky?' But, in justice to Debussy, I must own that I saw him only very infrequently in the weeks after *The Nightingale*, and perhaps he simply had no opportunity to tell me his true impressions. (132–3)

Laloy, writing in *Comoedia*, gave the work a heroic welcome: 'A masterpiece, as has been declared here right from the first. A pure masterpiece. Superhuman music … Supernatural music … The revelation of *Le rossignol* takes possession of our soul and renews it: only the revelations of *Parsifal*, *Boris Godunov*, *Pelléas et Mélisande* and [Debussy's *Le martyre de*] *Saint Sébastien* are comparable. What a fortunate time we live in, with so many unexplored perspectives being discovered one after the other!' (Priest 1999, 285–9).

Rabaud and Roussel

On 15 May 1914, just over a week before *Le Rossignol* was first performed, Henri Rabaud's *Mârouf* – one of the biggest popular successes of prewar French opera and now largely forgotten – had its premiere at the Opéra-Comique. Rabaud came from a family with strong operatic connections: his great-aunt was the singer Julie Dorus-Gras, who had created major roles in operas such as *Robert le Diable*, *La Juive*, *Les Huguenots* and *Benvenuto Cellini*. After studies with Massenet, Rabaud won the Prix de Rome in 1894 and during his time in Italy became an enthusiastic admirer of Verdi and Puccini. But his Wagnerian roots went deep and *Mârouf* is a diverting amalgam of oriental story-telling, perfumed and exotic orchestral colours, and structures which owe much to Wagner. In 1922 Rabaud succeeded Fauré as Director of the Paris Conservatoire and his *L'Appel de la mer*, based on J. M. Synge's *Riders to the Sea* (also the basis for Vaughan Williams's opera) was first performed at the Opéra-Comique in 1924.

Albert Roussel was another composer for whom the Orient was an irresistible lure. He wrote the 'opéra-ballet' *Padmâvatî* during the First World War, to a libretto by Laloy – a man of prodigious talent whose importance as a critic has tended to overshadow his activities as a scholar and writer. Roussel and Laloy had known each other for almost twenty years, having met in the composition classes at the Schola Cantorum. Both were fascinated by the Orient: Roussel had spent several months during the autumn of 1909 on a voyage to India and Cambodia with his wife Blanche; Laloy had published a good deal on the music of the Far East, including an article on music and dance in Cambodia (1906) and one of the first books in French on Chinese music (1912). In 1914, following the success of

Roussel's ballet *Le Festin de l'araignée*, Jacques Rouché, recently appointed as Director of the Paris Opéra, commissioned Roussel to write a new stage work. Inevitably, the war disrupted creative activity and progress was sporadic, since the composer was serving as a transport officer on the Somme and elsewhere in 1915–18. And while *Padmâvatî* was finished in 1918, it was to be another five years before the piece received its first performance, at the Opéra on 1 June 1923. An 'opéra-ballet' in two acts, it clearly reflects Roussel's love of India, not least in terms of the influence on his musical language. Nicole Labelle has summarized the work's significance:

> *Padmâvatî* represents the culmination of Roussel's fascination with India, in its subject matter – the legend of the Queen of Chitor – and in its masterful integration of an Indian modal language into the composer's harmonic style. Dark, brooding orchestral colours, emotionally effective choruses and danced numbers, and poignant solo writing all evoke the majesty of Hindu temples and the tragic destiny of the characters. (2001, 808)

Critical reaction was enthusiastic. Dukas wrote: 'I believe sincerely that of the new generation of musicians, M. Albert Roussel is one of those who makes the strongest impression, through the combination of traditional skills and the most daring harmonic experimentation' (*Le Quotidien*, 7 June 1923). André Messager in *Le Figaro* was equally impressed, drawing particular attention to the primordial power of Roussel's rhythm, and other composers who wrote admiringly of the work included Florent Schmitt and Darius Milhaud (see Hoérée 1938, 57–8).

L'Enfant et les sortilèges

Ravel's collaboration with Colette on *L'Enfant et les sortilèges* produced a one-act opera which is extraordinarily touching, funny and filled with a sense of the marvellous. First performed at Monte Carlo Opera on 21 March 1925, it has been described by Richard Langham Smith as 'high on the list of works which at one level deal with the child within the adult' (2000, 200). Parodistic humour is an important feature of the score, but the work is far from lightweight. Ravel was characteristically self-effacing about it, but Colette certainly saw beyond the fun to the opera's deeper realms:

> How can I describe my emotion when, for the first time, I heard the little drum accompanying the shepherd's procession? The moonlight in the garden, the flight of the dragonflies and bats … 'Isn't it fun?' Ravel would say. But I could feel a knot of tears tightening in my throat. (Quoted in Nichols 1987, 58)

Ravel's handling of the orchestra in *L'Enfant* is breathtaking – a mixture of the dazzling and the delicate which results in a highly original and astonishingly beautiful sound-world quite unlike that of any other opera. His use of eccentric instrumentation, notably the Swanee whistle in the scene in the garden, was another inspired touch. The vocal writing is far more overtly melodic than in *L'Heure espagnole*, though Ravel's characteristic care over word-setting is apparent throughout. The close of *L'Enfant* – as The Child sings 'Maman' – is remarkable for its simplicity and its lack of obvious finality despite being a mildly coloured perfect cadence. This gesture is typical of the whole work: ostensibly simple means deployed to ends that seem effortlessly to fuse the childlike and the profound.

Milhaud

Darius Milhaud composed almost forty operas and ballets, and in several of these dramatic works he is at his most original and inventive. His first operatic project was *La Brebis égarée*, composed in 1910–14 during his years as a student at the Paris Conservatoire, to a libretto by Francis Jammes. It was first performed at the Opéra-Comique on 8 December 1923, almost a decade after its completion. The audience was hostile, as was much of the subsequent press reaction, but an exception was the typically thoughtful review by Dukas. While recognizing that Milhaud had come a long way in the ten years since writing the opera, he found much to admire:

> The basic material of the work is as simple, banal and barren as it could possibly be, and most likely it is this way on purpose. Apparently the reason is to make vivid the utter contrast between the radiant souls of the protagonists and the miserable platitude of their lives … Nevertheless, the two elements are expressively unified at those moments where the poetry intensifies and the dramatic situation reaches a climax, as in the church scene where Pierre is at prayer, and in the one in which Françoise, on her hospital bed, reads Paul's long letter of forgiveness. These two scenes mark the culminating points of the score as well as of the play. They are also the ones which made the most striking and profound impression on the audience. They reveal in M. Darius Milhaud a born musician of the theatre.
>
> (1948, 663–7)

Les Malheurs d'Orphée was written in the autumn of 1924. Its subject is a contemporary reworking of Orpheus's desolation following Euridice's death; despite being designated an opera in three acts, the work lasts no more than forty minutes. The music which Milhaud wrote to Armand

Lunel's libretto is generally terse, austere and economical. Paul Collaer described it as follows:

> Each section is brief, concentrated, stripped to the bone, completely devoid of development. It is as though 'mere music-making' is superfluous in the face of such sorrow. Measure after measure represents a cry, a sigh, or a shiver, as though the heart were being torn out piece by piece. Each note must sound true, necessary, beautiful. This is a work of quality rather than quantity, a concentration rather than a diffusion of sentiment. Moreover, the music must be performed as a kind of offering, a ritual prayer to console and soothe the wounded spirit. (1988, 81)

Another admirer was Ravel, who discussed the work in an interview with Roland-Manuel first published in *Les Nouvelles littéraires* (2 April 1927). Ravel praised Milhaud at the same time as taking a swipe at an old enemy of his own, the critic Pierre Lalo:

> It is with respect to Darius Milhaud and his *Malheurs d'Orphée* that M. Lalo attains the height of impertinence. Here is a moving, magnificent work, Milhaud's best, and one of the finest achievements that our young school has produced in a long time. M. Lalo seeks in vain for 'something vibrant and expressive.' He complains that 'the progression is almost always slow,' while at every moment I find rapid progressions which indicate extraordinary rhythmic inventiveness. The orchestration of *Les Malheurs d'Orphée* is always very skilfully balanced. M. Lalo declares it to be abominable. (Orenstein 1990, 446)

Three years after finishing *Les Malheurs d'Orphée*, Milhaud began another series of compact little operas, the three 'opéra-minutes', none lasting more than ten minutes. The first was *L'Enlèvement d'Europe*, written at the request of Paul Hindemith and first performed at Baden-Baden in July 1927, on the same programme as Hindemith's own *Hin und Zurück*. *L'Abandon d'Ariane* and *La Délivrance de Thésée* complete this trio, all of which were written in 1927.

Esther de Carpentras was a project particularly dear to Milhaud's heart, concerning as it does a Provençal tradition to celebrate one of the great Jewish Festivals. Based on a libretto by Armand Lunel, the work is a comic opera in two acts, composed in 1925–7. But as well as moments of carnival atmosphere for the staging of the story of Queen Esther and a rich seam of melodic invention, the opera also explores the tensions between the Jews of the Carpentras ghetto and the Catholic cardinal from whom permission to celebrate the festival had to be obtained. The end of the opera, where a joyous song of praise from the Jews mingles with an anthem sung by the departing Catholics, is a remarkable moment, before the curiously subdued close where the character Cacan announces that 'the masquerade has ended up as a sermon' ('La mascarade s'achève en sermon'). The first performance was planned for the opera in Monte Carlo, but this fell through and the work had to wait ten years for its premiere, at the start of February 1938 at the Opéra-Comique (having already been broadcast from Rennes in the previous year). One pleasing juxtaposition was the review by a great Catholic composer of a work by his older Jewish colleague: Olivier Messiaen wrote about the opera for the Brussels magazine *Syrinx*. He was enchanted by the 'exuberant gaiety' of the score, with its 'orchestration which is comical, powerful, and joyously unbuttoned', and he attempted to summarize its particular quality: 'The spirit is not at all Rabelaisian, but Provençal, with all that word suggests in terms of light and of good humour. It is this quality with which Milhaud has infused so many places in his score' (Messiaen 1938, 25–6).

In 1928, Milhaud completed the first of his epic operas based on historical characters in the Americas. *Christophe Colomb* was first performed in Berlin (5 May 1930) under Erich Kleiber and it has come to be viewed by many, including Milhaud's friend Collaer, as one of his greatest achievements. (For a detailed discussion of the work, see Collaer 1988, 128–37.) It was followed by *Maximilien* (composed in 1930, first performed in 1932) and *Bolivar* (composed in 1943, first performed in 1950). *Médée* (1938) received its premiere in Antwerp (7 October 1939), and the first performance in Paris (on 8 May 1940) was a poignant occasion: it was the last new work to be performed at the Opéra before the German Occupation.

Milhaud continued to produce a seemingly unstoppable flow of music after the Second World War and this included several dramatic works. The grandest of these was the five-act *David*, a commission from the Koussevitzky Foundation for a work to celebrate 'the 3,000th birthday of King David and of the foundation of Jerusalem'. Dedicated to 'the people of Israel', this epic work was first performed in concert in Jerusalem on 1 June 1954, and the stage premiere took place a few months later, on 2 February 1955, at La Scala, Milan. Milhaud's next operatic venture could hardly have been more different: *Fiesta* was, on Poulenc's suggestion, a collaboration with Boris Vian – poet, songwriter, jazzman and one of the iconic figures of St-Germain-des-Prés in the 1950s. The short (twenty-minute) one-act opera resulting from this rather unlikely partnership was commissioned by Hermann Scherchen for the 1958 Berlin Festival and first performed there on 3 October 1958. In 1966 Milhaud returned to the world of *Le nozze di Figaro*. The trilogy of 'Figaro' plays by Beaumarchais ended with *La Mère coupable*, widely considered to be a dud, but clearly Milhaud thought it had potential. Madeleine Milhaud's libretto cleverly tightened up Beaumarchais's text, but the story never comes alive, and

Collaer was forced to conclude that the score – Milhaud's last conventional opera – was 'tiresomely monotonous' (1988, 156).

Honegger

The theatre was one of Arthur Honegger's abiding passions, but his operas are not widely performed. A prolific composer of incidental music for plays and of pioneering film scores, as well as of 'dramatic oratorios' which lent themselves to staged presentation (such as *Le Roi David* and *Jeanne d'Arc au bûcher*), his first opera was *Antigone*, composed in 1924–7 to a libretto by Jean Cocteau (after Sophocles). This was first performed at the Théâtre de la Monnaie, Brussels, on 28 December 1927. Greek tragedy was very much *à la mode* at the time, with Satie's *Socrate* and Stravinsky's *Oedipus Rex* near contemporaries. Honegger himself wrote that he chose the story 'because it is not the standard anecdote of love which is the base of nearly all lyric theatre' (Spratt 1987, 94). The composer's declared musical intention, set out in the preface to the score, was 'to envelop the drama with a tight symphonic construction without the movement seeming heavy.' Equally significant was the attention Honegger gave to word-setting, in particular the accentuation of particular syllables in order to achieve a natural and dramatically compelling prosody. Much later Honegger discussed the challenge which this presented: 'What I had to work at at all costs was the means whereby I might make others *understand* the lyric text: that, in my opinion, was the rule of the game in the realm of the lyric. French dramatic musicians show an exclusive concern for the melodic design and a quite subordinate care for the conformity of text and music' (Honegger 1966, 96). He goes on to discuss specific details which concerned him in *Antigone*, for instance:

> What is important in the word is not the vowel, but the consonant: it really plays the role of a locomotive, dragging the whole word behind it ... In our time, and for a dramatic delivery, the consonants project the word into the hall, they make it resound. Each word contains its potential, its melodic line. The addition of a melodic line in opposition to its own paralyses its flight, and the word collapses on the floor of the stage. My personal rule is to respect the word's plasticity as a means of giving it its full power.

Contemporaneous reaction to Honegger's word-setting in *Antigone* was generally positive, not least because the audience was able to hear all the words clearly. Some critics felt that Honegger's theories on prosody had restricted the melodic invention in the opera. Certainly the musical language of *Antigone* is notable for its austerity – severity, even – and for its avoidance of lyricism in any conventional sense. But it is precisely this lack of obvious allure, and the nature of Honegger's text-setting, which mark it out as a work of decisive importance in the history of French opera after *Pelléas*. Its failure with the public was a blow to Honegger and his next stage projects were very different.

Amphion (1929) was an unusual melodrama written for Ida Rubinstein and first performed by her and Charles Panzéra at the Opéra on 23 June 1931. Also in 1929 Honegger started work on *Les Aventures du Roi Pausole*, an operetta completed the following year and first performed on 12 December 1930 at the Théâtre des Bouffes-Parisiens – the celebrated birthplace of many of Offenbach's operettas. Honegger's operetta was based on a story by Pierre Louÿs which was originally intended for Debussy, who had asked his friend for an operetta text in 1916. Honegger's deft and utterly delightful score pokes amiable fun at operettas by Offenbach, Messager, Chabrier and others, but does so with a complete understanding of the genre as well as a real affection for it. The solemn and earnest composer of *Antigone* is replaced by one whose lightness of touch here resulted in a major box-office success: the original production of *Les Aventures* ran for 500 performances at the Bouffes-Parisiens. His later operettas were collaborations with Jacques Ibert: *L'Aiglon* (1936–7) and *Les Petites Cardinal* (1937). The remainder of Honegger's music for the lyric stage is not strictly operatic at all: the 'dramatic oratorios', of which *Jeanne d'Arc au bûcher* (1933–5, with a prologue added in 1944) is much the most spectacular, also included *Nicholas de Flue*, a kind of pageant written for the Swiss National Exhibition in 1939.

Canteloube's *Vercingétorix* and other French operas from the 1930s

Among the oddities of the French repertoire in the 1930s, none is perhaps odder than *Vercingétorix*, the most lavish operatic venture of Joseph Canteloube. Over a fifteen-year period, from 1910 until 1925, he worked on his first opera, *Le Mas*, which won the Heugel Prize in January 1926, but then had to wait another three years before receiving its premiere at the Paris Opéra (on 3 April 1929). After the modest theatrical success of *Le Mas*, Canteloube turned to *Vercingétorix*, an 'épopée lyrique' (lyric epic) in four acts. This was composed in 1930–32 and first performed at the Paris Opéra on 22 June 1933. The large orchestra includes real novelty with its parts for four Ondes Martenot to evoke, according to the composer, 'the mystic moments in the score'. *Vercingétorix* is a tale of Celtic heroism – the eponymous character was the leader of the Gauls who freed France from Roman occupation – and its visionary world was described by Emile Vuillermoz in his review for *Excelsior* published on 26 June 1933:

> The libretto of *Vercingétorix* is exactly what Richard Wagner, the author of *Siegfried*, would have written if he had been a Frenchman. The same preoccupations with deeply rooted ethnicity, the same philosophical and historical viewpoints ... the same moral and religious mysticism, the same theory of renunciation and of atonement through sacrifice, the same conception of heroism, the same suspicion of human love, and the same exaltation of Parsifal-like chastity.

Wagner's influence on the French lyric theatre was still at work in the 1930s, especially in an opera like *Vercingétorix*: Canteloube's nationalist epic is one of the most conspicuous (and grandiose) examples of this enduring legacy. The score is ripely post-Romantic, full of aspirational leitmotives, one of which (beginning with a rising fourth) evoked for one early critic not only the spirit but also the tune of *La Marseillaise*. While it is easy to smile at a cast-list which reads like the characters from the Astérix stories, and while the setting of the opening – on the summit of the Puy de Dôme, the 'montagne sacrée' – suggests a decidedly Wagnerian approach to stage mysticism, there is a certain nobility in Canteloube's music (quite unlike his more familiar folk-song arrangements) which is genuinely impressive. This vast score could be an interesting candidate for revival.

A glance at the list of operas first performed in Paris during the 1930s reveals a number of other works which have lapsed from the repertoire. 1930 saw Ibert's *Le Roi d'Yvetot*, Marcel Delannoy's *Fou de la dame* and Manuel Rosenthal's *Rayon de Soieries* at the Opéra-Comique, and Raoul Brunel's *La Tentation de Saint-Antoine* at the Opéra. The following year, the Opéra staged *Virginie* by Alfred Bruneau, the last in a long line of operas by a composer who had made his name in the 1890s thanks to his collaborations with Zola; 1931 also saw the posthumous premiere at the Opéra of *Guercoeur* by Albéric Magnard (composed in 1897–1901). In 1932, Milhaud's *Maximilien* and Alfred Bachelet's *Un Jardin sur l'Oronte* were the novelties at the Opéra, while 1933 saw the premiere of Rosenthal's operetta *Bootleggers* (libretto by Nino) at the Art-Déco Théâtre Pigalle. At the Opéra, Rabaud's *Rolande et le mauvais garçon* was first performed in 1934, followed by Reynaldo Hahn's *Le Marchand de Venise* (after Shakespeare) in 1935. The arrival of Enescu's *Oedipe* at the Opéra in 1936 meant that, after several years of near-misses, the company had a major new work on its hands. It was not until 1939 that the Palais Garnier put on another novelty of comparable scale: Henri Sauguet's output was dominated by several successful ballets for Diaghilev, Roland Petit and others, such as *La Chatte* and *Les Forains*; but his largest stage work was the opera *La Chartreuse de Parme*, composed over a period of ten years (1927–36), dedicated to Milhaud and first performed at the Paris Opéra on 6 March 1939. The libretto is by Milhaud's friend Armand Lunel (after Stendhal) and, though the opera is in most respects traditional, the music has a melodic grace which raises it well above the level of some of the works composed in the years immediately before the outbreak of the Second World War.

Progressive Italian opera between the wars: Malipiero and Dallapiccola's *Volo di notte*

> Through harmonic writing nourished by the old Venetian contrapuntists, through instrumentation meticulously crafted and modern, through the original development of ideas ... the musical quality of the operas of Malipiero is superior to anything which has been seen in Italian theatres since Verdi.

This ringing endorsement of the operatic output of Gian Francesco Malipiero, proclaimed by Massimo Mila (1947–8, 109), is ample encouragement to re-evaluate these largely neglected works, widely recognized at the time as an important new departure for Italian opera, making as they did a definitive and highly imaginative break with the *verismo* tradition. Malipiero's triptych with the collective title *L'orfeide* was composed in 1918–22 and comprises three works: *La morte delle maschere*, *Sette canzoni* and *Orfeo, ovvero L'ottava canzone*. Of these, perhaps the most striking is the first to be composed, *Sette canzoni*, consisting of seven miniature operas unconnected by plot and 'threaded together like beads on a string' (Waterhouse 2001b, 699). It was first performed at the Paris Opéra, conducted by Gabriel Grovlez, on 10 July 1920, but this was an unhappy occasion, as René Dumesnil reported ten years after the event:

> Francesco Malipiero has taken up the battle against Mascagni, Leoncavallo and Puccini ... He is also a friend of d'Annunzio, and his works, the cause of violent controversy, have been the most courageous manifestations against *verismo*. It would be reasonable to think that the *Sette canzoni* contained something really subversive, since the audience at the Paris Opéra heard them against an uproar and it was necessary to wait for Mme Bériza to revive them at her theatre in order to be able to listen to them.

> In truth, because it is both sincere and original, this music stays in the
> memory. It contains passages ... which made a lasting impression, even
> at the first performance, on anyone who didn't systematically refuse to
> understand it.   (1930, 77–8; see also Dumesnil 1946, 50)

Despite these unpromising beginnings, the opera was soon recognized as
a work of considerable significance and as early as 1929 it was the subject
of a collection of essays entitled *Malipiero e le sue Sette canzoni*
(Ciarlantini 1929), written by some distinguished Italian contemporaries
including Franco Alfano, Alfredo Casella and Mario Castelnuovo-
Tedesco. Malipiero's fondness for operatic triptychs is reflected in other
works from the 1920s and 1930s: *3 commedie goldoniane* (1920–25),
Il mistero di Venezia (1925–8) and *I trionfi d'amore* (1930–31). Usually
the author of his own librettos, Malipiero did collaborate in 1932–3 with a
leading Italian literary figure, the great Luigi Pirandello, on *La favola del
figlio cambiato*. Malipiero's interest in earlier music, especially
Monteverdi, is reflected in *San Francesco d'Assisi* (1920–21) which received
its first (concert) performance in Carnegie Hall, New York, on 29 March
1922. *Merlino, mastro d'organi* (1926–7) is rather more of a curiosity
given its bizarre and tortuous plot: credulity is strained by a story-line
in which a vast magic organ kills all who hear it; its evil-doings are only
brought to an end when a deaf mute murders the organist and then turns
out to be a reincarnation of his own victim. A good deal more plausible is
the brooding *Torneo notturno* (1929), considered by Mila to be 'perhaps
Malipiero's operatic masterpiece, which deploys a number of expressive
possibilities: Goldonian comedy, mixed with a bitter dose of sarcasm,
religious fervour and mystical elevation, and above all a love of the
fantastic and of the artificial which is a constant theme, the motor, so to
speak, of his artistic creativity' (1947–8, 109–10). John Waterhouse has
characterized the music of this opera as 'hauntingly enigmatic ...
another of Malipiero's supreme achievements, in which the obsessively
recurring "canzone del tempo" evokes the inexorable destructiveness of
time' (2001b, 699).

Antoine de Saint-Exupéry's largely autobiographical novel *Vol de nuit*
was first published in 1931 and its influence at the time was considerable,
even inspiring such ephemeral delights as the 'Vol de nuit' perfume by
Guerlin, as well as the film *Night Flight* (1933) starring Clark Gable. One
of the pioneers of commercial flying, Saint-Exupéry worked during the
1920s in Africa, then South America where he was a director for
Aéropostale in Argentina. *Vol de nuit* was also to serve as the inspiration
for a remarkable one-act opera composed by Luigi Dallapiccola in 1937–9
and first performed at the Teatro della Pergola in Florence on 18 May

1940 (conducted by Fernando Previtali). Dallapiccola had discovered the music of Debussy – especially *Pelléas* – in his teens, and its impact was such that he stopped composing altogether for three years (1921–4). His enthusiasm for French music was thus an important early influence, and his encounter with Berg in 1934 was to prove decisive. Dallapiccola's older compatriot Casella wrote admiringly of *Volo di notte* in his memoirs (first published in Italian in 1941), praising it as among 'the fruits of one of the richest imaginations in music today, not only in our country but even in the whole of Europe ... Dallapiccola ... represents one of the greatest energies to which our musical future can be confided' (1955, 200). This was the composer's first stage work and its visionary qualities are perhaps its most enduring feature. The opera

> re-uses material from [Dallapiccola's] *Tre laudi*. This transference of music originally associated with medieval religious texts to an opera about night flying in the Andes is less incongruous than it may seem, for Dallapiccola's libretto contains a strong element of religious symbolism. When, at the climax, the pilot Fabien rises above the storm and, just before death, glimpses the infinite, eternal beauty of the stars, his experience has mystical connotations: for Dallapiccola the stars were a symbol of God.
>
> (Waterhouse 2001a, 855–6)

In terms of sheer novelty, the most startling feature of the opera was the introduction to the lyric stage of modern technology, but this was complemented by music of genuine modernity. Mila's article (referred to above) in the progressive French journal *Polyphonie* described this successful combination: '*Volo di notte*, drawn from the masterpiece by Saint-Exupéry, is one of the most compelling of modern operas. It goes without saying that its modernism is not only evident in the appearance of aeroplanes and radio transmitters on the stage, but it extends to the score, which it penetrates deeply' (1947–8, 112).

Paris Occupied

Paris was under German Occupation from June 1940 until August 1944, but the Opéra continued to flourish, albeit under the ultimate control of the occupying authorities. Visits by German companies attracted a good deal of notice (including the celebrated Bayreuth production of *Tristan und Isolde* which was brought to Paris in May 1941, with Max Lorenz and Germaine Lubin in the title roles, conducted by Herbert von Karajan), and German repertoire was to dominate the programme, including modern works like Pfitzner's *Palestrina* (1917) and Werner Egk's *Peer Gynt* (1938) as well as generous helpings of Wagner. No new French opera was put on at the Opéra under the Occupation – a striking contrast with the ballet repertoire which included important new works by Poulenc (*Les Animaux modèles*) and Jolivet (*Guignol et Pandore*) – though there were new productions of Fauré's *Pénélope* and Honegger's *Antigone* in the spring of 1943.

Elsewhere in Paris things were a good deal livelier – indeed a production from the Opéra-Comique formed the basis of a heroic affirmation of French culture: the first major recording project in France during the period was the famous set of *Pelléas et Mélisande* featuring Irène Joachim, Jacques Jansen and Henri Etcheverry, conducted by Roger Désormière. It was made by Pathé-Marconi between 26 April and 26 May 1941 and originally issued on twenty 78rpm discs. Music by Offenbach, who was Jewish, was banned during the Occupation, but at the Opéra-Comique Désormière chose another enchanting example of French light opera, Chabrier's *L'Etoile*, to coincide with the composer's centenary in 1941. Extracts from *L'Etoile* were recorded by Opéra-Comique forces in 1943. The company also put on a new work which enjoyed considerable success at the time. Commissioned by the state in 1938, Delannoy's *Ginevra* was finished in 1942 and first performed at the Opéra-Comique the same year (25 July). For some of the musical material, this work draws on a source which would have had nostalgic resonances for the audience of the time: French Renaissance *chansons*.

Poulenc

Poulenc's first venture into opera came after more than two decades of working as a composer of ballets and of incidental music for the theatre. His setting of *Les Mamelles de Tirésias* – by turns uproarious and radiant – is based on a text by Guillaume Apollinaire, who had been such a decisive influence on Poulenc's work. Poulenc had attended the first performance of Apollinaire's play in June 1917, when he was in good company, as the audience also included Matisse, Picasso, Braque, Dufy, Cocteau, Eluard, Satie, Diaghilev and Breton. Composed during the war years, Poulenc's 'opéra-bouffe' on *Les Mamelles* was first performed on 3 June 1947, though Poulenc had performed it privately *autour du piano* as early as November 1944. His own assessment of the work (for which he declared 'a passionate fondness') was that it was 'one of the few things I have done where I wouldn't change a single note' (Schmidt 1995, 354). Perhaps more than most of his extended pieces, it combines brilliantly the different aspects of Poulenc's musical personality: farcical humour and rapturous tenderness happily co-exist in a score which is both exuberant and touching.

The climax of Poulenc's output of religious music (from 1936 onwards), as well as his zenith as an opera composer, is *Dialogues des Carmélites*, based on an unused film script by Georges Bernanos and first performed at La Scala, Milan, on 26 January 1957 (when it was sung in Italian). The work has been criticized for its episodic construction and its short-breathed musical phrases, but Poulenc's score burns with that most highly prized of qualities among French composers – 'sincérité' – and at its best, the music is inspired. This is Poulenc's longest work and it is thus no surprise to find it full of the self-borrowings (from a bewildering diversity of earlier works) which make pinning down his elusive expressive and aesthetic intentions so problematic. The religious nature of the work is underlined by the inclusion of sections setting Latin liturgical texts. The most famous – to some, notorious – of these is the remorseless 'Salve Regina' sung by the nuns as they make their way to the guillotine (immediately preceded by a march which has its origins in *Deux marches et un intermède*, a short orchestral work written for a dinner party at the 1937 Paris Exposition); elsewhere a kind of rapt ecstasy can be found in these moments of semi-ritual. The Priest's farewell Mass, where he and the Sisters sing the 'Ave verum corpus', is a memorably beautiful case in point.

Poulenc's last operatic venture is also his most unusual. Based on a libretto by his old friend Cocteau, *La Voix humaine* (first performed on 6 February 1959) is a monologue for one singer – Poulenc wrote it for the soprano Denise Duval – with a set comprising a couch and, crucially, a telephone. The result is a gripping one-act drama which has a sustained, claustrophobic intensity rare for Poulenc.

Later French opera

The Paris Opéra was plunged into administrative chaos after the Liberation of the city in September 1944 and this inevitably led to a rather cautious attitude by the management. While new ballets continued to appear regularly, new operas were few and far between. The company itself was constantly dogged by strikes: the theatre closed for a month in 1945 due to industrial action; the musicians were on strike for several months in the first half of 1946; the stage technicians followed suit in 1947 to protest at Serge Lifar's return to the company and a new dispute closed the theatre for a month in 1948; the musicians were on strike from 28 November 1949 until 10 January 1950; and six weeks later the technicians withdrew their labour for over a month. The fire which broke out on Christmas Day 1950 was just one more reason to close the theatre, this time until April 1951. In almost every season for the next two decades, there were more disputes, including a three-week lock-out in October–November 1953. Finally, in 1969, the theatre closed, ostensibly for repairs, but primarily in an attempt to sort out working practices, contracts and artistic policy. The following year there was no attempt to disguise the reasons: on 30 July 1970 the theatre closed and it was not until 14 months later, on 30 September 1971, that performances resumed in the Palais Garnier. Given the precarious state of the Opéra, its appalling industrial relations and its ageing infrastructure, it is perhaps unsurprising that few important new works saw the light of day there during these turbulent years. The announcement that Rolf Liebermann was to become administrator of the Opéra in 1973 led many to hope that there would be a more innovative artistic policy, and this turned out to be the case.

It was a commission from Liebermann which produced one of the grandest of French operas composed since 1945: Messiaen's *Saint-François d'Assise*, first performed at the Palais Garnier on 28 November 1983, after almost a decade of work on the composition and orchestration. Messiaen's position on opera was ambivalent: while Mozart, Wagner, Gluck and Debussy's *Pelléas* had been among his earliest inspirations (and recurred frequently in his own teaching) he declared more than once that he would never write an opera, but admitted elsewhere (even as early as 1948) that it was something he wanted very much to attempt. His mammoth *Saint-François d'Assise* was conceived on a *Parsifal*-like scale, and while the music has been greatly (and rightly) admired, the work has been criticized for being too static, too monumental. However, while Messiaen's intention was never to write a fast-paced drama, to claim that *Saint-François* is a kind of glorified oratorio is to miss the point: the human drama of the story, the passionate engagement with nature by the principal character and the composer, and the blazing fervour (and incredible beauty) of the music suggest that this is very much an opera, albeit an opera as only Messiaen could (or would) compose – and the work, despite its huge instrumental and vocal demands, has started to make its way into the international repertoire.

Other French operas from the second half of the century include several by Marcel Landowski. A member of the Académie des Beaux-Arts from 1975 (and its Secrétaire Perpétuel from 1986), his works for the lyric stage included *Le Fou* (1948–55), the one-act *Le Ventriloque* (1954–5), *Les Adieux* (given its first staged performance at the Opéra-Comique on 8 October 1960), the children's opera *La Sorcière du placard aux balais* ('The Witch of the Broom Cupboard', completed in 1983), and three full-length operas. The first of these, *Montségur*, received its premiere in Toulouse on 1 February 1985 and was described by Landowski as 'born of the meeting between the passionate story of an impossible love and the equally stirring one of the bloody conflict between two absolute and rival religious faiths' (*Landowski* (catalogue of works), 1996). *La Vieille maison* (1987), to a libretto by the composer himself, was first performed at Nantes on 25 February 1988. *Galina* (1995), jointly commissioned by the French Government and the Opéra de Lyon and first performed on 17 March 1996, is a most unusual work: Landowski's own libretto is based on the autobiography of the Russian singer Galina Vishnevskaya, and Vishnevskaya herself was present in the audience at the opera's premiere. Despite quite a prolific operatic output, Landowski – whose music is rooted in tradition but is sometimes rather anonymous – has failed to make any real impact beyond France. His importance perhaps lies as much in his work as an administrator: he appointed Liebermann to the Paris Opéra and his reforms of musical education, and policy of decentralization, have made a lasting impact on French cultural life.

The Romanian-born Marcel Mihalovici wrote several operas. Apart from the early *L'Intransigeant Pluton* (1928), these include *Phèdre* (completed in 1949) and *Le Retour* (1954), based on a story by Guy de Maupassant. In 1959, Mihalovici composed what is perhaps his most intriguing opera, *Krapp, ou la dernière bande*, a setting of Samuel Beckett's *Krapp's Last Tape*, lasting about one hour. Described as an 'opera', it has a cast of one (like Poulenc's *La Voix humaine*), in this case a single baritone. The role features quite extensive use of *Sprechgesang*, and the otherwise small orchestra includes a large percussion section, notably a part for vibraphone requiring four players. This work is noteworthy not least because operatic settings of Beckett are so few and far between. It was first performed in a concert version given by Radio France forces under Serge Baudo on 13 February 1961, and the first stage performance took place 12 days later at the Bielefeld Opera.

Claude Prey studied with Messiaen and Milhaud at the Paris Conservatoire and the vast majority of his works were written for small experimental groups specializing in music theatre. The composer of at least 30 such pieces, he had a great deal of fun inventing new operatic sub-genres. His stage works (all to his own texts) include an 'opéra-cruciverbal', an 'opéra-d'appartement', a 'mono-mimo-mélodrame', an 'opéra-test', an 'opéra-epistolaire', an 'opéra-kit', an 'opéra opus Proust' and – with a kind of lunatic inevitability – an 'opéra-opéra'. Prey's brilliant games with music (parodies and allusions to Wagner, Beethoven, Fauré and others) and with written and spoken language (for instance using only the 12 letters in the title of *L'Escalier de Chambord*) can be seen at their most elaborate in *O comme eau ou L'ora dopo* (1984), subtitled an 'ode homophone'. Set in an underwater world after the drowning of Venice, this piece employs the vowel 'o' throughout, since it is the only sound which the inhabitants can remember. Prey's works in some ways look back to much earlier innovations like Milhaud's 'opéras-minutes', but their wit, cleverness and their modest scale also ensured that – unlike most of the more grandiose ventures of the 1980s and 1990s – they were quite widely performed. The Prix de Rome for music – intended above all as a nursery for future opera composers – was awarded for the last time in 1968. It had become an anachronism and the student uprisings, the 'évènements', of that momentous year brought about its abolition. The work of Prey and others offer the possibility of some intriguing new directions a century on from Debussy's *Pelléas et Mélisande.*

9 Austria and Germany, 1918–1960

GUIDO HELDT

Just over 14 years went by between the end of the First World War and the Nazis' seizure of power, a short span for the high cultural repute Weimar culture has been accorded in twentieth-century popular and academic imagination – a repute particularly relevant to Berlin, which is still deriving much of its fragile self-confidence from that mythical decade. Opera is part and parcel of these images, but in a limited sense: we think of Bertolt Brecht and Kurt Weill, the Golden Boys of the Golden Twenties, of *Die Dreigroschenoper* (1928), *Aufstieg und Fall der Stadt Mahagonny* (1930) or Paul Hindemith's *Neues vom Tage* (1929); we think of the Kroll Opera and its controversial productions under the musical direction of Otto Klemperer; we think of a pointedly urban, sassy modernity. But it may be the range of personalities and events rather than any *couleur locale* that made Berlin such a musical hotbed at the time. There was the premiere of Alban Berg's *Wozzeck* in 1925; there were the antagonistic figures of Ferruccio Busoni and Hans Pfitzner, both teaching masterclasses at the Academy of Music since 1920; there was their superior, Academy director Franz Schreker, who had come from Vienna in the same year; there was Hindemith, who joined the Academy as a professor in 1927; there was Alexander Zemlinsky, who came from Prague in the same year to conduct at the Kroll Opera and taught from 1931 to 1933 at the Academy of Arts – composers with wildly different approaches to opera, embodying a disintegration of stylistic common ground that is the main characteristic of twentieth-century music. In popular musical theatre, too, the Berlin operettas by Walter Kollo were balanced by the Berlin premieres of Viennese composers such as Oscar Straus, Robert Stolz, Ralph Benatzky and Franz Lehár, whose *Zarewitsch* (1926), *Friedrike* (1928), *Das Land des Lächelns* (*The Land of Smiles*, 1929) and *Schön ist die Welt* (*Beautiful Is the World*, 1930) were first shown in Berlin.

The musical scene in Vienna proved more conservative than that of Berlin after 1918, the Second Viennese School notwithstanding, of whose operas only Schoenberg's *Die glückliche Hand* was premiered in Vienna, in 1924. Schoenberg himself had moved to and fro between his hometown and Berlin since 1911; in 1926, he finally left Vienna to teach composition at the Prussian Academy of Arts. (Even Franz Schmidt, who remained in Vienna, had his second opera *Fredigundis* premiered in Berlin in 1922.) So

Richard Strauss's *Die Frau ohne Schatten* in 1919 was indeed the only other influential operatic premiere in Vienna between the wars. The largest part of new musical theatre was made up of operettas: works by Paul Abraham, Benatzky, Julius Bittner, Leo Fall, Emmerich Kálmán, Lehár, Stolz and others. Though it would be simplistic to imply a straightforward causal connection, it is intriguing to note the parallel between Vienna's diminished roles as musical and as political capital. What in 1914 had been the hub of a major European power comprising a wide variety of peoples found itself by the end of the war on the fringe of a small country landlocked between Germany and Italy.

The end of the war brought major changes for the opera houses in Germany and Austria. After the breakdown of the monarchies, often within a few months the former court operas were transformed into national, state or municipal operas, which meant new financial structures and a new public accountability of institutions which had been fortresses of conservative culture. But new conditions had already been set by the outbreak of war, which meant the loss of subsidies and the necessity to attract larger audiences, something at which non-musical theatre was more adept than opera. Due to the fact that in a standard *Dreispartentheater* – a theatre comprising opera, ballet and *Sprechtheater* – opera tended to soak up two thirds of the funds, its need to spend less and attract more customers was direst. The ensuing attempts to popularize pro-grammes reinforced a trend towards operetta as a financial mainstay of musical theatre which had already begun before the war (Walter 2000, 71–130; 79).

The financial problems of opera were intensified through the hyper-inflation of the early 1920s, which hit hardest those whose disposable income was based on savings (which were devalued profoundly), among them large parts of the educated bourgeoisie who had made up the core opera audience. Conservative misgivings about postwar theatre were in part misgivings about changes in the audience structure – the diminished role of a former cultural elite and the larger role of new groups: workers who came to the theatre through union-organized cultural programmes and, after 1923, the 'new middle classes' of executives, teachers, civil servants, etc. who had profited from an economic stabilization. Such changes fuelled an interest in emphatically modern operas, which were written in Weimar Germany in larger numbers than either before or since, though they rarely achieved lasting success. In the 1926–7 season, new works accounted for 20 percent of opera productions, but only for 4.5 percent of performances (Walter 2000, 103–4). The repertoire of older operas, though, remained stable and was in 1927 not much different from that in 1917 or 1907. Most frequently performed were the works of

Wagner, Verdi, Mozart and Lortzing; Bizet, Weber and Offenbach also figured prominently. The rise of Puccini (in third place in the German statistics in 1926–7) was the most conspicuous development in this respect (80–83, 104–5; see also Köhler 1968).

More than their political and social counterparts, music historians have tended to focus on all things new emerging after the war; and perhaps justly so. But the anti-republican conservatism of parts of the German elites which helped to undermine the Weimar Republic played its role in musical life as well. When the Berlin State Opera reopened on 14 November 1918, it did so with Wagner's *Meistersinger*, an opera recommending openness to the new as much as a central role for an established culture and community – a mixed message which was played out with increasing intensity during the Weimar years.

Conversely many works which made their name after 1918 and are part of our idea of postwar opera had been conceived before the war. Schreker's *Der Schatzgräber* (*The Treasure Seeker*), first shown in Frankfurt in 1920, had been composed between 1915 and 1918; Berg's *Wozzeck*, first shown in 1925, had been begun by 1914; Rudi Stephan's *Die ersten Menschen* (*The First Humans*) had been written in 1914 and was premiered in Frankfurt in 1920; Walter Braunfels' *Die Vögel* (*The Birds*) had been begun in 1913 and was premiered in 1920, after the composer had converted to Catholicism and up-ended the moral of the plot (Kienzle 2000, 100–101). Pfitzner's *Palestrina*, first shown in Munich in 1917, became a national success after the productions in Vienna and Berlin in 1919; but the libretto had already been finished by 1911 and the whole opera in June 1914.

Palestrina may serve as an entry into the maze of German opera between the wars because, though maniacally conservative, it attempts something characteristic also of much self-professedly modern art of the time: as an answer to a confusing present and recent past, it claims to re-establish foundations, to find a new or find anew an old starting point for artistic integrity. And it is not so much ironic as logical that, in the year of *Palestrina*'s premiere, Busoni (whose *Entwurf einer neuen Ästhetik der Tonkunst* (1907) was the main target of Pfitzner's *Neue Ästhetik der musikalischen Impotenz* in 1919) brought out in Zurich both *Arlecchino* and *Turandot*, representing his radically different version of opera renewed by harking back to operatic traditions of the eighteenth century and of a playful use of dramatic and musical construction to hold the story told and the way of its telling at arm's length.

Nowhere in *Palestrina* does the attempt to re-establish foundations become more obvious than in the *Vorspiel*, reinventing step-by-step basic elements of tonal musical language. But *Palestrina* performs its ideological programme as a tightrope walk: it sings the praise of art by inspiration through re-imagining a music rigidly rule-bound; and it praises the work of art transcending all time and purpose through re-imagining a Mass, an emphatically functional genre (though in a context centred on transcendence). Pfitzner's need to philosophize in music on music – though traditional enough: see the *Meistersinger* of Pfitzner's hero, Wagner – may have betrayed an insecurity as to the state of the art counteracted in the ostentatious conservatism of *Palestrina*.

Křenek

Only a few years later, the musical reflection on music (as in *Palestrina*) and the idea of opera literally com-posed of heterogeneous elements (as envisioned by Busoni) shaped one of the most successful German operas of the 1920s: Ernst Křenek's *Jonny spielt auf* (*Johnny Strikes Up*, Leipzig 1927). Grown up in Vienna, Křenek too had come to Berlin in 1920 as a student of Schreker's. *Palestrina* extrapolates to the salvation of music itself a Wagnerian obsession with salvation stories – an obsession shared by Pfitzner's *Der arme Heinrich* (*Poor Heinrich*; Mainz, 1895) and *Die Rose vom Liebesgarten* (*The Rose from the Garden of Love*; Elberfeld, 1901), and by his later operas *Das Christelflein* (*The Little Elf of Christ*; Dresden, 1917) and *Das Herz* (*The Heart*; Berlin and Munich, 1931). *Jonny spielt auf* also shares this theme, but without the Wagnerian trappings. Instead of alleviating dissatisfaction about the way music was going by the invocation of old certainties, *Jonny* uses uncertainty: by breaking up the unity of style, by confronting shimmy, foxtrot and Stephen Foster's 'Swanee River' with allusions to eighteenth- and nineteenth-century opera and by confronting composer, virtuoso and jazz musician. But, in the end, Křenek reclaims certainty no less than Pfitzner: it is the 'vitality' of jazz violinist Jonny's musicianship that shows Max the way to America, the new cultural lodestar – in an eerie premonition of the forced emigration of so many European composers only a few years later.

In contrasting lost operatic self-sufficiency with a new musicality, *Jonny* seems to mirror Křenek's own meandering course as an opera composer. Already in *Der Sprung über den Schatten* (*The Leap over the Shadow*; Frankfurt, 1924) he had experimented with parody and popular music; but *Orpheus und Eurydike* (Kassel, 1926) harks back to the expressionist stance of the scenic cantata *Die Zwingburg* (*The Stronghold*; Berlin, 1924) and to a more unified, atonal musical language. It was followed by a set of programmatically diverse one-act works: *Der Diktator* (*The Dictator*), *Das geheime Königreich* (*The Secret Kingdom*) and *Schwergewicht, oder Die Ehre der Nation* (*Heavyweight,* or *The Pride of the Nation*; all Wiesbaden, 1928). In *Das Leben des Orest* (*The Life of Orestes*; Leipzig, 1930), Křenek again deconstructed a Greek myth; and again the music alludes to popular styles. In *Karl V.* (Prague, 1938), Křenek is back in the Catholic south, and here the search for foundations has curious consequences: to musicalize his imagination of Catholicism as a unifying force in a fractured world, he uses Schoenberg's dodecaphony, making *Karl V.* the first completed large-scale twelve-tone opera.

That Schoenberg himself had first employed dodecaphony in opera in the marital comedy *Von heute auf morgen* (*From One Day to the Next*, 1930) seems surprising less because of any inherent unsuitability of the technique to comic subjects but because the other dodecaphonic operas of the time share *Karl V.*'s striving for greatness – nowhere more so than in Schoenberg's *Moses und Aron*, also wedding dodecaphony to a desperate invocation of roots. Berg's *Lulu*, the other great dodecaphonic torso, seems more of its day with its elements of *Zeitoper*, but here too we find an ambitious, large-scale opera on a subject that, through G. W. Pabst's film adaptation of Frank Wedekind's *Die Büchse der Pandora* (1929), had been reaffirmed as a topical story of modern morals and sensibilities. That *Lulu* and *Moses* remained unfinished again says less about dodecaphony as a basis for opera than about the ravages of time which killed Berg in the midst of composing and which brought the Nazis to power, forcing Schoenberg into exile. Křenek had only marginally more luck. The premiere of *Karl V.* in Vienna in 1933 was cancelled: it was premiered in 1938 in Prague, and the composer of this grand vision of European history had to flee to America.

Schreker

The historically fluid nature of modernity is perhaps best illustrated by Schreker. His first opera *Der ferne Klang* (*The Distant Sound*; Frankfurt, 1912) was seen as heralding a new modernist alongside Strauss and Schoenberg. But the modernism meant here was soon to be refashioned into 'late romanticism', a label that stuck in music historiography, which tended to preserve 'modernism' for the later Schoenberg, for Berg, Webern, Stravinsky, Bartók, Varèse, etc. *Der ferne Klang* illustrates the operatic characteristics which fitted the tenets of literary modernity as proclaimed by the Viennese playwright and critic Herrmann Bahr in the 1890s (see Bahr 1890 and 1891). Against the social determinism of naturalism, Bahr wanted literature to focus on states of the soul, on the inner life (which a few years later exploded into expressionism). Composers of this modern persuasion turned away from *verismo* or Wagnerian mythologizing and composed dreams, hallucinations and hysteria, right alongside Sigmund Freud, who published

Studien über Hysterie (*Studies in Hysteria*) in 1895 and *Die Traumdeutung* (*The Interpretation of Dreams*) in 1899. The 'distant sound' of Schreker's opera, obsessively pursued by musician Fritz, is a metaphor for his submerged love for Grete; and Schreker employs music of immense opulence and subtlety to make sound and psyche mesh. Schreker's *Das Spielwerk* (*The Glockenspiel*; Munich, 1920), *Die Gezeichneten* (*The Stigmatized Ones*; Frankfurt, 1918), *Der Schatzgräber* (*The Treasure Seeker*; Frankfurt, 1920) and *Irrelohe* (Cologne, 1924) follow that path, mixing psychology, mysticism, medievalism (or in *Die Gezeichneten*, one of the fashionable Renaissance settings also found in Max von Schillings' *Mona Lisa* (1915), Korngold's *Violanta* (1916) and Zemlinsky's *Eine florentinische Tragödie* (1917)), magical instruments (the glockenspiel, the lute in *Der Schatzgräber*), expansive melodies, rich chromaticism and orchestral grandeur in varying proportions.

Meanwhile, war had intervened and changed the rules. The musical buzzwords were 'new objectivity', 'linearity', 'popular music', 'neo-classicism', 'young classicism' (Busoni 1920 and 1956, 34–8); the interest in psychological intensity and fine gradations of musical means was replaced by an interest in irony, parody, hard contrasts and pastiche. Within a few years, the former moderns came to represent a culture from which a younger generation wanted to distance itself, a culture associated with the world which had so willingly slithered into war. In 1928, Schoenberg wrote in a tribute to Schreker: 'Dear friend, we are from those good old times when unsympathetic people showed themselves as such through calling us "modernists". How are we to find our way in a time that calls us "romantics"?' (1928a, 82).

So the failure of Schreker's *Irrelohe* in 1924 was caused as much by its lack of a new modernity as by its abundance of an old one – by its overblown plot around sex and violence and its dense chromaticism. In subsequent operas Schreker tried in different ways, though without success, to adapt to the spirit of the times: elements of *Zeitoper* and self-reflexivity in *Christophorus, oder Die Vision einer Oper* (*St Christopher, or The Vision of an Opera*; the Freiburg premiere in 1931 was cancelled and did not take place there until 1978); counterpoint and modal harmony in *Der singende Teufel* (*The Singing Devil*; Berlin, 1928); and in *Der Schmied von Gent* (*The Blacksmith of Ghent*; Berlin, 1932) a folk opera – ironically a genre the Nazis, who quickly dismissed Schreker in 1933, would try to foster themselves soon afterwards.

Korngold

But the old modernity could still prove triumphant, as it did in Erich Wolfgang Korngold's *Die tote Stadt* (*The Dead City*; Cologne and Hamburg, 1920). Korngold, only 23 at the time, had already composed two one-act operas, *Der Ring des Polykrates* (*The Ring of Polycrates*) and *Violanta* (both Munich, 1916). He was the quintessential musical child prodigy; and as other child prodigies like Mozart or Chopin he had a flawless command of the musical language he had grown up with. So *Die tote Stadt*, yet another opera about dream-states and intense interiority, became one of the most successful works of the 1920s. Maybe a story about retrospection, mourning and the need to go on struck a chord after the war. But perhaps the reason was just Korngold's mastery of this style, hardly matched even by Schreker or Strauss: securely tonal, but richly chromatic; expressionistically intense, yet balanced by lucidity and relaxation; melodically appealing, but kaleidoscopically flexible. Yet the *Zeitgeist* prevailed. *Das Wunder der Heliane* (*The Miracle of Heliane*; Hamburg, 1927) largely failed, not least due to its hazily mystical plot. An anecdote pinpoints the situation: Korngold's father, the music critic Julius Korngold, campaigned against Křenek's *Jonny*; and a Viennese cigarette manufacturer used the fuss to market two new brands: the cheap *Jonny* and the luxurious, golden-tipped *Heliane*. Korngold's last opera *Die Kathrin* (*Catherine*; Stockholm, 1939), reflecting the operetta arrangements he had made since the early 1920s, merges opera and operetta, aiming at a popular music theatre, not unlike Schreker had with *Der Schmied von Gent*.

Yet the gap in the reception history of Schreker, Korngold or Zemlinsky between 1933 and the 1970s is more than the echo of an ageing modernism, and demonstrates the influence of history on music history, whose 'relative autonomy' (see Dahlhaus 1977, 173–204) is very relative indeed. For the Jewish composers, recognition of their work was bluntly cut off; and the gap was not bridged until a new generation became curious about the origins of Schoenbergian modernism.

The comparison with Schoenberg and Strauss puts this in perspective: Schoenberg's musical sensibilities were no less than those of Schreker or Korngold out of touch with the *Zeitgeist* of *Zeitoper* which he satirically adopted in *Von Heute auf Morgen* – the parody of a parodistic genre. But his internationally recognized role as Schoenberg the Progressive made him after 1945 a link to a past which could be defined as inherently forward-looking, telling a progress story that skipped the apparent aberration of Nazism. And Strauss, with *Salome* and *Elektra* (Dresden, 1905 and 1909) prime examples of prewar modernism, had by the 1920s become his own one-man genre, largely impervious to the developments around him.

Strauss after the First World War

After his co-directorship of the Vienna State Opera from 1919 to 1924, Strauss went freelance and continued his prewar collaboration with

Hugo von Hofmannsthal in *Die Frau ohne Schatten* (Vienna, 1919), *Die ägyptische Helena* (Dresden, 1928) and *Arabella* (Dresden, 1933). The historical refractions of *Der Rosenkavalier* (Dresden, 1911) and *Ariadne auf Naxos* (Stuttgart, 1912) have been read as foreshadowing neo-classicism; the mundane subject of *Intermezzo* (Dresden, 1924) has led to its categorization as an early *Zeitoper*. But though *Intermezzo*'s extrapolation of recitative styles into Strauss's musical language is as interesting as some quasi-filmic cuts between scenes – also found in Berg's *Wozzeck* and Zemlinsky's *Die Kreidekreis* (*The Chalk Circle*; Zurich, 1933) – the subject is not new for the composer who had dealt with his home life already in the *Sinfonia Domestica* (1903). And for all the diversity in Strauss's later operatic output, the differences are overshadowed by a music that renounces all claims to contemporaneity and draws on a rich pool of tried and tested means. Unlike those of Schreker, Zemlinsky or Korngold, Strauss's operas have remained a staple of the repertoire, giving him a role in twentieth-century operatic history that only Puccini can rival.

But though Strauss had leaned towards a (self-)classicizing attitude since *Der Rosenkavalier*, the postwar situation presented him with a context for it. He and Hofmannsthal became involved in the foundation of the Salzburg Festival. In 1919, Hofmannsthal outlined his ideas to the festival association, and he envisioned a new capital of central European culture born of Austro-Bavarian spirit, for him the root of the best in German-language theatre: 'Salzburg is the heart of the heart of Europe ... and it was here that Mozart had to be born' (Hofmannsthal 1919, 6–7). Mozart and Goethe were the pillars of his vision of a culture connecting the aristocratic and the popular, East and West, country and city, old and new; and beside their works Strauss's operas were, from 1926 onwards, central to the festival repertoire. That the imagination of this spiritual empire coincided with the political end of the Austro-Hungarian empire is hardly accidental – an Austrian echo of the German idea of itself as a *Kulturnation*, a 'cultural nation', which had consoled German patriots during the eighteenth and nineteenth centuries about the political disarray of their country.

Zeitoper and the reclamation of form

Against such dreams of continuity, *Zeitoper* positioned itself as a new dawn after the abdication of the *ancien régime*. Yet *Zeitoper* was (and is) another buzzword, implying a clearly defined phenomenon, whereas in fact it has been associated with operas as different as Weill's *Die Dreigroschenoper*, Max Brand's *Maschinist Hopkins* (*Hopkins the Factory*

Worker), Berg's *Lulu* and Schoenberg's *Von Heute auf Morgen*. Contemporary and mundane subjects, gramophones and ringing telephones on the stage and allusions to popular music are one level, and a relevant one. But to listen to these operas in comparison makes palpable that the label covers up profound differences. And the sheen of the new hides the manifold ways in which these 'operas of their time' were connected to other operas of their time and to music history.

Insecurity about what it meant to be an artist links *Jonny spielt auf* with *Palestrina*, Hindemith's *Cardillac* and *Mathis der Maler*, also with Schoenberg's *Moses und Aron*, whose religious subject can easily be translated into a discourse on artistic truth and popularity, and perhaps with the glut of Orpheus re-readings since the mid-1920s: Gian Francesco Malipiero's *L'Orfeide* (Düsseldorf, 1925), Darius Milhaud's *Les Malheurs d'Orphée* (Brussels, 1926), Křenek's *Orpheus und Eurydike* (Kassel, 1926), Weill's cantata *Der neue Orpheus* (Berlin, 1927), Alfredo Casella's *Favola di Orfeo* (Venice, 1932). But more typical were libretti about modern *mores* or with openly political intent. Of course *Jonny*'s different musical spheres mean more than music, and allegorize a broader cultural renewal. But it would overly functionalize the new rôle accorded to popular music in these operas if it were seen as a mere cipher for a socio-political project. The idea of the special power of popular music which developed at the time changed music history itself – something we feel strongly today, when to understand 'music history' as 'art-music history' seems ever more ridiculous. When the uneducated heroine of Irmgard Keun's novel *The Artificial Silk Girl* (Berlin, 1932) mocks the scheming behind the scenes of a serious theatre production she witnesses as an extra, yet describes her experiences in cheap Berlin dance-halls in hypnotically beautiful language, she illustrates a sea-change in which opera merely participated.

If the use of songs seems one of the most idiosyncratic aspects of *Zeitoper*, it also fits into a wider trend to reclaim distinct musical forms for opera. The idea that a renewal of opera would have to be achieved against Wagnerian music-drama, against the strategy of overwhelming the listener through dissolving the (theatrical) world in musical boundlessness, had been a staple of the discussion since the turn of the century. That the future might be won through harking back to older models of music theatre and the supposed autonomy of traditional musical forms was a corresponding conclusion. Not accidentally, *Die Dreigroschenoper* started as an adaptation of *The Beggar's Opera* (London, 1728); Hindemith's publishers Ludwig and Willy Strecker, too, had suggested *The Beggar's Opera* to him in 1923, before he settled on E. T. A. Hoffmann and *Cardillac*.

So on one level the song-style could be seen as only the most radical exponent of a widespread tendency in postwar opera to regain firm

Figure 9.1 Busoni's *Doktor Faust*: poster for Hans Neuenfels' production at Frankfurt Opera, 1980. Reproduced by permission of Professor Günther Kieser.

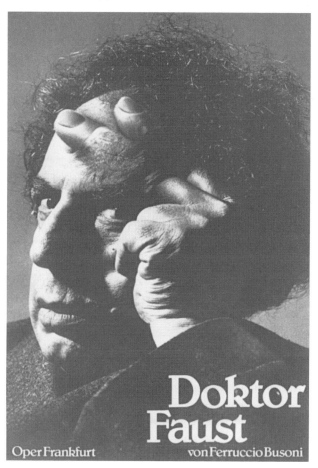

formal ground. Hindemith based *Cardillac* (Dresden, 1926) on the models of aria, concerto, passacaglia, etc.; already in *Mörder, Hoffnung der Frauen* (*Murderer, Hope of Women*; Stuttgart, 1921) and *Sancta Susanna* (Frankfurt, 1922) he had used sonata and variation as frameworks. Berg uses sonata, rondo, fugue, passacaglia, cavatina, chorale, etc. in *Wozzeck* and *Lulu*; sometimes as unrecognizable background structures, sometimes with semantic intent (the fugue in Act II scene 2 of *Wozzeck*; the film music in *Lulu*). Zemlinsky composes closed vocal numbers and dance sequences in *Der Zwerg* (*The Dwarf*; Cologne, 1922); and Busoni structures parts of his *Doktor Faust* (Dresden, 1925) after a dance-suite, scherzo, fugue, etc. To compare Weill's 'Moon of Alabama' from *Mahagonny* with the sonata movement underlying Act II scene 1 of Berg's *Wozzeck* strains the meaning of 'musical form' and cuts out the question of listening comprehensibility;

nevertheless both may be linked by a shred of common historical sensibility.

Busoni was a pivotal figure. In the *Entwurf einer neuen Ästhetik der Tonkunst* he developed his vision of anti-Wagnerian opera: not an imagined world suffused by music, but a spectacle of many means and attractions – a concept which already outlined the 'epic' quality of many postwar operas, the foregrounding of narrative technique we usually associate with Brecht. The break-up of stylistic unity allowed the clash of different musics, used in Křenek's *Jonny* as well as in Brand's *Maschinist Hopkins*, which differentiates between aspects of the plot through employing tango and jazz, Puccinian *cantabile* and neo-classical bustle. Weill in *Der Dreigroschenoper* uses, inter alia, a neo-baroque overture, music from *The Beggar's Opera* (Peachum's 'Morning Chorale'), and a musical idea by Brecht ('Pirate Jenny'), and alludes to Eduard Künneke's operetta *Der Vetter aus Dingsda* (*The Cousin from Doodah*; Berlin, 1921), Puccini's *Madama Butterfly* (Milan, 1904) and his first composition teacher Engelbert Humperdinck's *Hänsel und Gretel* (Weimar, 1893): see Hinton 1990, 33–41.

Busoni's ideal was Mozart's *Die Zauberflöte*, combining 'education, spectacle, solemnity and entertainment' (Busoni 1956, 19). It is no wonder that his student Weill could adapt to Brecht's aesthetics. Were we not used to the successes of Brecht/Weill, the blithe combination of political agitation, sharp dialogue and catchy tunes would seem an unlikely idea. But it did provide education, spectacle and entertainment (though not much solemnity) and appealed wildly. The catchiness of texts and tunes made the shocks of their spiky parodies all the more effective – dialectics at work.

Not by chance do at least three of Busoni's terms refer to an opera's relation to its audience: the idea of a new kind of musical theatre was the reaction to the weakening of opera's social moorings, of a socio-cultural role which had been damaged together with the culture that had underpinned it. 'Whither opera?' was a ubiquitous question in the German musical press of the 1920s. Weill was convinced in 1927 that 'opera has to take note of the interests of that wider public for which it ought to be written in the near future if it is to have any right to exist at all' (2000, 60). And Křenek saw *neue Sachlichkeit* (New Objectivity) defined by its capacity to affect the 'outer world', whereas the 'romantic individualism' of expressionism had 'isolated the creative artist and made him ideologically independent of success' (quoted in Grosch 2000, 135).

That Křenek with *Orpheus und Eurydike* and Weill with *Der Protagonist* (Dresden, 1926) had delivered their own expressionist calling cards throws their new attitude into sharp relief. It is more than a demotic allergy against bourgeois delusions of operatic grandeur. Given opera's need to acquire new audiences, it is intriguing to note how the socio-aesthetic maxims followed economic necessity like a shadow – a neat illustration of Marx's ideas about foundation and superstructure. The problems of opera were exacerbated by the increasing importance of new media which appealed to a far wider public. With the formation of the conglomerate UFA (Universum Film Aktiengesellschaft) in 1917, film production in Germany reached a new level of industrialization; and with the establishment of a regular radio programme in 1923 in Berlin, opera acquired a whole new channel of dissemination. Many operas took the bull by its horns: in *Jonny spielt auf* Anita's aria and Jonny's music are presented as radio transmissions. The protagonists of Ernst Toch's *Der Fächer* (*The Fan*; Königsberg, 1932) listen on the radio to music from the same composer's *Die Prinzessin auf der Erbse* (*The Princess on the Pea*; Baden-Baden, 1927). And for *Der Zar lässt sich photographieren* (*The Tsar Has his Photograph Taken*; Leipzig, 1928), Weill had the 'Tango Angèle' marketed as a record before the premiere, so that the record could be used as pre-existing music in the opera (and became a success, though after the premiere rather than before). Underscored by such techniques, the pastiche structure of the operas mirrored an increasingly multi-faceted media culture.

But born of its time, *Zeitoper* was short-lived. Brecht's, Weill's and Elisabeth Hauptmann's *Happy End* (1929) failed utterly, not least due to its agitprop finale; *Mahagonny* already deviates from the *Dreigroschenoper* mode towards a broader, more elaborately operatic structure. In *Der Jasager* (*He Who Says Yes*; Berlin, 1930), the penultimate Weill–Brecht collaboration, the stark text forbids any playfulness; and Weill is at his most grainily sober. In *Die Bürgschaft* (*The Surety*; Berlin, 1932) this new sobriety is taken up in a far more varied and relaxed manner – Weill's version of a style that could combine a new accessibility with the grand sweep of traditional opera. *Der Silbersee* (*The Silver Lake*) returns to the smaller scale of *Die Dreigroschenoper*, but not to its all-pervasive irony; after the parallel premieres in Leipzig, Madgeburg and Erfurt on 18 February 1933, the Nazis quickly banned it, and Weill fled to Paris.

Křenek's way from *Der Sprung* and *Jonny* to *Karl V.* has been mentioned; Hindemith took a similar path. He too had meandered through the fashionable styles: the parody of expressionism in *Das Nusch-Nuschi* (Stuttgart, 1921), neo-classicist strictness in *Cardillac*, prototypical *Zeitoper* in *Neues vom Tage*. His ostentatious (re)turn to roots was *Mathis der Maler* – written in 1934–5 in reaction to the new conditions set by Nazism, which cut through German and soon Austrian opera history incisively.

Opera under Nazism

Yet how incisive Nazism really was for opera is a matter of perspective. One could stress the continuities: the pillars of the repertoire were still Wagner, Verdi, Mozart, Puccini and Lortzing. Performances of French operas had been decreasing since 1918, not least in favour of Italian ones; so the ban of music from enemy nations in 1939 was less palpable than it might have been. Even the sacking of Jewish musicians was not necessarily very obvious to audiences: against 3 percent of musicians dismissed in 1933 for being Jews stood a general fluctuation of musical personnel of 25 percent (Dussel 1988, 196). On the other hand, state funding and the number of theatres and their employees drastically increased between 1933 and 1944, though mostly due to the general economic recovery after the depression (Schreiber 2000, 667). In any case, opera was not a major occupation of Nazi cultural politics, certainly not of the system's higher echelons. Goebbels poked fun at Furtwängler and Strauss for their puny audiences, compared to the millions listening to the radio or to Lehár operettas (Egk 1981, 318, 343). If a mark was overstepped, though, the reaction could be swift: when in June 1935 the Gestapo intercepted a letter from Strauss – president of the Reich Music Chamber – to Stefan Zweig, the Jewish librettist of *Die schweigsame Frau* (*The Silent Woman*; Dresden, 1935), in which he adopted the wrong tone in describing his musical politics, Goebbels sacked him immediately (Riethmüller 2003). Whether Strauss's *Friedenstag* (*Peace Day*; Munich, 1938) was meant as an anti-war statement or a celebration of endurance is not clear; in any case it was a celebration of diatonicism and final C major jubilation. Strauss's last operas *Daphne* (Dresden, 1938), *Capriccio* (Munich, 1942) and *Die Liebe der Danae* (*The Love of Danae*; Salzburg, 1944) did not add anything substantially new to his stature, though *Capriccio* interestingly revived the narrative playfulness of *Ariadne*.

But one could as easily stress the break Nazism meant. Just listing émigré opera composers makes the loss strikingly obvious: Goldschmidt, Hindemith, Korngold, Křenek, Schoenberg, Toch, Weill, Wellesz, Wolpe, Zemlinsky... Such spectacular impoverishment can be found in all fields of German culture. Historically ironic was the case of Hindemith. *Mathis der Maler* implied Hindemith's willingness to accommodate to the new conditions, musically reaching back to folksong, Gregorian chant and modal harmony. But the opera about the sixteenth-century painter torn between his artistic calling in the service of Catholic author-ity and his religious and political convictions made its conciliatory point so tortuously, and Hindemith's sins as a former young Turk were so glaringly obvious, that he stood no chance. Similarly, moderately expressionist painters such as Max Pechstein, Ernst Barlach, Karl Schmitt-Rottluff and Emil Nolde had hoped in vain during the early years of the Nazi reign that they could position their art as particularly Germanic (Willett 1970, 196–219).

But Nazi opera policies never added up to a concerted programme; different factions within the cultural apparatus pursued their own agenda (see, for example, Schubert 2003). Hindemith's failure had not least to do with a trial of strength over Furtwängler's public defence of the composer. Where *Mathis* failed, Ottmar Gerster's *Die Hexe von Passau* (*The Witch of Passau*; Düsseldorf, 1941) was a moderate success (though less so than his *Enoch Arden* (Düsseldorf, 1936), with its 500 performances): a story around a fifteenth-century peasants' revolt using a musical language not too far from Hindemith's, an example for the tempered (and folksy) modernity that was acceptable to a Third Reich that, for all its regressive traits, did not want the restoration of Second Reich culture. Rudolf Wagner-Régeny harked back to the sober tone of Weill's *Die Bürgschaft*: his *Der Günstling, oder Die letzten Tage des großen Herrn Fabiano* (*The Favourite, or The Last days of the Great Fabiano*; Dresden, 1935) was hailed as a model of clarity, and *Die Bürger von Calais* (*The Burghers of Calais*) was produced lavishly at the Berlin State Opera in 1939. Even material generally deemed degenerate could occasionally be used. Paul Klenau used dodecaphonic structures (though with tonal echoes) in *Michael Kohlhaas* (Stuttgart, 1933), though he was criticized for it. Schoenberg's student Winfried Zillig used dodecaphony in *Rosse* (*Horses*; Düsseldorf, 1933), *Das Opfer* (*The Sacrifice*; Hamburg, 1937) and *Die Windsbraut* (*The Whirlwind*; Leipzig, 1941). Werner Egk's successful *Peer Gynt* (Berlin, 1938) used song style and jazz rhythms from the 1920s – but used them to characterize the demonic world of the trolls, justifying the stylistic choice through its denunciatory purpose.

Mostly, though, conservatism reigned, thematically and musically. Staging the Nazi movement itself, common in film and drama, was frowned upon in opera; the image of NS martyr Horst Wessel 'as an opera tenor, surrounded by his SA friends singing baritone and bass' struck terror even in Nazi hearts (Schmitz 1939, 381). Instead, we find folk tales (e.g. Heinrich Strecker's *Ännchen von Tharau* (*Ann of Tharau*), Breslau, 1933), fairy tales (e.g. Egk's *Die Zaubergeige* (*The Magic Fiddle*), Frankfurt, 1935), comic operas (e.g. Edmund Nick's *Das kleine Hofkonzert* (*The Little Court Concert*), Munich, 1935; and Mark Lothar's *Schneider Wibbel* (*Tailor Wibbel*), Berlin, 1938) or classic subjects (e.g. Paul Graener's *Der Prinz von Homburg* (*The Prince of Homburg*, after Heinrich von Kleist), Berlin, 1935; and Hermann Reutter's *Doktor Johannes Faust*, Frankfurt, 1936).

Carl Orff's solution was both opportunist and original. His neo-folk, neo-medieval style served up what was wanted by the regime: roots, simplicity, physicality, communality. The scenic cantata *Carmina burana* (Frankfurt, 1937) sets medieval texts collected in a Bavarian monastery; *Der Mond* (*The Moon*; Munich, 1939) and *Die Kluge* (*The Wise Maiden*; Frankfurt, 1943) are based on fairy tales; *Agnes Bernauer* (Stuttgart, 1947) on Bavarian history. But his music was clearly an offspring of *neue Sachlichkeit*, transposed from city to country, from 'now' to 'then', avoiding the *Asphaltromantik* vilified by the Nazis but retaining some of the historical momentum of 1920s hope for a new popularity. *Carmina burana* was duly castigated by critics for being experimental and 'un-German'; but despite or because of this it became a success to rival *Die Dreigroschenoper*, its country cousin, its dark shadow.

Some of the most topical operas of the Third Reich were never part of its official music history. Karl Amadeus Hartmann wrote *Simplicius Simplicissimus* (*The Simplest Simpleton*, after Grimmelshausen's picaresque novel of the Thirty Years War) in 1934–5, using the pastiche and alienation techniques of the 1920s. He knew that it could not be performed at the time and chose to fall silent as a composer until better days; the opera was premiered in 1948. Viktor Ullmann, a student of Schoenberg's and Alois Hába's and composer of two previous operas – *Der Sturz des Antichrist* (*The Fall of the Antichrist*, 1935; premiere Bielefeld, 1995) and *Der zerbrochene Krug* (*The Broken Pitcher*, 1942; premiere Dresden, 1996) – wrote *Der Kaiser von Atlantis, oder Die Todesverweigerung* (*The Emperor of Atlantis, or The Refusal to Die*) in 1943 in the concentration camp at Terezín, where Hans Krása had written his children's opera *Brundibár* a few years before. Ullmann's work was never performed there and had to wait until 1975 for its premiere. The story about emperor Overall who declares total war and thereby appals even Death invites the obvious comparisons. The music is equally telling: encompassing allusions to Mahler, Schoenberg, Weill, cabaret songs, protestant chorale, Reichardt, Bach and Brahms, Ullmann looks back at the multi-faceted structure of *Zeitoper*, but also composes a compendium of German music, as if he refused the Nazis' attempt to take this tradition away from him.

After 1945

Music has its own geography; and in 1945 it changed irrevocably. No longer could Austria and Germany claim to be its centre. The international operatic success of the year was English, a phenomenon inconceivable before the war, particularly from a Germanocentric perspective: Benjamin Britten's *Peter Grimes* heralded an opera composer who would outshine his German and Austrian contemporaries.

Indeed, the mid-century might seem a watershed: in 1949, the German Democratic Republic (GDR) and the Federal Republic of Germany (FRG) were founded; in the same year Strauss and Pfitzner died, followed in 1950 by Weill and in 1951 by Schoenberg. In 1947, the Salzburg Festival for the first time premiered an opera by a living composer: Gottfried von Einem's *Dantons Tod* (*Danton's Death*), the first opera of the 29-year-old who had spent the Third Reich waiting for its end, studying privately with Boris Blacher. But the next Salzburg premiere, in 1949, was Orff's *Antigonae*, pointing out that the past was not done with. Orff had smartly changed tack, continuing his style, but moving away from Germanic subjects towards antiquity, an interest that had begun with *Catulli Carmina* (Leipzig, 1943). *Antigonae* was followed by *Oedipus der Tyrann* (Stuttgart, 1959), *Prometheus* (Stuttgart, 1968) and *De temporum fine comoedia* (Salzburg, 1973). Success during the Third Reich did not *per se* constitute a career impediment: Egk was performed in both East and West Germany and wrote operas until 1966; Gerster's *Die Hexe von Passau* for its peasants' revolt became a GDR favourite; Reutter made a career in the FRG. Wagner-Régeny became an influential composition teacher in the GDR, but received no opera commissions; the scenic oratorio *Prometheus* (1959) was written for Kassel and *Das Bergwerk von Falun* (*The Mine at Falun*, 1961) for the Salzburg Festival.

The past was present in other ways as well. Some of the émigrés returned, with mixed results. When Korngold's *Die Kathrin* had its Vienna premiere in 1950, audiences reacted favourably, but the critics condemned it as a dinosaur. Křenek stayed in the USA, but wrote operas for German theatres, which continued his penchant for diversity, oscillating between political engagement in *Pallas Athene weint* (*Pallas Athene Weeps*; Hamburg, 1955), which uses the fate of Socrates as a mirror image of McCarthyism, and *opera buffa* in *Sardakai* (Hamburg, 1970), taking its cue from Mozart's *Così fan tutte* – though again with political overtones. Hindemith moved to Switzerland and wrote *Die Harmonie der Welt* (*The Harmony of the World*) for the 1957 Munich Opera Festival, using Johannes Kepler's theories of planetary motion as a mirror of his own theories of musical harmony.

Particularly thorny was the rémigré situation in the GDR. Alongside Brecht, Hanns Eisler and Paul Dessau had been expelled from the USA under McCarthyism and returned to Berlin. Eisler had never composed an opera, but collaborated with Brecht on numerous plays. In 1951–2,

Eisler wrote his own libretto for a *Johann Faustus* opera. But after publication of the text, it was dragged into a heated debate about the role of intellectuals in German history, disheartening Eisler so much that he refrained from setting the text. Dessau, too, had worked with Brecht. Now he followed Roger Sessions in setting Brecht's radio play *The Trial of Lucullus*. Its anti-militarist message did not go down well with the GDR authorities; but the carefully selected public of the premiere in Berlin in March 1951 liked it nevertheless, raising the political stakes. The Central Committee of the party charged the opera with the blanket condemnation of 'formalism', curiously inappropriate with regard to the colourful, extrovert music. Brecht and Dessau reworked the opera (changing the title from *Die Verurteilung des Lukullus* to *Das Verhör des Lukullus*), and it became a staple of the GDR repertoire. It took Dessau until 1966 to write another opera, *Puntila*, again after Brecht; but three more works – *Lanzelot* (Berlin, 1969), *Einstein* (Berlin, 1974) and *Leonce und Lena* (Berlin, 1979) – developed his flamboyant musical style and an epic theatre of complex relationships between representation and comment.

The Eisler and Dessau affairs did not bode well. After Stalin's death in 1953 the problematic heritage of 'socialist realism' was widely debated when, paradoxically, GDR opera increasingly fell under the influence of Soviet models, imitated by composers such as Max Butting (*Plautus im Nonnenkloster* (*Plautus in the Nunnery*), 1959) and Ottmar Gerster (*Die fröhliche Sünder* (*The Happy Sinner*), 1963). But still, the post-Stalinist operatic scene was far from uniform. Conservative composers such as Robert Hanell polemicized against Western 'made-up modernisms' (Neef 1992, 216); but after 1960 some GDR composers made them up too: Siegfried Matthus cautiously introduced serial structures into *Lazarillo von Tormes* (*Lazarillo of Tormes*; Karl-Marx-Stadt/Chemnitz, 1964) and more openly into *Der letzte Schuss* (*The Last Shot*; Berlin, 1967); Udo Zimmermann in *Die weiße Rose* (*The White Rose*; Dresden, 1967, revised version Hamburg, 1986) and Rainer Kunad in *Old Fritz* (Radebeul, 1965) used serial structures as well. The conflict between an international orientation and the insistence upon disassociation, especially from the estranged big-brother FRG, was to run through GDR operatic history. Whether much of that history can be retrieved after the re-unification – and cultural re-colonization – of the GDR in 1990 is, sadly, doubtful.

After Nazism had brutally interrupted the 'normal' course of (music) history, West German and Austrian composers in 1945 had the chance to re-connect with the avant-garde of the 1920s – that, at least, is the authorized version. But the tale has its holes, even beside the continued work of composers who were not much interested in taking up pre-war progress. In the spectrum of New Music, opera was positioned awkwardly: bound to big institutions with their own inertia and with more conservative audiences than other modes of music. And the rediscovery of prewar avant-gardes was selective: after Nazism's exercises in artistic communality (re-staged in the GDR), Weill's vision of opera for 'that wider public' appealed less than Schoenberg's insistence on the artist as avant-gardist. German critics were shocked by Weill's Broadway career and preferred 'the old, real Weill, smelling of Russia leather and tobacco' (Fiechtner 1961, 217). Adorno (1950) even denied that the Broadway Weill could be called a composer. But the threat that was rhetorically warded off in such statements came anyway: the influx of swing, jazz, then rock'n'roll from America was the most influential development in European postwar music; but one that, other than in the 1920s, hardly affected opera anymore.

The intensification of the prewar trend towards *Literaturoper* assured opera of a cultural worthiness which could be taken for granted even less than after 1918. So Orff sets Sophocles' *Antigonae* and *Oedipus* in Hölderlin's translations and Aeschylus' *Prometheus* in Greek; Egk uses Kleist's *Die Verlobung in San Domingo* (*The Engagement in San Domingo*; Munich, 1963); Boris Blacher sets *Romeo and Juliet* (Berlin, 1947); von Einem sets Büchner's *Dantons Tod*, Friedrich Dürrenmatt's *Der Besuch der alten Dame* (*The Visit of the Old Lady*; Vienna, 1971) and has Heinz von Cremer adapt Kafka's *Der Prozess* (*The Trial*; Salzburg, 1953); Giselher Klebe uses Schiller in *Die Räuber* (*The Robbers*; Düsseldorf, 1957) and Shakespeare in *Die Ermordung Cäsars* (*The Murder of Caesar*; Essen, 1959); Zillig composes *Troilus und Cressida* (Düsseldorf, 1951); Wolfgang Fortner develops into a Lorca specialist with *Die Bluthochzeit* (*Blood Wedding*; Cologne, 1957) and *In seinem Garten liebt Don Perlimplin Belisa* (*Don Perlimplin's Love of Belisa in his Garden*; Schwetzingen, 1962); Hans Werner Henze adapts Cervantes for *Das Wundertheater* (*The Magic Theatre*; Heidelberg, 1949), Prévost's *Manon Lescaut* for *Boulevard Solitude* (Hanover, 1952), Kafka for *Ein Landarzt* (*A Country Doctor*; Hamburg, 1951), Carlo Gozzi for *König Hirsch* (*King Stag*; Berlin, 1956), Kleist for *Der Prinz von Homburg* (*The Prince of Homburg*; Hamburg, 1960), and so on.

Perhaps the proven credentials of the texts were the permission charge for musical experiments; disoriented audiences could fall back upon a secure literary base. If GDR composers had to deal with official restrictions, their Western counterparts were spoilt for choice. The range of musical options is hard to summarize, encompassing atonality, dodecaphony, different tonal idioms, pastiche and parody, later electronic music and *musique concrète*. They are perhaps best encapsulated by the figure of Boris Blacher, teacher of Klebe, von Einem and Aribert Reimann.

He, too, used serial techniques and, from the mid-1960s onwards, electronics; but his ballet opera *Preussisches Märchen* (*Prussian Fairy Tale*; Berlin, 1952) is a virtuosic pastiche of songs, marches, waltzes, polkas etc., while the *Abstrakte Oper Nr. 1* (*Abstract Opera No. 1*, 1953) builds on the nonsense syllables and isolated phrases of Egk's libretto soundscapes of 'pure' emotions – abstract expressionism in music.

But the representative German opera composer after 1945 is Henze, for better or worse. He begins playful, satirical, sarcastic in *Das Wundertheater* (satirizing racism and nationalism), *Boulevard Solitude* and the radio operas *Ein Landarzt* and *Das Ende einer Welt* (*The End of a World*, 1953) using everything from eighteenth-century parodies to Bergian atonality and dodecaphony, cabaret songs and big-band jazz. In 1953, he flees the busy Germany of the economic miracle and the gathering serialist orthodoxy as represented by Boulez, Stockhausen and Nono and settles in Italy, re-inventing himself as an Italian composer, drawing on folk music as well as on Italian opera tradition. The controversial *König Hirsch* (1956) seemed to aim at a renewed grand opera, using every means at hand for a glittering musical tapestry – and effectively shutting Henze out from the inner avant-garde circles. Henze continued on his colourful way in *Der Prinz von Homburg*, *Elegie für junge Liebende* (*Elegy for Young Lovers*; Schwetzingen, 1961), *Der junge Lord* (*The Young Lord*; Berlin, 1965) and *Die Bassariden* (*The Bassarids*; Salzburg, 1966), by and by – and rather like Strauss – becoming his own classic; the *Elegy* is even dedicated to the memory of Hofmannsthal. But in step with West German society, in the late 1960s and 1970s Henze again re-invented himself, now as a left-wing political composer in works such as *El Cimarrón* (1970), *La Cubana* (1973) and *We Come to the River* (London, 1976).

10 Eastern Europe

RACHEL BECKLES WILLSON

Once upon an ancient time . . .
A story introduced in rhyme . . .
The tale is old, the moral new,
Even the players could be you
Yourselves, Ladies and Gentlemen.

You're watching me, I'm watching you,
But which is which and who is who?
Consider, safely in your beds
Is the theatre here, or in your heads
Ladies and Gentlemen?

Here there is a generous ration:
Crimes of violence and passion –
In wars outside the blood runs redly:
Here is something far more deadly,
Ladies and Gentlemen.

The prologue to *Duke Bluebeard's Castle* (John 1991, 46) invites the audience to use the opera as a mirror for itself, to observe connections between spectator and spectated and also to look beyond the surface of the bloodied castle for its meanings. We do well to think similarly when considering 'Eastern Europe', which unlike other 'Topographies' in this volume, was not a politically unified entity before the Soviet Union occupied it in 1949. The region's agglomeration of nations has nonetheless been characterized as a whole in various ways, regarded frequently as an aspiration, but equally often as a problem (see, for example, the editors' preface to *Central Europe*, 1/1 (May 2003), 3). It has been viewed as a 'Kingdom of the Spirit' (Garton Ash 1989, 161–91), a region of people sharing 'thought-styles and thought-worlds' (Schöpflin 2004) or just a myth constructed by Western Europe (Wolff 1994). Eastern Europe's citizens themselves have had far from straightforward relations with their so-called homeland – many emigrated beyond its apparent provinciality or lived in deeply nostalgic, enforced exile. And at times, people have been placed there by sheer brute force.

What follows will, despite these cautionary remarks, identify some common elements in the region's operas, focusing on the countries where an operatic tradition in the nineteenth century led to the richest fruits in the twentieth: Czechoslovakia, Hungary and Poland. (In Yugoslavia, Bulgaria, Albania, Macedonia and Greece operatic institutions developed more recently, and no operas from these countries have been successful internationally; for an excellent overview of the varying contexts for music in the region, see Beckerman and Samson 1993.) In the first half of the century operas are predominantly serious in spirit and a large number are set in villages. Most are shaped by the ambition to explore the question of human destiny, several of them do so through tragic plots that unfold with an irreversible teleology. Many libretti are specific to national pasts or presents and music regularly draws on, even if it does not actually quote, indigenous folk music. Others, where composers were concerned to forge closer links with European traditions, are shaped by ancient Greek myth. For related reasons, most operas have absorbed some elements from French nineteenth-century grand opera, Strauss or Wagner.

Yet if these tendencies shape a large number of operas, then there are many exceptions which deserve to be taken on their own terms, rather than seen as anomalies. With the benefit of hindsight, these operas turn out to be ahead of their time, carrying the most premonitions of the latter part of the century in their probing of tragedy and temporality. Some are written by exiles, which this chapter includes without claiming that they 'belong' to Eastern Europe, but rather in the interest of exploring what links they retain. Others are written by 'insiders'. Viewing Eastern Europe is indeed like viewing Bluebeard's Castle. Let us open its doors.

Door One: Czechoslovakia (I)

Whereas a strong sense of Czech tradition was continued in the operas of Ostrčil, Novák and Foerster in the first part of the twentieth century, Janáček moved beyond this romantic style (see Tyrrell 1988 and 1992). His *Jenůfa* (1894, c. 1901–08), which Chew (2003) situates in the context of Czech Decadent and Naturalist drama of the turn of the century, retained strong links with the past yet transcended local reference in both the depth of its subject matter and its musical treatment. Although the opera is framed by Moravian folk dances, guaranteeing a sense of realist 'rural tragedy', and follows the prose writing of Gabriella Preissová in a naturalistic 'speech melody', the final act in particular pushes beyond the local characterization with profound questions of human morals and motivation.

Tragedy unfolds in the first three acts, by the end of which Jenůfa has lost her beauty (disfigured by a rejected suitor), her preferred partner (no longer captivated by her looks), her purity (she is pregnant by him) and her baby (secretly murdered by her stepmother). As Jenůfa's personality develops, however, she becomes reconciled to the lover who had slashed her face and – in the heart-rending climax of the opera – even comes to understand and forgive her stepmother when she confesses to the murder of her child. The interweaving musical threads of 'locality' (such as an ostinato representing the turning of a mill wheel, folk-type dances and songs), human passions and fate (dialogues, passionately lyrical monologues and powerful orchestral interludes) are bound with an extended tonality that uses dissonance as a poignant and ominous undercurrent. The strength of Jenůfa's character, which breaks the interweaving cycles of retribution, is mirrored in the final resolution to a more settled tonality and texture.

Janáček revisited personal tragedy in *Kát'a Kabanová* (1921), which is also framed by its rural setting. Kát'a is unhappily married into a family which bullies her, while she is attracted to someone else (Boris); her husband's temporary absence allows her to become intimate with Boris and struggle violently with her conscience thereafter. Her consequent 'confession' echoes that of Jenůfa's stepmother, but does not resolve her situation at all. Feeling guilty at having brought Boris into disrepute and doomed, herself, to an interminable domestic imprisonment, she leaps into the Volga; her husband releases his grief by hurling the blame on his mother. The opera is thus a more pessimistic portrayal of humanity than *Jenůfa*, setting the forces of society's pressures and their restrictions into sharper relief. Unlike Jenůfa, Kát'a does not transcend her miserable surroundings. Janáček's musical vision, however, is all the more powerful once released from the 'up-front' Moravian folk dances. The music sets up the apparent inevitability of the tragedy from the start in portentous timpani beats, ostinati and Kát'a's passionate pleas (she fears her own transgression) that her husband not travel away. Her confession, taking place during a tumultuous rainstorm, is the musical response, the balancing frame, to that anxiety; and the wordless choir haunting her from then until her death is a tugging thread that draws her beyond the village in which we see her.

Door Two: Hungary (I)

Bartók and Kodály each made a clear break from Hungary's nineteenth-century grand opera, but in very different ways. Kodály wrote a number of nationalist Singspiels, each setting a string of (newly discovered) Hungarian folksongs and dances, and each based on a national theme: *The Transylvanian Spinning Room* (1924–32), *Háry János* (1926, revised

1937–8 and 1948–52) and *Czinka Panna* (1946–8). Contrarily, Bartók's early opera *Duke Bluebeard's Castle* (1911) plunges into the inner life of humanity. A symbolic dialogue, rather than dramatic action, shapes the work, the tension between newly wed Judith and her husband Bluebeard manifested in their discussion of seven doors within his Castle. Each time Judit persuades Bluebeard to let her open a door, a highly colourful musical tableau evokes the scene behind it. Stage realizations tend not to reveal these scenes (which range from a torture chamber to a lake of tears) because they are intended to represent Bluebeard's character, rather than his physical castle. Suggestive lighting changes allow their symbolic nature to remain intact, through which the music provides a sense of progression, leading from dark pentatonic hues, to bright tonal ones and back to the pentatonic when Judit herself is enclosed behind the seventh door.

This dialectic between darkness and light is interwoven with that of closure, control and rationality (Bluebeard's speech-like utterances, his pulling Judit back into pentatonicism at the end of the opera) against openness and emotion (Judit's wide-ranging and ornamental vocalizations). Judit attempts to open Bluebeard out, but destroys herself entirely in the process: understood thus, 'man' is by definition lonely, and 'woman' is too curious to respect or withstand the necessary – if tragic – loneliness of his position. Yet if the opera is indeed such a projection of a 'male' centre, repeatedly penetrated by a 'female' inquisitor, then the male centre nonetheless colludes in her presence, even invites her in. The 'male' longs for 'female'; or rather, the 'rational framework' longs for 'irrational, unconscious invigoration', while also perceiving it as something needing to be repressed, crushed into a monolithic framework. In this sense *Bluebeard* offers a metaphor for Bartók's intoxication with peasant music, coupled with his need to make it palatable for the city. At the time he wrote the opera his interest in folk music was primarily creative and idea-forming rather than nationalistic: in 1910 he expressed in a letter to Delius his enthusiasm for the 'vivid reality' of Romanian music, and mentioned that his interest in folk music was not 'the thirst for scientific knowledge' (Demény 1971, 106). At the same time he was anxious about the reception of his work, which was already indicted by some as expressing 'frenzy' and 'insanity' (97). *Duke Bluebeard's Castle* is a pessimistic commentary on the possibility of such synthesis.

Door Three: Poland (I)

Like *Bluebeard*, and although written shortly after Poland gained autonomy, Szymanowski's *King Roger* (1918–24) makes no statement regarding national history or identity. Neither does it resource nineteenth-century Polish models, nor quote folk music. Rather its concern is with universal questions of human nature and it is often read as a quasi-autobiographical reflection on personal development: Stephen Downes suggests that it 'dramatises Szymanovski's struggle with the nature of his personality and his art' (1995, 258). Comparison with the Hungarian work is rewarding because there is a basic similarity: the central character, functioning within an established framework, finds a way to come to terms with irrational forces. *King Roger* is based on a loose reworking of Euripides' *Bacchae* by poet Jaroslaw Iwaszkiewicz and Szymanowski himself.

The framework here is the Orthodox Church, powerfully evoked by the opera's opening with hymn singing and, frequently, a Byzantine Chapel scene on stage. King Roger is informed by the Archbishop that a shepherd is leading people astray by preaching a new faith; when the shepherd enters (with his music of free lyricism) we learn that his 'faith' is the pursuit of ecstatic Dionysian joy. The tension between the poles of rationalized religious authority and the dark, elemental energies of eroticism are played out on several levels in the opera. In part, they are seen as externalizations of the King's own personal conflicts: here the link with *Bluebeard* is manifest. King Roger fares better: unlike Bluebeard he does not ultimately rejoin the medieval scholasticism of the church and thus return to the state where he was before encountering the irrational. Nor does he simply turn away from the rational side of his existence and pursue an unfettered life of indulgence. Although the end is somewhat ambiguous, there is no doubt that he is fundamentally altered: the harmony at the close synthesizes the diatonic (representing the church) with the (disruptive) whole-tone collection. Where Bluebeard remained in darkness, King Roger found a capacity to choose his own path between orthodoxies.

Door Four: Romania

Enescu's *Oedipe* (1910–22, orchestrated 1931–2) was written while its composer divided his time between Romania and Paris. Edmund Fleg's libretto comprises a reworking of Sophocles' *Oedipus Tyrannus* and *Oedipus at Colonnus*, preceded by two acts drawn from legend but not hitherto available as drama. Changes made to Sophocles are significant, especially the riddle of the Sphinx. Rather than asking Oedipus 'what goes on four legs in the morning, two legs in the day and three legs in the evening?', she asks whether there is any force which can withstand destiny. The answer is the same for each, and Oedipus' correct response,

'Man', paves the way for the rewriting of the tragedy. Although Oedipus does kill his father unwittingly and does blind himself, he recovers his sight and dies in a pastoral grove amid a blaze of light, while the Eumenides chant: 'Happy is he who is pure in soul: peace be with him'. The tragedy is redeemed by a Judeo-Christian note of hope.

Enescu shaped the tragic impulse of the early acts with motives associated with 'fate' and 'parricide', and used orchestral effects to magnificent dramatic consequence. The music of the Sphinx, with extraordinary timbres from ordinary instruments as well as celeste and harmonium, builds up towards her 'death shriek', which is extended by a musical saw. While drawing on the Romanian *doina* for the leitmotiv of the Shepherd's flute, Enescu refrained from exoticizing the origins of his libretto: he 'decided to remain ignorant' of Greek music (Malcolm 1990, 150). His experimental vocal techniques are notable, however, all of which are put to dramatic effect. Oedipus resorts to a quasi-*Sprechgesang* when standing blind before his people, for instance; in other areas quarter-tones – deliberately 'out of tune' singing – emerge as if as a consequence of fear or horror. In that the entire span of Oedipus' life is presented, and that he passes from great hopes through horrendous disaster to final rest, the opera represents an archetype for human life in general. Enescu projected something akin to Szymanowski: the ability of humankind to transcend, or at least modify, the mythology according to which it lives.

Door Five: Czechoslovakia (II)

Whilst the operas of Enescu, Bartók and Szymanowski share some elements with *Jenůfa* and *Kát'a Kabanová*, Janáček's comical *The Excursions of Mr Brouček* (1923) is rather different. It includes a journey to the moon, as well as faintly absurd reflections on the aesthetics of artistic creation: its closest relatives probably lie in the work of the composer's compatriot Martinů. Comparison with the more light-hearted music of Martinů is nonetheless more revealing of the composers' differences, rather than their similarities. A 36-year gap in their ages was probably contributory, but their operas also bespeak vastly different places of composition. Whereas the libretto of *The Excursions* is closely related to Prague and fifteenth-century Czech history, Martinů's three comedies of the 1920s are influenced by the arts in Paris at the time. (The cultural exchange between the two countries is mapped, in relation to Martinů's *Les trois souhaits ou Les vicissitudes de la vie* (1928–9) in Chew 2000.) Their music maintains a distance from its subject matter: set against Janáček's powerfully expressive tone they are determinedly cool, evading overt subjectivity. They are also highly eclectic, drawing on operetta, French jazz and surrealism, and as such, they might seem overly derivative or even slightly *passé* to some.

Viewed from the perspective of European operatic development, however, they emerge in a very different light. Martinů's collaborations with the poet Georges Ribemont-Dessaignes led him to create what is probably the first Dadaist opera: *The Tears of the Knife* (1928). This represents a 20-minute destruction of the medium's most basic qualities. Operatic singing style may be forced into a tempo in which it sounds ludicrous rather than powerful or anguished; such moments are juxtaposed with tango, foxtrot and Charleston; and scenes change as if they were film clips (see Pečman 1967, 127–58). The 'plot' is an anti-plot and the frequent appearances of Satan's head – popping out from other heads as they split open – alert us to the source of the forces of destruction. Any potentially dramatic event collapses into a grotesque situation. The heroine is in love with the body of a hanged man; she stabs herself to death; the hanged man comes to life; a pair of legs (only) begins to dance; it then juggles with a smiling head. The parody of contemporary idioms is comparable with Stravinsky's *Oedipus Rex* and Honegger's *Antigone*, but the parody is here more destructive. Thus, for instance, within the orchestration of four woodwind, four brass, three strings, piano, banjo, accordion and tom-tom, the instruments associated with jazz (saxophone, banjo and tom-tom) are almost always silent in the jazz-like sections. The work actually consisted of its own obliteration, in that it was completely unstageable: only through film and stage technology beyond the capabilities of the 1920s could this extraordinary and path-breaking spectacle be realized.

Whilst aiming for something far less radical, Janáček's final three operas are nonetheless also highly individual. If myth functioned in several works discussed above as a means to come to terms with the limitations of human capabilities during their lives, then here a related question is posed rather more explicitly: how can humanity come to terms with its own death? *The Cunning Little Vixen* (1922–3) and *From the House of the Dead* (1927–8) are set in diametrically opposed contexts: one in a scene of vital pastoral renewal, the other in a Siberian prison camp where death is an everyday event. *The Makropulos Affair* (1925), lying between them, is set in early twentieth-century Prague, where the heroine's interminable life provides not only the solution to a legal case, but also a reminder of death's function within life.

The focus of Rudolf Těsnohlídek's novel on which Janáček based his libretto for *The Cunning Little Vixen* is a vixen's escape from human captivity, and her rearing of a family thereafter. The vixen is Janáček's central character, forming the focus for his characteristic explorations of women and their trapped domestic situations; although she is eventually shot by a poacher, the opera proffers solace in the natural cycle of the seasons and by the large family of cubs she has had. This positive message can be traced throughout the music, whether in the various dances of animals (grasshoppers perform a waltz, for instance) or in the use of an off-stage choir that invokes not death (as in *Kát'a Kabanová*) but rather the natural life of the forest. This idealized forest dominates the opera, which is something of a tribute to nature's diversity and fantastical capacity for creation. The use of children's voices for animals also lightens the tone of the score; and ballet and mime add a delicate humour.

In contrast, Dostoyevsky's novel drawn upon for *House of the Dead* has no central role, and no significant female characters. Relegated to equal servitude and suffering, individuals emerge at intervals from the chorus and then sink back into it. They are distinguished from one another only by their pasts, established mainly in three lengthy monologues describing their brutal crimes. Harmonic writing is harshly dissonant; the opera does contain moments of warmth and hope, but closes with a return to the unremitting hard labour of the camp (see Wingfield 1999, 56–78).

Nonetheless, this ending, in which individual death has been subsumed into a larger flow, invites comparison with *The Cunning Little Vixen*. Moreover, musical textures and structures in the two operas are unified similarly: each is sustained by an orchestral continuity that allows vocal parts freedom to explore the naturalistic speech-melody that Janáček had been developing since *Jenůfa*. Finally, the two operas are linked by their analogously complex exploration of captivity, which renders them distinct from Janáček's other operas. Apparently more strictly bound than the vixen, the prisoners in *House of the Dead* cannot escape. But they themselves have a captive: an eagle which they torture, while admiring its defiance and regarding it as a symbol of freedom. It is their 'vixen'.

The vixen and eagle are linked, symbolically and through allusion, to human roles and aspirations. In *The Cunning Little Vixen* the animal and human spheres are linked in fantasy: the vixen dreams of being a girl, while the forester is lonely without her; at the same time the schoolmaster and priest pine for earlier loves (who, we infer, 'escaped'). In *House of the Dead*, the fate of the eagle is made to entwine with that of the prisoners: when a prisoner is released, the remaining prisoners release the eagle, which soars above them to the accompaniment of the musical theme associated with freedom earlier on. Just as these separate realms are suggestively linked, the past protrudes into the present in each opera. Even when the vixen is dead, her children taunt the forester. And in *House of the Dead*, prisoners' tales of being flogged in the past are related almost synchronically with actual floggings; and a character from someone's past turns out to be present in the camp – unrecognized until he has died.

The notion of the past in the present, and the mysterious passage of time, is central to *The Makropulos Affair*. Janáček's characteristic ostinato technique finds particular resonance here: sustained, yet constructed through the repetition of very short melodic cells, it evokes the paradoxical temporalities of the opera plot. In the opening scene a lawyer wakes up with a start ('is that the time?') and, while rushing about to a 'ticking' ostinato, ruminates on the family inheritance dispute that has run on through generations for over a hundred years. The fragmentary melodic style, with sudden harmonic lurches and pulsating orchestral interruptions, sets the tone of hasty preparation. Yet into this chaos steps the heroine, who has lived for 327 years so far. Her lengthy life has brought misery to several of the opera's characters, past and present. Some fell in love with her beauty, some with her voice, but none found their warmth reciprocated, and none found happiness in their admiration. Her name becomes associated with a rising and falling musical theme of longing. Yet we learn gradually that unless she can obtain another dose of the magic elixir, she faces death. Her own melodies come to express the musical longing associated with her name; and the other characters, instead of admiring or coveting her, come to pity her. The final resolution – her death – brings her relief, for she has come to realize that without the measure of death, life can find no system of values: it has no point.

Janáček had moved a long way from overtly national expression by this stage, while Martinů, still living in Paris, dedicated himself to it afresh when he returned to opera (after a considerable gap) in 1933. *The Plays of Mary* (1933–4) combined miracle plays with medieval drama; and his radio opera, *The Voice of the Forest* (1935), quoted folk song in an ambition to fashion a folk theatre for the time. *The Comedy on the Bridge* (1935), also a radio opera, treats instruments, gestures and rhetorical figures with remarkable witticism: recitative is parodied, solemn 'highly confidential' choral sections are satirized and the absurd plot is bound together with marches reminiscent of – and sometimes quoting – the Rákóczi March, the Hungarian national march in nineteenth-century Austro-Hungary. This provides the listener with a reference to Central Europe, even if the opera is a distant mockery of the Dionysian passions explored elsewhere in the region.

Martinů's best-known opera, *Julietta* (1936–7), touches more penetratingly on the more mysterious aspects of destiny than elsewhere in his work. In *Julietta* the border between fantasy and reality is treated with considerable nuance, even though it is still indebted to his less subtle earlier influences: the disruption to expectations of narrative and our understanding of the flow of time are distinctly surreal. Michel arrives in a town where he has been before, in search of a woman he once loved. Nobody in the town has any memory at all, however; they do not even remember what they just said. The situation renders not only his search fruitless, but also his (and our) ability to discern dream from reality, fantasy from truth. 'Truth' lost, the whole opera becomes a projection of human longing, whether for 'Julietta', 'reality' or 'truth'. Even the characters cease to be protagonists in action, because their actions are entirely inconsequential – forgotten the instant they are committed. Michel is merely the embodiment of longing, a vehicle for the composer to appraise rational, irrational and emotional values through him (see Pečman 1967, 160–82). If it is typical of Martinů's light touch, his rhythmic prodigality and folk-like extended tonality, it is nonetheless more unsettling than much of his work. Variously communicating through lyrical lines, recitative and spoken words, the characters become bizarre, their very vacillation between half-sung and half-spoken statements embodying the borderline of their plausibility (Macek 1993, 120–25).

Martinů fled to Provence in 1940 and to New York in 1941. Shortly afterwards, the Nazi camp at Terezin saw the composition of Viktor Ullmann's *Der Kaiser von Atlantis*. The work is composed into the German tradition in which Ullmann, a pupil of Schoenberg's born in Teschen, was trained, but in using the tritone 'death' theme from Suk's 'Asrael' Symphony throughout also provides specifically Czech references. It is a transparent parody of the regime which would exterminate both him and Ullmann within a few months. The librettist, the poet Peter Kien, nonetheless conjured up an opponent more powerful than the 'Emperor' of his tale, namely the character of 'Death'. 'Death' refuses to cooperate with the despotic Emperor and thus obstructs his plans to eradicate his subjects. The problem recalls the question raised by Enescu's Sphinx and destiny's eventual overturning by the faith of Oedipus: Ullmann's and Kien's message is defiant.

Opera took a new direction in Czechoslovakia with the performance in 1949 of Eugene Suchoň's *The Whirlpool* (1941–8). The libretto's probing of love, murder, pregnancy and guilt in a rural situation recalls Janáček, as does the use of short melodic and rhythmic figures combined with ostinato. The atmospheric and psychological dimension of the work might have alienated it from the newly implemented Communist regime, and its expressionistic music is often dissonant. The realism of the tale, however, coupled with the regime's desire for highly visual and articulate moralizing artworks, secured it significant support. The chorus is used as a formal and moral framing device; the anti-hero's sense of guilt overwhelms him, for example, in a scene when he hears the chorus (symbolic of the idealized 'village community') in the distance. A socialist interpretation of his decision to face up to his wrong-doing and perform self-criticism would not have been difficult to construct, and *The Whirlpool* enjoyed widespread success in the Soviet Republics. Suchoň was to be outstripped by Ján Cikker in quantity of operas produced: the latter's *Resurrection* (1962) continues the line of themes of childbirth, murder and betrayal, adding to the tendency towards psychological exploration with monologue interludes in which characters reflect privately on their situations.

Martinů did not return to Czechoslovakia, although he remained in close contact with the country and considered relocating there many times in his last, unsettled years living variously in the US, France and Italy. Written during this period, his last opera was originally intended to be on a Czech theme, but eventually set a compacted version of Kazantzakis' novel *The Greek Passion* (original version (discussed here) 1954–7; revised 'Zurich' version, 1957–9). The rural village setting involves many elements from operas discussed above; the villagers' preparation for their annual Passion play draws into that context the use of myth in shaping human development and destiny. The village is put to a test when a starving group arrives looking for protection, having been banished from their own village by Turks. The villagers' responses take on rôles of Christian mythology linked increasingly obviously with their designated rôles in the passion. Most (including a priest) turn them away; a woman (Mary Magdalene) shows kindness and compassion; and a shepherd (Jesus) insists – at the cost of his life at the hand of a villager (Judas) – that the village welcome the strangers into their fold. The individuality of their characters is expanded into the larger fabric by their characterization through families of instruments: wind for the priest, strings for 'Jesus', for instance. The two choruses – villagers and refugees – have prominent dramaturgical roles too, so that the tension between societies and individuals is played out with some complexity.

The Greek Passion is Martinů's most 'realist' opera and his shaping of music through dialogue brings him as close as he ever came to Janáček. His libretto (in English) contributed to the intonation of speech-like sections which move the action forward very rapidly; he also drew on quasi-liturgical intonation for the priests. Rapid shifts from everyday to liturgical reflect the tension characterizing the whole opera. As Martinů expressed it in a letter to the Guggenheim Foundation written in 1956, 'the two themes are like thin trickles of blood: the heritage of man's Christian virtues and his obligations to humanity' (reproduced in the Royal Opera House Covent Garden's programme book (2000), 13).

Relations between the two themes gape wide with irony. The moral framework of the Orthodox Church is presented as too rigid to offer compassion to the refugees in their sick, needy, earthly reality. Meanwhile 'Jesus' also renounces aspects of life on earth, abandoning petty thieving and sexual gratification to aspire to spiritual purity. There is a bleakness here in stark contrast to Janáček's welcome of the passing seasons in *The Cunning Little Vixen*. The village, celebrating Christmas some months later, has apparently forgotten their spring murder, which renders their real tragedy useless on a spiritual level.

Door Six: Poland (II)

Socialist realist tragedy set the heroic individual against the oppression of society, a tendency which Witold Rudziński's *Janko the Musician* (1953) demonstrates particularly clearly. On the other hand, Tadeusz Baird's *Tomorrow* (1964–6), based on Joseph Conrad's short story, harks back to the rural operatic tragedies of the region, while moving beyond them in musical dramaturgy. The opera is set in a remote fishing village and based on human longing: an ageing father longs for his son to return home; the son returns and another ageing father longs for him to wed his own daughter; the daughter falls in love with the son. The music's investigation of Mahlerian and Bergian harmony was a departure for Polish opera, as was the use of the chamber orchestra as a vehicle for the human subconscious, in which emotions such as joy, anger and frustration are represented by certain musical motives. Characters' actions are delineated by instrumental groups, but the most striking dramatic effect is that the son never sings, but only speaks. He destroys all hopes of happiness on the parts of the other characters, raping, robbing and abandoning the girl.

The operas of Penderecki take a more critical stance of the society around themselves and, as if attempting to drive the messages home as firmly as possible, they maximize the exposure of violence, torture and exorcism, frequently within a libretto rich in scatological reference. In *The Devils of Loudon* (1966–8), based on John Whiting's dramatization of Huxley, the battle of the individual against society's pressures underlies the plot: a priest has opposed the King's strategy for obliterating resistance to royal supremacy. Simultaneously, he is the target of the sexual fantasies of a convent of nuns. Innocent of the charges of debauchery against him, he refuses to 'confess' even under torture of leg-breaking and fingernail-pulling. The sexual and religious obsession of the society around him condemns him to the stake, an event anticipated in the dream of the convent's Prioress at the opening of the opera which sets up the dramaturgical tension.

Penderecki's characteristic instrumental effects such as tone clusters, glissandi and woodwind 'clucking' are further enhanced by contributions from electric guitar and taped bell sounds; their unpleasantness ensures that the priest's calm resistance is set into maximal relief. In the meantime the church is represented by monotone chanting. All four of Penderecki's operas communicate directly rather than subtly: the use of quotation from other music serves to make specific points rather than blend into a seamless dramatic whole. *Paradise Lost* (1975–8), *The Black Mask* (1984–6) and *Ubu Rex* (1990–91) continue to explore humanitarian concerns, the last two with a more specific focus on Poland (see Schwinger 1989).

Door Seven: Hungary (II)

Communist Hungary's two most successful operas were realist tragedies: Emil Petrovics's *C'est la guerre* (1961) and Sándor Szokolay's expressionist *Blood Wedding* (1964). Whereas the latter concentrated on tragedy in human relations, once again in a rural setting, *C'est la guerre* explored the unhappiness of Hungary's Nazi participation in the Second World War. It cast the misery as an indomitable condition in which human love struggled in vain to survive. Tacitly avoiding the fact (transparent in 1961) that Hungary's 'liberation' from fascism had brought a further regime of oppression, it participated in, rather than opposed, the official climate of denial in which it was written (see Beckles Willson 2003). (Penderecki's *The Devils of Loudon* is a pointed contrast.) Zsolt Durkó's *Mózes* (1977) returned Hungarian opera to the more mythical passion-type narrative of nineteenth-century grand opera, whilst Péter Eötvös's chamber opera *Radames* (1975) demonstrated the composer's close contact with progressive currents in Germany where he studied and worked – while in close contact with music in Budapest – from 1966.

Ligeti's *Le Grand Macabre* (1974–7), on the other hand, while a response and contribution to music in Europe, marked the beginning of a rapprochement with the composer's earlier influences from Hungary. Along with 'deep-frozen' musical ideas from the past (Ligeti 1983, x), the theme of despotic destruction is an obvious sign, although its exploration of human fate is different from operas discussed so far. Only *The Emperor of Atlantis* set up a tragic situation and then stuck a spanner in its works in a way that might be compared with *Le Grand Macabre*. In Ligeti's opera, disaster is announced blatantly at the opening: no mere individual crisis is predicted, rather, the end of the world is to occur at the stroke of

Figure 10.1 Ligeti's *Le Grand Macabre*, directed by Peter Sellars with set designs by George Tsypin (Salzburg Festival, 1997). By permission of Ruth Walz.

midnight. Death is pronounced for all. As the plot proceeds, further ominous predictions confirm that it is indeed on the way, while a stream of grotesquery, frivolity and debauchery flows without check. Yet at the foretold hour of doom the disaster does not take place at all and life continues along its banal course.

The sense of disorientation that this creates is present from the first prediction of catastrophe, because the character who makes the announcement confounds all notions of such characters. He is no Jonah or Noah figure suggesting reform will bring redemption, and no Faustian devil who offers a contract for an alternative path to would-be salvation. Rather, he is the personification of death itself, seemingly able and prepared to bring an end to all around him. Thus there is no potential even for Ullmann's notion of resistance to a despot from 'Death' itself. The obliteration of norms and also of drama is played out in the endless parodies of the music, conjoining an 'imperfect' twelve-tone theme with Beethoven's *Eroica* Symphony, Scott Joplin with a Greek Orthodox hymn and folksong, and Monteverdi's *Orfeo* in a passacaglia of car horns. Even a pair of lovers is satirized, provided with overblown lyricism and elaborate ornamentation. There is no 'good' to set all the 'bad' against, no framework within which to see it: the disaster is a disaster, but lacks the tension and longing of a tragedy.

Thus, whilst understood as a *post*-anti-opera, and so as an opera 'for' rather than 'against' opera as medium, *Le Grand Macabre* does scorn serious opera's prime concern: the burden of humanity's sense of destiny. The opera's final scene makes this very clear. Nekrotzar, it seems, was simply too drunk to bring about the end of the world at the appointed time: the question remains as to whether he really was Death (in which case Death 'died' and the characters are in eternal life), or he wasn't (in which case there is a further period of respite). Either way, 'death' turns out not to be so important after all. The two lovers who have been enjoying one another in private during the central section re-emerge to celebrate the joys of love which remove all unnecessary fears of Judgement Day. The rest of the characters join them to sing of the futility of worrying about death. The moral is simply to 'live merrily!' *Le Grand Macabre* therefore initially recalls Martinů's *Tears of the Knife* – which prevented tragic expectation from being set up despite two deaths – and later, his *Julietta*, which came to question whether or not anything at all had ever happened. *Le Grand Macabre*'s 'affirmative' moral chorus at the end, despite its debt to epilogues in historic operas such as *Don Giovanni*, *Falstaff* and *The Rake's Progress*, scorns all the fear, tragedy and serious-ness that have been the themes of opera for so long.

Such mockery finds a gentle echo in the last major opera of the century, Eötvös's *Three Sisters* after Chekhov (1997), which in many respects brings us full circle to *Duke Bluebeard's Castle*. The world of the sisters is presented as a semi-closed society, from which only 'out-siders' (their admirers) might rescue them; in fact only their brother Andrej's wife really penetrates it, and simply causes grief. The sisters long for something apparently out of their reach (to go and live in Moscow), without being able to bring it about: each of their lives, as well as that of Andrej, constitutes a mini-tragedy, a path of unfulfilled ambition and hope. The inevitability of this self-perpetuating closure is established by the opera's cyclic structure. Rather than following Chekhov's gently directed narrative, three 'Sequences' present extracts of the play from the perspectives of Irena, Andrej and Masha. Causality of actions and events is completely undermined. The lack of a temporal line is emphasized by symbolic events such as a clock being smashed (in two separate Sequences) and the quasi ritualistic nature of such repetitions. Casting the sisters as countertenors abstracts them yet further from their representation of 'sisters', the sound of the accordion evokes a nostalgia for Russia, from which the opera is nonetheless remote. Hints of irony, such as Masha's constant whistling – a callousness in the face of the misery around her? – contribute further to the distancing strategies.

The opera thus sets itself against realist tragedy, yet strives to comment on reality. It suggests that some lives seem tragic, but that they actually have a universality which makes them normal, rather than exceptional. In the prologue of the opera (the epilogue of Chekhov's play) the sisters try to find a reason for their torment, and present themselves as suffering on behalf of the future of humankind:

> A time will come when we shall know the reason for our suffering. Our suffering will turn to joy for those who live after us, and they will remember those who live now with kind words.   (Chekhov 1959, 329–30)

But at the close of the opera, Masha's whistling, now her defence-mechanism against the sadness she feels on the departure of her lover, renders the tragedy comical. Suffering and longing, in all its absurdity, are simply the substance of life itself.

11 Russian opera: between modernism and romanticism

MARINA FROLOVA-WALKER

The first stirrings of modernism

The twentieth century began with Rimsky-Korsakov firmly established as the grand old man of Russian opera, with a catalogue of 11 operas to his credit, many of them regularly performed in St Petersburg and Moscow and throughout the provinces as well. His *Legend of the Invisible City of Kitezh* (completed in 1904 and premiered in 1907) acts as a summation of the nationalist operatic tradition of Glinka and The Five; aside from the characteristically Russian mixture of history and legend, realism and the supernatural, Russian and Oriental, Rimsky-Korsakov also introduced Wagnerian elements – to the extent that the opera became known as 'the Russian *Parsifal*'. But in two other operas from these last years of his life, Rimsky-Korsakov was laying the foundation for modernist opera in Russia and beyond. In *Kashchei the Immortal* (completed and premiered in 1902) and especially *The Golden Cockerel* (completed in 1907 and premiered in 1909 – after Rimsky-Korsakov's death) the fairy-tale characters are presented as dehumanized, puppet-like figures, while the elements of The Five's nationalist idiom are presented in an exaggerated, parodic manner. Chromatic harmony is pervasive, but this is used by Rimsky-Korsakov in a most un-Wagnerian way, since the music is designed to leave the audience's emotions unengaged.

The modernist potential of the *Cockerel* spilt over into the staging when it was performed by the Diaghilev company in Paris in 1914: at the suggestion of Alexandre Benois, the singers sat throughout the opera, leaving dancers to provide the action; Benois called this divorce between music and action the 'destruction of the synthesis' of opera. This device was assimilated by Stravinsky, a pupil of Rimsky-Korsakov's, who employed it in *Renard* (completed in 1917 and premiered in 1922 in Paris), while in Russia it was applied by the modernist director Vsevolod Meyerhold to Stravinsky's *Nightingale* (Mariinsky, 1918). In *Les Noces*, Stravinsky took the device further, by placing the singers out of view in the orchestra pit, leaving only the dancers on stage. But there were other possibilities opened up by Rimsky-Korsakov in the *Cockerel*, in particular the anti-psychologistic and absurdist approach that became known as 'anti-opera'.

Two anti-operas: *The Love for Three Oranges* and *The Nose*

It would not be an exaggeration to say that Russian modernist theatre in general and opera in particular were born of Meyerhold, the most eminent avant-garde theatrical director of his time. For all his influence, he still remains largely unknown in the West. Indeed, the fundamental ideas of modernist theatre that are usually associated with Brecht generally had their origins in Meyerhold's revolutionary practices, which predate their Brechtian incarnation by several years. There is a direct line of influence between Meyerhold and the theories of Russian formalists such as Shklovsky on the one hand, and Brecht on the other (see Leach 1989, 170–72).

In the case of Prokofiev, the connection with Meyerhold is evident even in the title of his celebrated anti-opera, since it was Meyerhold who had rediscovered Carlo Gozzi's fable, adapted and then published it as a kind of manifesto piece in the first issue of his journal, in 1914; Meyerhold went so far as to call the journal *The Love for Three Oranges*. Although this journal was short-lived, and the play itself was never staged by Meyerhold, the idea of appropriating *commedia dell'arte* principles in the struggle against the naturalist theatre of Stanislavsky became for a time a central strategy in the practices of Meyerhold and his followers. In 1917, Meyerhold himself suggested *Three Oranges* as an operatic subject that Prokofiev might like to take up; the opera was completed two years later, by which time Prokofiev was already in New York (it was premiered in Chicago in 1921, while the first Russian production was in Leningrad in 1926). The opera took the dehumanization principle to new heights: the 'characters' are not even puppets, but mere playing cards. Their destinies are decided in a card game between Fata Morgana and Chelio (Celio), two sorcerers who are so woefully inadequate in their craft that 'members of the audience' (the High-Brows, the Low-Brows, the Eccentrics, the Empty-Heads and others written into the score) have to interfere from time to time in order to bring the play to a satisfactory conclusion. The story is ruled by chance and makes no attempt to engage the audience through interest in the unfolding of the narrative, let alone through sympathy for the characters. It needs theatrical gimmicks – and Prokofiev's music – to keep the public in their seats to the end.

The music of the opera is fragmented in a patently anti-Wagnerian manner: it consists effectively of nothing but a long string of *visions fugitives*, of roughly two-minute independent pieces, individuated by their texture, rhythm and melodic material. Only a very few non-leitmotivic themes turn up more than once. *Three Oranges* uses a variety of approaches to text-setting, and its vocal style is randomly eclectic – including humorous references to operatic clichés of any provenance. Both on the musical and the dramatic level, the opera is therefore a Meyerholdian 'montage of attractions' ('attractions' in the fairground or circus sense; this is film director Sergei Eisenstein's term). The attractions are of extremely varied nature but always deliberately superficial: we may chuckle at the list of illnesses enunciated by the doctors in unpunctuated, unmetred quavers, at the chorus of little devils that reminds us of five-finger exercises, at Chelio, who exhibits Rimsky-Korsakov's octatonicism taken to an extreme, at the cross-dressed Cook (echoing another cross-dressing cook in Stravinsky's *Mavra*), or at the total absurdity of the situation with the oranges and dead princesses when the narrative veers off the road and has to be salvaged by an extraordinary intervention of the 'audience'. These chuckles, however, seem rather weak when compared to the 'programmed' audience responses to which both Meyerhold and Eisenstein aspired.

For Gozzi, *Three Oranges* was directed against Goldoni and Chiari, and for Meyerhold against Stanislavsky and the naturalist tradition; but, for Prokofiev, *Three Oranges* seems divorced from any theatrical or operatic debate. If it is taken as a satire, then it is curiously unfocused, since Prokofiev simply pokes fun at anything that happens to come his way, whether operatic clichés of the most general kind (the unison incantations 'Fata Morgana!', the typical duet inserts 'Que faire! Misère!'), or the last scene of Bizet's *Carmen* (the plaintive counterpoint to a joyful march which points to the presence of a dissatisfied character), or the musical style of Debussy's *Pelléas et Mélisande* (the brief occurrences of 'love' music). This disengagement, however, is understandable, since Prokofiev was an émigré who had not yet rooted himself in any particular cultural milieu outside Russia. *Three Oranges* was just as disconnected from the Chicago operatic scene of the premiere as it was from the revolutionary Russia that Prokofiev had left behind. In 1926, however, when the opera came to the Soviet Union, it fortuitously found itself at the centre of a cultural polemic: it was hailed by the 'modernists' and derided by the 'proletarianists'. It was too late for the opera itself to have a significant following in Soviet Russia at this stage: the First Five-Year Plan, the cult of Stalin and the imposition of Socialist Realism were only a few years away, and the frivolity of *Three Oranges* would soon find itself unwanted. Nevertheless, the overwhelming popularity of the opera's catchy March ensured that Prokofiev's name was inseparably associated with his early fun creation, even though *Three Oranges* bore scant resemblance to most of his subsequent output.

It was during these last years of artistic freedom and experimentation in Soviet Russia that Shostakovich wrote his own anti-opera, *The Nose*, which was also inspired by Meyerhold. During its composition,

Shostakovich worked as a pianist in Meyerhold's theatre and even rented a room from him. He later collaborated with Meyerhold on Mayakovsky's play *The Bedbug* (1929), and Meyerhold also planned to produce *The Nose*: the eventual production, for various reasons, had to be shifted from Moscow to Leningrad, and so the Moscow-based Meyerhold was not involved. Even Shostakovich's inspiration for *The Nose* was drawn from Meyerhold's daring 1920s production of *The Government Inspector* (1926), based on Gogol, which fired Shostakovich's imagination; the production had been a critical *cause célèbre*, drawing responses from Trotsky and Walter Benjamin, and polarizing the critics of the day. Shostakovich likewise took Gogol as his source and attempted to translate the Meyerholdian approach to the musical stage. For example, the Meyerhold production had notably featured clusters of characters crammed on to small platforms that could be moved across an otherwise empty stage. Shostakovich also worked with clusters of characters: eight janitors, ten policemen, seven gentlemen, eight students and so forth. As the opera progresses, elaborate ensemble scenes become increasingly important: the scene in the small ads department (Act II) culminates in the octet of janitors enunciating eight different advertisements simultaneously as a pointillist atonal canon; the ambush scene (Act III) contains a variety of ensemble writing with a complex interaction of several groups; the letter-reading scene (Act III) is a quartet where two pairs of characters are reading a letter and a reply to it at the same time; finally, the Intermezzo of Act III begins as an unaccompanied septet with chorus and, as the wild rumours about the fortunes of the Nose keep accumulating, it turns into a brilliant comic-opera finale echoing the riotous finale of Meyerhold's production.

Shostakovich also managed to reproduce Meyerhold's trademark 'estrangement' effect – the deliberate laying bare of the artificiality of a stage production, in opposition to naturalism. (Again, this is usually credited to Brecht, whose term *Verfremdung* is normally translated as 'alienation'.) Shostakovich achieved this in two ways. First, the very act of putting Gogol's novella onto the stage meant that the absurdities of the story had to be fully worked out in visual terms; in Gogol, the tale of Major Kovalyov's runaway nose could be understood simply as a dream or tall tale, but on Shostakovich's stage we see all the ludicrous details of the missing nose showing up as a high-ranking civil servant, 'praying ardently' in the Kazan Cathedral and being placed under arrest (in Gogol, the arrest is only a rumour). There is no way in which the audience can square this with the real world; they are never asked to believe in the characters, let alone sympathize with them. Second, the music takes Gogol's own deadpan approach and turns it into another estrangement device: the most ridiculous lines are accompanied often by the gravest and most earnest music. In the Kazan Cathedral scene (Act I), for example, we are presented with the dialogue between the bewildered Kovalyov and his nose; since the nose has somehow gained a higher social rank, he demands due respect from Kovalyov. But this lunacy unfolds against the background of a haunting wordless chorus that teeters on the brink of atonality. The chorus of sleeping soldiers from the last act of Berg's *Wozzeck* (performed in Leningrad in 1927) was probably the inspiration here. Another sign of *Wozzeck*'s influence can be found in the grotesquely high notes in several male parts, especially those of police officers who, Shostakovich said, tended to shout. And of course Shostakovich's decision to begin with a shaving scene signals his debt to Berg's opera from the outset.

In another respect, however, Shostakovich draws from a tradition that predates Meyerhold, namely the Russian naturalistic tradition in opera of scrupulously following the prose of the literary original (Meyerhold felt free to alter his originals), which began in the mid-nineteenth century with Dargomïzhsky's *Stone Guest*, which had used the complete text of Pushkin's 'little tragedy', word for word. Other 'little tragedies' that offered the right amount of text for one-act operas were subjected to similar treatment by Rimsky-Korsakov (*Mozart and Salieri*, 1898), Cui (*A Feast during the Plague*, 1901) and Rakhmaninov (*The Miserly Knight*, 1906). The naturalistic, word-for-word tradition found its most famous advocate in Musorgsky. His first attempt was *The Marriage*, which, like *The Nose*, used a comic Gogol text. He had not long begun the first act before he realized that the text would prove unmanageably long. The original version of *Boris Godunov* (1869) preserves the best of *The Marriage* while circumventing the pitfalls.

In Shostakovich's case, the fact that this device was originally associated with operatic naturalism may seem to conflict with Meyerholdian anti-naturalism, but given the inescapable absurdity of Gogol's story at every turn, such a conflict never arises. Shostakovich preserved nearly all of Gogol's original dialogue, and elsewhere carefully adapted the original narrative passages for stage use. On the other hand, there were some additions, all but one of which were drawn from elsewhere in Gogol. In his only borrowing from outside Gogol (Ivan's song from Act II), Shostakovich used Dostoyevsky; but since the latter was Gogol's celebrated disciple, the stylistic integrity of the libretto was not harmed. Shostakovich's principles of text-setting are close to those displayed in Musorgsky's *Marriage*; accordingly the music follows natural speech rhythm and intonation, while assigning a distinct idiom to each character; the closest correlation is to be found between Shostakovich's

Praskovya Osipovna and Musorgsky's Fyokla, who both exemplify the feisty and loquacious middle-aged female characters popular in Russian literature. This approach provides Shostakovich with a default, throwing into relief those passages where the text-setting is decidedly unnatural for comic purposes. The only significant passage from the novella that Shostakovich omitted was precisely an estrangement device: Gogol undermines his own story, shaking his head at the ludicrous subject matter, and pointing out various loose ends. But given the degree to which Shostakovich had already produced Meyerholdian estrangement effects, it would have been quite superfluous to mirror Gogol at this point (a consideration apparently overlooked in the 1974 Moscow revival, where Gogol's closing words were re-inserted).

How topical, however, was this Meyerhold-inspired satire for a Soviet Union in which Stalin was consolidating his power? Certainly much more so than anything to be found in *Three Oranges*. The flourishing of a bureaucracy in which the ruthlessly ambitious could rise rapidly through the ranks is reflected in the character of the Nose; likewise, the ubiquity of policing is mirrored in the constant presence of policemen of various ranks in the opera. But it would be wrong to look for any serious, sustained political critique; Shostakovich clearly enjoyed the opportunities afforded by the anarchic plot for the production of striking musical and dramatic effects in every scene (and, as in Prokofiev, primarily for their own sake). Like *Three Oranges*, Shostakovich's anti-opera became the immediate subject of vigorous debate, until Shostakovich was condemned for his modernist 'formalism' in 1936, when it disappeared from view. It did not resurface in the Soviet Union until 1974, although there were some Western productions in the 1960s because musicians had been able to take the score and parts abroad once the Khrushchev Thaw had set in.

The retrieval of the human element: *Lady Macbeth of Mtsensk* and *The Fiery Angel*

Neither Prokofiev nor Shostakovich continued in this anti-opera vein. Their next two operas were both large-scale tragedies that engaged seriously with the tradition: Prokofiev's *The Fiery Angel* (completed 1927, concert performance 1954, staged premiere 1955) and Shostakovich's *Lady Macbeth of Mtsensk* (completed 1932, premiere 1934). Both operas also sit uncomfortably between modernism and romanticism, and while for long stretches they wholeheartedly embrace tradition, elements of parody also re-emerge; likewise they both show a mixed attitude towards their characters, sometimes inviting sympathy, sometimes deliberately distancing them from the audience. In spite of these unresolved conflicts, both operas are masterworks that are capable of giving their audiences much greater satisfaction than the aesthetically coherent anti-operas we have just discussed.

As it happens, it was in the more conservative *Lady Macbeth* that Shostakovich took truly Meyerholdian liberties with his source text, a novella by Leskov, adapting it ruthlessly to his own vision and even conflating the central character of Katerina with another Katerina of Russian classical literature, from Ostrovsky's drama *The Storm*. If Leskov's Katerina is a multiple murderer who is completely dehumanized by the author's dispassionate newspaper prose style, the changes carried out by Shostakovich are directed at exonerating and elevating her as a strong woman rebelling against oppression, struggling for her own happiness passionately and impulsively and perishing tragically after being betrayed, ridiculed, and finally overcome by the 'black waves' of her own conscience. To achieve this, Shostakovich had to remove one of Katerina's murders, of an innocent child (this would have been impossible to explain away), and also added a scene in which she saves a peasant woman from potential rape.

Ostrovsky's Katerina was dubbed 'a ray of sunshine in the kingdom of darkness' by the critic Nikolai Dobrolyubov ('Luch sveta v temnom tsarstve', *Sovremennik* (1860), vol. 10). But if Shostakovich wanted to elevate his own Katerina to this exalted level, these alterations to the story would not have sufficed; the music had to carry the main burden. Accordingly, he set Katerina into relief by casting the music for other characters in his grotesque or parodic style, representing a world of darkness; for Katerina, by contrast, he reserved a concentrated, serious lyricism. The only exception to this scheme is the Old Convict, who at the close offers Katerina some Dostoyevskian compassion; because of this, he is less a character within the narrative than a representation of the authorial voice. Everyone around Katerina, including her victims, is dehumanized by waltzes, polkas, galops and melodramatic operatic clichés – by this means, Shostakovich prevents these characters from engaging our sympathies, just as he had done in *The Nose*. On the other hand, we are given every encouragement to sympathize with Katerina, whose character is built up through a series of reflective ariosos. In Act I, her social status is indicated: she is a merchant's wife, hence the drawing-room romance, but she had come from a poorer background, hence the folk/popular song style on another occasion. In Act II, her love is represented by Mahlerian lyricism, and finally, in Act IV, her despair is represented in a bleak D-minor arioso; here Katerina stands alone at the front of the stage, and her music is stripped of references to genre that would place her in any particular time or place. This is abstract tragic music for a heroine of Shakespearean stature, and Shostakovich has ensured that at this moment our hearts are unequivocally with Katerina.

The two styles thus allow Shostakovich to shape our attitudes towards the different characters, but present him with a problem of musical cohesion. At times the strain shows, as in the Act III policemen's scene, where the farcical, cabaret style stretches the opera's integrity almost to breaking point (although it is interesting that Shostakovich inserts dramatically redundant scenes ridiculing the police in both his operas). But the duality is generally more deftly handled: Act IV, for example, convincingly alternates between passages of music in inverted commas and passages intended seriously; Shostakovich even moves confidently between 'good' and 'bad' melodrama, somewhat in the manner of Mahler (who was another major influence on his music).

Lady Macbeth is still eclectic in the range of musical styles it exhibits, but it sheds all of the more pronouncedly modernist idioms that appeared in *The Nose*. Indeed, we can see Shostakovich's mature style beginning to coalesce in *Lady Macbeth*, above all in Katerina's ariosos. As in *The Nose*, Musorgsky is the most important musical inspiration, but now Shostakovich looks towards the products of Musorgsky's retreat from naturalistic text-setting: the later strata of *Boris* and *Khovanshchina*, where arioso predominates. Apart from this pervasive influence, there are some more specific references to Musorgsky. There are distorted quotations, such as the scene in which Katerina laments over the body of Boris Timofeyevich: this is a clear parody of the first chorus in *Boris Godunov*. Here we have a direct cerebral reference: we note that in both cases the lament is forced and insincere. In Act IV, through musical associations with Shchelkalov in *Boris* or Shaklovitïy in *Khovanshchina*, we realize that the Old Convict, in his arioso, is speaking on behalf of the author; the same associations also prompt us to apply his words to Russia ('vast steppes, endless nights, joyless thoughts and merciless gendarmes').

The story of *Lady Macbeth*'s reception is a striking illustration of the twists and turns of cultural policy under Stalin: it was the first Soviet opera to enjoy true popularity, and it also won official critical acclaim, being held up as a model Soviet opera; but within two years of its premiere, it had been condemned by the same critics, and banned from the stage. It reappeared on the Soviet stage only after the death of Stalin, under the title *Katerina Izmailova*, with light revisions by Shostakovich, for artistic rather than political reasons (see Fay 1995). The condemnation of *Lady Macbeth* had lasting and wide-ranging effects on Shostakovich's career and musical style; not least of these was his decision to avoid opera thereafter, to concentrate instead on the safer course of writing symphonies and string quartets (instrumental music was policed much less than the literary, dramatic and pictorial arts). Nevertheless, *Lady Macbeth* was already a move in the direction of Socialist Realism *avant la lettre*: Shostakovich here uses a simpler musical idiom than anything to be found in *The Nose*, and Katerina's music often looks back to the nineteenth-century Russian classics. Shostakovich's retreat to a more conservative manner therefore began several years before it was politically required of him, since it was not yet decided at this stage precisely what Socialist Realism entailed for music.

Prokofiev's *The Fiery Angel*, by contrast, received no attention, either supportive or hostile. Disregarding the advice of various friends, Prokofiev worked on the opera without any commission, only to find that no one was interested in staging it; indeed, there were no complete performances of the opera during the composer's lifetime. Beyond the lack of any commission, the *The Fiery Angel* was already handicapped by its failure to engage with any contemporary artistic currents. The source text was a symbolist novel by Valery Bryusov based on the author's personal experience: a love triangle consisting of himself, Nina Petrovskaya and Andrey Bely. Bryusov placed the narrative in medieval Germany, which enabled him to use a palette of dark Gothic hues, and to employ his skills as historian and master of literary pastiche; the occult practices of Ruprecht and Renata reflect the spiritist séances popular in symbolist circles (see Morrison 2002). But this novel was already considered old-fashioned by the time Prokofiev set to work on it, and his idea of parodying its symbolist preoccupations scarcely improved matters – who would be interested in a parody of an artistic trend that no longer held sway? No-one in the West, where Bryusov was unknown, but even less so in the Soviet Union, where artists had forcefully rejected the Russian symbolism of pre-Revolutionary years. On the musical level, Prokofiev's harmonic complications and often dense orchestration, together with his revival of nineteenth-century operatic forms and principles (there are Wagnerian leitmotives, for example) also seemed out of touch with the times in the West, where neo-classicism was the dominant current in new music. Yet, unwanted by its contemporaries, the opera finally won an audience at the end of the twentieth century, and was hailed as a uniquely powerful work.

It appears that Prokofiev was attracted by the operatic potential of the novel, and could not imagine that interest would be lacking in what he quite correctly judged to be his masterpiece, whatever its musical and literary styles. He was fascinated by Bryusov's occultism, and relished the musical task of depicting the 'endless orgies' of the plot, as he called them in a letter to Myaskovsky (Kabalevskiy 1977, 276). These 'orgies' of increasing intensity can readily be seen as the central strand of the opera. In Act I, we have the wild behaviour of the demon-possessed Renata, and then later the bizarre fortune-telling scene. Act II offers us the invocation of the infernal spirits, and eventually we have the spectacular collective insanity of the final act. In all of these scenes Prokofiev uses multiple layers of hypnotic ostinato patterns (after the manner of Stravinsky's *The Rite of Spring*), and in the final tableau this principle is elevated to a colossal scale, with terrifying effect. Especially where these scenes are concerned, the orchestra plays the leading role in shaping the audience's perceptions, so it is not surprising that Prokofiev was able to assemble his Third Symphony (1928) from the material of the opera. This is particularly true of Act II scene 2, where Ruprecht is interviewing the scholar of magical arts, Agrippa of Nettelsheim. The rather prosaic and at times even comic dialogue is set to one of the raging orchestral 'orgies', without obvious motivation (unless we imagine the demons working feverishly behind the scenes). To some extent this scene is indicative of how this opera works: however sceptically we might regard the plot, the power of the orchestra sweeps all before it.

If scenes of hysteria, both musical and dramatic, provide the modernist side of the opera, there is also a more conservative side, found in the parallel development of a psychological drama. As in Bryusov's original, this drama is experienced through Ruprecht, the robust and rational knight who falls under the spell of the seductive Renata and begins a stormy relationship with her. Whether she is a visionary, or simply mentally ill (we are not told), she gradually takes control of Ruprecht's will. Tormented by love for her and jealousy for an invisible third party (the Fiery Angel, also known as Madiel and Count Heinrich), he is prepared to serve Renata blindly, to kill and to die for her if necessary. Their psychological battles are played out in a string of scenes which are essentially duets with a minimum of action. Occasionally, Wagnerian models are in evidence: for example, Renata's Tale is shaped similarly to Elsa's Tale in Act I of *Lohengrin*, and Elsa's tactics of emotional blackmail in Act III seem to be a prototype for Renata's behaviour throughout the opera. In spite of all his sacrifices, Ruprecht loses his battle and Renata leaves him for the convent. But if this train of events has lulled us into thinking that this is a fundamentally romantic opera, a surprise is in store: the opera changes its course in the middle of Act IV, beginning with the insertion of an unexpected comic scene featuring Faust and Mephistopheles; Simon Morrison calls this a 'visitation from another opera' (2002, 260). This strange pair offers to spirit Ruprecht away to the convent so that he can observe Renata's exorcism.

With the failure of the exorcism, and the frenzied spread of the demons to the assembled nuns, the opera comes to an abrupt end with a death sentence pronounced upon Renata by the Grand Inquisitor; Ruprecht observes, but appears impassive. This ending has often been criticized, although it is no more illogical than the ending of Berlioz's *Symphonie fantastique*, where the seductress has been exposed as a witch, thereby healing the victim of her snares. Because we too have been intoxicated and hypnotized by Renata, we fail to realize until now that the story has unfolded from Ruprecht's perspective alone; while we were party to all his private thoughts, Renata's terrible visions were never shared with us. The device of the comic interlude enables Prokofiev to lead us outside the confines of the psychological drama, so that we can observe the punishment of the seductress dispassionately. Ruprecht does not intercede on behalf of Renata as Faust did on behalf of Margaret; instead, he is once again simply a voyeur, just as he was in the opera's opening scene. This last-moment subversion of the opera's apparent 'romanticism' is a strikingly modernist negation: after becoming deeply engaged with the plight of the characters, we are suddenly dumped in an emotionally neutral location, with Renata dehumanized and no more sympathetic to us than the Chosen One in *The Rite of Spring*.

The return of grand opera: *War and Peace*

In an interview from 1927, Prokofiev contemplated the possibility of a Soviet production of *The Fiery Angel*. Perhaps it could have happened during the 1920s, but when Prokofiev eventually returned to his homeland in the mid-1930s this was clearly an impossibility. *Lady Macbeth* was condemned shortly after he arrived, and restrictions were placed on the subject matter and musical style of new operas. Opera was now a showcase genre, intended to extol the virtues of the Stalinist state after the completion of the first Five-Year Plan. The first opera based on a specifically Soviet subject was *For Red Petrograd*, by A. Gladkovsky and Y. Prussak, first performed in Leningrad in April 1925: it was a historical chronicle of the events of 1919, presented as a realistic spectacle; the music was eclectic, and included many quotations of Red and White songs. The subject matter and format were chosen freely by the composer and his collaborators. By the mid-1930s, however, the authorities were demanding that composers should use Soviet subjects for some of their operas; there was often official interference from choice of subject through to the dress rehearsal.

Stalin himself had now begun to pay close attention to opera, and in 1936 the negative example of *Lady Macbeth* was counterbalanced by a new opera officially regarded as the model for future efforts, namely the 'song opera', *Quiet Flows the Don*, by Ivan Dzerzhinsky, whose musical language was very undemanding. In the same year, official culture had turned towards the open celebration of various episodes in Russia's pre-Revolutionary history. As a corollary, the classics of nineteenth-century Russian opera were elevated in importance, both as models for new operas, and also as works deserving of the most lavish, monumental productions themselves, as Stalin began to amass all the paraphernalia of imperial grandeur that the Tsarist past could offer. Tendencies towards monumentality had become readily discernible since the 1928 production of *Boris Godunov* and the 1931 *Maid of Pskov*; in the 1930s, the grand-opera manner became *de rigueur*, as in the productions of *Prince Igor*, *Sadko* and *A Life for the Tsar* – the last refashioned as *Ivan Susanin* (see Gozenpud 1963, 215–20).

Prokofiev composed his own Soviet opera, *Semyon Kotko* (1939, premiered in 1940), based on a Socialist Realist novel by Katayev about a Ukrainian soldier during the Civil War. But this attempt met with a mixed reception: while some aspects were praised, the preponderance of recitative and a lack of heroic monumentality were cited as substantial shortcomings. But over the following years, during the composition of *War and Peace*, Prokofiev must have looked upon such criticism as mere friendly banter, for his chosen subject had guaranteed that his work would be subject to the full scrutiny of the Soviet bureaucracy. Such attention was drawn for several reasons. Marshal Kutuzov, in command of the Russian troops facing Napoleon, was seen to prefigure Stalin, who now invited comparisons between himself and various figures from the pre-Revolutionary past. The scenario of the foreign army advancing far into the territory of Mother Russia had immediate parallels in the Nazi invasion of 1941. And where the libretto was concerned, Tolstoy had come to occupy first place in the Soviet literary pantheon – this placed a third burden of responsibility on Prokofiev's shoulders. Prokofiev had considered the novel as the possible basis for an opera for several years, and he had approached *War and Peace* simply as his own pet project, with little thought that it would become an artistic endeavour of gravest national significance which could not be allowed to go wrong in any detail. Prokofiev was desperate that the work should not meet the fate of *The Fiery Angel*, and he submitted five substantially different versions to various committees, incorporating hundreds of the changes they had called for (the Committee for Artistic Affairs had the last word, but bodies such as the Bolshoi Theatre were also involved). Even so, *War and Peace* was never performed in its entirety during Prokofiev's lifetime; the final version was in two parts, and only the first was performed since the second, featuring Napoleon and Kutuzov, was still considered to be too risky by the committees involved in the project.

Prokofiev's original intentions were remote from this sprawling grand opera. He had originally been attracted to Tolstoy's complex heroes and his attention to the seemingly trivial details of everyday life. Tolstoy's prosaic, unoperatic language was another attraction for the composer. Dialogue was to be represented through Musorgskian speech intonation and rhythms, with musical characterization of each of the *dramatis personae*. At the same time, Tolstoy's frequent examinations of a character's mind were used by Prokofiev for arioso asides. 'It is impossible that they won't take a liking to me', sings Natasha before meeting her prospective in-laws. 'How can they execute me, kill me, take my life away – me, Pierre Bezukhov, with all my thoughts, hopes, strivings, memories?', sings Pierre in what he thinks are his last moments. Such arioso asides are strikingly fresh on the operatic stage, and suit the medium perfectly. The size of the novel, however, meant that Prokofiev could not even attempt to follow the psychological development that Tolstoy provides for each of characters. Even Natasha is only sketchily outlined, let alone Pierre and Andrey; to appreciate their complex interactions, a prior acquaintance with the novel is indispensable. This, of course, was not a problem where Prokofiev's Soviet audience was concerned; indeed, it was quite normal for Russian 'literary' operas.

By April 1942, Prokofiev had completed the vocal score of his first version, a patchwork of brief episodes, largely in dialogue, alternating declamatory passages with arioso; we can form an idea of Prokofiev's original conception from the scene at Dolokhov's, which survived almost unchanged through to the final version. The sharp contrasts between these episodes is still reminiscent of the *visions fugitives* manner that characterized *Three Oranges*. However, there are two features already present in the first version which were unusual for Prokofiev but *de rigueur* for Socialist Realist opera, namely a range of musical styles leaning heavily on the nineteenth century, and also the various set-pieces, such as the choral songs in the war scenes. It is notable that Prokofiev borrowed several of the opera's most prominent themes from the Tchaikovskian incidental music he had written for a stage version of *Eugene Onegin*, which had never been performed; examples are to be found in the opening theme of Scene 1, usually referred to as 'Natasha's theme', and the second theme of Andrey's first arioso, known as 'Andrey's theme'. The use of set-pieces and the tuneful retrospective style came to predominate in the later revisions, bringing the opera closer to the Socialist Realist ideal; the Ball scene, for example, added during the revisions of 1945–6, consisted almost entirely of period pieces (as ever with characteristic Prokofiev touches in the harmony and orchestration).

It was the 'war' section of the opera that had to undergo the most drastic changes. The everyday aspects of Tolstoy's account, especially the telling details that humanized Kutuzov, were not welcome on the operatic stage: the Committee for Artistic Affairs deemed them a trivialization of the Russian people's struggle and, even worse, Marshal Kutuzov's banter was considered shockingly inappropriate for the character who was to represent Stalin. Prokofiev was given the task of creating a grander Kutuzov, without the humanizing tics; with great reluctance, he composed a new scene, 'The Council at Fili', with a central aria of a suitably heroic type. Although at odds with the course of the drama at this point, the aria's 'Moscow theme', majestically evoking the Russian classics, was perfect, as far as the authorities were concerned; even better, the same Moscow theme was to make a triumphant return in the choral apotheosis at the close of the opera. After much deliberation, Prokofiev took his Moscow theme from a passage in his music for Eisenstein's film *Ivan the Terrible*, Part I (1942–4).

Prokofiev's first version of *War and Peace* was also lacking in another essential Socialist Realist quality: 'organic unity' was too little in evidence among the string of *visions fugitives*. Prokofiev had not been entirely oblivious to this requirement and had tried to link the 'peace' and 'war' sections by various means: for example, the scene at Mïtishchi, where Natasha meets the dying Andrey, was a crucial overlap between the two worlds, from the first version onwards. But this was not nearly enough for the authorities, and so Prokofiev had to incorporate many thematic reminiscences. Unfortunately, a degree of exasperation seems to be in evidence, since Prokofiev sometimes rent the delicate fabric of a scene simply to insert one of the recurring themes, which must have satisfied the authorities, albeit at the cost of greater offences against unity at the local level. One such jarring moment occurs in the Mïtishchi scene, where Andrey's last thoughts are interrupted by the intrusion of the 'Moscow theme'; the reminiscence of the 'first waltz' theme from the Ball scene is more justifiable, but hardly less incongruous stylistically.

There is certainly much evidence of the opera's tortuous path of revision for those who look carefully enough; in spite of this, Prokofiev's eclectic epic is not only viable, but has proven one of the most successful of twentieth-century operas. The committees involved in the project in all probability contributed to this, since Prokofiev's original, more Meyerholdian vision, could hardly have won such wide acceptance as the grand opera that he eventually produced at the authorities' behest. Nevertheless, much of the sophistication and intricate detail of the original version survived the revision process, which also resulted in the addition of much excellent music. Prokofiev had always prided himself on his ability to clothe the same melodic material in difficult or easy-going garb, according to circumstance. While the revisions of *War and Peace* severely tested his patience, he was generally able to make a virtue of necessity, to produce one of the handful of Socialist Realist classics that retained their classic status long after Socialist Realism had been consigned to the dustbin of history.

The waning of Socialist Realism

While *War and Peace* managed to transcend the limitations of Socialist Realism, dozens of its contemporaries did not. The only other monumental historical spectacle that rivalled *War and Peace* in Soviet theatres was Yuri Shaporin's *Dekabristï* (*The Decembrists*, 1953), but most new operas of this kind deservedly had a much shorter lifespan. Comic opera yielded more works of quality and enduring popularity, including Kabalevsky's *Kolas Breugnon* (1939), Prokofiev's *Betrothal in a Monastery* (1940) and Shebalin's *The Taming of the Shrew* (1957). But the repertoires also included a number of duller efforts which had been judged Socialist Realist classics without winning any real affection from critics or audiences. Each of the USSR's seventy-eight opera houses had at least one of these 'classics' in its repertoire; even after *perestroika* was under way, the Moscow Bolshoi still glumly persisted with two such operas, regardless of the meagre audiences: Muradeli's *October* and Molchanov's *The Dawns are Quiet Here*. During one tour in the 1970s, the Bolshoi even played Molchanov's opera in New York, where it caused great puzzlement both for audience and critics (see Taruskin 1976). The effects of Khrushchev's Thaw on Russian operatic life were felt in the rehabilitation of both of Shostakovich's operas: in 1963, *Lady Macbeth* returned as *Katerina Izmailova*, and *The Nose* followed in 1974. With the return of *The Nose* in the small basement auditorium of the Moscow Chamber Opera, a real alternative to the grand 'imperial' stages was established; in a way, *The Nose* proved to be more pointed a weapon in 1974 than in 1930 since it was now, in effect, directed against the edifice of Socialist Realist grand opera. Thanks to *The Nose*, anti-opera came back into fashion; one of the better-known later examples was Schnittke's *Life with an Idiot* (premiered in 1992 in Amsterdam), a brusque satire of the Soviet way of life. Nevertheless, Denisov's *L'Ecume des jours* (also premiered in 1992, in Paris), based on a surrealist novel of the same name by

Boris Vian, continues in the tradition of large-scale serious opera, albeit in a fully modernist idiom.

For late and post-Soviet composers, both anti-opera and serious opera have provided a basis for major works – the former most often satirizing aspects of late Soviet Socialist Realism, the latter departing altogether from Socialist Realism in favour of Western modernist idioms. One important recent opera consciously attempts to draw the two strands together: Vladimir Tarnopolsky's *Wenn die Zeit über die Ufer tritt* (*When Time Overflows Its Banks*, Munich 1999). At first, Tarnopolsky's characters seem to have stepped out of a Chekhov play – they even utter lines selected from various Chekhov sources. But these characters are progressively dehumanized by the accumulation of estrangement techniques; they move from *cantilena* to *Sprechstimme*, then sentences are fragmented and shared out between the characters; finally, verbal communication breaks down altogether, and the characters are left with the disembodied vowel sounds of the Jews' harp. While this process makes use of characteristic anti-opera devices, the work is seriously intended as a bleak view of future prospects for Russia or the human race – among other things, a refusal to countenance the mendacious optimism of Socialist Realism.

12 American opera: innovation and tradition

ELISE K. KIRK

American opera of the twentieth century encompasses a great diversity of styles that vividly reflect the wide landscape of America's social and cultural life. In an opera world dominated by European tastes and traditions, American composers have reached out for their own individual voices. Some have turned to indigenous sources – Native American motifs, black culture, jazz forms, American literature or Hollywood cinematic effects. Others have found a voice in non-narrative ideology, preferring ritual to description, and symbol to an unfolding storyline. But whether in mellifluous melody, romantic-hued harmony or acerbic atonality, American composers melded music and drama within the vital framework of life around them. They saw their art as individual and American, but they also understood music's powerful role in defining character and propelling the drama forwards.

Belonging to a nation of explorers and rugged individualists of many ethnic origins and modes of thought, Americans wrote opera as they travelled along a historic road of many twists and turns. The eclecticism of this opera – its panorama of styles, subjects and moods that seem to know no boundaries – both reflects and defines its people. With the possible exception of Gian Carlo Menotti, who was especially influential in the 1940s and 1950s, there is essentially no enduring 'school' of American opera. Whether William Henry Fry or Walter Damrosch in the nineteenth century, or Virgil Thomson, George Gershwin, Philip Glass or Carlisle Floyd in the twentieth, each composer – each opera – is distinctive. And each offers an element of surprise along the path to discovery that lies at the heart of American opera.

From Wagner to the vernacular

The most profound influence on American operatic life as the nineteenth century turned was Richard Wagner. If American composers were caught up in the spell of the Wizard from Bayreuth, they had no intention of leaving their American roots in his shadow. They wrote 'Wagnerian' operas, but gave them American settings. Damrosch, conductor of the New York Philharmonic for forty years, based his grand opera *The Scarlet*

Letter (1896) on Nathaniel Hawthorne's brooding psychological romance. Though the story is set in New England, Wagnerian aspects come to play in the work's harmonic language, orchestral fabric, leitmotivic imagery and continuous structure. Another opera influenced by Wagner was *Poia* (1910) by the Pennsylvanian composer, Arthur Nevin. *Poia* received its premiere in Berlin under the baton of the great Mahler and Wagner interpreter, Karl Muck. Its rich, sonorous scoring and pervasive use of symbolism were inspired by Wagner, but its libretto is based on a colourful, dramatic Native American legend (see Kirk 2001, 142–7).

Poia's performance overseas illustrates the attention American operas were now receiving both at home and abroad. As the United States became an internationally recognized economic and political force, its culture, too, began to achieve wider notice, and prominent Americans reinforced this through their composing, conducting, teaching and performing. Many were also builders of large-scale dramatic structures – post-romantic grand operas, such as *Azara* (1898) by John Knowles Paine and *Mona* by Horatio Parker, which was given its premiere at the Metropolitan Opera in 1912. George Whitefield Chadwick's sensual score for his *Judith* (1901) is heightened by exotic and erotic musical imagery. In the extraordinary scene in which Judith slays Holofernes, following the apocryphal tale, Chadwick uses percussive effects, cross rhythms and explicit orchestral contrapuntal figures to intensify the drama. Nothing quite like it had ever been conceived for the American stage.

As they searched for new, expressive sonorities and colourful subjects for their operas, many composers of the early twentieth century turned to Native American sources. The intensive research into the culture of Native Americans by scholars such as Natalie Curtis and John Fillmore (Kirk 2001, 140 and 412 n.1), provided the springboard for the 'Indianist' operas of Victor Herbert (*Natoma*, 1910), Mary Carr Moore (*Narcissa*, 1912), Charles Wakefield Cadman (*Shanewis*, 1918) and many others. While most of these operas were romanticized and tended to ignore ethnographic authenticity, they served an important purpose. Their popular subjects attracted large audiences: Cadman's *The Willow Tree* was the first American opera to be composed specifically for radio, being first aired in an NBC broadcast on 3 October 1932 (149). Operas inspired by Native American music and legend also drew audiences of thousands to an art form many had never before experienced. Thus, in using these novel indigenous sources, American composers opened a new frontier for opera.

If audiences flocked to operas shaped by Native American elements, they responded to those that employed jazz much more tentatively. The cultural picture in America was changing rapidly. By 1920 more than half the population resided in cities – thriving, bustling urban centres that shaped the values, attitudes and behaviour of the nation. Along with a dramatic change in the size of American cities came an increase in the ethnic mix of its people. Many black composers settled in New York City during what was known as the 'Harlem Renaissance'. Some of these composers wrote grand operas that utilized jazz elements – notably Harry Lawrence Freeman in his *Voodoo*, a work infused with blues, spirituals and lively cakewalks within an aria-recitative framework. While *Voodoo* was composed in 1913, it had to wait fifteen years for a performance (in New York in 1928) and then was promptly forgotten. Audiences not only ignored blacks as opera composers, but considered jazz a 'low-class' art form unworthy of the elevated art of opera.

Another work written by a black composer had a similar start, but a happier outcome – though half a century later. When Scott Joplin presented his *Treemonisha* unstaged with piano accompaniment in 1915 in New York, it failed miserably. But after its highly successful staged premiere in Atlanta in 1972, orchestrated by William Bolcom and later Gunther Schuller, it has enjoyed frequent performances. *Treemonisha* surpasses Freeman's opera by virtue of its excellent crafts-manship in the balance and integration of musical forms and styles, which include overture, ragtime, sentimental parlour tunes, Italian lyricism, recitative, barbershop quartet and dance, together with deft musical characterization. The story, moreover, is timeless and relevant: the opera's young heroine is a startlingly early voice for civil-rights causes, notably the importance of education and knowledge to African-American advancement.

Non-black composers, too, soon realized that jazz carried American opera far adrift from the powerful Wagnerian currents. Jazz idioms gave their works vital new dramatic dimensions and moved their creative processes beyond the outmoded nineteenth-century melodrama and into the realms of realism, expressionism and social commentary. Early *verismo* operas – Frederick Shepherd Converse's *The Immigrants* (1914), Frank Harling's *A Light from St Agnes* (1925) and Hamilton Forrest's *Camille* (1930, which starred Mary Garden) were heightened dramatically through the excitement and colours of jazz. But no jazz-inspired opera ever reached the heights of popularity of Gershwin's *Porgy and Bess*. For no composer of the time melded jazz, drama, symphony and song as seamlessly as Gershwin. Even so, the opera closed shortly after its pre-miere at New York's Alvin Theatre on 30 September 1935, and many years passed before its treasures took hold. Today *Porgy and Bess* is the most popular and longest-running American opera in history, and the nation's most successful cultural export.

Porgy and Bess is based on the novel *Porgy* (1925) by DuBose Heyward, who also wrote the libretto for Gershwin's opera, and is set in a black community on the Charleston waterfront in the 1920s. The opera's main characters are victims of uncontrollable forces that tear at their love. Porgy is marked by disability, frustration and jealousy, and Bess by her attraction to drugs and inability to leave an abusive relationship. Yet both characters are elevated to heroic heights in the arias and dramatic recitative Gershwin gives them. Indeed the staying power of this opera lies in the composer's gift of melody. But it also reflects America's fascination with the *verismo* tradition. In this style of opera, everyday characters, caught up in powerful, often tragic, crises, are enlarged and defined by richly expressive music. And like the characters themselves, the orchestra plays a vital rôle throughout. In Gershwin's opera, it highlights Porgy with a jazzy blue note, provides thematic recurrence at key spots in the drama and sets up important passages of dialogue and recitative, very much like a film score that reaches a chilling crescendo before the murderer opens the door.

Realism

Verismo (realism) is a term commonly applied to Leoncavallo's *Pagliacci*, Mascagni's *Cavalleria rusticana* and, in the early twentieth century, certain works of Puccini's. But it also applies to numerous American operas from about the mid-twentieth century to modern times. The dramaturgy of American *verismo* stems from the nineteenth-century American melodrama and the graphically explicit orchestration of both Wagner and the motion-picture score. But the stories are often drawn from modern realistic American literature. *Verismo* characters achieve a special focus: they are not only transcriptions of life, but embodiments of it. Aria forms and lyric declamation no longer merely serve the action, they define the characters by allowing them to express in song their innermost thoughts and emotions.

Most of the finest, most frequently performed American operas are cast in the *verismo* tradition. During the 1940s and early 1950s, three important composers – Menotti, Kurt Weill and Marc Blitzstein – composed works that reflected different aspects of the new realism that was also infusing film and musical theatre at the time. Although the characters in both Weill and Blitzstein develop and deepen in their interaction with one another, Menotti's characters go a step further and explore the inner, symbolic elements of life itself (Kirk 2001, 249). Menotti's realism, moreover, usually contains a spiritual message, while Blitzstein and Weill prefer to accent social and political themes. But in the ability to penetrate deeply into human feelings with music that underpins the characters' plights, Menotti is a master. His *The Medium* (1947), *The Consul* (1950), *The Saint of Bleecker Street* (1954) and *Maria Golovin* (1958) remain as sombre and shocking today as when they were first performed. More importantly, Menotti discovered a way to communicate with his audiences. His operas were not only performed on Broadway, but also recorded and televised. *Amahl and the Night Visitors* (1951) was the first opera to be commissioned for television and remains a national icon today.

Rooted in the Italian romantic tradition, Menotti also avoided spoken dialogue and the extended use of American traditional or popular music, which served Weill's *Street Scene* (1947), and Blitzstein's *The Cradle Will Rock* (1937) and *Regina* (1949) so effectively. Weill composed *Street Scene* after coming to America from Germany in 1935 following a six-year collaboration with Bertolt Brecht. Based upon Elmer Rice's Pulitzer Prize-winning play of the same title, the opera revolves around life in New York's hot and faded tenement district. Though Weill's use of operatic and pop techniques may not assimilate as smoothly as they do in Gershwin, the various solos, scenes and ensembles nevertheless flow powerfully into one another. *Street Scene*'s stylistic traits also played a formative role in the theatrical works of Blitzstein. A great admirer of Weill, Blitzstein does not always share Weill's gift for memorable tunes. Blitzstein's *The Cradle Will Rock* is a biting political satire that uses a vernacular musical idiom. His *Regina*, however, is a more ambitious work with a wider, fuller dramatic range. Derived from *The Little Foxes* (1939) by Lillian Hellman, it abounds in themes of greed, money-grubbing and hate-filled family conflicts. And in his use of spirituals, Victorian parlour music, dance forms, ragtime, aria and a large, symphonic score, Blitzstein tells his tale and paints his characters in the new American *verismo* tradition.

The Met

During the early part of the twentieth century, the city of New York could boast an artistic life as lively and varied as any large European urban centre. From the opulent glamour of the Ziegfeld Theater to the aquatic shows in Madison Square Garden, New York seemed to have it all. And with the opening of the elegant 3,625-seat Metropolitan Opera House on 22 October 1883, a new era of American operatic history began. Through the backing of the Morgans, Vanderbilts and other wealthy patrons, the

Metropolitan Opera reflected the nation's changing face of finance and industry. This, in turn, enlarged the power-base for the arts, encouraging a cultural hierarchy around opera that has, for better or worse, defined its image and created notions of class distinctions that are peculiar to Americans even now.

No single organization did more for the cause of American opera in the early days of the twentieth century than the Metropolitan Opera. Under the ambitious management of Giulio Gatti-Casazza from 1910 to 1935, the Metropolitan produced fourteen new American operas. These included Frederick Converse's *The Pipe of Desire* (1910), Victor Herbert's *Madeleine* (1914), Cadman's *Shanewis* (1918) and Joseph Breil's *The Legend* (1919), starring the young Rosa Ponselle. Among the most successful productions were the popular operas of Deems Taylor: *The King's Henchman* (1927) and *Peter Ibbetson* (1931) enjoyed exceptionally long runs of nearly four years at the Met (Kirk 2001, 172). With its libretto by the Pulitzer Prize-winning poet, Edna St Vincent Millay, *The King's Henchman* was also the first opera to be broadcast from the Metropolitan Opera on the newly formed CBS radio network in 1927.

Gatti-Casazza not only gave a boost to the visibility of the American composer, he also brought highly innovative stage designs to his American works in the creations of Norman Bel Geddes, Frederick Kiesler and others. The stage designs for Howard Hanson's *Merry Mount* (1934) and Louis Gruenberg's *Emperor Jones* (1933) were created by Jo Mielziner, who managed to capture the dark symbolism of both operas – works that were as contrasting musically as they were visually. *Merry Mount* was essentially lyrical, with arias and ensembles cast in clear-cut musical forms; *Emperor Jones* (which featured Lawrence Tibbett) was a freely conceived work with pounding syncopation, conflicting tonalities and expressionistic imagery that vividly reflected the terror of its tormented protagonist. Through huge phallic images in a ghostly jungle setting, Mielziner's fantastic sets explored the opera's symbolism as it evolved in the play by Eugene O'Neill.

New horizons

But it was not at the Metropolitan Opera that the most innovative operas of the time were performed. During the interwar years, experimentation and social commentary brought new avenues of creative thought to music. George Antheil worked in Germany during the 1920s and knew very well the experimental theatre movement of the Weimar Republic – a cultural rage that diminished only when Adolf Hitler's reactionary policies towards society began to take hold. *Transatlantic* (Frankfurt, 1930) is a surrealistic satire about an American presidential election. In the *Zeitoper* (opera of the times) manner, it weaves many aspects of the era into its plot, including neon signs, a Salvation Army band, jazz motifs and a soprano who sings in a bathtub. The staging of *Transatlantic* was a brilliant feat of original design for the time, requiring four simultaneous scenes and a large central cinema screen.

Like Antheil and many other Americans of the era, Virgil Thomson went to Europe to study and compose. In Paris – a city that teemed with Dadaism, Futurism and all the other 'isms' of the time – he met the radical poet from California, Gertrude Stein. Stein wrote the libretto for two of Thomson's operas, *Four Saints in Three Acts* (Hartford, 1934) and *The Mother of Us All* (New York, 1947), a pageant-like work about Susan B. Anthony, the late nineteenth-century American reformer and champion of women's suffrage. Both works show Thomson to be a highly original composer with a true genius for understanding the important element of prosody, or the rhythm of language – a talent American opera composers often lacked. Thomson chose melodic lines, harmonic progressions and rhythmic momentum that tied in closely with Stein's syllables, words, phrases and stanzas. *Four Saints in Three Acts* has virtually no plot, but its absence of leitmotivic techniques and musical characterization give it an enigmatic charm. A great success at its premiere, Thomson's joyous *Saints* lives on through many revivals, including a magical staging by Robert Wilson at Lincoln Center in 1996.

After the Second World War, Americans enjoyed unprecedented prosperity during the 1950s. The arts were beginning to develop and thrive as never before, with increased sources of patronage, both public and private, and ever-expanding audiences. And with the new long-playing microgroove recordings, the music industry was booming. The war also encouraged the hiring of fine American singers, well educated in their native environment and less expensive than foreign artists. In addition, more black singers were cast in wider roles, women appeared on the roster of conductors, new works were commissioned on a large-scale basis and several American works were recorded or telecast. Some opera companies even devoted entire seasons to operas by American composers.

Whether composers were conservative or innovative, eclectic or individual, there was always something fresh about the American operatic sound. Recognizing this, college and university workshops across the nation – less dependent on full houses and box-office receipts – regularly produced new works. Several hundred premieres of both full-length and shorter, chamber operas took place on these creative academic stages. Many were written by prominent composers at the start of their careers, such as Leonard Bernstein, Dominick Argento, Carlisle Floyd and Jack Beeson. One pioneer programme, Columbia University's Opera Workshop, staged at least fifteen American works between 1941 and 1958, including the premieres of Menotti's *The Medium*, Thomson's *The Mother of Us All* and Douglas Moore's Pulitzer Prize-winning *Giants in the Earth* (1951).

This academic phenomenon, in turn, brought about a new kind of democratization of opera. From north to south, east to west, small companies sprang up and gave new life to the American theatrical scene, including Kentucky Opera (1952), Tulsa Opera (1953), Santa Fe Opera (1956), Seattle Opera (1962) and Minnesota Opera (1964). Larger companies, too, opened their doors during this period. Dallas Opera was inaugurated in 1957 with a gala concert by Maria Callas. With verve and daring, Lyric Opera of Chicago (1954) and Houston Grand Opera (1955) eventually established traditions of featuring contemporary American repertoire. By the year 2000, Houston could boast twenty-five world premieres. Four were composed by the popular and prolific Floyd: *Bilby's Doll* (1976), *Willie Stark* (1981), *The Passion of Johnathan Wade* (new version, 1991) and *Cold Sassy Tree* in 2000 (Rich 2000, 15 and 17). Other important Houston premieres ranged from Bernstein's *A Quiet Place* (1983) and John Adams's *Nixon in China* (1987) to Meredith Monk's *Atlas* (1991) and Mark Adamo's *Little Women* in 1998 (29–30).

With a rich and varied repertoire as its signature, New York City Opera also reached out to America's operatic tastes, traditions and fresh approaches, showcasing many works that became enduring staples. Throughout its history of more than half a century, the company has staged some sixty American operas, twenty-three as world premieres. Under the direction of Julius Rudel, twenty-one American works comprised the Ford Foundation American Opera Series of 1958 and 1959. New York City Opera also produced the first major premiere by a black composer: *Troubled Island* by William Grant Still in 1949. Premieres of such works as Aaron Copland's *The Tender Land* (1954), Hugo Weisgall's *Six Characters in Search of an Author* (1959), Moore's *The Wings of the Dove* (1961), Robert Ward's *The Crucible* (1961), Beeson's *Lizzie Borden* (1965), Argento's *Miss Havisham's Fire* (1979) and Anthony Davis's *The Life and Times of Malcolm X* (1986) opened the door to new, compelling opera for many audiences. Several of the company's productions have also enjoyed repeated performances. *Street Scene*, for example, has been revived at New York City Opera more than fifty times.

What styles, subjects and moods draw people to American opera today? The question of what makes American opera 'American' is far less important than what makes it moving. American folk-like figures – Porgy, Baby Doe, Susannah – are at the core of the most popular American operas. While these characters are down-to-earth – more flawed than heroic – they breathe, grow and are humanized through their music. Indeed American locales and subjects provide colourful elements in the stories, but it is the composer's skills in musically interpreting these elements as drama that make them part of the nation's cultural legacy. Moore's *The Ballad of Baby Doe* and Floyd's *Susannah*, both staged for the first time in 1956, remain with *Porgy and Bess* the nation's most popular American operas. Though the characters themselves are indeed credible, it is through their lyricism and song that we come to know them.

Opera, film and musical theatre

Broadway and the Hollywood film have played a formative role in many operas by twentieth-century American composers. When Gershwin's *Porgy and Bess* was first performed in 1935, critics argued vehemently about whether it was an opera or Broadway musical. Today the term 'crossover' is often used to describe works that share or meld elements of vernacular and classical style. Both operas and musicals can have spoken dialogue or be sung throughout. Both can have full symphonic textures or smaller, pop-style ensembles, and either complex musical scenarios or simple tunes. And as modern musicals have picked up elements of opera – musical dramaturgy, grandiose spectacle and melodramatic conflicts – opera often draws from the folk, jazz and other vernacular styles of Broadway. Sometimes the determining factor in deciding what to call a work is the venue and audience the composer wrote for. More important than terminology, however, is the dramatic and musical integrity of the work. Whether Broadway or opera, Bernstein's *Candide* (1956) and Stephen Sondheim's *Sweeney Todd* (1979) and *Passion* (1994) are strong, effective theatre under any terms (see Kornick 1991, 294–5).

The United States has long been a world leader in the art and industry of the motion picture. And as Hollywood and television invade American lives in multiple ways, it is not surprising that many of the nation's operas should fall under the spell of the ideology, dramaturgy, visual techniques and musical approaches of the motion picture. During the silent-film era, John Philip Sousa used actual film clips in his opera, *The Glass Blowers* (1909). But with the advent of sound, the motion picture approached a new artistic genre, and by 1940 the studio symphony orchestra had become as important an ingredient in the film as speech and sound effects. Most movies, in fact, contained orchestral scores with near-continuous music following the mercurial needs of the drama so closely that film composer Erich Korngold called them 'operas without singing' (Kirk 2001, 5).

In modern times, many of the most successful American operas display not only strong characterization and rhythmic energy, but also a vividly coloured orchestration that – like a film score – both follows and motivates the action. Often it is the orchestra that tells more about the struggles and feelings of the characters than the characters themselves. A good example of this occurs at the close of Act II of Samuel Barber's *Vanessa* (1958), a Pulitzer Prize-winning work commissioned by the Metropolitan Opera with a libretto by Menotti. When Erika bitterly comes to realize Anatol's deception, the leitmotiv associated with her anguished, distorted mind appears in the orchestra and is pitted against the simple hymn sung in the chapel offstage. Expanding into a darkly hued countermelody, the orchestral motif allows a glimpse into Erika's soul by shrouding the simple diatonic harmonies of the hymn with grotesque clashes of tonality.

Bernard Herrmann takes a somewhat different approach in his *Wuthering Heights* (1951), a remarkable work based on Emily Brontë's strange, haunting tale of the Yorkshire moors. Herrmann's explicit scoring for *Wuthering Heights* follows the dark moods of the story throughout, but it is also coloured with passages of intensely dramatic 'lyric speech', to use Herrmann's term. Though he wrote the scores for many of Alfred Hitchcock's movies, Herrmann's music for *Psycho* (1960) is perhaps his most influential. Shades of this thriller can be found in the scores of certain American operas from the 1960s, notably Beeson's *Lizzie Borden* and Marvin David Levy's *Mourning Becomes Elektra*. *Wuthering Heights* is Herrmann's only opera, and it had to wait nearly forty years for its premiere. True to his penchant for self-borrowing, the opera uses material from some of his film scores, among them *The Ghost and Mrs Muir* (1947) and *Jane Eyre* (1944) – which he called his first 'screen opera' (Kirk 2001, 268 and 426 n. 26).

In more recent operas, both orchestral and vocal styles fall under the influence of the motion picture, where direct communication and the expressive use of words keep the drama in motion. Many composers prefer an actively moving lyric declamation to the traditional action-stopping aria. In *A View From the Bridge* (1999), William Bolcom thrusts the action forward through a variety of vocal techniques – lyrical lines, recitative, pitched speech or merely dialogue. In so doing, he provides the action, pacing and passion that are the hallmarks of American *verismo* opera.

Many composers today admit that the cinema has greatly enlarged their dramatic perspectives. André Previn (*A Streetcar Named Desire*, 1998) claims he learned about the capabilities of the orchestra from his work in Hollywood. Libby Larsen, who has composed nine operas, found techniques from the motion picture and television created strong characterization and moving modern metaphors, notably in her *Frankenstein* (1990). Having studied screen-writing, she is acutely aware of the way films and television condition theatre audiences, changing even the perception of how emotion unfolds in a human being.

Jake Heggie, Tobias Picker, Stephen Paulus, Lowell Liebermann and many others have virtually grown up with the ubiquitous, all-powerful culture of the American screen. Many of their operas are based on famous works of literary realism that were made into motion pictures before they wrote their operas. Among these are Lee Hoiby's *Summer and Smoke* (1971, after Tennessee Williams), Floyd's *Of Mice and Men* (1969, after John Steinbeck), Bolcom's *A View From the Bridge* (1999, after Arthur Miller), John Harbison's *The Great Gatsby* (2000, after F. Scott Fitzgerald) and Previn's *Streetcar* (after Williams). Thus the realism of American literature has shaped both the narrative style of the American motion picture and the *verismo* tradition of contemporary opera. Both give modern American opera its characteristic strength and drawing-power.

Many directors and designers make use of filmic techniques to heighten the visual and symbolic interest of their productions. *The Ghosts of Versailles* (1991), by composer John Corigliano and librettist William Hoffman, was the first opera to be commissioned by the Metropolitan Opera in twenty-five years. A large part of its extraordinary success can be attributed to its phantasmal stage designs. Called a 'grand opera buffa', it abounds in seventeenth- and eighteenth-century imagery with singing statues, trapdoors, flying apparitions and an enormous, colourful twelve-foot pasha. Director Colin Graham felt the opera was written like a film script, constantly rolling from one world into another. For Argento's *The Dream of Valentino* (1994), John Conklin projected Valentino's face onto multiple screens, where it became surrealistically distorted and broken into pieces to reflect the actor's tragic lost dreams.

Experimental multi-media effects have long fascinated Meredith Monk and Laurie Anderson, who broke ground with their exciting, angular operas born of the latest technology. But the century's most successful innovative venture since Thomson's *Four Saints in Three Acts* was Philip Glass's and Robert Wilson's concepts for *Einstein on the Beach* (1976). *Einstein* is an abstract work that combines music, dance, spoken text and singing in a series of tableau-like pantomimes (Kornick 1991, 116–18). The unique atmosphere of minimalism in Glass's score, moreover, serves the opera's mystical style effectively. With *Satyagraha* (1980) and *Akhnaten* (1984), Glass's *Einstein on the Beach* forms a trilogy representing heroic figures from science, politics and religion. Cinematic illusions, holographic projections, silent-movie techniques and other influences from film are aspects of later Glass operas also. But with his large-scale *The Voyage* (1991), commissioned by the Metropolitan Opera to celebrate the 500th anniversary of Columbus in the New World, Glass has written his most ambitious single work. *The Voyage* uses a large cast and orchestra and shows more harmonic complexity and chromaticism than is normally associated with his style.

Where is American opera going? What lies in its future? With the start of the new millennium, more operas by Americans are being commissioned, produced, recorded and published than ever before. Many are also being performed overseas with great acclaim, as the operas of Floyd, Menotti, Bernstein, Weill, Ward and Elliott Carter attest. In addition, co-commissioning and joint staging have helped sustain American opera as federal support has declined. Still, while the audiences for opera in America have increased dramatically over the past decade, stagings of *Figaro*, *La Bohème*, *Carmen*, *La traviata* and other staples remain the major box-office draws. American works are slow to carve a place in the repertoire. But more new works are being repeated, and frequently. Indeed American works appear as often on company season lists as some operas of Massenet, Donizetti, Bellini, Meyerbeer and Janáček. American opera, still a younger art form than its European counterpart, is indeed alive and well. And for the nation of sturdy explorers, new avenues and fertile creative paths lie just around the bend.

13 Opera in England: taking the plunge

CHRISTOPHER MARK

My dear Imogen,

  Thank you for your kind letter about Peter Grimes. I am so glad that the opera came up to your expectations, & it is sweet & generous of you to write so warmly about it. I must confess that I am very pleased with the way that it seems to 'come over the foot-lights', and also with the way the audience takes it, & what is perhaps more, returns night after night to take it again! I think the occasion is actually a greater one than either Sadler's Wells or me, I feel. Perhaps it is an omen for English Opera in the future. Anyhow I hope that many composers will take the plunge, & I hope also that they'll find as I did the water not quite so icy as expected!   (BENJAMIN BRITTEN, 26 June 1945)

Britten's comments about the wider significance of his first successful opera in this letter to Imogen Holst written nineteen days after its premiere (Mitchell and Reed 1991, 1268) were indeed prescient. Opera had in fact figured strongly in the worklists of British composers in the first half of the twentieth century: the genre was central to the work of Charles Stanford, Ethyl Smyth, Gustav Holst and Rutland Boughton, while Frederick Delius's *A Village Romeo and Juliet* and Ralph Vaughan Williams's *Riders to the Sea* contain some of their composers' best music. But Britten's *Peter Grimes* excited an unprecedented degree of faith in opera's possibilities, sustained to this day. Since the Second World War, few British composers of any substance have been able to resist the siren call of what is still probably the most risky of all compositional undertakings, beset as it is by the dangers of multiple collaboration and the strong possibility that, because of the scarcity of funds, the fruits of many months' (if not years') labour will fall silent after the first production. For some composers (Peter Maxwell Davies, Harrison Birtwistle and Judith Weir are a few examples, along with Britten and Michael Tippett) opera has been crucial in forging or honing a distinctive style; sometimes (as in the case of Tippett's *King Priam*) it has been the catalyst for momentous stylistic shifts. For others – Jonathan Harvey, for instance – opera has been less central, though this is not necessarily to say that their work has been less powerful. Indeed, such is the volume and variety of operatic achievement in twentieth-century England that, rather than attempt a comprehensive survey, I have taken a snapshot approach, focusing for the most part on a few key aspects of the most influential works of just three composers – Britten, Tippett and Birtwistle – whose operatic outputs are especially remarkable in range and quality. Consideration of them is preceded by sketches of earlier works that are too often overlooked, and succeeded by brief samples of recent developments.

Delius, Holst and Vaughan Williams

It is difficult to find many opera composers working at the turn of the twentieth century who do not have something to say about Wagner, in words or compositional approach or both, and English opera is no exception. As Anthony Payne has observed, the music of Delius is 'based to a large extent on Wagner, whose endless flow and harmonic aura Delius attempted to emulate'. This is tempered by Grieg, 'whose airy texture and non-developing use of chromaticism showed him how to lighten the Wagnerian load' (Payne 2001, 164). There is in Delius little of the long-range harmonic momentum without which the unrelenting power of Wagner could not exist: as Peter Evans has written, Delius's 'chords are essentially local phenomena, sensitively coloured and spaced but accountable for their nature only in terms of immediate chromatic adjacencies' (1995, 180). So it is that the final bars of his best-known opera, *A Village Romeo and Juliet* (1901), are more a contemplation of the socially isolated lovers' fate than a *Liebestod*-like denouement. Evans's comment would seem to imply severe limitations in Delius's technique. But in this particular instance Delius's tendency to celebrate 'the moment' almost to excess is ideal for the task in hand, since the lovers choose (as Sali puts it) 'To be happy one last moment, and then to die'. Nor is intense contemplation out of keeping with the rest of the work: Delius describes it as a 'lyric drama in six scenes', and, as Payne observes, 'each scene is more concerned with presenting a spiritual state' than furthering a dramatic plot line (Payne 2001, 164). Given the importance of mood, it is no surprise that the evocative orchestral interludes, including 'The Walk to the Paradise Garden', well known as a concert piece, have a signal role to play: it is in these that the key emotional moments of the work are to be found.

Wagnerian principles, if not the Wagnerian harmonic vocabulary as such, continued to inspire composers born in the next decade whose nationalistic impulses drew them away from the perceived hedonism and individualism of Austro-German late romanticism. That Holst started out as a committed Wagnerian is evident from *Sita* (1900–06), the eighth of his thirteen theatrical works. This derives its subject-matter from the *Ramayana*, the Sanskrit epic, and is nothing if not Wagnerian in scale. As this extract from a 1903 letter to Vaughan Williams shows, Holst was unable to see an alternative position: 'I do feel sometimes inclined to chuck *Sita* in case it is only bad Richard I [i.e. Wagner]. Unless one ought to follow the latter until he leads you to fresh things. What I feel is that there is *nothing* else but Wagner excepting Italian one act horrors' (Vaughan Williams and Holst 1959, 12). Wagner did indeed lead him on to new things, for Holst seems to have realized through the experience of *Sita* that he was precisely the opposite kind of composer to the German master – one whose voice would best be served by understatement and a fundamentally modal, rather than chromatic, language (though chromaticism still has an important role to play). The new approach was essayed in Holst's next work, *Nine Hymns from the Rig Veda* (1907) for voice and piano, and consolidated in his finest opera, *Sāvitri* (1908–09).

Based on another Sanskrit epic, this time the *Mahābhārata*, translated and adapted again by Holst himself, *Sāvitri* might seem designed as the very antithesis of Wagnerian music-drama. It is a one-act chamber opera of thirty minutes' duration with a tiny cast of three plus a small chorus of female voices and twelve instrumentalists. The story is romantic (it is a variation of the topos, especially associated with Wagner, of 'woman as redeemer'), and there are aspects of the musical style that clearly evoke Wagnerian practice (Sāvitri's impassioned, surging hymn to Life and a limited leitmotivic technique stand out in this regard). But the most significant debt to Wagner, the principle of endless melody, is for the most part allied to a flexible modal usage, sometimes involving folk-like material, as in Sāvitri's song to Satyavān as he lies on the ground on the cusp of death. This is essentially a love song, accompanied only by flutes and (later) double bass. Its detached simplicity is representative of the work as a whole. Generally speaking, textures are spare, and nowhere more so than at the opening, when Death, unseen, states his purpose unaccompanied. The tenor of the work is established to no small extent by entrances: that of Death, just mentioned; that of the first instrument to be heard, the melancholic viola (which repeats Death's opening intonation); and that of the mysterious, unseen wordless chorus (supporting the first mention of the mystical concept of Maya). It is in such tellingly simple moments that the music most fully approaches the hieratic tone of the Sanskrit original.

The most impressive opera by Vaughan Williams, *Riders to the Sea* (1925–32), based on the play by J. M. Synge, is also small in scale – only some seven minutes longer than *Sāvitri* and with a cast of only two more characters, though it does require a somewhat larger (but still chamber) orchestra. Little comfort might be expected at the end of this grim venture into realism, and little is offered. But Vaughan Williams does create a remarkable sense of release at the exhaustion of the possibility of further tragedy. This results chiefly from the quality of the E major that emerges as the tonic at the end. There is no sense of inexorable progression; rather, E is gradually and gently asserted in a number of steps, fully emerging, occasionally inflected with the Lydian fourth, at Fig. 47. The key does not go unchallenged: there are threatening reminiscences of the stormy opening up to the final page. But it manages to maintain its tenuous authority, even though the work ends with the E major triad in its least stable, second-inversion position.

Boughton and the Glastonbury Festival

Born slightly later than Holst and Vaughan Williams, Rutland Boughton achieved astonishing success with one of his operas – or music-dramas, as he described them (Boughton and Buckley 1911, 15–20) – even though he failed to forge a language distinctive enough to build a sustainable reputation. His utopian socialist vision of the *Gesamtkunstwerk* led him to set up a Glastonbury Festival in imitation of Bayreuth in 1914. As Michael Hurd has written, Boughton's ideas 'had grown out of William Morris soil and were primarily concerned with creating a healthy union between art and ordinary people. Boughton proposed a community of artists, living and working on the land and exploding into "festivals" of artistic celebration at regular intervals' (1984, 435). The first project was to be a Wagner-inspired five-opera cycle on the exploits of King Arthur, the first one of which, *Uther and Igraine*, he had already written. The extent of Boughton's ambition is apparent in his extraordinarily bold introductory essay to this work:

> The following pages contain a half-taste of a work which achieves what Wagner failed thoroughly to achieve. I do not intend to depreciate Wagner, to whose work Buckley and I are so greatly indebted; but neither will I depreciate our work by affecting modesty in regard to our continuation of the German master's drama. Wagner has opened the way to the perfection of modern dramatic art.
> (Boughton and Buckley 1911, 1)

Unsurprisingly, perhaps, Boughton's initial vision for the Festival had to be scaled down (a number of performances were accompanied by piano rather than orchestra, for example), and it finally folded in 1927 – well before the Arthurian cycle was finally completed in 1945 – after one of the scandals that dogged the composer's career (Hurd 1984, 437). But the 350 staged perform-ances, including six works by Boughton himself and early English musical dramas by Matthew Locke, John Blow (*Venus and Adonis*) and Henry Purcell (*Dido and Aeneas*), represent an impressive testimony to Boughton's and his supporters' energy and determination (White 1983, 392–402).

It was at the first Festival that Boughton's best-known work, *The Immortal Hour* (1910–13), was first performed. The work adapts a verse drama by William Sharp (1855–1905), writing as 'Fiona Macleod'. Most of the music is not especially remarkable, but much of it is atmospheric and attractive, though one frequently finds oneself wishing for more incident and dramatic engagement. The opera had a staggering success in London, running for 216 consecutive performances beginning in 1922, with a revival of 160 performances in 1923. Eric Walter White's explanation of this as escapism for an audience starved of music during the First World War (398) may seem plausible, but is perhaps unduly dismissive, since one of Boughton's express purposes was to maximize the work's accessibility. Much, though by no means all, of the musical material is modal, and a folk-like simplicity is cultivated in a number of set-pieces, such as Etain's 'Fair is the moonlight' (Act I scene 1: quoted in Rye 1995, 347, where it is incorrectly attributed to Act I scene 2) and the 'faery' tune 'How beautiful they are' (sung by 'Unseen Voices' at the end of Act I scene 2 and repeated by Midir towards the end of Act II). The chromatic passages clearly have their provenance in Wagner, but the symphonic development that is at the heart of Wagner's musical language is not pursued to any significant extent.

Britten

As Hurd points out, Boughton's Glastonbury Festival anticipated the festival founded at Aldeburgh by Britten and Peter Pears in a number of ways (Hurd 1978, 31). Aldeburgh's greater success, and Britten's greater operatic achievement, is due in no small measure (over and above the sizeable matter of sheer talent) to the unremitting professionalism that informed all his musical activities. Once he had decided, after the success of *Peter Grimes*, that opera would become central to his career, he devised a working method – Imogen Holst's description (in Blyth 1981, 55) makes it seem like a factory assembly line – that allowed him to produce new works at a speed which, if hardly approaching that of Rossini, was nevertheless remarkable for the twentieth century.

Peter Grimes and *Death in Venice* (1973), Britten's first and last ventures in the genre, have in common with *Billy Budd* (1951), *Gloriana* (1953) and *Owen Wingrave* (1970) one of the most rehearsed of the recurring themes in Britten's operas: the isolation of an individual from the society in which he or she moves. This is especially evident in *Grimes*, in which the gulf between the eponymous anti-hero and the townsfolk is made palpable by the fact that, as Philip Rupprecht has pointed out, 'Grimes and the chorus in fact share the stage only twice – during the opening inquest scene, and then in the Act 1 pub scene'; as Rupprecht goes on to say, 'the remainder of the opera is a pattern of non-encounters' (2001, 34). In the pub scene the dichotomy is projected musically in two ways. First, Grimes's 'Great Bear' aria opens up vistas of musical expressiveness utterly at odds with the habitual small-talk of the towns-folk – an expressiveness matched in intensity, if not in visionary tone, only by Ellen in Act II scene 1 and the quartet of women in 'From the gutter' later in the same scene. Second, Grimes's off-tonic entry into the round 'Old Joe has gone fishing' (started by Ned Keene as a way of achieving community order) disrupts the flow, as Evans notes (1989, 113), by augmenting and diminishing the rhythmic patterns, and creates considerable harmonic tension before the Borough, *en masse*, wrenches the music back to its original key, overwhelming Grimes's voice in the process. Foreground and middle-ground harmonic tensions such as these have an immediate effect. Less obvious to the listener, but a vital con-tribution to the overall atmosphere of incompatibility, is the construction of the work at the background level of structure around the tritonal poles of A and E flat, though these do not often engage each other directly. As Evans argues, no hard-and-fast symbolic function can be attached to either key (this is, after all, likely to be lost on the listener who does not possess perfect pitch): it is the tension inherent in the interval that is symbolically significant (121–3; see also Payne 1963).

The viewpoint of *Grimes*'s audience is the traditional one of the all-seeing spectator, who has direct access to the thoughts and feelings of all the principal characters. The audience of *Death in Venice*, however, sees events only through the eyes of its protagonist, Gustav von Aschenbach. Thus, in contrast with *Grimes*, in which narratory reflection plays such an important role (above all in the famous 'sea interludes' and the passacaglia), 'We hear the environment as Aschenbach experiences it, we hear his gaze, as it were … everything the orchestra plays reveals Aschenbach's sensory perceptions, and there is no independent orchestral voice' (Rupprecht 2001, 253). (There is, I would suggest, a pre-echo of this in the so-called 'mad scene' of *Grimes* – Act III scene 2 – which Britten encourages us to experience from inside Grimes's head. After all, the women's voices' soothingly triadic, *dolce* 'Grimes' four bars after Fig. 49 can hardly be regarded as 'reality', given the aggressive choral utterance of his name to that point; rather, it may signal his sudden thinking of Ellen.) There are exceptions, however, as Rupprecht goes on to mention, and they are not easily dismissed. One of them is the final orchestral passage of the opera, which begins at the moment Aschenbach dies, and so may be regarded as an external view-point. Coming at the end, it inevitably colours our view of the whole.

Whittall describes 'this extraordinarily atmospheric ending' as con-veying 'the exaltation of Aschenbach's release into death', and points to the differences between the technical resources of the two operas by outlining the means by which this release is achieved: 'The inescapable disquiet inherent in the total chromatic, however securely rooted, is dissolved into modal ethereality rather than resolved into the solidly hierarchic planes of the tonal system. We most definitely do not "progress" from one to the other, but the music evolves the conditions whereby the transformation can be effected' (1990, 262). As this implies, there is no tonal scheme as such in *Death in Venice*; rather the musical drama is created through developments and transformations of motives and through contrasts and interactions of different types of material. In none of Britten's other operas is the material more vividly or economically characterized. Particularly remarkable is the music first heard in Act I at Fig. 73 that, one might say, embodies Tadzio: this transcends its gamelan provenance (see Cooke 1998, 220–44) to provide what Rupprecht describes as 'a transfixed "sonic gaze"' (2001, 246).

In its swift movement – in effect, cross-fading – from one short scene to another, *Death in Venice* draws on Britten's (and his production team's) experience of creating what is still arguably the most distinguished opera commissioned for television thus far, *Owen Wingrave*. Indeed, it is difficult to see how the effect of 'that other, *external* reality – the world around Aschenbach – [having] operatic life only as an object of his perceptions' (245) could have been conceived without a televisual (or, at least, cinematic) model of how to melt away the substance of that external reality – the stage apparatus as well as the music – as Aschenbach's thoughts and feelings shift. Meanwhile the harmonic and textural organization of both *Wingrave* and *Death in Venice* owe much to the innovations of *Curlew River* (1964), the first of Britten's three 'parables for church performance'. In taking on board aspects of both its Nō-play model and the heterophonic textures of other types of traditional Japanese music (Cooke 1998, 130–89), this work dispenses with the progressive apparatus and textural alignment of conventional tonality that, even in his most radical vein, Britten had still drawn upon to some degree up to that point.

Tippett

Eric Crozier, Britten's librettist for *Albert Herring* (1947) and the co-librettist (with E. M. Forster) of *Billy Budd*, made it clear that, as far as he was concerned,

> a librettist is a craftsman working for an artist. He may also be an artist himself, but his main job is not to write as the poet must write . . . but to provide his composer with words, ideas, emotion, actions that are all true to character, true in style, and *infinitely capable of formal modification and reshaping to musical ends*.
> (Herbert 1979, 137; emphasis added)

It appears that, after various problems with Auden (librettist of *Paul Bunyan*, 1941), Montagu Slater (*Peter Grimes*) and Ronald Duncan (*The Rape of Lucretia*, 1946), Britten had found the ideal working relationship, later to be reduplicated with William Plomer (*Gloriana* and the church parables) and Myfanwy Piper (*The Turn of the Screw*, 1954, *Owen Wingrave* and *Death in Venice*). Many other English composers preferred to write their own libretti. In his essay 'The words of Wagner's Music Dramas', published in *The Vocalist* of June 1902, Vaughan Williams comes to the conclusion that 'there is only one man who can write the words of a musical drama, and that man is the composer of the music, for the drama must generate in the music' (Vaughan Williams and Holst 1959, 35). He had obviously changed his mind by the time he composed *Riders to the Sea*, which sets Synge's play with only a little pruning. But these sentiments were shared by a good number of other English composers.

Chief amongst them was Tippett, who had already written the text for one musico-dramatic work, his oratorio *A Child of Our Time* (1939–41), before beginning work on *The Midsummer Marriage* (1946–52). The shortcomings of Tippett's texts have often been observed, not least by Derrick Puffett: 'I well remember reading, with mounting dismay, the libretto of *The Knot Garden* when it first came out, in 1969 (it was published before the score), and wondering what sort of music its author could possibly set to it' (2001, 139). However, it is clear from Tippett's own accounts of his working practices that he could not operate in any other way; that his holistic approach (and, more specifically, an approach in which Jungian symbology played such an important role) demanded the possibility of words responding to musical or theatrical ideas (Tippett 1974, 50–66). But whatever problems there may be with the libretti, Puffett's other main criticism of the operas – that the later ones peddle a personal mythology rather than a collective one – seems more serious:

> In pursuing the need to transmute his traditional, mythological material into images corresponding to 'an immediate experience of our day', Tippett has lost sight of the equally powerful need for these images to be based on something collective ... Peter Brook never gave better advice ... than when he counselled the composer to 'choose a public myth and not a private one' for his new opera [*King Priam* (1958–61)]. It is not simply a matter of the audience being able to follow the composer without difficulty, as Brook averred. Perhaps Brook was too tactful to say what he really felt: that without the stabilising force of a mythological subject, Tippett's work was likely to go off into a fantasy world of eccentricity.　　　　(2001, 147)

It would certainly be over-reacting to dismiss the three operas Tippett composed after *King Priam* (*The Knot Garden*, 1966–9; *The Ice Break*,

1973–6; and *New Year*, 1986–8) on the grounds that they do, indeed, 'go off into a fantasy world of eccentricity', for, as Puffett acknowledges, they contain some impressive stretches of music. But it is equally clear that Tippett's first two operas achieve much of their considerable power from tapping into 'collective, mythological material' – a nexus of common inheritance including (to mention only the most obvious) Mozartian opera and the symbology of the Jungian collective unconscious in *The Midsummer Marriage* (see Kemp 1984, 209–77, and Mellers 1999), and the Greek myths concerning the Trojan war in *King Priam*.

Much can be learnt about the essences of *The Midsummer Marriage* and *King Priam* from their endings. *The Midsummer Marriage* centres on the psychic and spiritual journeys that the main characters, Mark and Jenifer, have to undergo in order to achieve 'wholeness'. As the dominance of sonata form in the history of common-practice tonality demonstrates, music is particularly good at enacting the progression from 'division' to 'wholeness'. However, as is often the case with Tippett, it is not easy to discern the systematic manipulation of tonal centres that one associates with sonata form (and common-practice masterworks in general), and it seems more productive to regard the *type* of music employed – and, as Kemp suggests, its sonorities – as being of the greatest significance (Kemp 1984, 237–9). Thus it is the sheer energy of the final pages, born of madrigalian cross-rhythms (the finale is in essence a series of madrigals) and unexpected shifts of harmonic area – by turns transfiguring, as at Fig. 514 when the stage gradually fills with light, or explosive, as at Fig. 519, or both, as at Fig. 520 when 'The stage is now in bright sunlight' – that embodies and celebrates the completion of the quest.

The Midsummer Marriage has clear parallels with earlier and contemporaneous English operas. Though Boughton's direct influence seems doubtful, the chorus comes close to fulfilling his ambitions for its operatic role, while the pastoral, magical and Celtic aspects have precedents in *The Immortal Hour*. Although Tippett's plot is a good deal removed from Britten's customary realism, the orchestral interludes take as central a role as those of *Peter Grimes* – and, like Britten's, were also later extracted to form a popular concert work, the *Ritual Dances*. The more explicitly modernist tone of *King Priam* is easier to relate to the work of later generations. Its ending is one of the most disquieting 'conclusions' (a singularly inappropriate word) in all opera, and is as different from that of *The Midsummer Marriage* as can be imagined. Indeed, though there are moments of luminosity during the course of *Priam* – pre-eminently in Hermes' hymn to Music (during the Interlude between scenes 3 and 4 in Act III), where Hermes (as Tippett's mouthpiece) states why the tale is being told through music – the ending is untypical of Tippett in that most of his big, public statements offer unambiguously affirmative statements. The aftermath of Priam's death is portrayed with what Tippett has described as 'a few curious sounds that might represent *our* inward tears' (1980, 230) – desiccated sonorities with the merest hint of lyricism in the cello. As Whittall has shown, connections can be made with pitch structures from other parts of the work (1999, 63–4). However, while these cannot be dismissed, it could be said that they are beside the point, for it is the numbed disassociation with what has gone before that counts. The break with the previous music is the most extreme instance of the most discussed aspect of the opera, its mosaic form. Unrelated blocks of music, very often non-developing and (more significantly) habitually non-concluding, are placed against each other. The 'cut-off' points frequently seem arbitrary, giving the overall impression that the music is not, so to speak, in control of its own destiny: the decision to move on to the next block is not intrinsic, but external. This is as powerful a symbol (again, almost an embodiment) of the hand of Fate – arguably the true central 'character' of *King Priam* – as one could imagine.

Birtwistle and after

Tippett's mosaic approach has its provenance in Stravinsky (whose *Symphonies of Wind Instruments* of 1920 (revised in 1945) is the *locus classicus* of the form), and Stravinsky is also the model for the highly ritualistic mosaic usage in the first opera by Birtwistle, *Punch and Judy* (1967), commissioned by Britten's English Opera Group for performance at the 1968 Aldeburgh Festival. It may be felt that what Robert Adlington terms a 'compulsive short-windedness' (2000, 11) born of the abrupt discontinuities lends itself particularly well to depicting the notorious violence, as well as the comedy, of the traditional puppet show. But, as Adlington has argued, it is the absence of recitative that gives the opera (styled by Birtwistle and his librettist Stephen Pruslin as 'a tragical comedy or a comical tragedy') its unique flavour:

> In *Punch and Judy* the lack of recitative only emphasises the extent to which this is indeed a 'toy opera'. The 'characters' – puppets, after all – in being denied recitative are thereby largely denied opportunities for character development or the exercising of volition. Instead they are deployed in a succession of static situations, just as a child deploys toys in play. The motivation for the deployment is not apparent to the toys, but exists only in the child's imagination. Their violent interactions, similarly, are best seen not as representative of some potentially cathartic, archetypal conflict, but as reflective of the more quotidian brutality of motiveless, childlike play. (12)

A good deal of the comedy is to be found in the wordplay of the libretto itself, though it is difficult fully to appreciate the wittiest moments in the theatre: 'Punch, that virtuoso of villainy, plucks pizzicati of panic and glissandi of gore in a toccata of torture' from 'Proclamation III' in 'Murder Ensemble III' is readily assimilated by the ear (most of it is recited, by the Doctor and the Lawyer, on an octave E), but 'Two times too lost four her sake./ Totem stool for hearse ache' from 'Passion-Chorale II' demands to be seen on the page. As Adlington notes, the music itself 'comes close at times to a succession of comedy turns', with 'many of the opera's numbers [fashioned] into mini exercises parodying historical styles or forms' (11). Not the least comical moment occurs when the putative narrator, Choregos, is himself tricked by Punch into being hanged. And in such moments of challenge to the 'normal' course of operatic events the work triumphantly asserts the capacity for modernism to continue to breathe new life into the genre.

But it is Birtwistle's second opera (or 'lyrical tragedy in three acts') that most fully demonstrates its composer's remarkable capacity for reinvention. While *Punch and Judy* was conceived, on one level, as (in the librettist's own term) a 'source opera' – in fact, *the* source opera, as if it had somehow travelled back in time to create the conventions that, in its own time, it is parodying – *The Mask of Orpheus* (1983), based on one of the favourite topics of opera composers through the centuries, begins with the birth of music itself. It is a highly complex work, with a threefold representation of the central characters (Orpheus, Eurydice and Aristaeus are each played by singer, mime and puppet), frequently dense counterpoint of orchestral layers, and various electronic components (brilliantly realized by Barry Anderson at IRCAM in Paris). But it is the non-linear plot, resulting from the concatenation of various Orphic myths and from events being revisited and seen from different angles, that most fully characterizes the work. The discontinuities can be over-emphasized, however. Adlington notes that 'the directness of the music is potentially a surprising revelation for a work whose notoriety since its premiere came to rest largely on the fastidious complexities of its libretto' (1998, 43). Later he writes of the 'unapologetically goal-directed musical structure', and notes elsewhere that the music 'frequently takes a stake in the raw drama of the narrative, in just the manner that the rigorous formalism of Zinovieff's text denies. The music's very continuousness does much to maintain the unbroken theatrical spell – the tinge of realism – that was so consistently disrupted in *Punch and Judy*' (2000, 20). The listener's (if not the spectator's) final impression of the work, looking back over the whole, is likely to be a progression towards what Whittall has described as 'the archetypal Birtwistle conclusion, establishing an equilibrium between focusing and dissolving which, for all its reliance on centricity, creates no "tonal" hang-ups' (1998, 55). The centre referred to here is the E that recurs, often spread over several octaves, during Act III (it provides the starting-point for the various returns of the Love Duet, for example). Significantly, E is always a point of departure, never a point of contraction (which explains why there are no '"tonal" hang-ups'). Always unheralded, its various appearances seem to be in the manner of external intrusions similar to the imposed breaks between the blocks in *King Priam*. Again, the symbolism suggests the hand of Fate: Birtwistle's and Zinovieff's underlying metaphor for Act III is the inexorable movement of the tides. The effect, though, is rather different: as most commentators have observed, the central concerns of *The Mask of Orpheus* are Time and Memory, and in Jonathan Cross's words, 'by the end of the Act, events have become so attenuated that the E of the tides is about all one can fix on. Fragments are layered on top of this ... but we are left in something like a dream world, an eternal present, the product only of memory' (2000, 107).

While the quality of the music of *The Mask of Orpheus* (which in Act III ranks as high as anything the composer has written) may be equalled in his ensuing operas (*Yan Tan Tethera*, 1984; *Gawain*, 1991; *The Second Mrs Kong*, 1994; and *The Last Supper*, 1999), Birtwistle's second opera is likely to remain at the core of discussions of his achievements, and its originality and colossal ambition should ensure that it remains a benchmark of late twentieth-century musical theatre of whatever provenance. The operas of the other members of the so-called Manchester School, Peter Maxwell Davies and Alexander Goehr, are less spectacularly innovative and, while containing much that is impressive on a purely musical level, generally lack Birtwistle's dramatic sensibility. Thus Davies's *Taverner* (1962–8), which follows the composer John Taverner's betrayal of his art through misguided political idealism, suffers from pressing its central concern – the transformation from one state into its opposite – rather too laboriously. And it makes impractical demands on the audience's powers of perception, requiring a highly tuned ability not only to detect markedly transformed versions of the plainchants that are Davies's basic material, but also to recall their texts, if the fundamental symbolism is to be appreciated. (Introducing a BBC studio recording broadcast on 2 April 1997, Davies talked about the 'slight optimism' at the end of the work, which depends on the listener spotting an easily missed reworking of a fragment of a plainchant for the Resurrection in the cello at six bars after Fig. 290.)

Given my commentary so far, it might seem that, although parallels can often be observed between different works by different composers, little emerges in the way of an English operatic tradition as such. The work of subsequent generations – composers like Robin Holloway, Jonathan Harvey, Oliver Knussen, Judith Weir and Mark-Anthony Turnage – reinforces this view. All of these figures, who have come to prominence in an era of unprecedented pluralism, display a degree of indebtedness to one or both of Britten and Tippett, but the differences between them are more striking – from the luscious romanticism of Holloway's *Clarissa* (1976), to the playful and manifold allusions of Knussen's *Where the Wild Things Are* (1979–83), the electronically under-pinned psychic journey of Harvey's *Inquest of Love* (1991–2), the multiple rôle-playing of Weir's *King Harald's Saga* (1979), and the ingenious mixture of kitchen-sink drama (with its references to popular culture) and Greek myth in Turnage's *Greek* (1986–8). *King Harald's Saga* might seem out of place in this chapter, since it is written for just one performer; yet it achieves a sense of breadth (and an engagement with the essential features of 'grand' opera, actually being entitled 'grand opera in 3 acts') that belies the length of its cast-list and its duration. Weir has said of the singer's task:

> I find that making a singer play several characters draws out much more interesting work from them, and they begin to define their characters in much more scientific ways. In the classic operatic production there are stock characters and the singers have rather trivial, anecdotal ways of getting into them. So if a singer is suddenly plunged into *King Harald's Saga* where they have to be about nine characters, they have to think hard about making these characters different people. (Ford 1993, 109–10)

Multiple rôle-playing is also required in Weir's *A Night at the Chinese Opera* (1987), a work that shows pluralism to its best advantage in its mixture of comedy and moral seriousness couched in a language that, whilst drawing chiefly on materials and procedures familiar from the extended-tonal past, rarely takes the easy expressive option. Harvey's *Inquest of Love*, with its resonances of *The Midsummer Marriage* in its 'strange story of weddings, murders, and the quest for understanding, healing, and forgiveness in the afterlife' (Harvey 1999, 54), exemplifies the continuing relevance of the modernist legacy to an institution that Boulez famously decreed should be blown up. That operatic composition in England should survive his injunction might never have been in serious doubt; that English composers continue to take the operatic plunge with such variety and inventiveness despite the infrastructural problems men-tioned at the beginning of this chapter is testimony to the continuing potential of the richest of all musical genres as well as the strength of English composition in general.

PART FOUR

Directions

14 Music theatre since the 1960s

ROBERT ADLINGTON

Avant-garde music and theatre

Of all the performing arts, none has been more circumspect about its theatrical nature than classical concert music. A romantic ideology that located musical content in sounds rather than actions or locations, and that accordingly identified composer rather than performer as the primary origin of that content, came to ensure that the act of performance was, as far as possible, rendered invisible. The theatre of musical performance was largely limited to a carefully circumscribed ritual of dress and behaviour; the performer who sought to assert his or her individuality over and above this ritual risked accusations of charlatanism.

On the face of it, the postwar avant-garde in Europe and America, while enthusiastically dispensing with other aspects of musical tradition, represented the apotheosis of this downplaying of the business of performance. Here was a music that elevated the abstract sonic configuration to the status of a fetish, that finally eradicated the pleasure of the performer as a compositional consideration, and that seemed more at home in the lecture room or the computer lab than the concert hall. As Paul Griffiths has noted, 'in the 1950s ... few young composers wanted to work in the theatre. Indeed, to express that want was almost enough ... to separate oneself from the avant-garde' (1995, 171). And yet this apparently arid terrain for theatrical endeavour was soon touched by developments that, conversely, prepared the ground for quite new sorts of musical theatre. During the second half of the 1950s, the music of the avant-garde became, albeit frequently unwittingly, suffused with the spirit of theatre.

This occurred in a number of ways. First, the virtuosity demanded of performers by avant-garde scores in itself served to highlight the very act of performance. A new generation of performers – including figures such as David Tudor, Cathy Berberian and Severino Gazzelloni – became renowned specifically for championing modern music, and grateful composers, including Berio and Cage, responded by devising solo works that celebrated performance virtuosity as much as compositional technique. These and other works frequently experimented with extended instrumental and vocal techniques; the theatrical element of all musical performance was thus enhanced as a performer set about his or her instrument in ways that intruded upon and transgressed the 'neutral' codes of the concert ritual.

A second important development in 1950s avant-garde music also assumed an active rather than passive interpreter: namely, indeterminacy. Aristotle, in his *Poetics*, declares that dramatic character is a product of the choices made by an individual (Dorsch 1965, 41): by this reckoning, the ceding to performers of an element of compositional decision-making brings a particularly theatrical quality to musical performance. Indeterminacy or aleatoricism appears in the music of composers of all hues at this time – be it the carefully delimited alternative routes prescribed in Boulez's Piano Sonata No. 3 (1957), or the more generous freedoms of Cage's music – initiated by the notorious 'silent' piece *4'33"* (1952), which 'may be performed by any instrumentalist or combination of instrumentalists and last any length of time'. Intriguingly, though, this elevation of the performative act also seemed logical to composers who, conversely, preferred to retain more total authorial control. For Stockhausen, the movement of performers' bodies was deemed a legitimate concern for the composer precisely because of the desire for optimum integration. According to Stockhausen's spokesperson Karl Wörner,

> The basic tendency is to integrate into the composition every phenomenal aspect of music, everything that can be observed by the senses. In this way one necessarily comes to the idea of 'musical theatre'. (1973, 187)

The same rationale lies behind Stockhausen's fondness for unconventional stage layouts; and this utilization of space as a musical parameter constitutes a third characteristic of avant-garde music that predisposes it towards theatre. Occasional precedents had been set in the music of Ives and Harry Brant, but it was Stockhausen who was largely responsible for establishing it as accepted practice in contemporary music. *Gruppen* (1957) and *Trans* (1971) are both essentially orchestral pieces, but in deriving much of their musical motivation from the unorthodox spatial disposition of the musicians they knock at the door of music theatre. Spatial layout was to become central to the music of a number of other composers: it reinforces the explicit instrumental theatre in Birtwistle for instance; and it can also contribute to the sense that the vocal music of György Kurtág, though not actually labelled as music theatre, nevertheless comprises what Adrienne Csengery has termed 'camouflaged opera' (quoted in Griffiths 1995, 283).

A final germane development in 1950s avant-garde music from the viewpoint of theatre is the advent of electronic composition. Stockhausen was particularly influential here too. His landmark contribution to the genre, the *Gesang der Jünglinge* (1956), reinforced the theatre implicit in the speech and song that are the piece's primary sound source with a spatial dimension: the music is bounced between four speakers placed around the auditorium. The electronic alteration of speech later formed the basis of works written especially for radio broadcast by Berio (*Thema – omaggio a Joyce* (1958) and *Visage* (1961)), works which, in the words of David Osmond-Smith, 'explore the borderline where sound as the bearer of linguistic sense dissolves into sound as the bearer of musical meaning' (1991, 62). The imaginary theatre conjured up in such works is not wholly dependent upon an origin in spoken or other 'found' sounds, however. The attraction of wholly synthesized tape pieces often lies precisely in their tendency to connote real-world objects, actions and scenarios. It is difficult to hear the original version of Stockhausen's *Kontakte* (1960), for instance, without imagining a journey through a futuristic landscape. In more recent electronic music – such as Gilles Gobeil's remarkable *Le vertige inconnu* (1993) – synthesized sounds can conjure up a 'virtual' world of machinery and motions with such immediacy that they almost relinquish their claim to be 'music' at all.

Music theatre: definitions

As composers awoke to the dramatic potential of their evolving compositional concerns, so the theatrical aspect of their work became more pronounced. Indeed, this theatrical orientation permeated music of the 1960s and early 1970s sufficiently thoroughly to make the distinguishing of a separate genre of 'music theatre' rather problematic. An indication of this difficulty is given by Griffiths' suggestion that the genre's death-knell was sounding in 1972 (1994, 334), despite the fact that the majority of Stockhausen's and Henze's 'music theatre' pieces (for example) had yet to be written.

It cannot be assumed, for instance, that the presence of a human voice is a prerequisite for music theatre. Many of the standard exemplars of the genre, at least as defined in dictionary accounts, have no vocal component: see, for example, Kagel's *Match* (1964) and Peter Maxwell Davies's *Vesalii icones* (1969). The question then arises as to whether *any* work that contains an element of purely instrumental theatre must count as music theatre. There are distinctions to be drawn even within this sub-genre. The sorts of enaction involved in Kagel's and Birtwistle's instrumental music, for instance, differ markedly. Kagel's works, in accommodating facial expressions and bodily gestures over and above those required for instrumental performance, invite closer comparisons with the spoken theatre; Birtwistle's rôle-play is largely limited to stage placement and sharply characterized musical material. These works, in possessing characteristics shared with many *vocal* theatre works, are clearly candidates for discussion in the present context. Other variants on the theme of instrumental theatre – in the music of composers as disparate as Berio, Tan Dun and Rebecca Saunders – will not be discussed here; but this is more a reflection of their limited relevance in a book about opera than an indication of some fundamental discontinuity with the tradition of postwar music theatre.

The line between music theatre and instrumental composition is thus not easily drawn. The same is true for music theatre and chamber opera. Music theatre has often been distinguished from opera simply on the basis of its reduced scale and the altered performance venues and conventions that this entails. Music theatre, it might be argued, concerns the introduction of practices of the theatre into the sphere of chamber music; alternatively – to entertain an even more general definition – it comprises 'theatre' pieces intended for performance in a concert hall. Such definitions nicely accommodate those music-theatre pieces that involve dance or mime rather than staged song, while not discriminating against the latter. There was often a financial explanation behind this turn to the small scale and the less elaborate (Clements 1992, 529). Opera houses were well aware that their audience had become firmly attached to a repertoire of endlessly repeated classics, and that the presentation of costly new works usually meant box-office disaster; composers therefore had to resort to other, cheaper means. However, these financial constraints were felt by avant-garde and 'conservative' composers alike: a sizing-down in scale should not be taken as indication of a fundamental antipathy to opera. Britten's chamber operas, most notably, capitalized on the intimacy that smaller forces allowed; more recent years have seen a healthy flow of small-scale theatre works (from figures such as Thomas Adès, Martin Butler, Mark-Anthony Turnage and Judith Weir in Britain alone) that are at least as much 'opera' as 'music theatre'. Conversely, imposing works have been produced in the opera house that are more 'music theatre' than 'opera': Berio's *Passaggio* (1962) and Birtwistle's *The Mask of Orpheus* (1983) fall into this category. Scale is a far from wholly reliable indicator of genre.

One of the primary reasons why both *Passaggio* and *The Mask of Orpheus* strain at the boundaries of their putative genre is their manner of story-telling. Both works adopt an overtly non-naturalistic and (in certain respects) anti-narrative approach. At earlier stages of its history, opera had been the most affectedly artificial of theatrical genres; but developments in the second half of the nineteenth century came to ensure that, from the perspective of the middle of the twentieth century, opera was seen as a vehicle for the essentially realistic portrayal of dramatic situations and psychological states. Music theatre, by contrast, is often characterized as being pre-eminently anti-realist – and, thereby, as representing (paradoxically) something of a throwback to early opera.

In some ways this propensity for anti-realism is a better criterion for distinguishing between music theatre and other genres than the others explored here. It is a propensity that can take two forms. First, narrative cogency may be deliberately exploded – whether by presenting a succession of situations that refuse reduction to a simple narrative sequence, or by combining material that is not clearly related so that the drama appears internally divergent or contradictory. Such challenges to narrative cogency may be found in abundance in the music-theatre works of Salvatore Sciarrino, where pre-existing stories may be reassembled in the 'wrong' order, as in *Lohengrin* (1982), or all pretence of narrative focus is abandoned in favour of a 'surrealist montage' of ideas and text-sources, as in *Cailles en sarcophage* (1979) and *Vanitas* (1981) (Osmond-Smith 1992, 268). Sciarrino's focus on the disturbed psychological states of his 'characters' means that his theatrical works sometimes resemble staged songs as much as they do traditional narrative opera; this is true of *Lohengrin* and the more recent *Infinito nero* (1997), for instance.

Second, taking a cue from Bertolt Brecht, composers have set about the disintegration of the stage illusion that forms such a central part of traditional theatre. Brecht's proposition that theatre should provoke critical thought on the part of the spectator, and that to do this it needed to resist 'seducing [him] into an enervating … act of enjoyment' by stressing the artificiality of the enaction (Willett 1964, 89), finds a resonance in music theatre's fondness for placing singers and instrumentalists on the same platform, and for withdrawing naturalistic scenery. Birtwistle's *Bow Down* (1977), with its tight circle of actor-singers defining the performance space in the centre of the stage, is emblematic of this pared-down, functional approach. Indeed the disassemblage of 'the pretence of opera' has been viewed as intrinsic to the 'whole nature of music theatre' (Griffiths 1994, 326).

Even here there are occasional exceptions. Hans Werner Henze's *La Cubana* (1974) is described by the composer as 'a "vaudeville" … in which all the music is employed realistically. Music can be heard and seen in it only where it would also be heard and seen in real life', a conceit made possible by the fact that the piece is about a chanteuse and the bar in which she sings (Henze 1982, 207). Here music theatre seeks to oppose operatic illusion, not through stylization, but rather with an almost clinical realism. Henze's piece serves to make the point that music theatre is perhaps ultimately best seen as an 'anti-genre' – which is to say, as characterized by a refusal to conform to traditional or pre-existing genres and categories, rather than by any other consistent traits. Music theatre tends to illuminate the awkward interstices between art forms, the gaps between existing aesthetic categories. This tendency is most obviously apparent in the compositions of the American performing artists who, during the early 1960s, came to be known collectively as 'Fluxus'. The text pieces of George Brecht, for instance, which instruct the performer to undertake some sort of action, have been described not as multimedia but as 'intermedia', in that 'they inhabit the area *between* poetry and perform-ance' (Nyman 1999, 79; emphasis added). Along similar lines, LaMonte Young justified his *Composition 1960 No. 2*, in which a fire is built in front of the audience, on the basis that it is good for someone to 'listen to what he ordinarily just looks at, or look at things he would ordinarily just hear' (84). The active involvement of European composers, notably Nono and Berio, with experimental theatre companies in the mid-1960s, suggests the degree to which they, too, were willing to loosen the bound-aries of their activities.

This 'anti-conventional urge in music theatre' has been viewed as containing the seeds of an eventual demise: a settling into generic patterns and clichés was never an option (Griffiths 1994, 334). Yet, as we have already seen, claims of the death of music theatre may have been pre-mature. Younger generations of postwar composers have undertaken theatrical ventures that are often strikingly consistent with the 'classic' works of the 1960s and 1970s. This consistency is easier to perceive if we look, not for similarities of style or technique, but instead for some wider preoccupations that appear to unite much of what has been called 'music theatre'. The remainder of this discussion will address a number of these preoccupations. First, it will look at the relation of music theatre to politics – and particularly the cultural politics of 'classical' and avant-garde music performance. Second, it will examine the ways in which the musical and performance styles of much music theatre have revelled in allusions to and affinities with the practices of different cultural tradi-tions. And third, it will draw attention to music theatre's interest in focusing our minds on certain existential universals: specifically, time; the human body; and space.

Music theatre and politics

For more than a few avant-garde composers in the 1960s and 1970s, music theatre's refutation of traditional genres, especially opera, had an explicitly political edge. Music theatre was the beneficiary of two related developments in the avant-garde at the start of the 1960s. The first was the awakening of a belief that avant-garde musical idioms found their validity and legitimacy not in appeals to abstract notions of structural cogency, but rather in their political function. The growing dissemination of Theodor Adorno's writings helped propagate the idea that the rejection of historical musical languages and forms, tainted as they were seen to be, was politically progressive. At the same time, many avant-garde composers were feeling a profound (if less explicitly voiced) hunger to engage once again with the realm of human affairs, after a decade of obsession with the abstract shaping of the molecules of musical material.

Music theatre thus provided an answer to two important developments in avant-garde music, by allowing a re-engagement with dramatic enaction in a form that explicitly refuted bourgeois theatrical conventions. This was the ideal medium for the overtly political messages of early music-theatre works such as Nono's *Intolleranza 1960* (1961) and Berio's *Passaggio* (1962), both of which commented gravely on political oppression. Elsewhere in Europe, the 'political' element of music theatre took a more introspective form, focusing first and foremost upon classical-music institutions and conventions rather than the world outside the opera house or concert hall. Part of this critique was implicit in the modest scale of many music-theatre works, which could be construed as a riposte against the expense and extravagance of bourgeois opera. But commentary on the rituals of classical performance could also take the form of an increased elaborateness. This is the case in Stockhausen's first full-blown excursion into music theatre, *Originale* (1961), which incorporates excerpts from the revised version of *Kontakte* (including live performers) and surrounds them with 'a polyphony of actions, involving music, drama, film, photography, painting, recording, street theatre and street music' (Maconie 1990, 115). Stockhausen's juxtaposition of the *Kontakte* extracts against the everyday activities of a recording engineer, a painter and a host of other miscellaneous characters, naturally served to highlight the artificiality of the conventions of classical musical performance: it is as if the presentation of the earlier piece was placed in inverted commas. The experience may have unnerved Stockhausen, for it exposed the historical contingencies – in the form of assumptions about concert presentation – upon which his supposedly forward-looking compositional output largely depended. For the rest of the 1960s he largely limited his theatricalisms to matters of stage placing and sound diffusion, devices that represented less of a challenge to the ritual of concert performance.

No composer has undertaken a more concerted examination of the business of musical performance than Mauricio Kagel: indeed, classical-music practice constitutes the principal subject of his music theatre. Kagel has been described as setting out to 'demystify the ritual' of the classical concert (Perrin 1981, 11), and this he does especially by highlighting the absurdities of virtuoso performance. On the face of it, then, here is a good example of an avant-garde attack on a cornerstone of the nineteenth-century performance tradition – one that appeared to be underlined in *Staatstheater* (1970), Kagel's exhaustive analysis of the absurdities of grand opera. In actuality, though, the real critical edge of Kagel's theatre arises from the way that his critique of the nineteenth-century virtuoso blurs into a ruthless nose-thumbing at the performative challenges of contemporary music. This tendency was already apparent in the early *Transición II* (1959) for pianist, percussionist and tapes. Ostensibly the piece is an attempt to fuse musical past, present and future through the use of tape recordings. But its conjunction of taped extracts from earlier in the performance with the continuing frantic actions required of the percussionist in real time – with the result that 'there are too many sounds to be accounted for by the actions one sees' (Toop 1974, 37) – seems more intended as sarcastic comment on the excessive difficulty of much avant-garde music. Griffiths appropriately describes the work as 'a caricature of contemporary avant-garde endeavour' (1995, 139).

Later works by Kagel play more openly on this theme. In *Sur scène* (1960), a speaker accompanies the bizarre musical gestures of a baritone and three instrumentalists with an absurd parody of a learned treatise on contemporary music (see Attinello 2002 and Heile 2002). *Match* 'for three players' (two cellos and percussion) emphasizes in its very title the proximity of virtuoso musical performance to spectator sport. That both this piece and the later *Siegfried P* (1972) are intended specifically as salvos against avant-garde music, where virtuosity tends to be lost on all but the most schooled of listeners (as opposed to the nineteenth-century virtuoso tradition, where technical achievement is likely to be more widely appreciated) is strongly suggested by the discrepancy between the performers' heroic actions and the relative banality of the sounds that result (Toop 1974, 37).

Satirical comment on the eccentric behaviours required of performers by avant-garde composers may not be completely absent from Ligeti's *Aventures* (1962–6) and *Nouvelles aventures* (1965–6) either, and this time it is vocalists rather than instrumentalists who are subject to examination. Although originally intended as concert pieces, Ligeti later allowed these two works to be staged, an apt move in view of the overt theatricality of the three soloists' bizarre, wordless vocalization. The rapid mood-changes and extended techniques of the nonsensical vocal parts can certainly be read as a critique of the clichés of much contemporary opera of the time (Griffiths 1994, 330). They also have their own strangely compelling poetry, however, an impression strengthened by the refined and focused music of the accompanying chamber ensemble.

As noted earlier in this chapter, musical theatre is in many ways intrinsically at odds with the aesthetics of the avant-garde. The referentiality of staged enactions compromises the autonomy that avant-garde composers like to claim for their music; as Eric Salzman has suggested, music theatre 'reverses the purism of modern art' (1988, 245). It is notable that the most ardent champions of modernism have remained resistant to theatrical ventures – at least until very recent times. The absence of theatre works in the output of Pierre Boulez is consistent with his notorious diatribe (in 1967) against the institution of the opera house; and although an operatic project was mooted in the 1990s (see the composer's interview in Ford 1993, 22) his suspicion of the theatrical projects of his contemporaries is indicated by his reported dismissal of music theatre as 'opera of the poor' (Clements 1992, 529). Like Boulez, Milton Babbitt has written extensively for the voice, but his only theatrical work is a now unknown musical, *Fabulous Voyage* (1946), whose style uncharacteristically reflects Babbitt's life-long enthusiasms for jazz and Tin Pan Alley. Only in very late life has Elliott Carter penned a chamber opera, and its title, *What Next?* (1999), seems to allude to the erstwhile unlikelihood of such a development. Other prominent carriers of the modernist flame, such as Brian Ferneyhough and James Dillon, have likewise only recently ventured into music theatre (Ferneyhough's *Shadowtime* and Dillon's *Philomela* both received first performances in 2004).

It was in keeping with the prevailing modernist suspicion of theatrical endeavour during the 1970s that prominent composers of music theatre at that time should set themselves far more openly in opposition to the modernist avant-garde. Works from this period by composers such as Henze and Louis Andriessen owe more to the tradition of Weill and Brecht than to the hermetic constructions of the Darmstadt school – constructions that underpin even Kagel's and Ligeti's theatre works. In his writings, Henze is unambiguous that the theatrical impulse in his music is concerned to 'drive out abstraction and inhumanity', that his music 'sees itself as drama, as something that inwardly belongs to life, and could not exist in tidy abstinence or in the private domestic realm' (1982, 207 and 230). For Henze, bourgeois musical life and the institutionalized avant-garde are merely two sides of the same coin. This is made explicit in the 'show for seventeen performers', *The Tedious Way to Natascha Ungeheuer's Flat* (1971), which tells of a bourgeois leftist revolutionary who is tempted away from active participation in the social struggle by the siren-like artist Ungeheuer. In addition to a *musique concrète* tape and a brass quintet, the work features on stage the ensemble of Schoenberg's *Pierrot lunaire*, part-dressed in Pierrot costumes and part-dressed as doctors carrying various injuries. As Henze comments,

> The significance of the two types of costume points to one thing: sickness, the sickness of the bourgeoisie, its music, its morality, the suffering of a class that has made itself sick. What they have to say has its origins in Schoenberg's construct, but has departed from it and broken with it, beyond the point of parody towards a new kind of denunciatory analytical music-exercise. (1982, 191)

In *Natascha Ungeheuer*, then, the *Pierrot* ensemble acts as a cipher for the political quiescence of progressive intellectualism. The subtle critiques offered by Kagel and Ligeti are here replaced with an explicit protest against avant-garde art.

Andriessen's *Matthew Passion* (1976) and *Orpheus* (1977), conceived in collaboration with the experimental Dutch Baal Theatre Group, ostensibly take as their primary points of reference the revered 'classical music' tradition of Bach and Monteverdi–Gluck–Stravinsky. Both works' self-consciously raw and irreverent scenarios and theatrical style are certainly designed to jar with the refined sensibilities of the traditional concert-going audience: in the first, Jesus is depicted as a Jewish female prostitute (the brothel in which she works is managed by 'Magdalena'); in the second, Orpheus is a spoilt mother's boy who is deliberately betrayed by a vengeful Eurydice. But Andriessen's music, with its highly eclectic musical idiom and idiosyncratic scoring, also pitches itself against the modernist avant-garde. The score to *Matthew Passion* is, in the words of Willem Jan Otten and Elmer Schönberger, 'a musical minefield of irony, parody, paraphrase' scored for an ensemble that includes music students, a jazz horn player and a gypsy violinist (1978, 25). *Orpheus*, meanwhile, intimates that the hero is a pop singer, and the work includes a Shirley Bassey-like 'Lied van Orpheus', jazz-rock music accompanying the first appearance of Aristaeus, and a 'Grand ballet en mi-bemol majeur avec choeur with respectful greetings to Steve Reich, Phil Glass and the others' (32).

The waning of musical modernism's institutional power during the 1980s and 1990s was accompanied by a softening of both Henze's and Andriessen's musical and theatrical outlook. Works such as Henze's *Das verratene Meer* (1989) and Andriessen's *Rosa* (1994) were written for the opera house and place a higher premium on stylistic consistency and narrative continuity. In so far as the more innovative and colourful approaches to music theatre were driven by an essentially political desire to refute the drab monotony of much avant-garde music, they were never guaranteed to flourish in the postmodern age.

Mixing traditions

One of the ways in which music theatre became symbolic of a move away from the priorities of the avant-garde was its tendency to encourage an intermingling of different musical traditions. The comparatively small scale of many music-theatre works was important in this respect, for it allowed more direct comparisons with musical cultures from outside the classical tradition, and indeed from beyond the Western world. A connection with folk music was already clearly present in important early twentieth-century precursors to music theatre – notably Stravinsky's *Renard* (1916) and *L'Histoire du soldat* (1918). This precedent was enthusiastically taken up by Harrison Birtwistle, not just in his theatre works *Punch and Judy* (1967) and *Down by the Greenwood Side* (1969), which drew on historical popular entertainments for both their subject matter and, in the latter case, instrumentation, but also in his creation (with Maxwell Davies) of the Pierrot Players, a flexible and transportable ensemble that formed a kind of 1960s parallel to the *théâtre ambulant* of *L'Histoire du soldat*. In both Birtwistle's and Maxwell Davies's music theatre, considerable importance is given to mime and dance, theatrical forms that carry a certain primitivist or folk-like connotation. Maxwell Davies's *Vesalii icones* (1969) for male dancer, cello and instrumental ensemble and *Blind Man's Buff* (1972) for vocalists, mime and instrumental ensemble, are indicative of this predilection, which reached a massive culmination in Birtwistle's *The Mask of Orpheus* (1973–83), with its panoply of puppets, actors and dancers. Mime and dance remained important in the music-theatre works of younger British composers in the 1970s and 1980s, including Nicola LeFanu, Roger Marsh and Trevor Wishart.

In the case of Marsh, the desire to incorporate certain sorts of physical movement and stage disposition was as much the result of an interest in non-Western performance traditions as it was an urge to tap into primeval forms of expression. Marsh's interest in Japanese music and theatre, in particular, informed the extreme vocalizations and movements of *Dum* (1972–7) for solo vocalist-actor, and the unusual stage layout of *Kagura* (1991) for chamber ensemble. It also led him to create the Centre for Japanese Music at the University of York. Marsh's turn to the Far East is representative of a wider trend in music theatre; few composers remained completely immune to the fascination of Japanese, African or other non-Western traditions as they became more widely known during the 1960s. Exposure to such influences had both specific and general consequences for composers' own works. An obvious example of the former is Britten's *Curlew River* (1964), which draws its story and stage layout from a Japanese Nō play (see Cooke 1998, 130–59). The importance of masks, and of stylized movement and vocalization to many music-theatre works by younger composers reflects a more general influence. W. Anthony Sheppard has suggested that one of the principal attractions of such conceits (which, for many composers, derive also from an interest in ancient Greek theatre) is the way in which they deflect attention away from the performer, who is denied any real opportunity to express his or her individuality, and towards the composer, who emerges as an unchallengeable 'High Priest' figure (2001, 19–20). An interest in the practices of other cultures was thus by no means always motivated by a sense of creative modesty.

Music theatre's emphasis upon the theatricality of musical performance also brought contemporary classical music closer, in certain respects, to the ambit of contemporary pop. As Simon Frith has pointed out, pop performance involves 'a process of double enactment', in which singers 'enact both a star personality (their image) and a song personality, the role that each lyric requires ... the pop star's art is to keep both acts in play at once' (1996, 212). Much music theatre involves a similar double enactment. It can achieve this by foregrounding the theatricality of its own means – sometimes at the expense of projecting the drama of its subject. In Birtwistle's *The Mask of Orpheus* the elaborate staging and other theatrical paraphernalia required to realise it properly reflects the title's allusion to 'masque', the sixteenth- and seventeenth-century genre whose *raison d'être* was the celebration of spectacle and artifice (Adlington 2000, 16–17). Alternatively, music theatre may expose the theatre of conventional classical performance rituals – rituals to which we more usually turn a blind eye. Some examples of this sort of approach in the work of Kagel and Henze have already been discussed.

Whichever 'foreign' musical tradition is involved, the attraction of alluding to it is frequently the same: it facilitates a redrawing or disintegration of the boundaries that define classical music. These boundaries may concern the nature of the performing space, the particular duties assigned to performers, or the authorial control of the composer. For Henze, such redrawing has a demystificatory function: 'In music-theatre, as I envisage it, music is incorporated into the drama, is performed on the stage rather than invisibly in the pit, is a concert dissolved into movement and action: demystified music' (1982, 207). So, music theatre frequently reconfigures the classical performance space by placing instrumentalists and actors on the same stage. This arrangement suggests that the instrumental music can no longer be presumed to have a subordinate or supporting function (as is implied by the consignment of the orchestra to the pit), and it also enables a greater interaction between performers. In some instances the instrumentalists actually become *dramatis personae*, crucial to the action. This is the case in Maxwell Davies's *Eight Songs for a Mad King* (1969), for instance, where the instrumentalists represent the caged birds owned by the dying King. In Henze's *La Cubana*, the on-stage instrumentalists form the chanteuse's accompanying band and are given strict instructions as to how to play their music 'in character'.

Alternatively, sharing a stage simply allows a type of interaction not possible when instrumentalists are placed in a pit. Maxwell Davies's *Vesalii icones* sets one of the instrumentalists (the cellist) apart from the rest of the ensemble; while the cellist does not literally participate in the danced 'action', the solo dancer interacts with him or her as a second character. Birtwistle's dance piece *Pulse Field* (1976) takes the idea a little further: the actions of the dancers are now partly governed by cues from the instrumentalists, who are positioned symmetrically around the edge of the stage.

Breaking down the barriers between instrumentalists and actors or singers is one important respect in which music theatre encourages a rethinking of standard performance arrangements; breaking down the barriers between performers and audience is another. Berio's *Passaggio* established a precedent in this regard by planting a speaking chorus amongst the audience, with the intention that their contributions should 'give brutally self-revealing voice to the inner thoughts of a cultured, bourgeois audience' (Osmond-Smith 1991, 92). The bringing together of performer and audience is particularly characteristic of the theatre of John Cage. For Cage, 'theatre takes place all the time wherever one is and art simply facilitates persuading one that this is the case' (cited in Nyman 1999, 80); as a result, audience and performers are not to be kept apart but should be allowed to interact. The theatre should be arranged, says Cage, 'so that the physical circumstances of a concert do not oppose audience to performers but dispose the latter around – among the former' (Schmitt 1982, 21). In particular, the frontality and single focus of the conventional theatre, in attempting to present everyone with the same experience, contradicts Cage's desire to emphasize the equal validity of different individual experiences. The format of the circus was exemplary in this respect, and the circus became an important guiding influence for Cage's own theatrical events. His *Musicircus* (1967), in which musicians were invited to perform independently but simultaneously in any way they desired, went beyond the in-the-round arrangement of the traditional circus and encouraged the audience to wander freely around the main floor of the pavilion (Pritchett 1993, 157–8). The same principle was applied both for further one-off performances – for example, a performance in November 1969 at the University of California at Davis entitled *Mewantemooseicday* – and more carefully structured 'works', such as *HPSCHD*, also dating from 1969 (Revill 1992, 225–32).

Thus music theatre may seek to undo the rigid arrangement of singers, instrumentalists and audience conventional in opera or classical concerts. It also serves to undermine the rigid specialization of performers. Instrumentalists are required to diversify; now, rather than simply playing a single instrument, they may have to play several, or sing, or act. Henze's *La Cubana*, with its 'in character' instrumental ensemble, has already been mentioned. Henze's other music theatre works demand a comparable flexibility on the part of his instrumentalists. *El Cimarrón* (1970), for instance, requires all four instrumentalists to play a number of instruments, and in *Natascha Ungeheuer* the solo on-stage percussionist is on occasion required to 'stand in' for the main vocal protagonist. Henze's desire to make his instrumentalists into actors finds a measure of correspondence in Birtwistle's *Bow Down* (1977), in which numerous versions of the fable of The Two Sisters are presented through song and dramatic enaction. In Birtwistle's piece, the actors are just as much musicians as the musicians are actors. The score admittedly describes each of the nine performers as either a 'musician' or an 'actor', but this indicates a relatively slight difference in emphasis: all the performers make music, often of a fairly rudimentary kind, and all the performers contribute to the acted drama. For Henze, this sort of departure from the narrow specializations that characterize classical music culture constitutes part of music theatre's liberating function:

> I would like the music to lay bare something of the history of the instrumentalists, which belongs to the history of the working people. I would like the instrumentalists to interpret themselves consciously, and to extend their scope, so that they see themselves as inhabiting a realm of increased possibilities – possibilities of self-realization and self-liberation, which are assuredly a prerequisite for liberation on a larger scale.   (1982, 215)

Fundamentals: time, body, space

Cage's belief that 'theatre is all around us' (Nyman 1999, 72) shared something of the democratizing motivation just identified in Henze and Birtwistle. Cage gave creative licence not only to the professional performer but to the audience as well. Indeed, he did so to the extent that the very distinction between art and reality, and certainly art's privileged status in relation to reality, started to collapse (79–80). Cage viewed all his creations as theatre, and if in certain respects they exist at one remove from music theatre as it is commonly defined – in Griffiths 1994, for example, Cage receives only a single brief mention as an influence on Stockhausen (334) – they nevertheless serve as a reminder of the extent to which music theatre has been nourished by a concern to replace old and exhausted categories of action with underlying fundamentals.

Thus for Cage a hard and fast distinction between music and theatre was untenable. Other composers of the 1950s and early 1960s sought 'new unions' of music and theatre, but for Cage these were not separate realms in the first place. Cage's primary interest was, instead, with that which underlay, and was articulated by, actions of any sort: namely, time. The meticulous structuring of time had been a prominent feature of Cage's early works; now, in his own theatre works and those of his followers, the organization of time comes to supersede the organization of sound as the composer's primary business. In works such as *4'33"*, *Water Music* (1952) and *Theatre Piece* (1960), not to mention the 'happenings' that Cage first organized in the early 1950s, 'music' comes to mean simply 'activities in time'. In 1961 Robert Ashley stated that

> Cage's influence on contemporary music, on 'musicians' is such that the entire metaphor of music could change to such an extent that – time being uppermost as a definition of music – the ultimate result would be a music that wouldn't necessarily involve anything but the presence of people . . .
> (Cited in Nyman 1999, 11)

Thus LaMonte Young would, in his *Composition 1960 No. 10*, 'draw a straight line on the floor and follow it'. In the words of Michael Nyman, 'the line piece becomes an extended metaphor. For a line is a "potential of existing time" and is therefore relevant to music' (83).

Few of Cage's European contemporaries went so far in erasing the boundaries between art and life. Nevertheless a parallel concern with the articulation of fundamentals of existence may be detected in many music-theatre works. For instance, works by composers as different as Stockhausen, Birtwistle and Harry Partch can be seen to involve a focus upon the human body. In the case of Stockhausen this focus originated in a perception concerning instrumental music, namely that 'musicians move about while playing; thus this movement will be endowed with an independent meaning too' (Wörner 1973, 187). Stockhausen's determination to incorporate this physical aspect of music-making in his composition results in works that are less concerned with amalgamating old genres, and more predicated upon an exploration of the potential of the performing body. Thus in *Inori* (1974), a solo part written in musical notation 'is interpreted by two dancer-mimers, who translate the notes and inflections of the solo line into an "action melody" of silent gestures drawn from world religions' (Maconie 1990, 230). *Harlekin* (1975) attempts to forge a unity between the music and danced action performed by a solo clarinettist, both of which present 'a large-scale wave form' (252). And *Musik im Bauch* (1975) deploys six percussionists in an enaction that blends instrumental performance and ritual activity; the 'bodily' focus is dramatized by the centring of the actions upon a mannequin that houses musical boxes in its belly (the 'Bauch' of the title).

This last work makes for an interesting comparison with Harrison Birtwistle's *Bow Down*. In drawing attention to the difficulties in maintaining absolute distinctions between words and music, or dance and musical performance, *Bow Down* effectively posits instead a wider and more sustainable category that emphasizes the common basis of all acts of performance in the human body. And, as with *Musik im Bauch*, Birtwistle's work dramatizes the centrality of the performing body in its very scenario, which revolves around a speaking harp fashioned out of a corpse (Adlington 2000, 24–6).

Like Stockhausen and Birtwistle, Partch's interest in emphasizing the bodily in his theatre works sprang partly from the influence of ancient and exotic theatrical traditions. In Partch's case, however, this influence gave rise to a more all-encompassing conviction that musical performance should be thought of as a fundamentally 'corporeal' act – and thus as an antidote to the abstraction and anti-physicality of the machine age (Sheppard 2001, 184). Partch's handcrafted instruments often required particularly marked physical motions on the part of the performer, and it was thus appropriate that the instruments should appear on stage in his music-theatre works *The Bewitched* (1955) and *Delusion of the Fury* (1966). In both pieces the chorus and soloists are given 'bodily', non-verbal vocal sounds rather than 'conceptual' words, and Partch specifies detailed choreography. As Sheppard has observed, the result in each case is a late twentieth-century *Gesamtkunstwerk* (180).

Bodily movements occur in space, and it is perhaps a matter of personal predisposition whether it is the body, or the space articulated by that body, that is seen as primary. The same could be said of sound's relation to space: a sound is qualitatively dependent on the space in which it is made and heard. Space is a third fundamental concern that has led composers to experiments in music theatre. Once again Stockhausen and Birtwistle are important figures. Both composers have been innovative in their use of unorthodox stage placements and movement in their instrumental music. Birtwistle has written a number of 'territorial pieces', wherein particular music is 'allotted to a space'. The idea in a piece such as *Verses for Ensembles* (1967) is, in the composer's own words, 'that *that* music happens here, in *this place*, and it doesn't happen in another place' (cited in Adlington 2000, 49). However, Birtwistle uses space largely in order to articulate his musical forms: the musical materials remain primary, and are largely unaffected by the chosen performance venue. The idea that, conversely, music might be used to articulate a space is one taken up more whole-heartedly in Stockhausen's *Alphabet für Liège* (1972). This piece, which is subtitled 'visible music', involves the performing of various theatrical and musical actions in different rooms of a building. As such, the space used is going to exert as much influence on the final product as the sounds made. To this extent, Stockhausen's piece directly foreshadows contemporary installation art.

A more extreme variant on the same idea is presented by Nono's *Prometeo* (1984). In this work, the auditorium takes the form of 'a specially constructed wooden shell providing stations for both performers (singers, speakers, instrumentalists, electronic technicians) and listeners'; the whole space 'would thus become a single musical instrument' (Griffiths 1994, 340–41). Space and sound are made indistinguishable. Paradoxically, Nono's work represents something of a return to the 'pure' listening that music theatre once seemed quite intent on leaving behind, for the composer requests that it should be performed in complete darkness. It is, in Nono's words, a 'tragedy of hearing', or as Griffiths puts it, 'an opera for the ears alone'.

Demise or evolution?

As noted earlier in this chapter, the demise of music theatre is a matter of some debate. Griffiths conceives of the genre as an inherently revolutionary medium; as such, 'it was inevitable that ideas would be exhausted, and that the anti-conventional urge in music theatre would lead to a world in which there were no taboos left to break, except the taboo against going back to tradition' (334). Ligeti, for one, felt that Kagel's music theatre had made possible 'anti-anti-opera' (336), and correspondingly a piece like Ligeti's *Le Grand Macabre* (1977), while undoubtedly 'more "opera" than opera' (337), is also arguably more 'opera' than music theatre. The revival of interest in opera amongst composers was certainly a remarkable feature of art music in the last two decades of the twentieth century. That said, the fact that composers have begun again to adopt the term 'opera' may simply be a matter of their having established some distance from old opera. It does not necessarily imply a refutation of music-theatre principles, which still speak through many of the contemporary operas written today. The seven works that make up Stockhausen's mammoth cycle *Licht* (1977–2003), each named after a day of the week, present a striking example. Stockhausen describes each of these works as an opera, and four have been premiered in opera houses. But in numerous regards they sustain the preoccupations explored so determinedly in Stockhausen's earlier music-theatre works. Instrumentalists feature prominently on stage, and physical gesture is carefully prescribed by the composer, rather than left to the whim of a director. Narrative continuity and direction are gleefully dispensed with, in favour of a 'ragbag' (Griffiths 1995, 245) of musical meditations that accommodates other, semi-autonomous works – such as *Klavierstück XIV* (played by a budgerigar) in *Montag* (1984–8) and the airborne transmissions of the *Helikopter-Streichquartett* in *Mittwoch* (1992–8). The loose mystical thread connecting all seven operas, which concerns the three 'spiritual essences' (Kurtz 1992, 210) – Michael ('the Creator-Angel'), Lucifer (his antagonist) and Eve (the source of mankind's rebirth) – represents a characteristically incautious continuation of music theatre's well-established engagement with existential universals.

A resurgence of interest in narrative and simpler modes of representation is, however, clearly evident amongst younger composers, especially in America and Britain, and this new-found confidence in story-telling makes many of the trappings of music theatre redundant. It is the opportunities afforded by new technologies that appear to hold out most promise of a continuation of some of the principal concerns of music theatre. To the extent that the main thrust behind technological developments is the overcoming of perceived realities and the presentation of 'virtual' alternatives, they have the potential to act as a counterbalance to the realistic and narrativistic tendencies abroad in other sectors of contemporary culture. Steve Reich's recent theatrical works – *The Cave* (1993) and *Three Tales* (2002) – decisively demonstrate how technology can give renewed impetus to the music-theatre tradition. In these works, video recordings, sampled speech, staging and live music, all skilfully combined through computers and click-tracks, contribute to a highly schematic dramatic presentation that unambiguously belongs to the mainstream of late twentieth-century music theatre. New technologies are also central to Heiner Goebbels' music-theatre works. The sampler, specifically, features prominently in *The Repetition* (1995), *Black on White* (1996) and *Hashirigaki* (2000), and it is in some ways symbolic of Goebbels' eclectic, 'pick and mix' theatrical style. The 'postmodern' musical instrument *par excellence* thus encourages a continuation, ironically, of some of the classic preoccupations of modernist music theatre: anti-narrativity and non-linearity; the incorporation of references to musics of other cultures and ages; and a 'political' rejection of the conventions of classical music performance (with its fetishization of the 'live' and acoustic). It is in the extension and development of such applications of technology to live performance that the future of music theatre's various preoccupations and motivations most probably resides.

15 Minimalist opera

ARVED ASHBY

Emerging from and ultimately belonging to the stage, minimalist music is an offshoot of avant-garde New York theatre. The style has been traditionally associated with American pop culture and African and south Asian music, but just as important are the early minimalist composers' connections with the innovative theatrical figures of downtown Manhattan in the 1960s. Indeed, musical minimalism and American theatre served to define each other at critical points in both their histories.

Before the 1970s, the signal innovations in American music and theatre certainly did not take place in the opera houses. But the minimalists have shown an extraordinary creative interest in music drama and other large-scale theatrical endeavours. The story of this operatic renovation really begins in the late 1950s and 1960s, when Philip Glass and fellow opera composer Meredith Monk were students in New York. The theatres of lower Manhattan were seething with revolutionary change at that time. Pioneering among non-narrative collaboratives in the city was the Living Theatre, founded in 1947 by anarchist free spirits Julian Beck and Judith Malina.

By Glass's own description, he had grown up with the 'progressive theatre' of Brecht, Genet, Pinter and Beckett rather than the traditional 'narrative, commercial' theatre of Eugene O'Neill, Arthur Miller and Tennessee Williams. 'The kinds of theater which spin familiar stories, moralizing, sometimes satirizing, occasionally comforting us about our lives, have never meant much to me. What has always stirred me is theater that challenges one's ideas of society, one's notions of order' (Glass 1987, 4). The greatest impact on his 'notions of order' came from the Living Theatre, which first exposed him to the style of marathon *tableaux-vivants* that would later be called 'the theater of images' when taken up by Robert Wilson, Richard Foreman and Lee Breuer. Glass remembers a decisive 1964 encounter with the Living Theatre's *Frankenstein* as 'the first theater work I had seen that so radically extended the accepted sense of theater time' (6–7). The *Frankenstein* productions comprised three to

This chapter is dedicated to Jeremy Tambling

five hours of fractured, de-centred and sometimes frantic stage action, beginning with a full half-hour of silence as the players tried to levitate a young girl on stage (Biner 1972, 123).

Whether by coincidence or not, Glass penned the first music that he acknowledges less than a year after seeing *Frankenstein*: this was incidental music for two saxophones to accompany Beckett's *Play* as staged by the Mabou Mines Theatre, the progressive group Glass himself was intimately involved with from its beginnings in the mid-1960s. As it began here, Glass's mature minimalist style was as radical an extension of 'the accepted sense of time' as anything the Living Theatre was doing. In the composer's own estimation, his music eschews 'colloquial time', which he describes as 'the time that we normally live in.' He continues: 'one of the first things that people perceive in my music is extended time, or loss of time, or no sense of time whatever. All that narrative structure of the Beethoven concerto is gone from my music' (Kostelanetz 1997, 164, 171).

While Glass approached opera through his work in the so-called theater of images, Meredith Monk came to opera from a rather different direction. Her roots are in the Fluxus movement and the Events and Happenings of the 1960s – and specifically the Judson Dance Theater, a Greenwich Village fixture since 1962. Monk's Fluxus background can be seen in the playfulness, whimsy and utopianism of much of her work, characteristics that can now seem old-fashioned. But Monk also came to reject some basic tenets of Judson's experimental theatre: as one might expect of a composer of self-declared 'operas', she is a story-teller at heart, and also interested in specific characters and characterizations. Perhaps paradoxically, she is also a kind of neo-structuralist who takes great care over the dramatic shape of her presentations. Either Monk retains the traditional Aristotelian idea of form as having a beginning, a middle and an end; or she works up a schema, a dramatic shape, of her own.

'I am not, like Glass, a theater composer', Steve Reich has said. 'I don't carry the theater around inside me' (Schwarz 1996, 103). Reich is indeed one of today's great constructivists, caring for formal process to such an extent that the only drama to be found in his music is structure-born. Or is it? We tend to forget the performance-art elements in Reich's decisive early work. *It's Gonna Rain* (1965) was his first example of the 'process music' by which he became famous. Playing two tapes of a Pentecostal preacher on cheap equipment, Reich heard one running slightly slower. In the phasing that resulted, he discovered 'an extraordinary form of musical structure ... It was a seamless, uninterrupted musical process' (Reich 2002, 20). As if to verify the performance-art aspect to the tape pieces, Reich turned immediately afterwards to conceptual works showing the influence of Fluxus, Cage and LaMonte Young. His *Pendulum*

Music (1967) was process music posing as performance art, or perhaps the other way around: four performers released individual microphones suspended above speakers, letting them swing back and forth until the feedback became constant from all four sources. Typically for Reich, the piece is outwardly technical-structural but at its basis theatrical-didactic.

The process might sound mechanistic, but in the 1960s Reich was utilizing 'phasing' repetition as much for psychological and emotional effect as for structural unity. In his own words, his early tape pieces represent 'a very rigid process, and it's precisely the impersonality of that process that invites this very engaged psychological reaction' (Reich 2002, 21). Also striking is the fact that Reich took as his ultimate goal a kind of realist experience that resembles Antonin Artaud's Theatre of Cruelty. Insistent repetition of recognizable speech enables the composer to retain the emotional power of the locution 'while intensifying its melody *and* meaning through repetition and rhythm' (20). In short, tape allowed Reich a concentrated form of theatre – and much the same can be said of his later use of sampling in *Different Trains* (1988), *The Cave* (1992) and *Three Tales* (2002).

John Adams, the youngest of these four composers, is not a minimalist strictly speaking, and was not privy to the downtown theatrical innovations of the 1950s and 1960s. His operas are relevant here because they show how Glass's and Monk's downtown remakings of opera were eventually brought back uptown, into the opera house proper. Adams also helped tie off the historical narrative of minimalist opera by demonstrating the latterday transformation of vernacular theatre through media. Sometimes called 'CNN operas', Adams's stage works show the way video and television have come to appropriate and supplant notions of theatre and theatricality: a shift in aesthetics and perception has been subsumed by a change of medium. The kind of wholesale theatrical innovation offered by the Living Theatre is no longer possible in today's monolithic situation of video-induced sensory and aesthetic saturation. Walter Benjamin could well have been foreseeing video culture when he spoke of 'the work of art the reception of which is consummated by a collectivity in a state of distraction' (1968, 241).

Minimalism, repetition, theatre

Minimalism is distinguished by repetition, and repetition is innately poetic in that it disrupts signification and literal meaning; it moves music from a system of signs to a world of symbols. For what is each individual statement of a repeated musical figure: an authentic expression of the moment or a simple replication of that which was just heard, hiding behind the fact of repetition? ('Because repetition differs in kind from representation', writes Gilles Deleuze (1994, 18), 'the repeated cannot be represented: rather, it must always be signified, masked by what signifies it, itself masking what it signifies'.) Repetition defines minimalism and late twentieth-century performance art alike, transforming both institutionalized musical idioms and everyday action into theatre: when Michael Nyman wrote *In Re Don Giovanni* (1977) by setting up internal repetitions within Mozart's 'Catalogue Aria', common practice became music about music; when Northern Irish performance artist André Stitt repeatedly and bit by bit chipped off the enamel surface of a cast iron bathtub, a plumbing renovation became theatre. In both instances, repetition served to disconnect the action from evident reason and rationality: Deleuze refers to 'an inverse relation between repetition and consciousness, repetition and remembering, repetition and recognition ...' (1994, 14).

Minimalism represented a kind of scorched-earth approach to aesthetics: the minimalist composers' rejection of Darmstadt modernism was the strongest generational rebuff in music history, and the most specifically contradictory. Minimalism's radically new proportion between small-scale detail and background event (as described in more detail below) can be heard as a wholesale rejection of modernism's distillation and concentration of local, small-scale event. Schoenberg and Darmstadt had also placed highest priority on avoiding literal repetition of pitch, motive and phrase. The alliances that modernists like Boulez and Stockhausen formed with John Cage in the 1950s might seem self-contradictory, but make sense in that the two parties considered repetition a common enemy: the former because it betokened a lack of thought, and the latter because it was symptomatic of *too much* thinking. The minimalists, on the other hand, foregrounded repetition in an attempt to annihilate ambiguity. Repetition in psychoanalytic terms is a symptom of the failure to integrate traumatic experience – and so repetition would seem to emblematize the anxiety of influence between minimalism and modernism. If we take the Lacanian view that all art is neurotic, we could say musical minimalism put the symptom of repetition compulsion in the foreground whereas modernism denied it.

Deleuze was writing about repetition at just about the same time that Reich, Glass and Terry Riley were writing within it. In his book *Difference and Repetition* (published in 1968), Deleuze works to flesh out Western philosophy's faulty conception of repetition by finessing it into two types:

> one which concerns only the overall, abstract effect, and the other which
> concerns the acting cause. One is a static repetition, the other is dynamic ...

One refers back to a single concept, which leaves only an external difference between the ordinary instances of a figure; the other is the repetition of an internal difference which it incorporates in each of its moments, and carries from one distinctive point to another.   (Deleuze 1994, 20)

This is the crux of the matter for minimalist composers, who – as practitioners of an art 'with no past tense', to borrow Carolyn Abbate's description (Abbate 1991, 52) – dare to encompass Deleuze's dichotomy in its most provocative form. Minimalism also confronts another problem that Deleuze describes, namely the difficulty of grasping the exact relationship between the now, the once-now, and the soon-to-be-now: 'We cannot wait, the moment must be simultaneously present and past, present and yet to come, in order for it to pass (and to pass for the sake of other moments). The present must coexist with itself as past and yet to come' (Deleuze 1983, 48). Confronting these dilemmas, minimalist form provocatively straddles structure and *style mécanique*. A minimalist composition is like a machine, in that it compels us to ask: when is repetition a positive, organic element – a triumph of reason, an acknowledgment of certainty and similarity – and when does it betoken mechanical imposition, a refusal to let the musical moment pass?

To phrase this duality specifically in musical terms: when Glass decides on a twenty-fold repetition of a nine-note phrase in *Einstein on the Beach*, to what extent does this become an inspirational passage – a whim, a capricious 'freezing' of the compositional software – and to what extent a heavily, dogmatically pre-cogitated compositional move? With the Darmstadt modernism that Glass rejected so strongly, choosing a tone row or row-class represented a pre-compositional decision that set the agenda for the piece – the music serving to realize the latent and inherent musical possibilities embodied in the row. This is perhaps equivalent to Deleuze's idea of static repetition, though the infinitely variable ways that the row actually comes to be heard in the composition amount to dynamic repetition. From either perspective, the row tends to retreat from immediate audibility. But with the modules and additive rhythms of *Einstein on the Beach*, say, repetition becomes a local event – and the overall consequence of repetition exactly equivalent, no more and no less, to the cumulative effect of local repetition.

In his essay 'The Automatic Message' (1933), surrealist André Breton discerned a similar duality in the practice of 'automatic writing' (*l'écriture automatique*). The question he raised also demands to be asked of the minimalist styles of Glass, Reich, Monk, Adams and Nyman: to what extent is this art automatic and habitual, and to what extent does it *mimic* the automatic and habitual? (Breton 1999, 125–43.) How much of this music is mindless and how much of it is mindful – not to use the words in a judgmental-aesthetic way? 'The head is the organ of exchange', Deleuze writes, 'but the heart is the amorous organ of repetition. (It is true that repetition also concerns the head, but precisely because it is its terror paradox)' (1994, 2). Breton praises the demystifying aspect of automatic writing as it urges quantity over 'quality', both within the work itself and in the way it recognizes no real difference between 'professional' and public writing. There are obvious analogies here with minimalism and minimalist expansion of musical dimensions, not to mention the arguments of those who have disparaged the style.

Glass, Wilson and *Einstein on the Beach*

Glass's new minimalist style of the mid-1960s was clearly sympathetic to protracted, non-narrative conceptions of theatre – and likely arose under their direct influence. But it was his co-operative efforts with director Robert Wilson, beginning with *Einstein on the Beach* (1976), that allowed him to refine and personalize his repetitive musical language.

Wilson's hypnotic power largely stems from the new relationships he effects between clock time, Aristotelian stage time (time as the characters on stage might feel its passing) and body time (the viewer's own breathing and heart-rate). Time and again, Wilson's audiences say he gives them a heightened perception of time. In similar fashion, Glass's compositions alter the listener's chronological sense by engineering an entirely new relationship between foreground event and background, large-scale structure. In *Einstein on the Beach* and his other works of that era, Glass's minimalism effects a new, disproportionate distance between quickened foreground activity and slower background motion: the fast (the figuration prolonging the harmony) becomes faster, the slow (the harmonic rhythm itself, the rate of change) slower. Both Wilson and Glass effect a quickened sense of small-scale motion (actors' hand motions in Wilson's case, and the obsessive semiquaver or quaver figurations in Glass's music) while change at the broadest level slows down (Sheryl Sutton became one of Wilson's favourite players for her ability to execute, effortlessly and seamlessly, slow and agonizingly drawn-out gestures; while in *Einstein on the Beach* Glass might stay with G major, say, for a half-hour at a stretch). The common-practice repertory tends to develop a different connection between figurational rhythm and harmonic rhythm: with sonata movements, but in other forms as well, thematic areas are harmonically stable and generally see moderate or slow rhythmic activity, while transitional and developmental sections are driven by quicker figuration and harmonic rhythm.

Eschewing narrative, Wilson stages in time strata. 'There is an additive process', he says, 'with layers and zones of activities and images and time ... In [*The Life and Times of Sigmund*] *Freud*, the turtle takes 22 minutes to cross the stage; the runner takes 18 seconds, Freud 6½ minutes. The woman sits in the chair for 31 minutes' (Kostelanetz 1994, 93). Wilson's slowest layers of on-stage action can give his work a dreamlike quality. In a now-famous description, surrealist writer Louis Aragon said of *Deafman's Glance* (1971): 'it is at once life awake and the life of closed eyes, the confusion between everyday life and the life of each night, reality mingles with dream, all that's inexplicable in the life of [a] deaf man' (Aronson 2000, 48). While Wilson radically slows down rhythm at the macro level, by way of compensation he increases the amount of localized, moment-to-moment information: 'by bombarding the senses', Arthur Holmberg writes of Wilson's *CIVILwarS*, 'Wilson vouchsafes the spectator a glimpse of the sublime, an emotion the modern world has suppressed' (1996, 27). Wilson disorients the viewer by thus realigning foreground and background, but supplies no help with verbalization or body motion: a viewer cannot hope to read the body motions of Wilson's players in any usual or functional way, and words also fail as a basic chronometer. He eliminates any absolute chronological sense, and thereby forces the viewer to devise entirely new ways of orienting him- or herself with regard to time. To return to Deleuze's phrase, Wilson demonstrates ways that the moment can be 'simultaneously present and past, present and yet to come.'

Music, unfolding in real time, is the reality to Wilson's dreams. Music that has a steady tactus precludes the floating, entirely relative chronology of dreams: it supplies the sense of time that Wilson lacks. In this sense, at least, Glass's music and Wilson's drama are complementary rather than analogous worlds. Does that collusion make *Einstein on the Beach* any more or less 'operatic'? Descriptions and evaluations of their collaboration, as well as Glass's stage works with other librettists and directors, always depend on how one defines opera – or, to state it another way, which repertory operas serve as the points of reference. Before he met Glass, even before he became involved with music, Wilson called his stage works 'operas'. Glass remembers their collaboration: 'He was much more interested in *Einstein* being like a real opera than I was. Bob wanted as much singing on stage as possible and he was very pleased that there was a duet in the night train scene and an aria for the flying bed' (Shyer 1989, 220). For Franco Quadri, *Einstein on the Beach* is the first opera – a true and seamless *Gesamtkunstwerk* – produced by this director or this composer. For Quadri, Glass's music for *Einstein* is 'a river that for almost five hours is the supporting element in the undivided whole of a composition

Figure 15.1 Four-act structure of Glass's *Einstein on the Beach*

```
Knee Play
Act I scene 1: TRAIN
Act I scene 2: TRIAL

Knee Play 2
Act II scene 1: DANCE
Act II scene 2: NIGHT TRAIN

Knee Play 3
Act III scene 1: TRIAL/PRISON
Act III scene 2: DANCE 2

Knee Play 4
Act IV scene 1: BUILDING/TRAIN
Act IV scene 2: BED
Act IV scene 3: SPACESHIP

Knee Play 5
```

where scenic action and musical score seem to unite so perfectly that it is impossible to tell which element comes first' (Bertoni *et al.* 1998, 20).

Like Gertrude Stein before him, Wilson eschews story-telling for a theatre of the continuous present. The iconic imagery of *Einstein on the Beach* and Wilson's complete reconception of stage blocking, scale and motion – these aspects recall Stein's idea of 'landscape drama', where the temporal aspect of stage illusion was jettisoned in order to concentrate on spatiality and motion. Wilson's theatrical concept – like Beck's and Malina's Living Theatre – is also indebted to Artaud's theatre of cruelty idea where words are given, to quote the French surrealist, 'approximately the importance they have in dreams' (Artaud 1958, 96). Albert Einstein never appears on stage in *Einstein on the Beach*, thus making that opera all the more enigmatic. Appropriately for its subject, *Einstein* offers a set of icons instead of a narrative – and even these icons are fluid, capable of morphing before our very eyes into other icons. (Also, they appear as cardboard cut-outs on stage, their obvious two-dimensionality underlining all the more *Einstein*'s status as series of *tableaux-vivants* rather than an opera in the Bellinian or Verdian sense. To borrow Arnold Aronson's description of Artaud (2000, 30), Wilson's is 'a theatre of relations rather than narrative'.) Wilson refuses to interpret the stage images, but lets us surmise their importance as emblems of Einstein's discoveries: a train (he used trains as examples in explaining relativity), a clock (indicating gravity's ability to 'bend' time), a bed (ideas came to Einstein in dreams), and a stylized spaceship (Einstein's discoveries making space travel possible). Wilson and Glass began their collaborative work on *Einstein* with a list of these symbolic images and *Einstein* follows this sequence (see Figure 15.1) rather than any story line.

There are basic differences between *Einstein on the Beach* and *Satyagraha* (1980), Glass's next opera – as one would expect given Wilson's deep involvement in the first and his lack of connection with the second. Unlike *Einstein*, *Satyagraha* does present the central character as a figure who sings on stage: the opera portrays Gandhi's years in South Africa as he develops the concept of *satyagraha*, or 'truth-force', in resistance to the British. Also important to the opera-ness of *Satyagraha* is its narrative plot – the piece weaves a six-part story around Gandhi, even if the six self-standing scenes are not arranged in chronological order. Musically focused commentators, perhaps taking Bellini and *bel canto* as an exemplar for music theatre, find *Satyagraha* more operatic than *Einstein* because of its considered vocal style. *Einstein* was indeed oriented more to the chorus than to solo voices. *Satyagraha* is also more operatic in that it calls for a real pit orchestra. For *Einstein* Glass had used his own ensemble, with its basis in keyboards and amplified winds. But *Satyagraha* was commissioned by a bona fide opera company, the Netherlands Opera, and Glass calls more or less for a true opera orchestra with triple woodwind, strings and organ.

By the time of his third opera, *Akhnaten* (1984), Glass had largely normalized the foreground-background relationship that had made *Einstein* so revolutionary. He also eschewed additive rhythms for modular repetition, cultivating a technique closer to the static repetition described by Deleuze. Scenes and acts are smaller in proportion, and the 'landscape drama' aspect less emphasized: the longest scene of *Akhnaten*, the Pharaoh's coronation in Act I, plays for only 17 minutes. Dramaturgically speaking, the on-stage figures in *Einstein* were two-dimensional as one expects in Wilson's work. In *Akhnaten*, which tells the story of the monotheistic Egyptian pharaoh and husband to Nerfertiti, Glass returned to some of that earlier iconicity. (The composer wrote his own libretto 'in association with' Shalom Goldman, Robert Israel and Richard Riddell.) The title role is given to a countertenor, thus making that character all the more distant and perhaps exotic. Adding to the sense of pageantry rather than opera strictly defined is the extensive role of the narrating Scribe, who seems both to 'own' the narrative and stand outside it.

With his projects of the later 1980s, Glass continued to distance himself from his own progressive theatrical roots – specifically the influences of Artaud, the Living Theatre and Wilson himself. With his next opera, *The Making of the Representative for Planet 8* (1988), Glass for the first time tapped a major literary figure as his librettist: adapting one of her own stories, Doris Lessing gives words something more than 'the importance they have in dreams.' As Tim Page observes, 'marking a change from his three previous large-scale operas, Glass's main concern in *Representative* was to set the text so that the words could be understood as fully as possible' (Page, *Grove Online*). Glass showed himself even more of a romantic, less a Wilsonian ascetic, with *The Voyage* (1992). None of his other stage works gives quite the same impression of a composer speaking and emoting through his characters – a ventriloquism that lies at the heart of opera as conventionally defined. Playwright David Henry Hwang worked from Glass's own story. The opera was commissioned to mark the 500th anniversary of Columbus's discovery of America, but the composer typically broadened the opera's subject to 'the concept of discovery'. As if further to emphasize the distance from the breakthroughs of *Einstein on the Beach*, musical repetition is often limited to two- and four-fold reiterations, nothing that would be terribly out of place in the music of Liszt or Wagner.

It is convenient to end this interim account of Glass's operatic career with *La Belle et la Bête* (1994), a unique and provocative opera 'gloss' on a pre-existing movie. The Nonesuch discs describe *Belle* as 'an opera by Philip Glass as based on the film by Jean Cocteau'. This is of course a self-contradiction, in that operas and films are by definition self-contained organisms, closed systems visually and aurally. What Glass has really done is sidestep George Auric's original music and produce an alternate soundtrack to Cocteau's 1946 film. Or one could say Glass has done the reverse of opera-loving filmmakers Ingmar Bergman and Hans-Jürgen Syberberg. While they turned operas into films that go beyond simple representation of the stageworks (*The Magic Flute* and *Parsifal*), Glass took Cocteau's film and transformed it into an opera that is both parasitic to, and in a sense distinct from, the original. In any event, Glass produced a delightfully memorable and cohesive musical work in spite, or perhaps because, of appalling compositional restrictions. His soundtrack – one can hardly speak of a score in the usual sense – accompanies three-quarters of the film.

Early in his opera career he had experimented with Wilson's reformulation of stage time as it relates to real time, while in *La Belle et la Bête* Glass did the opposite and managed to overlay a narrative in operatic time with a narrative in real (or at least cinematic) time. People do not sing at the same speed they speak – but they have to in this case, and Glass's singers dispatch words just as quickly as his *Einstein* chorus had chanted numbers and solfège. *La Belle et la Bête* combines the traditionally middlebrow genre of film with the relatively highbrow history of opera, and by force of that brilliant stroke may alter permanently the course of opera as a genre. It also encourages us to go back and ponder the operatic qualities of his own film soundtracks – his score for Godfrey Reggio's *Koyaanisqatsi* (1983) a landmark in the history of documentary scoring, the darker and more immediately expressive *Naqoyqaatsi* (2003) not far behind – and ask if any real, qualitative differences exist between an opera and a scored film. A complete rethink of opera as a genre, *La Belle et la Bête* conjoins the genres of opera and film in an entirely new way.

Meredith Monk

Before graduating from college – where she studied music, dance and theatre – Meredith Monk became involved with the Judson Theatre, which worked as a matter of principle to integrate the arts. Even compared to the Off-Off-Broadway groups in Manhattan, the Judson prided itself on functioning democratically as a collective. Sally Banes describes the group as 'a metacommunity of sorts where the different communities revolving around single arts disciplines coalesced and where interdisciplinary imagination flourished' (1993, 73).

Each of Monk's works betrays her basis in dance and performance art and blurs divisions between art forms and between collaborators' roles. 'I work as a mosaicist,' she says, 'building my pieces out of modules of music, movement, character, light, image, text, and object …' (Jowitt 1997, 171). Nevertheless, the mosaic originates with music: 'I think [music is] where everything starts for me', she says. 'I usually have the music written before I start working on the images' (81). Specifically, her clear-cut textures and narratives, reading like dimly recalled fairy-tales, spin off from simple instrumental ostinatos. The second cardinal element is her exploration of the widest range of vocal possibilities – in tone-colour, nonsense syllables, yodelling, glottal effects, vibrato and near-animalist characterizations. As Bonnie Marranca describes the vocal landscape of Monk's *Atlas*, 'Texture of the voice is more important than text in this opera that dances' (1992, 16). Many of these vocal techniques stem from folk idioms, and were hardly accepted in art-music circles – at least before the new music scene came to be influenced by Monk's very explorations in this area.

Glass has Brechtian views on music theatre – views that owe more to Beck and Malina than they do to Wilson, and yet which emerge most clearly in *Einstein on the Beach*. 'Early on in my work in the theater', Glass says, 'I was encouraged to leave what I call a "space" between the image and the music. In fact, it is precisely that space which is required so that members of the audience have the necessary perspective or distance to create their own individual meanings' (Kostelanetz 1997, 141). This resembles Brecht's concept of epic theatre and its desire to edify the audience and make them think – as contrasted with traditional drama and its empathetic goals. Signe Hammer turns to Brecht's idea of alienation to describe *Einstein*, and thereby contrasts the Glass–Wilson collaboration with a more humanistic Monk: '*Einstein* connects only to the disconnected, alienated, passive aspects of ourselves; it perpetuates the same radical dislocation of emotions from which the century itself has suffered' (Jowitt 1997, 70).

Of the two musicians, it is Monk who apparently shares Artaud's wish to reclaim drama as it might have existed before the advent of words. 'Words are a screen, a filtering device that takes us away from direct experience', Monk says. 'Having to articulate something verbally removes you from the experience, and what I'm trying to offer is something that blocks out the discursive mind. Once you quiet that habitual explanatory behavior, you begin to experience the work itself' (Monk and Smith 2002, 28). (Mikhail Yampolsky's analysis of Artaud makes especially clear his parallels with Monk's belief in a characterization lying beyond words: 'For Artaud, the mistrust of the audible word – the word that exists prior to its utterer – is central. Its origins are obscure, for it is as if prompted and spoken by someone else – a predecessor – and in it the speaker loses his identity' (Scheer 2004, 170).) For Monk the narrative is a large component of the 'work itself', and in pre-verbal fashion her storylines tend toward the archetypal, even the simplistic. Though Monk owes some of her operatic affinities to an abiding interest in narrative, her upbringing in experimental theatre has also made her indifferent to the idea of the proscenium stage – and that has in turn delayed her contribution to American 'opera' strictly speaking.

Quarry: An Opera (1976) was Monk's first large-scale work involving narrative, singing, characterization and a cast of any size. (This was the first time she worked with a chorus; the experience inspired her to found her own ensemble, which has since facilitated her practice of developing works through group improvisation.) *Quarry* enacts the rise of a totalitarian state, yet Monk prides herself in the fact that the dramaturgy creatively traces 'a circular, layered form' (Jowitt 1997, 81). A more linear story is told by *Atlas* (1991), which was inspired by the story of Alexandra David-Néel (1868–1969) – a Belgian adventurer and orientalist who (disguised as a Chinese monk) became the first woman to see Lhasa, the forbidden Tibetan capital, in 1912. David-Néel becomes Alexandra Daniels, whom we first see sitting in her parents' suburban house daydreaming of travel to far-off lands (echoing a remarkable statement David-Néel once made, referring to no country in particular, that she was '"homesick" for a land that is not mine'). Alexandra's rise to adulthood and travel to remote corners of the globe allow Monk and her collaborators to explore basic themes of, as she describes them, the 'loss of wonder, mystery and freshness in our contemporary life and the possibility of rediscovering our inherent clarity' (Loppert 1993, 4).

Because it translates that clarity directly into operatic terms, *Atlas* is an archaic work that begs off on Marshall McLuhan's all-important question of whether the medium isn't more important than the message it conveys. *Atlas* is an operatic anti-opera, offering a basic narrative but at the same time purposefully depriving the opera-goer of common-practice dramatic complexities, intrigue, melodrama and character development. Monk's wide-eyed, almost wordless view means that the malevolent agents – a trio of Ice Demons in Part II and later on a business-suited agent of the government-military-industrial complex – prove threatening only in a children's storybook way, and fail to imbue the story with any real tension. The travelling group escapes the doomsday scenario ('Possibility of Destruction') simply by 'ascending to a timeless, radiant place where they come into spiritual knowledge'. At the same time, there is little of Wilson's rich vocabulary of dreams and allusions.

Monk tellingly defines 'opera', and thus any reference to theatrical traditions, not in dramatic terms but as multi-sensory experience: 'Early on, I called my works "opera," not in the sense of the European model that we usually think of, but rather as a description of the multi-perceptual, mosaic form that I was envisioning' (Monk 1993, 1). Rather, any dramatic force that *Atlas* may have resides almost exclusively in 'the grain of the voice', to use Roland Barthes's famous phrase. Or, more specifically, the work depends on the character and personality that the actors/singers are able to convey only with their (non-operatic, and mostly wordless) voices. Monk's drama depends all the more on the audience's basic identification with and empathy for the characters on stage. In this way, her work aligns itself more with popular music than with institutionalized opera: to borrow Simon Frith's phrase about a pop singer's rôle for the listener (1996, 166), hers is an art of persuasion.

Steve Reich and speech-melodies

By all accounts, Glass became more of a romantic and less oriented to musical process when he approached the opera stage. As he himself said, 'it is surely no coincidence that it was at the moment that I was embarking upon a major shift in my music to large-scale theater works that I began to develop a new, more expressive language for myself.' Steve Reich's *The Cave*, on the other hand, grew directly and seamlessly from his preceding non-operatic work: Reich had already developed an intercession between instrumental music and speech patterns in *Different Trains* (1988) for string quartet and tape.

Reich's tape manipulations serve to concentrate the humanness of the person recorded, rather than offering an impersonalized kind of 'music' – the early *musique concrète* pioneers Pierre Schaeffer and Pierre Henry were less interested in individual people's inflections than in more objective rhythmic aspects. 'A human being is personified by his or her voice', Reich says. 'If you record me, my cadences, the way I speak are just as much me as any photograph of me' (2002, 21). Reich was directly inspired by Janáček's practice of notating speech-melodies, which the Moravian composer called 'windows to people's souls'. Reich takes even more care than Janáček over these intonations, such that *Different Trains* and *The Cave* almost become reliquaries. He faithfully observes the speakers' tonal qualities, rhythmic makeup and timbre, and the best his purely musical-formal impulses can hope for is a symbiotic relationship with the demands of the taped voices. In reality, composing *The Cave* involved a give-and-take between the desired dramaturgical order of the taped voices and the ideal musical sequence. Reich writes:

> What I've found is that if you're very sensitive to the documentary material, it can suggest many things. We've had an idea in western art about *objets trouvés*, which implies an abstaining of bringing your rational intellect to work; basically, just finding something and presenting it. There's an aspect of that here, but it interacts with one's ability as a composer to choose or reject speech melodies and then to put them in one's own musical context. That tension runs throughout this piece. (Schwarz 1993, 17)

The Cave is a hundred-minute opus that defies categorization. Reich himself describes the work as 'a new kind of documentary music video theater' (16). There is no action *per se*, no stage movement, and all characterization takes place – 'live' and unscripted – on five large video screens surrounding the eighteen musicians on stage (see Figure 15.2). The video feeds present people – both knowledgeable and ignorant of scripture and history – as they are confronted by four questions: who is Abraham? Sarah? Hagar? Ishmael? Like Glass, Reich seems to have become reconciled to the notion that *The Cave* and his other marriages of music, imagery and storytelling must perforce comment on – and in some sense be rooted in – opera history. Reich has always felt a strong need to speak to the present, and he now describes *The Cave* and *Three Tales* as necessary updates on opera. 'I'm not saying other composers shouldn't write bel canto operas, but I've pursued something that interests me now, here in America in the 1990s, which naturally doesn't sound like something from 18th- or 19th-century Italy or Germany' (Cott *et al.* 1995, 12). His speaking to the present entails not only topics that are relevant now, but also current technologies: 'I think the use of sampling and video in opera and music theater is clearly growing. It's simply an honest expression of the life we are living now. "Timeless" music theater has in fact always reflected its time and place' (Reich and Korot 2003, 11).

If Reich calls it an update on music theatre, *The Cave* can also be heard as a subversive work: Kyle Gann calls it 'an anti-opera, written inside out', a piece that shows its composer 'wisely scorning romantic-opera conventions' (1993, 99). Reich did take some time getting around to setting texts

Figure 15.2 Act III of *The Cave*, by Steve Reich and Beryl Korot. Photo: Andrew Pothecary, 1993, reproduced by permission.

for the pitched human voice. He did not bring words and voices together until *Tehillim* (1981), and even there he preceded the project with Jewish cantillation studies and elected psalms as the material to be sung. In *The Desert Music* (1984), Reich set words by William Carlos Williams for a chorus, but largely uses the voices as instruments. In his liner notes for the first *Desert Music* recording, the composer doubted a singer's ability to convey drama: 'You know, a voice can sing words – but does one hear the voice or the words?' (Reich and Cott 1985, 3). *The Cave* and *Different Trains*, as well as the later *Three Tales* (2002) which conjoins music and video, do serve to show that the performance-art aspect of using video footage – and the isolation and repetition of short instants – need not conflict with the works' more obvious documentary purpose. Korot focuses on the personality of each speaker in *The Cave*, devoting TV screens not only to the speakers' faces but also hands propped against jaws and such cognitively noisy marginalia as tapping pencils.

Perhaps the most unusual, or at least 'non-operatic', aspect of *The Cave* as it appears on stage is the projection of handwritten phrases. These are extracts from the interviewees' statements, written on the screens with commendable penmanship. The process represents a literal enactment of scripture (from the Latin *scriptum*, 'written'), the biblical Hebraic transmission of God's word as a mystical trace from on high. The written phrases might also drive home the point that the authorities filmed by Korot are engaged in hermeneutics, the science of interpreting scripture – except that Korot and Reich make *them* the interpretative objects. In any event, confronting the viewer/listener with literal transcriptions of the words is out of keeping with documentary and opera traditions. It can only squelch action, and thus kill the drama; or, if we choose to experience *The Cave* as a documentary, the writing belies the true-to-life, 'live' aspect of the production. But it seems more likely that Reich and Korot made spoken words visible for the most basic, musical reason: to help stitch together all the more firmly the speakers' speech-melodies and the musicians' doublings of them.

There is something deeply McLuhanesque about the *The Cave*'s array of sights and sounds as delivered by several media simultaneously: television-video, the handwritten word, text scripted out on computer screens, and electrified or amplified musical instruments. In such a situation, the written word is presented as the key that opened the mind to the idea of Euclidean space – the linchpin that made possible all visual (and thus video) representations. Perhaps Reich and Korot were out to demonstrate McLuhan's statement that 'phonetic writing translated tribal man into a visual world and invited him to undertake the visual organization of space' (1964, 96). If Reich and Korot recognize McLuhan, they also seem to acknowledge another seminal twentieth-century thinker on media: Walter Benjamin. *The Cave* obeys Jeremy Tambling's statement that 'opera must take its place amongst other late-twentieth-century media events as a distraction' (1994, 15). Here Tambling refers to Benjamin's definition of distraction as a state where 'the distracted mass absorbs the work of art', in contradistinction to the situation where 'a man who concentrates before a work of art is absorbed by it.

He enters into this work the way legend tells of the Chinese painter when he views his finished painting' (Benjamin 1968, 241). Architecture is commonly cited as the prime example of distractionist art: a building is lived in, much less thinkingly attended to than it is intuitively inhabited.

Resolutely non-dramatic, *The Cave* reduces opera to a kind of architectural design, isolating component parts from the experience and fastidiously balancing them against each other. Except for sections devoted to scripture and prayer, the work consists entirely of commentary: eschewing drama, *The Cave* incorporates spoken statements that do the thinking for us. Its wealth and variety of information – conceptual, historical, visual, musical, auditory, alphanumeric – are so constant and so 'present' that they become phenomenological walls and floors. The work is also architectural in its overall plan: the three acts of the opera (Jews answer the four questions in Act I; Muslims are asked in Act II; and Americans struggle to respond in Act III) contrast texturally and musically, offering a layout that functions more along the lines of a cantilevered weight and counterweight than a common-practice opera structure. A distractionist opera for the twenty-first century, *The Cave* invites inhabitation more than it does thought or empathetic exercise.

Adams and televisuality

John Adams is a post-minimalist, perhaps the first widely known composer who felt free to take Reich's and Glass's process-music concepts as a *fait accompli*. He has long appropriated the rhythms and modular repetitions of process music as a decorative façade without actually basing his forms in musical process. (And without necessarily showing himself versed in those process techniques, as Berg did when he recreated Schoenberg's twelve-tone system in his own image – an ostensibly appropriational and 'free' effort that in fact mandated even more binding precompositional strictures than Schoenberg's own 'strict' serial techniques.) Listeners will have to decide for themselves whether Adams's post-minimalism represents opportunistic hypocrisy – an Adorno would accuse Adams of a commodified surface of minimalist 'phantasmagoria' – or a loosening up of the objectivity that had proved suffocating in some earlier minimalist styles.

Compared to Glass and Reich, Adams's post-minimalism means that the repetitive and tonal aspects are free to underline the dynamics and surface emotions experienced on stage. In the first scene of *Nixon in China* (1987), when Nixon feels overwhelmed by his history-making arrival in Beijing and handshake with Chou En-lai, he is able to enthuse verbally in a way that would be unthinkable in a Glass or Reich work:

News news news news news news news news news news news news
Has a kind of mystery:
When I shook hands with Chou En-lai
On this bare field outside Peking
Just now, the world was listening.
And though we spoke quietly,
The eyes and ears of history
Caught every gesture,
And every word, transforming us
As we, transfixed,
Made history.

There are important ramifications of Adams's text-setting here. In the early music of Reich and Glass, 'minimalist' repetition had built forms, created manners of transformation unique until then in art music, and worked (perhaps subconsciously) to exorcize the militant variation techniques of the Darmstadt modernists. Now, repetition in *Nixon in China* had become a kind of pratfall, serving the relatively banal function of helping a stage character stutter in excitement.

As a counterexample, Michael Nyman makes rather smarter diegetic use of 'minimalist' repetition in his chamber opera *The Man Who Mistook his Wife for a Hat* (1986). The repetitions in Nyman's minimalist language are less DeLeuzian explorations of identity, difference and the passage of time than they are wry, pop-art allusions to the repetitiveness of doo-wop, classical and baroque styles. Nyman's stylistic references reflect his eclectic musical interests and his wide music-historical knowledge: in his student years he read musicology under Thurston Dart at King's College, London, and went on to write the standard twentieth-century text *Experimental Music: Cage and Beyond* (1974). Nyman's harmonies tend to move faster than Adams's: the harmonic rhythm is similar to Mozart's, and his repetitions are late twentieth-century updates on Alberti bass patterns in that they sustain chords rather than supplying structure and rhythmic detail. (Except for the rhythmic overlay in the accompaniment, *The Man Who Mistook* often sounds like Benjamin Britten.) The historical reference is spelled out unmistakably in the second scene when Dr P, a singer suffering from visual agnosia, is asked to sing Schumann's 'Ich grolle nicht'. Nyman chose to include this particular song, and the reason becomes clear in the opening bars: the reiterated chords in Schumann's accompaniment are identical to Nyman's basic texture, and so the composer reveals repeated quavers in groups of four as a kind of music-historical pun (Nyman 1986, 11).

In comparison with Nyman, at least, Adams's repetitions offer clear and obvious obeisance to surface and stage effect – with no possibility for rhythmic-stylistic inside jokes. In one respect, the what-you-see-is-what-you-get aspect helps make *Nixon in China* an up-to-date reflection of American culture. *Nixon* is not historically important because of its musical language or its dramaturgy per se, but because it is the first opera to recognize the operatic significance of television and video – or, more specifically, what mediologist John Thornton Caldwell calls the far-reaching cultural significance of 'televisuality', with its emphasis on public spectacle and idiosyncratic constructions of 'reality' and 'liveness'. As he describes the revolution of videotape, 'videotaped liveness has become a charged apparatus by which personal behaviors converge in public spectacle … Tape, masquerading as liveness, is now the recurrent mode by which the public intervenes in the private' (Caldwell 1995, 223). Working from film scholar Christian Metz's thoughts, Caldwell distinguishes between a cinematic 'fiction effect' which denies the artifice of video and the singular gaze, and a 'reality effect', which gives itself over to artifice and physicality: 'the picture effect packaged in the televisual documentary is out front, on the surface. Televisual spectatorship does not necessarily produce a subconscious or unconscious state. There is instead an explicit performance of style that directly addresses the viewer's presence in some way' (1995, 242–3).

In a brilliant essay on the televisual aspect of *Nixon in China*, Peggy Kamuf advances the President's first handshake with Premiere Chou as the archetypal media event:

> With that term is understood an event staged totally or in part for the media, especially television. As such, it is not identical to or coincident with the event it would appear to be, but at once more and less … By 'media event' we have come to understand this sort of empty image in which the camera records its own intervention at the center of an action that is thereby thrown off-center in an endless divergence from itself. In this sense, media events do not ever happen; they only recur.
>
> (1994, 88–9)

Televisuality having arrived in Beijing already in February 1972, the flesh-and-blood Nixon and Chou paused in freeze-frame as they allowed the photos to be taken, the video feeds to be made, the media event to happen. Actual life was disrupted, altered by the media event that span off it, and the latter became more natural and 'real' than the former. As Kamuf writes, in allusion both to Beijing and Walter Benjamin: 'The production of this first-time event, in other words, is not the condition but the effect of its reproduction.'

John Adams, librettist Alice Goodman and director Peter Sellars reinvented opera for the age of mass communication. *Nixon in China* is a brilliant and volatile mixture of history and kitsch, and owes its success to that juxtaposition – anomalous and bizarre in opera history, but television's daily bread. The daringly bourgeois foxtrot in Act III; the bumbling, politically partisan comedy of Henry Kissinger; Pat Nixon's crooked lipstick in Act III and her declaration that 'every day is Christmas' – these all serve to remove us from the historical importance of the President's visit and plunge us into the mundane details of its mass-mediated simulacrum, the banality of its televised form. As with the media event, though, the absurdity doesn't quite come to the foreground: despite Goodman's pretentious best efforts (her overbearing poetics appropriate only to Mao's heavier Act I locutions), it never really becomes clear if the kitsch is intended. ('I don't view this as a satirical opera at all', Adams has said in an interview, backing up his view with Goodman's description of the story as 'heroic' (Adams and Porter 1988, 27).) Kamuf hears Act II as an inextricable entanglement of opera and socialist-realist kitsch. As she writes regarding the performance of Madame Mao's socialist-realist play in Act II scene 2: '*Nixon in China* is no longer simply quoting (or pretending to quote) this other work, *The Red Detachment of Women*. Or, rather, the quoting function is still operating, but it is now unclear both where the quotation marks are exactly and which work is quoting the other' (Kamuf 1994, 104). Undirected but focused on effect, *Nixon in China* reads and sounds like twenty-first-century socialist realism: in short, as a stage spectacle with no underlying cause.

Adams has said repeatedly that opera must be made relevant to the present day, that it is the great modern political figures who are 'the mythological characters of our time' (Lieberson 1988, 35). His willingness to cut close to home, along with the corroborative daring of Goodman and Sellars, is seen acutely in *The Death of Klinghoffer* (1991). The work began with a conversation between Sellars and director Jean-Luc Godard on terrorism as a form of theatre (Adams and Porter 1988, 30). The story centres around the 1985 hijacking of the Italian cruise ship *Achille Lauro*, and the murder of Jewish-American passenger Leon Klinghoffer by the Palestinian terrorists. It was perhaps inevitable that Adams and company, given their interest in current events and televisuality, would focus at some point on terrorism, which is at its basis a media event. As N. C. Livingstone has written, 'Terrorism, as an extreme form of violence, is particularly newsworthy and well suited to the needs of television, which is a highly visual and compact medium with little time for exposition … It has been said, speciously but with some truth, that terrorism is so ideally suited to television that the medium would have invented the phenomenon if it had not already existed' (cited in Weimann and Winn 1994, 95).

Given the horrifying sensationalism of its subject, audiences are surprised to find *The Death of Klinghoffer* so slow, even ritualistic, on stage. The composer has said the opera resembles a Passion play, and much ink has been spilled on the 'Gymnopédie' and ballet that allegorize the descent of Klinghoffer's body when the attackers throw him overboard. *Klinghoffer* is frequently compared to an oratorio, partly because of the lack of immediate drama, and partly on account of the chorus's important role. Adams relies less on buoyant repetition and layered textures than he did in many earlier works, doubtless in reaction to the grim storyline. The singing, too, tends toward a gray arioso style. It is telling that the closest thing to an aria, or even a self-contained set piece, is also the closest that Adams comes to comedy. This is a short rumination in *Sprechstimme* by an Austrian passenger hiding in her stateroom – a number analogous to, and clearly influenced by, the Sprecher's narration in Schoenberg's *Gurrelieder*.

One accusation that has dogged Adams, Goodman and Sellars is that they have chosen volatile, pushbutton subjects that continue to bait and rankle – and then, painting with too fine a brush for their material, failed to come down on any side of the chosen issues. Some have gone on to question their ethics, but it would be fairer simply to call them nonoperatic. By its theatrical history and birthright, opera takes sides and courts absurdity by drawing the world in black and white: Don Giovanni is dragged down to hell with no second chances, Alfredo Germont's father (in *La traviata*) repents for his callousness by evening's end, and the Borough – drunk on its own vendetta – hunts down Peter Grimes like an animal. Given such a tradition, some opera-goers are upset by the facts that Adams and his colleagues present Nixon as neither a criminal nor a buffoon, and are unwilling to present a group of hijackers as bloodthirsty animals or lead them off to their just deserts in the form of a climactic *auto-da-fé*.

It is somewhat reassuring, then, that their next collaboration will focus on a rather more distant, if still knotty, subject: nuclear physicist J. Robert Oppenheimer and the creation of the atom bomb. The opera was commissioned by the San Francisco Opera, and its premiere is scheduled for the 2005–06 season.

Coda: opera and reform

To the question 'what is an opera?', Hans Keller replied that there could be no precise answer: 'It all depends on the next one, not the last one' (1994, 89). The history of opera is a forward-directed history of reform, which serves to contrast this genre with, say, the symphony – where composition has always had a curatorial, retrospective aspect. As Herbert Lindenberger notes, those reforms have habitually tried 'to rid opera of those elements most offensive to anybody holding an antitheatrical bias' (1984, 207). Over the centuries, from Jacopo Peri and Gluck to Puccini and Carlisle Floyd, there has been general and fairly constant agreement on just what realism – or, in other words, anti-theatricality – might mean in operatic terms. And, just as consistently, realism has been invoked in the name of modernity.

Against such a history, minimalist opera composers, librettists and directors of the 1970s and 1980s remade conceptions of reality itself. One couldn't have expected anything less ambitious, given the New York theatre revolutions of the 1960s and the new music-cognitive challenges of minimalism – its repetitiveness contravening basic ideas of narrative and refuting breath-based conceptions of the musical utterance. The minimalist opera 'reformers' turned opera into something that might seem more, rather than less, theatrical – and did so in the name of up-to-date-ness. With Glass and Wilson, realism became a matter of faithfulness toward dreams as the true, perhaps post-Freudian reality. According to Franco Bertoni, Wilson 'purifies in his illusory but authentic world the crudeness of matter, sees everything once again with the innocence of children and mad people, and gives us back – free of convention and restrictions – a vision of our everyday experience' (Bertoni *et al.* 1998, 180).

With Adams, Sellars, Goodman, Glass after about 1990, Reich and Korot, questions about realism became intertwined with questions of necessity. As these artists understood it, opera must serve a televisual reality, a world transformed by Walter Benjamin and Jean Baudrillard – in short, a reality of simulacra. Monk's new reality is sound-based: minimalism's focus on the individual moment and its minutiae freed her to explore the voice as a new kind of theatrical landscape. And this marked an imminent vocal emancipation: Monk has told the story several times of suddenly realizing during her dance training that 'the voice could be as flexible as the body' (Jowitt 1997, 82).

It is difficult to find a decade in opera history as decisive and portentous as that demarcated by the premiere of *Einstein on the Beach* and the first performance of *Nixon in China*. In the final analysis, the minimalist composers were able to take an art-form that has historically been resistant to musical avant-gardism – in 1967, Pierre Boulez famously suggested blowing up all the opera houses – and remake it in their own image. One sign of their success is Wilson's increasing acceptance and influence as a director of European, and to an increasing degree

American, opera productions. With Wilson's acclaimed minimalist stagings of Gluck's *Alceste* (Stuttgart, 1986) and Wagner's *Parsifal* (Hamburg, 1991) – the director working with the slow motion, abstract shapes, and ravishing and rarefied light effects already familiar from his collaborations with Glass – opera has become reconciled to *Einstein on the Beach* rather than the other way around.

One can only wonder how the minimalist opera 'reforms' will themselves someday be reformed upon: in short, what the next-next operas will be.

16 Opera and film

MERVYN COOKE

So why do we stick to a kind of theatrical activity which seems no longer to be viable? Granted, new and contemporary forms are continually arising, but in their lack of tradition they are naturally not exalted enough to meet with serious encouragement or to win favour with the cultivated! Isn't a good film to be preferred to a bad performance of Schiller? ALFRED ROLLER (1909)

Although this book is primarily concerned with operas composed in the twentieth century, space precluding a detailed consideration of how earlier repertoire has been reassessed in modern times, the present chapter will be concerned with filmed interpretations of operas written in various epochs. The relationship between opera and that quintessentially twentieth-century art-form, cinema, has been complex and potentially fruitful – but often fraught with difficulties, both real and imagined. Traditional repertoire has been reassessed from the cinematographer's perspective, the experience having been fed back into modern stage productions; film music was from the outset profoundly influenced by operatic techniques, before it in turn came to influence operatic music; and several operas were specially composed for the screen. This chapter looks briefly at those three topics, examining filmed treatments of existing operas, the relationship between opera and film music, and the select corpus of twentieth-century operas written specifically for film or television.

Opera on film

Cinematic interpretations of scenes from popular operas were widespread in the era of the silent film. By as early as 1904, extracts from Wagner's *Parsifal*, Rossini's *Barber of Seville* and Gounod's *Faust* had been recorded on film and projected with live music. The sumptuous Gounod film, *Faust et Marguerite*, was directed by pioneering film-maker Georges Méliès, who himself appeared as Méphistophélès. In 1908, two developments contributed towards a boom in such ventures: first, the founding of the influential *film d'art* movement in France (for which Saint-Saëns composed an original score for the launch film, *L'Assassinat du Duc de Guise*), which intensified interest in cinema as an art-form; second, the introduction of more stringent copyright legislation which henceforth compelled film-makers to plunder non-copyright classics of literature and the operatic stage in the interests of economy. A further consideration in the issuing of operatic extracts on film was the desire to promote gramophone recordings of the singers featured, a commercial concern that sat uncomfortably alongside the growing feeling that operatic source material could lend the medium of film a prestige that had formerly eluded it.

'Canned theatre' (in the parlance of the day) thus came to include 'canned opera', with both Pathé and Edison releasing new versions of Gounod's *Faust*, in 1909 and 1911 respectively; Pathé also made a film based on Verdi's *Il trovatore* in 1910. Other operas subjected to film treatment included Thomas's *Mignon*, Auber's *Fra Diavolo* and Wagner's *Siegfried* (all 1912). Appropriate musical extracts from the operas were suggested by the distributors to guide projection venues in fitting live performances to the images, and these performances generally lacked the vocal parts (Marks 1997, 72); venues were at liberty to use any other music of their choice, and often did. In the case of a film based on Mozart's *Le nozze di Figaro* (1914), the distributor declared in its trade advertisement that 'Music adapted from the famous Opera will be supplied gratis' (193). Biopics based on the lives of Wagner and Verdi appeared in Europe in 1913 and 1914 respectively, and operatic films continued to be produced in large numbers in France, Germany and Italy.

Bizet's ever-popular *Carmen*, already given a filmed treatment by Edison in 1910, formed the basis for a silent film starring operatic soprano Geraldine Farrar in 1915 – and wickedly parodied a year later by Charlie Chaplin in his *Burlesque on Carmen*. Produced by Cecil B. DeMille for Paramount, the Farrar film was launched in the USA to the accompaniment of arrangements from Bizet's score prepared by leading film-music pioneers Hugo Riesenfeld and Samuel L. Rothapfel. In 1917, Puccini refused to allow his music to be used for a film version of *La Bohème*, his gesture reinforcing the problem of tackling works still in copyright; but production of non-copyright opera films continued apace. By the 1920s silent films had grown longer in duration and relatively sophisticated in technique, and later operatic ventures were accordingly more satisfying. Among them, several films based on *La Bohème* finally appeared (in 1921, 1922 and 1926).

A silent film of Strauss's *Der Rosenkavalier* was made in 1925, and this is occasionally screened today – as it was at Aldeburgh in 2002, with live piano accompaniment. The film's production credentials were impressive, with direction by Robert Wiene (responsible for the legendary expressionist film *The Cabinet of Dr Caligari* in 1919), design by Alfred Roller (designer of Max Reinhardt's original staging of the opera) and the direct participation of both librettist and composer. Strauss originally intended to have little to do with the project, which was scheduled to be screened at the Dresden Opera House in January 1926; he agreed to compose a new march, but left the task of adaptation to Otto Singer and Karl Alwin. In December 1925 the librettist Hofmannsthal wrote to the composer to say: 'I must admit that your refusal to conduct the film in Dresden came quite unexpected and is a grave blow to me ... I cling to the hope that it may perhaps be tempered with "blessed revocability", but if it were irrevocable, I foresee for you (and consequently also for me) ... the loss of very considerable financial expectations' (Hammelmann and Osers 1961, 411). Hofmannsthal was impecunious at the time and clearly had a vested interest in generating revenue from the project: his awareness of its commercial potential is telling. In a later letter Hofmannsthal passionately argued that the film would provide 'a positive fillip and new impetus to the opera's success in the theatre' (quoted in Jefferson 1985, 123). Strauss duly relented, and conducted the shambolic first screening in which it rapidly became apparent that he possessed neither the technical expertise nor sympathy with the medium necessary to ensure accurate synchronization with the projected images: he suffered the humiliation of being forced to yield his baton to an experienced film conductor (London 1936, 69). In April 1926 Strauss was in London to conduct the first English screening, on which occasion he also recorded orchestral excerpts with the Tivoli Orchestra. Released by His Master's Voice, these recordings were an early example of a film 'tie-in'.

Reflecting on the tension between populist film music and modernist music 'driven into the esoteric' because of its minority appeal, Hanns Eisler – in a prejudicial study of film music co-authored with Theodor Adorno – took a hearty swipe at both *Der Rosenkavalier* and its composer:

> at the time when motion-picture music was in its rudimentary stage, the breach between middle-class audiences and the really serious music which expressed the situation of the middle classes had become unbridgeable. This breach can be traced back as far as *Tristan*, a work that has probably never been understood and liked as much as *Aïda*, *Carmen*, or even the *Meistersinger*. The operatic theater became finally estranged from its audience between 1900 and 1910, with the production of *Salome* and *Elektra*, the two advanced operas of Richard Strauss. The fact that after 1910, with the *Rosenkavalier* – it is no accident that this opera has been made into a moving picture – he turned to a retrospective stylized way of writing reflects his awareness of that breach. Strauss was one of the first to attempt to bridge the gap between culture and audience, by selling out culture.
>
> (Adorno and Eisler 1994 [1947], 57)

It is worth noting, however, that the first screening of the *Rosenkavalier* film took place in a prestigious opera house, not a picture palace, and that more elaborate presentations of silent feature films were often mounted in similar venues: in 1921, for example, Eugene Goossens conducted the London Symphony Orchestra in the Royal Opera House for the screening of a silent version of *The Three Musketeers*, starring Douglas Fairbanks. Goossens based his compilation score heavily on the work of an obscure composer, August Enna, whose music 'fitted anything, and also conveyed a spurious impression of great emotional depth, making it very suitable for my purpose' (quoted in Kershaw 1995, 128). The boundaries between art and popular entertainment were becoming blurred even at this early stage, and Adorno's and Eisler's 'breach' between the allegedly self-contained audiences for both is clearly an over-simplification.

Various attempts were made in the 1920s to improve synchronization between sound and image in operatic films, notably in Germany. In 1922 the first opera specifically intended for the silver screen, Ferdinand Hummel's *Jenseits des Stromes*, included musical notation as part of the projected image as a guide to the conductor, but the film has not survived (Evidon 1992, 196; Fawkes 2000, 27). In Berlin four years later, Carl Robert Blum exhibited his 'rhythmonome', which recorded sound in the form of a 'rhythmogram' charting the rhythmic course of the music diagrammatically and designed to be played back on the conductor's desk in exact synchronization with the moving pictures; this device found an application in live opera, being used for the first production of Křenek's *Jonny spielt auf* in 1927. Synchronized film sound first took the form of music recorded on gramophone records and played back in mechanical coupling with the image projector, and at the launch of the highly successful Vitaphone sound-on-disc system in New York in 1926 the feature film *Don Juan* was prefaced by a series of short films of musical and vaudeville performances: several star singers from the Metropolitan Opera had been signed up by Vitaphone specifically to make synchronized shorts of popular operatic excerpts.

As sound-on-film technology developed rapidly after 1927, Hollywood's penchant for glossy musicals resulted in the production of many filmed operettas, while films of 'serious' operas appeared mostly in Europe. An early highlight, which trod a middle ground between the popular and the esoteric, was G. W. Pabst's interpretation of Weill's *The Threepenny Opera*, shot in 1930 in both German and French versions using two different casts (Hinton 1990, 42–3). Pabst was a pioneer of cinematic *neue Sachlichkeit*, his innovative montage techniques developing methods of continuity editing still prevalent today. As with Max Ophüls's film of Smetana's *Bartered Bride* (1932), Pabst showed how a front-rank director could significantly enhance the impact of a stage work by skilfully adapting it to the new medium. The script for *The Threepenny Opera* was partly the work of Béla Balázs, librettist of Bartók's *Duke Bluebeard's Castle* and a noted film theorist, and the cinematography revelled in the restless, searching camera movements, high-contrast lighting and shady settings typical of Weimar cinema. Although the musical content was drastically pruned, it was treated inventively throughout: particularly effective use was made of diegetic cues, as when 'Mack the Knife' is accompanied by a barrel organ in a street scene (with the recording level manipulated to suggest distance in a long shot), and songs used in instrumental versions played in a tavern and brothel. A débâcle surrounding the film's contractual arrangements drew attention to the ongoing dangers in tackling copyright material: both Brecht and Weill were legally entitled to have exclusive control over alterations to the screenplay and music respectively, and both independently took the production company to court when their entitlement was openly flouted. Brecht lost his case, but Weill won his – securing in the process a hefty cash settlement and potentially lucrative options to score further films by the same company. On the film's release in 1931, Universal Edition issued a tie-in album containing four of the score's most popular songs (Hinton 1990, 44–6).

In the UK, the 1930s saw the production of two expensive opera films in colour, one based on Leoncavallo's *Pagliacci* (destroyed by the distributor, Trafalgar Films, after its completion in 1937 owing to the lack of revenue generated by its release) and the other of Gilbert and Sullivan's *The Mikado* (dir. Victor Schertzinger, 1939). The latter was intended as the launch vehicle for an ambitious series of G&S films featuring the D'Oyly Carte company and London Symphony Orchestra, but the series was halted by the outbreak of the Second World War. *The Mikado* met with mixed reviews, one critic declaring that 'the mechanical nature of the screen-photograph (added to its self-complete realism in its own sphere) precludes any direct inter-action between audience and performers' (quoted in Huntley [1947], 48). The most celebrated postwar British opera film was Michael Powell's and Emeric Pressburger's interpretation of Offenbach's *The Tales of Hoffmann* (1951), in which dancing and powerful special effects combined to create a new kind of cinematographic theatricality that appeared to be located in a fruitful middle ground between fantasy and reality, described by film theorist André Bazin as 'an entirely faked universe . . . a sort of stage without wings where everything is possible' (quoted in Joe and Theresa 2002, 51). Also in 1951, a film of Menotti's *The Medium* received critical acclaim and subsequently won an award at the 1952 Cannes Film Festival; this was an appropriate accolade for Italian filmed opera in general, the country having remained at the forefront of cinematic treatments of grand opera throughout the previous two decades.

Debate had by this time begun to rage on an apparently fundamental tension between filmic realism and stage theatricality. Because of the conceived incompatibility of the two approaches, several early commentators on film music bluntly predicted no future for filmed opera. Leonid Sabaneev identified the principal stumbling block as 'the fact that the art of the cinema ... is a photographic art, and is therefore obliged to be naturalistic and anti-theatrical' (1935, 26). Kurt London declared filmed opera to be 'impossible and intolerable', and continued:

> Those elements for which on the operatic stage even to-day allowance is made, under the influence of the personalities of live artists, must on the screen have an insipid, ridiculous, and anachronistic effect. The camera brings the singer's pathos much too close to the spectator; a close-up of a photographed high C, on which the distorted face of the tenor, with wide-open mouth, is to be seen, at once destroys the effect of even the most beautiful melody and resolves it into laughter or even disgust.   (1936, 139–40)

On the subject of the dubious value of close-up shots of singers' faces, which can be just as disconcerting on television as in the cinema, the problem has been wittily summarized by Mary Holtby in her satire 'The Pearl-flashers or *Simonna Boccanegra*':

> Fair face, in distant drama seen,
>   The source of sumptuous trillings,
> Avoid, I pray, the mini-screen,
>   Where I can count your fillings.   (Parrott 1989, 176)

In his account of the problematic nature of filmed opera, London concluded: 'The unreal world of opera and the naturalistic film have nothing whatever in common' (1936, 139–40). This view was elaborated by film theorist Siegfried Kracauer in the early 1950s, when he declared 'The world of opera is built upon premises which radically defy those of the cinematic approach ... Opera on the screen is a collision of two worlds detrimental to either' (quoted in Joe and Theresa 2002, ix).

Today's spectators are more aware that cinema is arguably the most artificial and manipulative of creative media – and potentially the most fantastic – and are far less desirous of realism. London's assertions that 'opera is static, film dynamic' and that 'well-known works of operatic literature have become rigid conceptions which may not be touched by the film' (1936, 140, 142) will amuse contemporary opera audiences, accustomed as they are to a spectacular diversity of production styles beyond the wildest dreams of both film and opera audiences in the 1930s.

As early as 1913, Schoenberg had explored the possibility of filmed opera in an unnaturalistic style when contemplating a hand-tinted silent film of *Die glückliche Hand*. Writing to his publisher, he characteristically stipulated that he should retain total control over all aspects of the live musical performance, and showed himself to be in sympathy with the exigencies of movie distribution by being prepared to consider the use of a cinema organ instead of an orchestra if dictated by the size of the projection venue. Schoenberg's comments on the style of the visual images were far-sighted in their experimental nature and awareness of the unlimited potential for illusion inherent in the medium of film:

> the basic unreality of the events, which is inherent in the words, is something that they should be able to bring out even better in the filming (nasty idea that it is!). For me this is one of the main reasons for considering it. For instance, in the film, if the goblet suddenly vanishes as if it had never been there, just as if it had simply been forgotten, that is quite different from the way it is on the stage, where it has to be removed by some device. And there are a thousand things besides that be easily done in this medium, whereas the stage's resources are very limited.
>
> My foremost wish is therefore for something the opposite of what the cinema generally aspires to. I want:
>
> *The utmost unreality!* (Hahl-Koch 1984, 99–100)

Significantly, Schoenberg was considering Roller as one of three possible designers (he was in good company: the other options were the expressionist painters Kokoschka and Kandinsky), having been impressed by the anti-realist tendencies he had shown in his production of *Tristan* for Mahler at the Vienna Opera in 1903. Roller's positive attitude towards cinema early in the century, as shown by the quotation reproduced at the head of this chapter, was revealed in the course of an essay bemoaning what he perceived as a general lack of interest in theatrical experimentation on the part of opera directors.

The film version of *Die glückliche Hand* remained unachieved, and Schoenberg's latent interest in the cinema was not successfully revived by abortive attempts on the part of Hollywood producers to entice him to compose film scores after his emigration to the USA. On one memorable occasion when Schoenberg attempted to secure entire directorial control over a picture he was asked to score by Irving Thalberg at MGM, Thalberg (much to his credit) declared: 'This is a remarkable man. And once he learns about film scoring and starts working in the studio he'll realize that this is not like writing an opera' (quoted in Silvester 1998, 188). In fact, the composer's curiosity about film music bore fruit only in his orchestral work *Begleitmusik zu einer Lichtspielszene* (1930).

A particularly prolific output of filmed opera was produced by the Soviet Union from the 1950s onwards, in tandem with a series of films of well-known Russian ballets. Following the stage-bound film versions of Rakhmaninov's *Aleko* (dir. N. Sidelev, 1953) and Musorgsky's *Boris Godunov* (dir. Vera Stroyeva, 1955), more creative cinematography was demonstrated in Tchaikovsky's *Eugene Onegin* (dir. Roman Tikhomirov, 1958). Tikhomirov later directed films of Tchaikovsky's *Queen of Spades* (1960) and Borodin's *Prince Igor* (1971). Other treatments of standard repertory items included two films by Vladimir Gorikker, of Tchaikovsky's *Iolanta* (1963) and Rimsky's *Tsar's Bride* (1964). The most notable Soviet opera film was based on a twentieth-century score: Shostakovich's *Katerina Izmailova* (the revised version of *Lady Macbeth of Mtsensk*, withdrawn in 1936 after the composer's infamous lambasting in *Pravda*). The opera was filmed in 1966 by director Mikhael Shapiro, working in close collaboration with the composer, and Galina Vishnevskaya took the title role as she had in the revised opera's first staging in 1963. Shapiro combined sophisticated montage techniques with two features common in later Soviet opera films: realistic settings and a double cast (one of actors, the other of dubbed singers; the only exception was Vishnevskaya, who fulfilled both functions). According to Tatiana Egorova, the film's only 'serious mistake' was the exclusion of naturalistic sound and sound effects from the final soundtrack, with the result that 'the visual element of the film resembled an animated illustration, a pantomime of the recorded opera' (1997, 190).

Outside the Soviet Union, the output of filmed opera had dwindled somewhat, being largely confined to straightforward filmings of staged productions, such as Paul Czinner's films of the Salzburg productions of *Don Giovanni* (1955) and *Der Rosenkavalier* (1961), or films designed for the greater intimacy afforded by the medium of television, such as Ingmar Bergman's *Die Zauberflöte* (1975) and Jean-Pierre Ponnelle's *Le nozze di Figaro* (1976). Also dating from 1976 was a more ambitious project in which Jean-Marie Straub and Danièle Huillet directed an austere outdoor version of Schoenberg's *Moses und Aron* that 'represented the zenith of the Brechtian anti-aesthetic trend in cinema' (Joe and Theresa 2002, 215). This film was too estoteric in both its choice of opera and style of presentation to be widely influential, and interest instead began to focus on the commercial viability of straightforward treatments of popular operas in lavish period settings.

The 1980s vogue for full-scale grand opera in the cinema was initiated by Joseph Losey's film of *Don Giovanni* (1979), performed on the soundtrack by the Paris Opéra under Lorin Maazel. The project was conceived by Rolf Liebermann, who considered Patrice Chéreau and Franco Zeffirelli as possible directors before deciding on Losey – who had never seen the opera. The action was shot entirely on location amongst the impressive Palladian architecture of Vicenza and in the Venetian islands, and viewers who merely revelled in the visual splendour of the cinematography may have been surprised to learn that, according to Marcia Citron, the stunning locations were used 'to erect a Marxist critique of class relations' (2000, 11–12). Critical responses ranged from Julian Rushton's curt dismissal of the project as an 'elegant imbecility' (1981, 80) – a remark which might also be applied to a good deal of the operatic repertoire itself, even in its unfilmed state – to David Caute's attempt to prove that this 'masterpiece ravishing to both ear and eye' is dramatically superior to a stage interpretation:

> Losey met the challenge by flooding the picture with sunlight and water, paintings and sculpture, his camera movements boldly responsive to Mozart's music, a dazzling fusion of the fine and performing arts. Confronted by the visual stasis of operatic convention, Losey eased apart the orchestral and the dramatic, reuniting them in the cutting-room on his own terms.   (1994, 431)

At the time of the film's release, the critical response in the UK and US was almost unremittingly negative. Only in France did massive publicity on the part of the producers (Gaumont) help the film to score an enormous success at the box office and receive the critical adulation that eluded it elsewhere. This was in spite of a major rift between Liebermann and Losey when the former objected to the latter's inattention to matters of dynamics in the score, and his tendency (in marked contrast to Shapiro's in *Katerina Izmailova*) to allow sound effects to dominate the singing; as Liebermann put it, 'Mozart did not compose film music' (430–31).

Zeffirelli brought his considerable stage experience, as both director and designer, to bear in a film version of Verdi's *La traviata* (1982), with a music track performed by the Metropolitan Opera under James Levine. Characteristic of its director were the opulent costumes and sumptuous interiors with warm lighting, and the simple use of stock cinematic devices such as flashbacks (to illustrate a character's thoughts), slow zooms in and out, and the occasional use of voice-over in soliloquys – the last a neat way of avoiding the intrusiveness of close-up photography of singing mouths. In the opening sequence, a flash forwards to the dying Violetta's dustsheet-clad apartment, and again during the Prelude to Act III, the combined effect of the mute visual images and Verdi's heart-on-sleeve music was remarkably similar to that of silent-film melodrama of the 1910s. A follow-up film of Verdi's *Otello* (1986), conducted by Maazel, took significant liberties with the score in the interests of serving the visual images, to the extent that the defensive director prevented music critics from attending the New York premiere (Citron 2000, 74). *Otello* failed to repeat the success of *La traviata*, even though (like the same director's *Romeo and Juliet* of 1968) it predictably netted the Academy Award for best costumes. In a television interview in 1997, Zeffirelli claimed that he felt opera to be the most complete artistic form, combining 'dance, drama, poetry, music and the visual arts' (R. Jackson 2000, 212); yet, in spite of their surface gloss, his filmed operas were deeply conservative in their production values and offered little to stimulate either the intellect or the emotion, treading a careful middle-ground between restraint and excess.

More successful was Francesco Rosi's version of Bizet's *Carmen* (1984), which also used traditional costumes and appropriate exterior locations. Produced by Gaumont and again featuring a music track conducted by Maazel, this flamboyant and colourful interpretation was distinguished by effective crowd scenes, several of which used voice-overs instead of mimed singing to achieve greater visual realism and freedom of movement. The main titles appear over a slow-motion bullfight to the accompaniment of crowd noise and distant snatches of music; the overture crashes into life at the precise moment when Escamillo's sword enters the bull's neck and the animal drops lifeless to the ground. An effective sequence in its own right, this prologue forms a symmetrical counterpart to the bullfighting climax with which the film concludes. Bizet's score proved to be admirable for cinematic adaptation in those instances where purely instrumental passages could be treated by Rosi as straight underscoring to the action on screen. As H. Marshall Leicester has shown, Rosi's refined cinematography – which at times purports to be as realistic as Zeffirelli's – subtly underlines the contrast in the score between vernacular musical idioms and conventional operatic gestures: 'Rosi converts "realism" into a textual element, making use of the rich reference to actuality in a way Zeffirelli, the exemplar he emulates and parodies, never dreamed of. He exploits the oddness of people singing in what looks so much like real life to specify and reinforce the psycho-social implications of a difference in musical style' (1994, 273).

The diversification of opera films in the 1980s resulted in several contrasting ventures entirely different from the heady energy of Rosi's *Carmen*. Hans Jürgen Syberberg's interpretation of Wagner's *Parsifal* (1982), played out on a massive set modelled on the composer's death mask, combined boredom and pretension in equal measure; singer Robert Lloyd (who played Gurnemanz) recalled that 'none of the cast really understood what Syberberg was on about, they simply did what he asked' (Fawkes 2000, 182). The portmanteau film *Aria* (1988) was a hotchpotch compilation of operatic excerpts interpreted by no fewer than ten different directors with varying degrees of flair and success; according to Derek Jarman, 'not one of the directors opened the music up; in nearly every case they used it as a backdrop for a series of rather arbitrary fantasies, none of which had the depth or complexity of the original work' (1989, xi). (For a detailed audio-visual analysis of the segment based on Lully's *Armide*, directed with characteristic idiosyncrasy by French New Wave director Jean-Luc Godard, see Cook 1998, 215–60.) Losey had been planning a film of *Tosca* before his death in 1984; Puccini's opera received an over-ambitious live-on-location filming in 1992, and an accomplished interpretation by director Benoît Jacquot in 2001 in which full-colour costumed scenes in luminous Zeffirellian settings were disconcertingly intercut with monochrome footage of the singers recording the soundtrack in modern dress – a rather gratuitous reminder that the singing in the film is, as usual, entirely pre-recorded.

Opera in film

Just as the choice of popular operas by composers such as Bizet, Mozart and Verdi for film treatment has always been a safer commercial bet than more modern or less familiar stage works, so early film music drew heavily on extracts from popular operatic scores rather than exploring new ground. To the three names just listed must be added that of Wagner, whose example is invoked time and again in contemporaneous commentary on music in the silent cinema. A journal proclaimed in 1911 that all movie-theatre musical directors were disciples of Wagner (Flinn 1992, 15), and the influence was manifested both in specific compositional techniques such as the use of leitmotives as both narrative and structural device – considered to be a cutting-edge technique in early film music and persisting to the present day, in spite of the attempts of later commentators to discredit it – and in an aspiration towards *unendliche Melodie* in the interests of musico-dramatic continuity. Not suprisingly, the Wagnerian ideal of the *Gesamtkunstwerk* was quickly applied to the new art-form as a whole, and the connection emphasized the vital role played by music in shaping the impact of filmed drama.

In the silent cinema, the live performance of well-known operatic gobbets (especially overtures) quickly became an audience attraction in its own right, and the introduction of compilation scores designed to accompany original narrative films occurred when the procedures used in the early filmed treatments of operatic tableaux were adapted for other genres. In 1911, for example, the commercially successful Italian film *Dante's Inferno* appropriated music from Boito's *Mefistofele* (Marks 1997, 73–4). Cue sheets and anthologies helped picture-palace music directors to select appropriate numbers for a wide range of films for which dedicated scores did not exist. As cue-sheet compiler Max Winkler recalled, 'extracts from great symphonies and operas were hacked down to emerge as "Sinister Misterioso" by Beethoven, or "Weird Moderato" by Tchaikovsky' (quoted in Karlin 1994, 157). A popular favourite was Rossini's *William Tell* Overture, which proved ideal for chases, while the bridal march from Wagner's *Lohengrin* was used for wedding scenes – two of the many silent-film clichés that persist in the popular imagination to this day.

When pioneering director D. W. Griffith collaborated with Joseph Carl Breil on an elebarate compilation score for his enormously influential epic *The Birth of a Nation* (featuring music by Wagner, Beethoven, Bellini, Grieg, Hérold, Mozart, Suppé, Tchaikovsky and Weber), reporter Grace Kingsley commented in the *Los Angeles Times* on 8 February 1915 that the film's music was 'no less than the adapting of grand-opera methods to motion pictures! Each character playing has a distinct type of music, a distinct theme as in opera . . . From now on special music is to be written in this manner for all the big Griffith productions' (quoted in Marks 1997, 137). Wagner's 'Ride of the Valkyries' was selected to accompany equestrian action in the film and, according to actress Lilian Gish, director and composer argued intensely over this particular cue. Griffith wanted some of the notes to be altered but Breil refused to 'tamper' with Wagner, whereupon the director remarked that the music was not '*primarily* music' but rather 'music for motion pictures' (140). (Wagner's famous 'Ride' was later used to memorable effect in Francis Ford Coppola's 1979 film, *Apocalypse Now*, where it is blared out from a tape recorder in an attack helicopter during the Vietnam War.) In an attempt to shed the ubiquitous Wagnerian idiom, which he detested, German director Fritz Lang commissioned an original score from Gottfried Huppertz for his *Siegfried* in 1923; much to the director's annoyance, however, the film was provided with a Wagnerian compilation score by Riesenfeld when screened in the USA two years later.

In the sound cinema, the mainstream style of Hollywood film scoring was heavily shaped by the work of immigrant composers from Europe who were steeped in the idiom of turn-of-the-century opera and operetta, to which dashes of exotic colouring from the styles of Debussy, Strauss and Rimsky-Korsakov were occasionally added. Given the strong early links between opera and film music, it is not surprising that several leading exponents of the latter were also accomplished operatic composers. Erich Wolfgang Korngold was one of the most respected and sought-after film composers working in Hollywood in the 1930s, and although his music was close to many of his lower-profile film colleagues in style, he was atypical because he already enjoyed a formidable reputation as a

European classical composer: as a result he was the leading celebrity of the Hollywood music studios, and commanded ideal working conditions of which the hack film composers could only dream. Korngold had begun composing operas in Vienna during his teens, and made his name with *Die tote Stadt* (1920), composed at the age of twenty-three. He wrote eighteen film scores in the period 1935–47, including music for a celebrated series of swashbuckling adventures starring Errol Flynn.

Korngold believed that film music was essentially operatic music without the singing, and he brought his colossal experience of operatic composition to bear in his work for the silver screen. Christopher Palmer aptly summarized Korngold's achievements in this regard:

> Wagner and Strauss were the immediate progenitors of a self-indulgent style wrought with a Puccinian lusciousness and luxury of invention and occasionally tinctured with Impressionist atmospherics. Korngold's melody was sweepingly lyrical, his harmony heated and opulent. His orchestration was creamy and full-flavoured. He had a lavish and superabundant talent, one that, fortunately, had enough inbuilt vitality to stop short of the kind of maggoty over-ripeness into which the idiom degenerated in the hands of less-accomplished practitioners ... The scores he wrote for pictures whose other component parts accorded perfectly with the inherent character of his music have survived the test of time to emerge as models of their kind ... (1990, 52–3)

Palmer noted, however, that the negative side of Korngold's achievement was the vindication it seemed to offer to hack composers who continued to churn out 'maggoty over-ripeness' when (as Adorno and Eisler would have wished) film music might better have embraced a more daring modernism. Yet Korngold's influence on film scoring has extended right up to the present day, with leading contemporary practitioner John Williams continuing to pay homage to the Viennese master's thoroughly outdated style in his superbly crafted scores to modern swashbucklers such as the *Star Wars* and *Indiana Jones* series.

More original than Korngold was Bernard Herrmann, whose film music was less indebted to well-worn leitmotivic principles and rooted in ostinato techniques and a dissonant harmonic language influenced by Stravinsky and the Second Viennese School; his best-known scores were written for Alfred Hitchcock's thrillers, including *Vertigo* (1958) and *Psycho* (1960). Like Korngold, Herrmann did not compromise the idiom of his concert music when working for films, and his film experience was carried over into operatic works, which included a full-scale opera based on Emily Brontë's *Wuthering Heights* (1952) – a project directly suggested by the experience of having composed a score for a film version of Charlotte Brontë's *Jane Eyre* in 1943, parts of which were reused in the opera's music. The libretto for *Wuthering Heights* was written by Herrmann's first wife, Lucille Fletcher, who also collaborated with him on the extraordinary diegetic operatic music he composed as part of his famous score for Orson Welles's *Citizen Kane* (1941). In this film, he was required to provide vocal music for Kane's second wife, Susan Alexander, who was an aspiring opera singer for whom Kane had an opera house specially built. Herrmann composed a pastiche segment from a fictional opera entitled *Salammbô*, designed to show how she was inadequate to the task of performing it: the music was wilfully over-scored and then deliberately recorded by a weak-voiced soprano (Palmer 1990, 261). In a montage sequence depicting Susan's perform-ances on tour, the music of *Salammbô* was brought into conflict with Herrmann's extra-diegetic music representing Kane's selfish ambition, 'which after one statement is reduced to an obsessive rhythmic hammer-ing on drums, as if beating poor incompetent but sensitive Susan to a mental pulp' (259).

The direct links between operatic composition and film music were perpetuated in the work of those composers from the classical arena who also worked occasionally in the cinema: these included Copland, Virgil Thomson, Philip Glass and John Corigliano in the US; Vaughan Williams, Walton, Britten and Michael Nyman in the UK; Hindemith and Henze in Germany; and Prokofiev and Shostakovich in the USSR. Britten's early career forms an interesting parallel with Herrmann's, since both worked in experimental radio drama in the 1930s and brought this experience directly to bear on their film work; in Britten's case, his apprenticeship with the GPO Film Unit supplied him with a formidable armoury of musico-dramatic techniques that bore fruit in his later operas – some of which have been aptly described as 'cinematic' (see below). Prokofiev's collaboration with director Sergei Eisenstein on *Alexander Nevsky* (1938) and the first two parts of *Ivan the Terrible* (1943–6) resulted in a close relationship between visual image and music, exemplifying the pioneering director's controversial theories of audio-visual counterpoint. Eisenstein himself regarded these films as essentially 'operatic' in conception.

Film music admitted a higher degree of dissonance and modernistic fragmentation during the 1950s, with composers such as Leonard Rosenman responding creatively to the atonal idiom of the Second Viennese School. Leading film composer David Raksin recounted an amusing episode when a producer approached him with an invitation to compose a 'powerful' film score based directly on the idiom of *Wozzeck*: 'To hear the magic name of Alban Berg's operatic masterpiece invoked by the man with whom I would be working was to be invited to be free!' (quoted in Kalinak 1992, 78). Raksin duly invited the producer to dinner and, when he arrived, *Wozzeck* was already playing on the gramo-phone. Clearly annoyed by the music, the ignorant guest curtly asked: 'What's that crap?' Berg had himself been interested in the musical potential of cinema, and reportedly wished that *Wozzeck* might be filmed in order 'to realise certain details to perfection by means of close-ups and long shots ... details that never emerged with the desired clarity in the theatre' (Willi Reich, quoted and discussed in Tambling 1987, 76–7). The cinematic nature of Berg's operatic language was noted by Joseph Kerman, and by Adorno and Eisler, who singled out the twelve-tone chord at the moment of the eponymous anti-heroine's violent death in *Lulu* as producing 'an effect very much like that of a motion picture' (1994 [1947], 37).

Berg's *Lulu* (1935) was one of several stage operas that imported a filmic element into their dramaturgy. Based on plays by Wedekind filmed by Pabst in 1929, *Lulu* features at its mid-point a palindromically scored film interlude depicting Lulu's incarceration and subsequent release from gaol: this device serves both as a convenient compression of stage time and as a graphic illustration of the turning point in the drama before various elements in the second half start to run in reverse. Filmed segments also featured in Satie's ballet *Relâche* (1924), in Hindemith's *Hin und zurück: eine Zeitoper* (1927) and in a production of Wagner's *Ring* in Berlin (1928). In Milhaud's *Christophe Colomb* (1930), according to the composer's wife, 'for the first time in an opera one could see moving films showing scenes a little different from what was happening simultaneously on stage' (Nichols 1996, 39). In 1994, Glass conceived his *La Belle et la Bête* as a simultaneous (silent) projection of Cocteau's 1946 (sound) film of the same title with a new musical accompaniment pro-vided by live but static singers (Joe and Theresa 2002, 59–73). Glass's novel venture was a follow-up to his *Orphée* (1993), an operatic version of another film by Cocteau.

Conversely, a steady succession of narrative films featured operatic excerpts in their screenplays. An opera-house setting was memorably used in the silent film of *The Phantom of the Opera* (dir. Rupert Julian, 1925), starring Lon Chaney, and remade with sound in 1943. The Marx Brothers incorporated an extended segment of *Il trovatore* in their riotous comedy *A Night at the Opera* (1935), but later cinematic appropriations of opera were generally serious in intent. The diegetic opera in *Citizen Kane* (see above) was a rare example of specially composed operatic music: more typical has been the use of pre-existing operas from the popular repertoire. In the film version of Peter Shaffer's play *Amadeus* (dir. Milos Forman, 1984), numerous lavishly staged extracts from Mozart's operas provided spectacular punctuation to the drama but somewhat impaired the narrative flow. In *The Godfather Part III* (dir. Coppola, 1990) a diegetic performance of Mascagni's *Cavalleria rusticana* forms an ironic and cohesive backdrop to a climactic series of killings. Nino Rota's music for the two previous films in the *Godfather* trilogy (1972 and 1974) drew heavily on the *bel canto* idiom of Italian opera, while Puccini's *Gianni Schicchi* was reworked in Alex North's score to the mafia comedy *Prizzi's Honor* (dir. John Huston, 1985) as a similarly 'ethnic sonority' (Joe and Theresa 2002, 107). Verdi's music appeared in many postwar Italian films (155–76), and remained a popular choice outside a specifically Italianate setting, notably in classic literary adaptations: it featured as a period-establisher in the film version of Dickens's *Little Dorrit* (dir. Christine Edzard, 1987), and indicated the force of destiny in the Pagnol diptych *Jean de Florette* and *Manon des sources* (dir. Claude Berri, 1986).

Several idiosyncratic uses of operatic subject-matter are to be found in non-Anglophone films. Krzysztof Kieślowski's *Personnel* (1975), in which a young man for whom opera represents a pinnacle of fantasy has his illusions cruelly shattered by the mundanity of working behind the scenes at an opera house, plays out a political metaphor of repression in Poland: according to the director, 'our dreams and ideas about some ideal reality always clash somewhere along the line with something that's incomparably shallower and more wretched' (Stok 1993, 96). In Jean-Jacques Beineix's *Diva* (1981), a fictional opera star is idolized by a young lad who records her singing illicitly, she having publicly declared that she will never preserve her voice on record. Her recorded voice almost becomes a separate character, and much play is made on the artificiality of extra-diegetic music in film: singing which appears to be extra-diegetic is twice revealed to be diegetic in origin when it ceases abruptly as the lad turns off the portable tape player that accompanies him on his bike rides. (Diegetic and extra-diegetic music in film are broadly comparable to Carolyn Abbate's conception of the 'phenomenal' and 'noumenal' in opera: see Abbate 1991.) In Werner Herzog's *Fitzcarraldo* (1982), the building of an opera house in the middle of a Peruvian jungle is 'paradigmatic of the desire for an opera and for an art generally to be situated outside the commercial pressures that have previously constituted the arts' (Tambling 1987, 18; see also Rogers 2004).

Disembodied recordings of operatic performances also feature prominently in narrative films. In *The Shawshank Redemption* (dir. Frank Darabont, 1994), a recording of Mozart's *Figaro* is relayed through prison loudspeakers to symbolize freedom – and this universal message is instantly comprehended by all classes of inmate. An identical device appears in *Life is Beautiful* (dir. Roberto Benigni, 1997), where recorded Offenbach similarly lifts the spirits of those incarcerated in a Nazi concentration camp. A recording of an aria from Giordano's *Andrea Chenier* illuminates various aspects of character and cultural context in *Philadelphia* (dir. Jonathan Demme, 1993). All these instances use an outdated musical idiom to suggest a sense of timelessness or nostalgic yearning, much in the fashion (as Caryl Flinn has persuasively argued) of the aural utopia conjured up by old-fashioned Hollywood film music. But, as Marc A. Wiener points out, operatic music can be used in films for diametrically opposed purposes according to context: 'When it represents particularity, opera signifies entrapment, and when it functions as a sign of the universal, it represents freedom' (Joe and Theresa 2002, 83).

The ongoing links between cinema and opera have been fostered not only by composers working in both genres, but also by a clutch of influential directors and designers whose work straddles both media. Directors of both staged opera and feature films include Baz Luhrmann, Chéreau, Eisenstein, Herzog, Nicholas Hytner, Losey, Rouben Mamoulian, Luchino Visconti and Zeffirelli. Film designer Georges Wakhevich worked on Peter Brook's 1948 Covent Garden production of Musorgsky's *Boris Godunov* – a staging which Ernest Newman explicitly condemned for its filmic qualities (Sutcliffe 1996, 20–21). Some opera singers have made a significant impact as screen actors, including Maria Callas in a magnificent interpretation of the title role in *Medea* (dir. Pier Paolo Pasolini, 1970) – described by one critic as 'an opera without music' (Walker 2001, 533) – and Teresa Stratas in a powerful performance as a self-absorbed singer who neglects her autistic-savant daughter in the Canadian production *Under the Piano* (dir. Stefan Scaini, 1995). Stratas had previously received critical acclaim for her interpretation of the title role in Götz Friedrich's film of Strauss's *Salome* (1974).

Opera as film

The first opera conceived as a sound film was *The Robber Symphony* by Friedrich Feher (1936), and it seemed to bode well for the genre's future. An anonymous contemporaneous critic commented: 'The intimate alliance of music and fantasy is in principle wholly commendable ... Here, perhaps, may even be opera's legitimate successor – the transmutation of that hitherto over-synthetic medium into something more complex and closely-knit' (quoted in Huntley [1947], 45). Ernst Toch went further, predicting that

> the focus of film music to come is the original film opera. This cannot be done by adapting old operas for the screen, for the conception of stage-opera music is bound to be different from what film-opera must be. To adapt existing

operas ... means to mutilate either screen action or the music itself. Music of film-opera has to create and develop its own forms out of typical screen action, combining its different laws of space, time and motion with constant music laws. The first film-opera, once written and produced, will evoke a host of others.

(1937)

As we have seen, however, later filmed operas were invariably based on existing repertoire, and the kind of creative vision demonstrated by Schoenberg's unachieved plans for *Die glückliche Hand* was reflected only in the Powell–Pressburger *Tales of Hoffmann* in 1951. That same year marked the birth of opera conceived for television, which bypassed some of the perceived problems inherent in filming opera for the big screen, but presented new challenges of its own.

The first television opera was Menotti's *Amahl and the Night Visitors*, commissioned by NBC in America and first broadcast live on Christmas Eve 1951. The opera's simple plot, family appeal and attractive music made it a considerable success, and it has been repeated and given new television productions numerous times in the past fifty years – generally with broadcasts taking place in the Christmas festive period. Menotti had already gained directorial experience with the cinema film of *The Medium*, a stage work which had been produced for CBS television in 1948. Even with the success of *Amahl* behind him, however, he considered that it worked best in a live theatrical staging; in 1963 he fell out with NBC because they had not involved him personally in a new production of the piece, and he prohibited future showings of the offending version (Barnes 2003, 37–8). *Amahl* was most recently produced on British television in 2002, when Francesca Zambello directed a straightforward intepretation for the BBC using Spanish locations as a naturalistic Biblical setting.

Amahl was the first in a major series of television operas commissioned by NBC: others included Martinů's *The Marriage* and *What Men Live By* (1953), Lukas Foss's *Griffelkin* (1955), Stanley Hollingworth's *La grande Bretèche* (1957) and Menotti's *Maria Golovin* (1958). Menotti later wrote *Labyrinth* for NBC in 1963 and *Martin's Lie* for CBS in 1965. CBS had first made its mark on television opera by commissioning *The Flood* from Stravinsky, which was broadcast in 1962. Although he later described the work as a 'musical play', Stravinsky showed a keen interest in the televisual medium, not only for its creative possibilities but also on account of the musical concision and economy the swiftness of screen drama seemed to demand: 'Because the succession of visualisations can be instantaneous, the composer may dispense with the afflatus of overtures, connecting episodes, curtain music ... [S]o far, I have not been able to imagine the work on the operatic stage because the musical speed is so uniquely cinematographic' (Stravinsky and Craft 1968, 79). This approach sat well alongside Stravinsky's contemporaneous interest in serial technique and the resulting score was characteristically compressed, lasting under thirty minutes. In spite of his comments on the work's 'uniquely cinematographic' nature, however, *The Flood* almost immediately received a theatrical production in Hamburg in 1963.

Television opera came into vogue in Europe in the late 1950s, with the BBC commissioning its first works for the medium from Arthur Benjamin (*Mañana*) and Malcolm Arnold (*The Open Window*) in 1956. The same year saw the establishment of the Salzburg TV Opera Prize, awarded triennially until 1986; Paul Angerer's prizewinning *Die Paßkontrolle* (1959) was one of several scores with topical subject-matter (Barnes 2003, 9). The BBC commissioned a further eleven television operas between 1957 and 1969, highlights including Arthur Bliss's *Tobias and the Angel* (1960) and Christopher Whelan's *Some Place of Darkness* (1967). While US television opera commissions dwindled after the 1970s, British television – after a barren decade in the 1980s – continued to elicit new scores throughout the 1990s (for a complete list, see Barnes 2003, 104). Especially notable was a series of six fifty-minute operas commissioned by Channel 4 in 1994–5 from Orlando Gough, Anthony Moore, Stewart Copeland, Michael Torke, Gerald Barry, and Kate and Mike Westbrook. Captured on film rather than video in accordance with 1990s production practices, these commissions were intended to be exclusively for realization on the small screen and 'unsuitable for live performance' (85). In contrast, some later BBC projects were jointly commissioned with opera companies so that the works received both televisual and theatrical productions: examples include Gordon Crosse's *Purgatory* (Cheltenham Festival and BBC TV, 1966) and Tippett's *New Year* (Houston Grand Opera, 1989; BBC TV, 1991).

One of the best-known television operas remains Britten's *Owen Wingrave*, commissioned by the BBC and first broadcast in May 1971. Prior to this, Britten had already gained considerable television experience from his involvement in the BBC's studio productions of his large-scale operas *Billy Budd* (dir. Basil Coleman, 1966) and *Peter Grimes* (dir. Brian Large, 1969). For the subject-matter of *Owen Wingrave*, Britten turned again to a ghost story by Henry James; significantly, his earlier handling of James's *The Turn of the Screw* in the medium of chamber opera (1954) had consistently been praised for its cinematic qualities (see, for example, the use of 'flashbacks' identified in Mellers 1984, 146), and it may not be coincidental that *The Turn of the Screw* had originally been suggested to Britten as the basis for an opera specially intended for film (Carpenter 1992, 331). The rapid scene changes, dissolves and evocative instrumental interludes of the *Screw* proved ideal for cinematic realization when it was stylishly filmed on location in Czechoslovakia by director Petr Weigl in 1982, the haunting images expertly dubbed with the music of a Covent Garden production conducted by Colin Davis. In *Owen Wingrave*, Britten adapted some of the freely aligned textures he had developed in his 1960s trilogy of Church Parables in the service of televisual montage; his attitude towards television as a medium fluctuated between a professed desire to avoid realism and a strong need to be able to visualize every single detail of the production, a paradox that lies at the heart of many of his stage operas. As in the case of Stravinsky's *Flood*, Britten's television opera quickly made its way onto the live operatic stage in a theatrical production at Covent Garden in 1973. A new television production of *Wingrave* was broadcast in the UK on Channel 4 in 2001, and a comparison of the two interpretations highlights some of the essential differences between a 1970s studio recording and a 1990s filmed opera.

The 1971 *Wingrave* was conducted by Britten in Snape Maltings Concert Hall, which had been transformed temporarily into a television studio. Directed by Brian Large and Colin Graham, the production was recorded using six video cameras running simultaneously and was edited in the same manner as the classic BBC TV literary adaptations and sit-coms of the 1970s. It is therefore inappropriate to compare the production with the techniques of Hollywood cinema – as does Shannon McKellar, who misleadingly states that the recording was situated 'within the boundaries of the classical Hollywood film genre. To a large extent, the work's film techniques and apparatus remain those one might have expected to find in the latest American movie' (1999, 394). As with studio drama, the sharp clarity of the videotaped image proved well suited to intimate scenes. There were only brief moments where the presentation departed from realistic studio norms, as in the greater abstractness of the Wingrave family's combined outcries of 'How dare you!' to Owen, which are addressed directly to camera against a stark black background, and the stylized regimental banners at the beginning of Act I scene 2. The camerawork is otherwise standard for its time, though McKellar has drawn attention to the careful editing of the crucial 'Peace Aria' which seems to suggest visually how Owen remains oppressed by his family background even as he ostensibly breaks free from it:

> the turning point in Owen's aria created by camera techniques is also the crux around which the opera revolves ... by embedding Owen's song within the actual diegesis of the work – with symmetrical design and shot length, and the greater amount of attention that the camera eye pays to the portraits – film techniques deny Owen the very quality that characterizes solo as aria. His song for peace is neither reflective nor wholly enclosed; he builds awareness only in relation to others, and sings, in effect, to the portraits and not to himself. His voice echoes from within the narrative space of the film, and not, like the [other characters] during moments of aria, from without.
>
> (1999, 409)

Figure 16.1 Britten's *Owen Wingrave*, directed by Brian Large and Colin Graham (BBC Television, 1971): the Wingrave family confront Owen. *Left to right*: Miss Wingrave (Sylvia Fisher), General Sir Philip Wingrave (Peter Pears), Kate Julian (Janet Baker) and Mrs Julian (Jennifer Vyvyan). Photo: Reg Wilson.

Figure 16.2 Britten's *Owen Wingrave*, directed by Margaret Williams (MJW Productions, 2001): the Wingrave family at the dining table. *Left to right*: Kate Julian (Charlotte Hellekant), Miss Wingrave (Josephine Barstow) and Mrs Julian (Elizabeth Gale). Photo: David Hobson.

Figure 16.3 Britten's *Owen Wingrave* (MJW Productions, 2001): Owen (Gerald Finley) enters the haunted family mansion. Photo: David Hobson.

In the few parts of the score which do not involve voices, it is intriguing to hear Britten adopting a musical idiom that at times seems directly redolent of modern film music: as Owen enters the family mansion in Act I scene 4, for example, the eerie twelve-note chord stacked up in the orchestra and topped off by a dash of glockenspiel recalls a standard spine-tingling gesture in 1960s film music. This seems appropriate to the stereotyped dramatic situation, described by Jeremy Tambling as 'playing on the way Owen comes to what seems to be an empty house; the device is out of any horror-movie, and appropriate as a reminder of the artificiality of the genre' (1987, 118).

The 2001 *Wingrave* was directed by Margaret Williams and shot on film in widescreen format, in accordance with the increasing vogue throughout the 1990s for television adaptations of literary classics to aspire to the often glossy production values of narrative cinema – especially in a heavy use of location filming. The action is updated to the Cold War of the late 1950s, which on the one hand makes the story seem more topical to a modern audience, yet on the other renders disquietingly anachronistic the strict Victorian family and military values at the heart of James's tale; in this version, Owen's personal predicament may seem less plausible than in the original production. The replacing of the latter's intimate theatricality with cinematic realism offers a challenge when it comes to creating the claustro-phobic intensity at the heart of the story; the opening sequence of family portraits, for example, brilliantly disturbing in the 1971 production (where it was closely synchronized with every detail implied by Britten's graphically programmatic orchestral prelude), is in visual terms no longer as threatening in the more expansive 2001 production. The filmic quality of Britten's orchestral music for the approach to the family mansion is well realized in this film, however, where the moody exterior shots include an additional appearance of the ghostly presence which will soon be implicated in the protagonist's mysterious death.

At the time of writing, the most recent opera film made specially for television was Penny Woolcock's interpretation of John Adams's *The Death of Klinghoffer*, shown on Channel 4 in 2003. With the exception of the surreally beautiful images of Klinghoffer's corpse sinking into its watery grave, the film cultivated a detailed cinematic realism consistently at odds with the extreme stylization in the music. Adams's score cries out for a corresponding degree of visual stylization, and the unnecessary realism in this film version paradoxically makes suspension of disbelief wellnigh impos-sible. A similar problem is encountered in the lavish cinema production of Andrew Lloyd Webber's rock opera *Evita* (dir. Alan Parker, 1996), where the attention to 1950s period details in the visuals often jars with the stylized 1970s idiom of the soundtrack, and where a greater degree of theatricality or fantasy might also have proved beneficial (as it invariably does in stage productions). In the case of *Klinghoffer*, realistic terrorists with realistic guns on a realistic ship in a realistic ocean seem a viable cinematic proposi-tion right up to the moment when the characters open their mouths and break into apparently diegetic song, and this problem seems far more acute in works with a topical modern setting than in the case of, say, Losey's period-dress *Don Giovanni*. The difficulties of negotiating the conflicting demands of cinematic realism and operatic theatricality remain as strangely problematic today as they did at the birth of the sound film over seventy years ago.

Operas specially written for film have always been exceptionally rare and, although rather more have been commissioned for television, the combined total is still small. This select repertoire has been notable for its surprisingly low level of dramatic and visual experimentation – possibly a consequence of understandable attempts on the part of those composers involved to write works which would transfer relatively easily to the live operatic stage and thereby stand a chance of securing a living future in the theatre. Clearly the commercial non-viability of filming modern opera for exhibition in cinemas has been a major factor contributing towards the paucity of original film operas. But the roots of the problem go right back to the 1930s when the film medium was generally perceived as too lowbrow to be applied to the interpretation of great works of art. The debate that raged in the 1940s on the subject of the relative merits of realism and theatricality in filmed opera productions singularly ignored the fact that the stunningly original Hollywood musicals of the 1930s had already shown what could be achieved when music and image were creatively combined and fantasy allowed free rein, and it is a considerable irony that this degree of artistic experimentation seemed acceptable only in the context of a popular and commercially viable genre.

Shortly before he completed *Peter Grimes*, Britten prophetically commented: 'I feel that with the advent of films, opera may turn its back on realism, and develop or return to stylisation – which I think it should' (1944, 4). Although from a modern vantage point we often view representative art that purports to be 'realistic' with suspicion, cinema was in the 1940s viewed as the realist art-form *par excellence* – and, just as the visual arts became less representative once photography became commonplace, so stage productions of opera and drama gradually yielded realism to the cinema and cultivated in its stead more compellingly stylized approaches to their raw material. Those who firmly believe in the artistic potential of cinema and television, and perhaps view film in particular as the ultimate collaborative *Gesamtkunstwerk*, will continue to regard filmed opera as something of a curiosity, that rarely – if ever – attains the creative heights of which it seems easily capable. If filmed opera is destined to remain an occasional presence in the margins of both cinematic and operatic history, the impact of cinema – both positive and negative – on the development of live stagings is nevertheless likely to be remembered as one of the defining influences on the theatrical arts of the twentieth century.

17 Popular musical theatre (and film)

STEPHEN BANFIELD

Spaces and genres

From Buxton to Ballarat, Manchester to Manaus, the London Coliseum to Central City, Colorado, the world is full of imposing opera houses built one hundred or more years ago that cause one to wonder just how much opera has gone on inside them. As architectural spaces, they have one and all catered for a mass public's aspirations towards plush velvet seating, regal insignia, the boudoir gilt, livery and privileged partial view (both in and out) found alike in private box and private coach, and the magical illusion of the proscenium stage. Theatrical magic is essentially that of a show, of the dazzle of a star, the virtuosity of a spectacle or the tension of a tragic or comic surprise; music adds magic of its own with the wondrous sounds proceeding from the star's mouth and, unseen or at least unobserved, from the orchestra pit. Some of the musical sounds and shows inhabiting such theatres have constituted opera proper; many of them have not. The dressing rooms, stages and musical cues have been prepared similarly for performing dogs and divas; from the tired businessman in the stalls to the gold prospector or Japanese tourist in the gallery, the men in the audience have ogled Melba, Mary Martin or a potential mistress, the women their men, their matinée idol or their neighbour's jewellery.

Those theatrical spaces, dedicated to lavish, alluring and clever multidisciplinary entertainment, have not changed much through the twentieth century and into the twenty-first. Nor perhaps has the range of upward and downward cultural – hence generic – pressures to which their types of entertainment are perennially subject, pressures basically towards high or low, serious or comic, clean or dirty. There remains a generic continuum between the sealed, concentrated world of sung melodrama that is opera and the serial entertainments of the variety show, and there remain supple exchanges between the two. But some time before 1900 a new audience contract had been drawn up when, as in late Victorian England, the rowdy critics of the pit and gallery were turned into respectable stallholders, and it was probably this that sealed once and for all the decorum of seriousness in opera. Spoken dialogue is not the issue, but no-one on stage smiles in Bizet's *Carmen*, and no-one in the audience applauds or laughs out loud to disturb the musical continuum in Verdi's *Falstaff* or Wagner's *Meistersinger*, which is where they differ from Rossini's *Barber of Seville*. Opera, in short, lost its wit, the comedy in Puccini notwithstanding. Theatrical presentation in the lower genres retained it, together with a vital ingredient of bodily allure, erotic or athletic in varying proportions, both continuing to sanction audible audience response – to language and to spectacle. Yet if opera, at least before minimalism, ceased to reach down, popular musical theatre kept reaching up, and to understand its styles one is obliged to identify the operatic dimension – the warbling heroine, the through-composed finale – until with rock opera and the mega-musical it becomes apparent that the vernacular succumbed to a patina of melodramatic amplification thrown over the entire production in more senses than one.

Is this a story of Americanization? Yes, up to a point, for popular musical theatre is above all commercial; and first Broadway, then Hollywood, and now what is simply known as the music industry have increasingly commanded our responses to it, as they have to popular music overall. And it could be said that the reaching out towards opera represents the survival of some kind of dignity, of an operetta tradition, in the face of the hype and merchandizing that affect everything in the popular theatre from the souvenir programme to the endlessly reprised hit song. Perhaps the best musicals manage to resist shipwreck on the rocks of commercial success on the one hand, subsidized cultural approval on the other, keeping away from both. *Show Boat*, *West Side Story*, *Sweeney Todd* and *Jesus Christ Superstar* would all fit that description. Conversely, only one work, Gershwin's *Porgy and Bess* (1935), appears large enough to bridge the gulf. Gershwin called it a folk opera, and its score is bigger, its musical demands greater, its style more intricate than those of any musical.

Even the American musical comedy had to become Americanized, for there is not much stylistic difference between, say, André Messager's *Véronique* (1898) and Victor Herbert's *Naughty Marietta* (1910). Both composers traded in common-practice tonal models but gave way to younger practitioners drawing on new music, dance and language from below. Thus the story is less one of national schools becoming submerged than of cosmopolitan urbanity giving way to folk signifiers. Or, to take a longer view, it was (in music) the gradual, sometimes sudden ousting of long-domesticated folk, parade and stage archetypes from central Europe – waltzes, polkas, country dances, marches and the daintiness of ballet – in favour of a new set of sounds and sights based on the great diasporas of the time. The white and black Atlantic were represented by gradually increasing modality of melody and parallelism of harmony on the one hand, sudden injections of ragtime, jazz and blues on the other, and the invention of 'belting' as folk-singing by reference to both. The Latin world made a greater contribution than is generally recognized with its sultry beguine rhythms and slow melodic triplets. The Jews changed male performance practice for ever with the influence of cantorial singing, backed up by more overtly emotional harmonic rhetoric.

Because of its increasing economic and cultural dominance, these changes were most noticeable and influential in the American musical, and (what is often not recognized) in many respects (for instance, singing styles) most influential after it had taken to film. Thus Jerome Kern incorporated ragtime into his songs, Gershwin highly syncopated rhythms, Cole Porter the eroticism of Latin dance, Richard Rodgers and Irving Berlin the cowboy inflections of an idealized past (in *Oklahoma!* and *Annie Get Your Gun*), Leonard Bernstein big-band jazz and something of the panache of rock 'n' roll in *West Side Story*.

European countries had nevertheless already made bargains with their folk traditions or with their musical 'Other' in order to establish a bourgeois musical theatre in the first place. Hence the gypsy element in Johann Strauss, highly symbolic of the Dual Monarchy in Austro-Hungary after 1866, and the satirical *couplets* in Offenbach, redolent of the café-concert with which *opéra bouffe* rubbed shoulders on the Champs-Elysées in the 1850s. Hence also the Cockney music-hall infusion on the West End musical stage hard on the heels of Gilbert and Sullivan's comic-opera restraint once that partnership had run its course. The very invention of musical comedy in the 1890s at the hands of impresario George Edwardes and with the help of his staff composers Lionel Monckton, Howard Talbot, Paul Rubens and Ivan Caryll operated to this formulaic blend, which at the start of *The Arcadians* (Monckton and Talbot, 1909) occasions a delicate, yearning chorus fit for ballet sylphs while by its end the audience is no doubt clapping if not singing along to 'All down Piccadilly' sung by a vulgar dandy. It could be argued that German operetta went further in the 1920s and brutalized its emotions from above rather than from below with modernist venom in the work of Weill and Brecht, its impetus the political challenge of cabaret rather than the liberal accommodation of vaudeville, but even when transplanted to the USA in Blitzstein's *The Cradle Will Rock* (1937), this was never the dominant voice of entertainment.

French, Austro-German, British and American traditions each had their social insignia. Doubtless so did the musical theatre of the Spanish world (including Latin America), Russia and possibly one or two other cultural units. But there was a good deal of interchange too. Austro-German operetta wasted no time in Americanizing (there is a cakewalk in Lehár's *Merry Widow*, 1905), as did British musical comedy – Coward's

Bitter Sweet (1929), with a double whammy, turns a Viennese waltz into a foxtrot. Gilbert and Sullivan had refashioned French *couplets* as patter songs, Gershwin echoed British music hall with his rattling 6/8 rhythms, and gypsy topics survive on the New York stage in *Anything Goes* and indeed as late as *She Loves Me* (1963), set in Budapest. The world's major cities have long had their stock exchanges; the major centres of vernacular musical theatre traded similarly in commodities for export and import, be they stylistic elements, the actual audiences (what proportion of these was native even one hundred years ago?) or entire repertoires when great shows went round the world.

The operetta formula

So much for operetta's mating habits. It is not difficult to identify it by its plumage, call and habitat as well, and the description will apply generally to operetta, comic opera, musical comedy and its outgrowth the musical before further distinctions need be made. Popular musical theatre, as implied at the start of this chapter, was and still is performed in metropolitan auditoria built and managed like opera houses, though on the principle of the 'run' rather than 'repertory' – that is, the same show will play night after night until failure makes it commercially unviable. Theoretically, a show can run for ever, which *Cats* looked as though it might.

A show is a whole evening's entertainment, divided into two or three acts: two became more or less standard, to proportions already fixed in Gilbert and Sullivan, entailing a longer first act which ends with the most substantial musical unit, a musically continuous finale. A medley overture begins the proceedings, and the audience talks through it, as they do through the instrumental *entr'acte* after the interval. The first-act curtain goes up on an extended chorus introducing the more or less choreographed mass beauties, the setting and one or two of the characters. Thereafter spoken dialogue, always in the audience's own language, alternates with songs until the finale; there is a repeated trajectory of spoken lines giving way to sung conversation in the 'verse' section of a song followed by more lyrical or soliloquizing poetry in its sung refrain, then a short dance refrain or coda without singing before applause marks off the next dialogue segment. Songs are most commonly solos and duets, though ensembles also occur and the chorus often supports an individual or couple. Until the 1920s there was generally one stage setting per act and the libretto was specially written or adapted from a recent play (often from another country – perhaps for copyright reasons); the operetta end of the spectrum could be more ambitious in its settings and starting with *Show Boat* (New York, 1927) began to turn novels into musicals and depict history rather than focus on the up-to-date; this could involve up to twenty scene changes within one show and tended to separate out the texture into 'book scenes' played before a backdrop while the set was being changed and more visually and musically driven 'production' numbers. Humour might similarly be more exploited in such book scenes, which can still run to complex vaudeville routines in some shows (the antics of Frosch the gaoler and Frank the prison governor in Act III of Johann Strauss's *Fledermaus* provide venerable examples).

The plot is drawn from Roman new comedy and represents the triumph of youth and beauty over impediments to a marriage laid down by age, authority or economics: parents, previous partners, criminals, difference of class or nationality, career expectations and monetary loss can all play their part in spinning out the plot. Mistaken identity causes humorous complications as frequently as the exchange of some object or sum of money, and these will come to a head in the first-act finale and probably once again just before the rapid final denouement in Act II. (Kay's emergence from the bedroom as the maid Jane in Gershwin's *Oh, Kay!* (1926) is an obvious reconstitution of Susanna's similar moment in Mozart's *Marriage of Figaro*.) In a genre where singing grates against the primacy of speech unless somehow justified, certain topics recur, often with the aim of making the music 'diegetic', that is, music that the characters know they are hearing or singing. A ball or restaurant scene (*Die Fledermaus, Hello, Dolly!*) is an obvious ploy, a show about putting on a show another, its heroine a star rising from obscurity *à la* Cinderella (*Sally, 42nd Street, Gypsy*). Psychological questing and fulfilment can be signalled by the solo ballad ('Someone to watch over me' in *Oh, Kay!*), often reprised in a finale or finaletto ('Bill' in *Oh, Lady! Lady!!*), or the tune which cannot be completed ('Ah, sweet mystery of life' in *Naughty Marietta*, 'My ship' in *Lady in the Dark*); or the opposite, reflection, nostalgia and loss, can equally be indicated by song (finale reprises once again, inarticulate with anger in the case of Danilo in *The Merry Widow*; the tune refashioned over time in *Bitter Sweet* and *Show Boat*).

Musical contrasts are important, and they operate on various axes as analogues to dramatic conflict. In *The Merry Widow*, Act I is set in diplomatic Paris, with fast, witty, urbane music to match, while Act II romanticizes Hanna's Balkan homeland *in absentia* with all-purpose Eastern folk topics in slow ballad and languid dance. Gilbert and Sullivan patented the contrapuntal double chorus – of lovesick maidens versus dragoons in *Patience*, peers versus fairies in *Iolanthe* – and this topic survives as late as *West Side Story* with the Jets and the Sharks. *West Side Story* is told very much from the point of view of the Jets, with the Sharks as musical Other (sultry hemiola dance rhythms in 'America'). In the dominant tradition, the Other will normally be somewhere farther East or South, the haunts of Mediterranean bandits being one favourite location (*The Maid of the Mountains*), Old England another (*A Damsel in Distress*, *Anything Goes*), Latin America a third (*El Capitán*, the Havana scene in *Guys and Dolls*, and Rio or Buenos Aires sequences or settings in countless musical films, most notably *Flying Down to Rio*). And when centre and periphery are reversed? Accounts of zarzuela (Spanish operetta) suggest that various Others, within and without the homeland, were enlisted to provide local or exotic colour (see Lamb 2000, 242–9). One wonders whether Soviet Russia ever co-opted the West in this role.

Overall setting and colour take these issues further. In certain periods (most obviously, New York in the 1920s) there are two types of narrative musical show (with non-narrative revue as a third): operetta and musical comedy. Musical comedy celebrates the here and now – Fred Astaire in white tie and tails, his sister Adele (or Ginger Rogers in the later musical films) in a fashionable gown – while operetta explores costume drama, set in a romanticized past or on distant geographical location. *Show Boat*, already mentioned, has precursors in the picaresque comic opera (German's *Tom Jones*, based on Fielding), and London witnessed a flood of musical comedies set in the East (*The Mikado*, 1885; *The Geisha*, 1896; *San Toy*, *Florodora*, *The Cingalee* and many more) prior to operetta's triumphant fusion with pantomime in *Chu Chin Chow* (1916), based on the Arabian Nights. Later Austro-German operettas likewise trade in exoticism (Lehár, *The Land of Smiles*, 1929; Abraham, *Victoria and Her Hussar*, 1930), American ones too: the Canadian Rockies in *Rose Marie*, Algeria of the Riffs in *The Desert Song* (1924 and 1926). This cunning amalgamation of exoticism and contemporaneity finds its classic expression in Ruritania, a generic name for the archetypal Balkan republic threatened by fascism (Novello's *Glamorous Night*, 1935) with its exiled or abdicating royal families (*Sally*, *Roberta*, *King's Rhapsody*), fairy-tale castles and hunting lodges (*Love Me Tonight*, a 1932 film musical actually set in France with a train hold-up as in any western), and glittering military uniforms. Novello even wrote a song called 'Uniform' for *The Dancing Years* (1939), and it ends with the words '. . . let's be gay!' *Brigadoon* has it all ways with a double exoticism of time and place, seventeenth-century Scotland and modern New York.

All this musical colour is supported by a standard theatre orchestra or some variant thereon: two flutes, oboe, two clarinets, bassoon, two trumpets, horn, trombone, strings and percussion. Commercial pits – or rather, in most cases until the 1950s or later, the curtained space in front of the stage – support unionized totals of between 20 and 30 players in the commercial centres, fewer as time goes on, though often more in the subsidized operetta houses. Mordden says (1997, 37) that you can tell an operetta from a musical comedy when there is a harp in the orchestra; conversely, pit pianos, especially two together playing 'novelty' syncopation in the *entr'acte*, increasingly characterize the 'rhythm' section of a musical comedy band in New York after the First World War. But the most important musical distinctions are between vocal types, and these correspond to the axes between humour and earnestness, allure and resourcefulness.

The basic contract in the operetta tradition involves virginal women romanced by worldly men, the virginity represented by a high, pure, trained singing voice and stiff acting, the worldliness the province of bluff humour, quick action and resourceful words. At its most extreme, this entails a soprano who can sing, a *parlando* baritone who can't (Julie Andrews and Rex Harrison in *My Fair Lady*, Adele and Fred Astaire with less extreme contrast). Operetta's greatest departure from opera is in its audiences' cultural suspicion of singing men, all exoticized in one way or another (Alfred the philandering tenor in *Die Fledermaus*, Georges Guétary a Frenchman introducing the Victorians to sex in *Bless the Bride*, Nelson Eddy the revolutionary pony-tailed aristocrat opposite Jeanette MacDonald in *The New Moon*, Richard Tauber perhaps the exception proving the rule). Instead, it highlights the singing (or croaking) actor, from George Grossmith senior, Rutland Barrington and Alexander Girardi, creators of the great comic roles in Gilbert and Sullivan and Johann Strauss, to latter-day beacons of reliable masculinity such as Topol, Yul Brynner and Zero Mostel in *Fiddler on the Roof*, *The King and I* and *A Funny Thing Happened on the Way to the Forum*. Admittedly Girardi was a tenor, but Rodgers' and Hammerstein's Curly in *Oklahoma!* and Billy Bigelow in *Carousel* already push male vocal allure 'just about as far as it can go' as baritones – and a real opera singer in *South Pacific* was cast as a Frenchman (see Clum 1999, 124–31). George Hearn honours the contract in *La Cage aux Folles* and *Sweeney Todd* by singing his heart out respectively as a transvestite and a serial murderer.

The music is basically a succession of quadratic (e.g. thirty-two bar) units, songs and dances with 'oompah' accompaniments of one kind or another (the second 'oom' missing in a beguine, for example), and it retains simple tonal plans permitting every word and witty rhyme to be heard, most commonly at the speed of speech, selectively elongated though it may be. The musical works wonders with such restrictions through the art of arrangement (Robert Russell Bennett the world's most prolific orchestrator of other people's musical comedy scores, though Weill orchestrated his own), stylistic updates (often a matter of harmonic 'moments' such as the blue chord) and a much more intimate reflexivity between word and tune, note and syllable, than in opera.

Changes

As the above makes clear, popular musical theatre inherited a strong set of archetypes from the nineteenth century and retained them wholesale or in part through two world wars and into the 1960s and beyond. Nevertheless, certain massive and signal changes are the most interesting and culturally indicative part of the story. There were perhaps four: the impact of jazz, the arrival of sound film, the achievement of United States hegemony with the Second World War, and the rock revolution in the 1950s. Two of these, Hollywood and rock, involved vocal amplification, the biggest single factor in generic transformation.

Jazz, as shorthand for three stylistic features of African-American origin – syncopation, blue-note inflections and minstrel-band orchestration – was a liberating force and secured for posterity the primacy of the New York stage's appeal, sealed as fast, loud, witty and soulful. Kern, according to Carl Engel (1922, 185), started a new era when he tinted 'The magic melody', a song in *Nobody Home* (1915), with the blue chord $IV^{\flat 7}$, but had already been exploiting ragtime syncopation, as had countless 'two-step' popular songs, as a way of turning text-setting colloquial with its casual cross-rhythms of three over two. (In 'You're here and I'm here, so what do we care', from *The Marriage Market* (1914), the last four words of this title line create a melodic rhythm of 3/8 atop the continuing 2/4 oompah accompaniment.) Gershwin took these techniques further in his 1920s shows, perhaps influenced by the vitality of the black musical *Shuffle Along* (1921), though one would be hard pressed to separate out the ethnographic factors in, say, 'The man I love' as black, Jewish or Russian, since a symbiosis of all three was at work. Theatre orchestration was slow to jazz up, the banjo in *Show Boat* no answer to the wholesale rearrangement of showstoppers in dance-band recordings of the 1920s. Swing-band sonorities (specifically, close-harmony chorus work from wind and brass) can be heard in musicals from Gershwin's *Girl Crazy* (1930) onwards as saxophones, three or four types of brass mute and drum kit enter the pit and 'reed' players begin to double on two, three or four instruments so that, for instance, a quartet of clarinets can accompany a certain song or section.

Radio, the technological craze of the mid-1920s, had already begun to change notions of vocal intimacy by inventing the male crooner before sound film faced its famous challenge (immortalized in *Singin' in the Rain*,

1952) of presenting its female silent stars' voices to their public. As any habitué of opera with spoken dialogue knows, female singers project their speech in a low register and sing in a higher one, the two blended (if one is lucky) by richness of sung tone. Lina Lamont in *Singin' in the Rain* has a grating high-pitched speaking voice to match her singing screech. Both have to be drastically lowered to convey the confidentiality of romance, and Kathy Selden dubs her singing an octave lower. This draws on the chest-voice 'belting' that child stars and 'coon shouter' comediennes such as May Irwin had long utilized in vaudeville but which Adele Astaire, for example, would have found difficult to recover on the adult soundstage had she followed her brother to Hollywood in 1933 rather than retired to marry a British aristocrat. Ginger Rogers, by contrast, epitomizes the new, tough, chest-voiced female lead singing in film with no gear change from speech in a contralto register that remains relaxed on its high notes because of the microphone. Thus the emblematic transition would henceforth be Judy Garland's, from child vaudevillian to young adult belter. The note a^1 (A above middle C) is the peak of her register and in (for example) 'The trolley song' from *Meet Me in St Louis* (1944) sounds a good deal higher than it is. Ethel Merman's apex was c^2, achieved on the stage in *Girl Crazy* without amplification but clearly (from her autobiography) after a good deal of soul-searching about resisting 'proper training' as a soprano (Merman 1955, 56).

The male crooner, a high baritone, was sexually subversive because erotically privileged (by the microphone's nuances) without the corresponding heroism of a tenor register (see McCracken 1999); his sound was accordingly blended in musical films with the more publicly persuasive emotionality of the Jewish cantor, made familiar above all by Al Jolson on stage and early sound screen (*The Jazz Singer*, 1927). Film singers such as Bing Crosby and Frank Sinatra resulted in the USA, while from Europe the cabaret and variety stage supplied corresponding models of new vocal allure, all with a flexible *parlando* as their amplified speech-to-song instrument: for example, Marlene Dietrich, Lotte Lenya, Edith Piaf, Maurice Chevalier and Vera Lynn. Chevalier, however, still played opposite a real soprano in the 'boudoir operettas' of film director Ernst Lubitsch, and the stage was similarly reluctant to trade operatic vocality for amplification in their entirety in the Rodgers and Hammerstein shows. These form a considerable portion of the Broadway canon, were later filmed, and showcase the virile baritone (Howard Keel, John Raitt, Alfred Drake) and the singing actress of soprano or mezzo range (Julie Andrews, Gertrude Lawrence, Shirley Jones) as well as the belter (Celeste Holm, Juanita Hall) in that canon's most fruitful compromise between the enchantment of operetta and the immediacy of film.

Rodgers and Hammerstein commanded a pivotal moment in twentieth-century culture when the vernacular enlisted tamed modernism for the expression of folk optimism. Ballet was the catalyst in the USA, and behind Copland's *Appalachian Spring* (1944) lie the liberal artistic policies of the New Deal conveniently perpetuating themselves in the nationalism of the Second World War. In other words, the nation needed artists to express its moment of community and artists both commercial and subsidized felt encouraged to do so. That moment was a delicate and sometimes contradictory balance of images rural and urban, past and present, culturally high and low, authoritarian and liberal, and Hammerstein has taken plenty of criticism for his exploitation of it in the musical, starting with the triumphant *Oklahoma!* (1943). Other countries had their own versions of this – symphonies in Soviet Russia, instrumental light music in Britain, for example – but where popular musical theatre is concerned, it sealed the international triumph of the American musical. Rodgers toned down his foxtrot rhythms and added folk signifiers: fiddling to open *Oklahoma!*, an unaccompanied mixolydian cowboy song at curtain up, oompahs, melodic repeated notes and country dances somehow more redolent of the barnyard and horses' hooves than urban frills and quadrilles in 'The surrey with the fringe on top'; even the waltz took on a new lease of country life under his pen. But he and Hammerstein attached this style to a bourgeois emotional manipulation that was at bottom what the 'integrated' musical meant: scenes and songs of sentimentally persuasive harmony to self-expressive, sincere (as opposed to witty) vernacular lyrics or prose that could wring your heart. When Hammerstein tried it in a weak father's reconciliation scene in *Three Sisters* in 1934 it was laughed off the London stage; a decade later, with American forces risking their lives in two hemispheres, what the public wanted from a musical had radically changed, and 'You'll never walk alone' (*Carousel*, 1945) was set to become a folk anthem.

Bourgeois realism, swing orchestration, belting and crooning and a good deal of residual operetta and musical-comedy technique in song forms, vocal types, dancing, humour and plot sustained the classic musical through the 1940s, 1950s and 1960s and beyond. Stephen Sondheim is perhaps its last great exponent. This applied not just in the USA but also with what little revival of fortunes Britain enjoyed through its Dickensian musicals (*Oliver!*, 1960; *Pickwick*, 1963) and their distant relations (*Half a Sixpence*, 1963; *Billy*, 1974). But the fourth change was more of a usurpation than a graft: the language of rock.

It was inevitable that youth would reassert itself in the Anglophone musical theatre. It had done so before – with the Princess Theatre shows at the time of the First World War, host to the Kern, Bolton and Wodehouse model of intimate musical comedy, and again with *Babes in Arms* (1937), featuring new actors still in their teens. But the youngsters in *Babes in Arms* are still members of a family community, indeed a theatrical community. Rock, by contrast, shifted teenage rebellion from the sociable conversation in the kitchen or on the back porch to the lonely guitar or transistor radio in the bedroom. Its depiction, indeed its essence, was as much a matter of inarticulacy, musical as well as verbal, often through class deprivation, as the essence of early jazz had been mockery. This would not generate eloquent, well-made musical plays, and most of the well-mannered tonal vocabulary, though not its song forms, was jettisoned, with modal tunes, chord progressions (including the reversed cycle of fifths) and primitivist traits (parallel triads, drones, ostinati) being substituted. What did fit was a heightened mode of presentation that prolonged the melodramatic stance of the rock concert number, and 'rock opera' eventually came into being with *Hair* (Galt MacDermot, 1968), *The Rocky Horror Show* (Richard O'Brien, 1973) and, as all-sung musical drama, *Jesus Christ Superstar* (Lloyd Webber, 1970) a decade or so after the musical films of Elvis Presley, the Beatles and others. The extraordinary anger and agility of the influential *West Side Story* had doubtless prepared the way; curiously, so had education, as school music bowed to fashion and supplied all-sung Biblical cantatas for young people. Lloyd Webber's *Joseph and the Amazing Technicolor Dreamcoat* (1968) sprang from this movement, an attempt by Christian authority to regain youth in the terminally secular 1960s. Stephen Schwartz's *Godspell* and maybe Bernstein's *Mass* (both 1971) need placing here, though the extreme emotionality of soul singing, supercharging the already amplified techniques of Broadway vocalists in *Jesus Christ Superstar* and taking male chest registers stratospherically high, betokened no religious revival. There was both showbiz and urgency in *Jesus Christ Superstar*, but already in *Evita* Che's sardonic heckling and Eva Perón's callous ambition feel like poor substitutes for the dramatic tension between Christ and Judas and the travesty cynicism of Herod. In later Lloyd Webber the show voice and its bodged fix between registers and harmonic styles, lyricism and drama, rock, modernism and romantic opera (epitomized by Christine and the Phantom) sounds arch and stale; similarly, the desperate earnestness of *Les Misérables* and *Miss Saigon* is a far cry from the lightness of operetta.

Canons

The repertoires to which these conditions and (sometimes) changes apply are as extensive as they are today elusive because of the commercial, vernacular and multidisciplinary nature of their materials (scripts and scores unpublished; only the songs, not the extensive dialogue, recorded;

theatre repertoires tied to their national language; screen versions radically different from stage versions). An overview would begin scarcely past the mid-nineteenth century with Hervé and Offenbach on a French/Austro-German axis, taking care to consider the latter's farcical, sometimes surreal one-act works (*Ba-ta-clan*, 1855; *M Choufleuri*, 1861) alongside the full-length ones such as *Orpheus in the Underworld* (1858), *La Belle Hélène* (1864), *La Vie Parisienne* (1866) and *La Grande Duchesse* (1867). Johann Strauss II entered the picture with *Die Fledermaus* (1874) and a series of less successful works including *Der Zigeunerbaron* (1885). Gilbert and Sullivan achieved the thirteen Savoy operas in the West End, *Iolanthe* (1882) and *The Mikado* (1885) their peak, the earlier *HMS Pinafore* (1878) their breakthrough to American markets, shortly after the triumphs of Offenbach and Strauss.

This was a tale of three capital cities – Paris, Vienna and London – though zarzuela had flourished in Madrid since the 1850s. A subsequent increase in metropolitan venues embraced Berlin (with Paul Lincke's *Frau Luna*) from 1899 and New York around the same time with Sousa, Kerker and Herbert. This was at first accompanied by a notable flourishing of international operetta trade. Late Victorian and Edwardian musical comedies travelled with ease to New York (*Florodora*, 1900), and Sidney Jones's *The Geisha* (1896) was popular until the Second World War in Paris and as far afield as Russia. Messager for a while lived and worked in London, as did Kern during part of his long apprenticeship of interpolating hit songs into other people's scores; in fact a list of the composers with whom Kern was thus associated spans almost the entirety of those active in three languages, English, German and French. Zarzuela was soon transplanted to Latin America; North American shows reached London (*The Belle of New York*, 1898), or their tunes became known (Sousa's *El Capitán*, 1895). Hungarians (Emmerich Kálmán) and Czechs (Rudolf Friml) contributed to German-language operetta, which remained vital until the 1930s (Leo Fall, Paul Abraham, Ralph Benatzky, Oscar Straus), while the French tradition after Offenbach produced exportable successors (Charles Lecocq, Robert Planquette, Edmond Audran) for a while only.

But the First World War strangled such international trade, for the established early twentieth-century repertoires then retreated within national boundaries and in many cases (as with Edwardian musical comedy) became lost even to the national canon. There were exceptions both old (*The Merry Widow*) and new (Benatzky's *White Horse Inn*, 1930), but even the American shows of the 1920s and 1930s (Berlin, Porter, Gershwin, Kern, Rodgers and Hart), whose songs and, in many cases, productions conquered London and to a lesser extent the continental capitals, did not form an ongoing canon, with the wholesale exception of *Show Boat* and partial ones such as *No, No, Nanette* (Vincent Youmans, 1924), *Girl Crazy* (altered in revival) and *Anything Goes* (Porter, 1934, rather flexible in contents). Other countries found it yet more difficult to compete.

After its victory in the Second World War, America's new musicals triumphed internationally while forming a nationalist canon. Rodgers and Hammerstein led the way between 1943 and Hammerstein's death in 1960, their later successes being *South Pacific* (1949), *The King and I* (1951) and *The Sound of Music* (1959); Lerner and Loewe formed a similar kind of team with *Brigadoon* (1947), *Paint Your Wagon* (1951), *My Fair Lady* (1956), *Camelot* (1960) and one notable film, *Gigi* (1958). Other masters included Jule Styne (*Gentlemen Prefer Blondes*, 1949; *Gypsy*, 1959), the still active Irving Berlin (*Annie Get Your Gun*, 1946) and Cole Porter, whose *Kiss Me, Kate* (1948) entered the central European operetta repertoire. Two crossover figures, Weill and Bernstein, emerged in the USA. They composed both opera and musicals, presenting audiences with stylistic and generic challenges where *verismo* depiction of New York was concerned (*Street Scene*, 1947; *West Side Story*, 1957), though Weill exchanged once and for all his European modernism (*The Threepenny Opera*, 1928; *Mahagonny*, 1930) for the common-practice tonality of Broadway (*Lady in the Dark*, 1941; *One Touch of Venus*, 1943; *The Firebrand of Florence*, 1945; *Love Life*, 1948; *Lost in the Stars*, 1949) while Bernstein moved back and forth between the two or sojourned in the middle (*Candide*, 1956). Other American practitioners included Jerry Bock and Sheldon Harnick (*Fiddler on the Roof*, 1964), Cy Coleman (*Sweet Charity*, 1966; *City of Angels*, 1989), George Forrest and Robert Wright (*Kismet*, 1953; *Grand Hotel*, 1989), Marvin Hamlisch (*A Chorus Line*, 1975), Jerry Herman (*Hello, Dolly!*, 1964; *Mame*, 1966; *La Cage aux Folles*, 1983), John Kander and Fred Ebb (*Cabaret*, 1966; *Chicago*, 1975; *Kiss of the Spider Woman*, 1990), Frank Loesser (*Guys and Dolls*, 1950; *The Most Happy Fella*, 1956) and Meredith Willson (*The Music Man*, 1957). Book and lyric writers not part of a regular team included Dorothy Fields, active from the 1930s, while directors (pre-eminently George Abbott and Harold Prince) and choreographer/directors such as Jerome Robbins, Bob Fosse and Michael Bennett reached fame on a flood tide of dance and staging, often at the expense of plotting in the 'concept' musical of the 1970s and often premissed on harsher musical idioms, including rock.

Rock, dance and concept proved shaky foundations for narrative musical theatre in the 1970s not least because of the expense of their often spectacle-oriented presentation and correspondingly long runs.

Four directions seemed to emerge. The 'yuppy revue' was often small-scale and played 'off Broadway' (Finn's *Falsettos* trilogy, 1979–90; Maltby and Shire's *Baby*, 1983, and *Closer Than Ever*, 1989). The all-sung mega-musical, at the opposite extreme, included Lloyd Webber's *Evita* (1978), *Cats* (1981), *Starlight Express* (1984) and *Phantom of the Opera* (1986); Boublil's and Schönberg's *Les Misérables* (1985), *Miss Saigon* (1989) and *Martin Guerre* (1996); and Abba's *Chess* (1986). Here Tim Rice was recurrent lyricist, Cameron Mackintosh recurrent producer. A third genre, the compilation show, ranged from pop (*Buddy*, 1989) and jazz (*Ain't Misbehavin'*, 1978) to earlier Broadway (Gershwin's *Crazy for You*, 1992; Kern's *Never Gonna Dance*, 2003). Finally, there was Sondheim, who wrote his yuppy revue with *Company* (1970) and has steered a lifelong course between saluting traditional Broadway styles and genres and subverting them in a dazzlingly intelligent but often resisted output that includes *Follies* (1971), *A Little Night Music* (1973), *Pacific Overtures* (1976), *Sweeney Todd* (1979), *Sunday in the Park With George* (1983), *Into the Woods* (1987), *Assassins* (1991), *Passion* (1994) and *Bounce* (2003). A fifth trend characterized the 1990s: Disney stagings of their earlier cartoon films (*Beauty and the Beast*, 1994; *The Lion King*, 1997). Like Sondheim, these had a knowing, retrospective stylistic range where music, lyrics and production images are concerned but took in a broader spectrum of idioms, including pop in *The Lion King* (already used in its unstaged film precursor, *The Jungle Book* of 1967). Alan Mencken and Howard Ashman deserve mention as composer and lyricist for *Beauty and the Beast*.

Reports of the death of Broadway have been circulating since the 1930s, but from the 1990s onwards there was probably real cause to wonder whether a genre was reaching the end of its life. Lloyd Webber's popularity, never matched by respect, was waning after *Sunset Boulevard* (1993) with *Whistle Down the Wind* (1998) and *The Beautiful Game* (2000). London showed little desire to import the latest New York shows (Yeston's *Titanic*, Flaherty's *Ragtime*, both 1997), though the rock musical had an extraordinary new lease of life with *Rent* (1996), the latest bid for a new, young audience occurring every thirty years or so. Jonathan Larson, composer of *Rent*, died as it went into production. Might he have been the new Lloyd Webber? No-one has obviously followed Sondheim, though Adam Guettel, Rodgers's grandson and clearly master of a new generic mix (*Floyd Collins*, 1996), is liable to discussion in those terms. Or are we looking in the wrong place? Broadway and West End mega-musicals have long been imported to northern Europe, especially Germany, which has its own magazine literature on the genre (Munich's *Musicals: Das Musicalmagazin*) but not yet, it seems, its own renewed creative tradition. Ruritania, however, is back in the picture as theatres in ex-Communist countries have lost their sub-sidies and turn to ways of making money. Croatia is creating musicals. Russia and East Germany, which during the Soviet years developed their own generic take on the classic musical film, may yet draw on such traditions. But the occasional travesty of an American musical that appears in programmes of TV trash from around the world, be it Egypt or Japan, is unlikely to herald additions to the canon. The real question is whether the canon is now fixed as a twentieth-century one. If it is, that would be convenient for the historian but bad for the propensity of agile wit of word and tone to appeal to a broad but, at its best, intelligent and critical public which wants to see its foibles reflected and its feelings articulated in a happy night out at the theatre watching and listening to something *new*. Musicals flourished when opera ceased to supply that need. If they now die, a sense of community will be lost, for opera has occupied the high ground for far too long to know how to reclaim the lower.

18 Opera in the marketplace

NICHOLAS PAYNE

I   Culture and Society

In 1945, as the Second World War drew to a close, the music publishers Boosey and Hawkes, who had acquired the lease of the Royal Opera House the previous year, issued a manifesto which would have a profound effect on cultural life in Britain:

> We hope to re-establish Covent Garden as a centre of opera and ballet worthy of the highest musical traditions. The main purpose will be to ensure for Covent Garden an independent position as an international opera house with sufficient funds at its disposal to enable it to devote itself to a long-term programme, giving to London throughout the year the best in English opera and ballet, together with the best from all over the world. If this ambition can be realized it is felt that it will be a great incentive to artists and composers, since it will offer to them an opportunity for experience in performing and writing of operas on a scale equal to that which has prevailed so long on the Continent but has been lacking so long in our musical life here in London.

The foresight and generosity of Leslie Boosey and Ralph Hawkes caught the spirit of a battered but renascent nation. Note that a primary purpose of the enterprise was to lay the ground for a creative burgeoning, which was harvested sooner than might have been expected. Over five successive seasons between 1949 and 1955, Covent Garden staged the premieres of Bliss's *The Olympians*, Vaughan Williams's *The Pilgrim's Progress*, Britten's *Billy Budd* and *Gloriana* (as well as reviving his *Peter Grimes*), Walton's *Troilus and Cressida* and Tippett's *The Midsummer Marriage* – a record not subsequently equalled in London, nor in many other cities. Another noteworthy aspect of the Boosey and Hawkes vision, especially at the time when the country was just emerging from a devastating war, is its adherence to the Continental example. For the model was unequivocally the German system.

Opera as social service

Opera may have been invented in Italy, but its industrial revolution took place in Germany. To this day, no other country is remotely as productive. Historically, every princeling had to adorn his court with an opera house and resident ensemble. That responsibility was inherited by every town of stature, and the system is enshrined in the federal nature of the German political system. During the twentieth century it has survived two catastrophic wars and economic ruin. The division into East and West Germany after the Second World War strengthened entrenched positions and increased inter-city competitiveness. Yet it has even survived reunification and has so far resisted the pressures to rationalize through economies of scale. It is bred in the bone.

The underlying philosophy is that opera, at the very centre of a theatrical tradition that also embraces plays, dance and symphonic music, is a social service. It sits alongside education and healthcare as something owed by responsible citizens to the rest of an identifiable society, but it is somehow more personal than its sister services, more closely representative of the town in which it exists. At the same time, the opera aspires beyond social service. Its loftiest examples set ideals for eternity, but it also holds a licence to criticize and satirize contemporary society. It is an entertainment with a moral force. No wonder that Wagner's *Die Meistersinger*, with its depiction of medieval Nuremberg, remains a symbolic icon.

This German system of 'repertory' opera is labour-intensive. It requires a permanent ensemble of artists including principal singers, chorus, orchestra, music and production staff and an almost equal number of craftsmen in technical and production-making departments. As an important local employer, it contributes to the economy through consumption and tax revenues. And it is dependent on state support for its survival.

State subsidy makes sense both as an economic investment and as a social duty. It enables ticket prices to be kept within reach of every citizen, and it funds enlightened access for schoolchildren. But the final decade of the twentieth century brought the strains of reunification between the consensus capitalism of the West and the bankrupt artificial 'full employment' of the East, leading to economic downturn, high unemployment and decreased tax revenues. Consequently the German system, which survived the most turbulent century in history and provided the inspiration for Covent Garden in 1945, is today under threat as never before.

While Germany may be the cradle of modern philosophy and its artists the legislators of society, it should be remembered that those same philosophers and artists have sought inspiration from the lands south of the Alps. Wagner owed as much to Greek drama as to Teutonic legend. Goethe, like his Mignon, yearned for the land where the lemon trees bloom. Mozart learned how to compose opera from the Italians.

At its zenith between the seventeenth and nineteenth centuries, the Italian system was incomparably prolific and volatile. First Florence, then

Venice, then Naples, then Milan enjoyed dominance, and the lack of national unity, as in Germany, was the mother of invention. Italian opera has always delighted in the sensuous beauty and expressiveness of the human voice. An impresario such as Domenico Barbaja in Naples would buy star singers as today's top football managers collect galácticos. He signed Rossini to compose operas for his *prima donna* Isabella Colbran, and Rossini adapted his style to hers. Verdi was more stubborn, and his insistence on the musico-dramatic integrity of his operas foreshadowed a shift in power from the star singer towards the star conductor. Its apogee came with Arturo Toscanini, whose two periods as Musical Director of La Scala in the first and third decades of the twentieth century set an example of moral seriousness whose profound influence reached far beyond his time and beyond Italy.

Gianandrea Gavazzeni was one of Toscanini's assistants at La Scala in the 1920s. Fifty years later, when he had become a doyen among conductors, he reminisced:

La Scala was completely re-organized for Toscanini, in respect to its rehearsal habits, to the way of conceiving its programme, to the method of making singers study, and also in respect to educating the public. The public with Toscanini during that era, was educated to consider the theatre not as something for amusement, but as something with a moral and aesthetic function, which enters into the life of a society, into the life of a culture. (Sachs 1978, 173)

Today, the conductor's name is still printed larger than anyone else's on an Italian opera poster. Riccardo Muti consciously adopted Toscanini's legacy at La Scala. The artistic directors who plan the *stagione* (season) of an Italian opera house are men – never women! – of refined culture and aesthetic awareness. But they are curators of a museum. Whereas Toscanini premiered new operas almost every season, that well is now almost dry. No Italian opera since Puccini's *Turandot* in 1926 has retained a hold in the repertory. Subsequently *verismo* declined into proto-Fascism. During the second half of the century, leading Italian composers such as Berio, Nono and Maderna deconstructed their heritage. Italian opera remains a glory, but a fading one.

If the traditional heartlands are weighed down by the burden of the past, their influence can still inspire the development of opera in a wider Europe. As might be expected, the German 'repertory' system has been the model for adjacent countries such as Denmark, Poland, Czechoslovakia and Austria, while the Latin countries have followed the Italian *stagione* system. Those nearer the Nordic fringes have tended to adopt a hybrid system, marrying an ensemble company with a semi-*stagione* approach to rehearsing productions. The vitality of opera in Europe today is best shown by examples from opposite ends of the continent.

Spain under Franco was an operatic graveyard, and its best artists worked abroad. After his death in 1975 and with the subsequent advent of democracy, Madrid's Teatro Real could at last be restored to life after more than half a century's slumber. Barcelona's privately owned Teatre Liceu, rebuilt after a fire, was reopened as a public facility and has increased its subscribers fivefold. Seville's new opera house La Maestranza will soon be emulated by the Palau de les Arts in Valencia. Spain's operatic rebirth has run in parallel with a creative explosion in cinema and theatre, and it engaged the interest of a new audience rejoicing in the relatively recent release from censorship and relishing the expression of its new freedom.

Scandinavia is also rebuilding its opera houses. Copenhagen celebrated the new millennium with *The Handmaid's Tale* by Poul Ruders, the first commission from the Royal Danish Opera for over thirty years and the first of a regular series leading up to the opening of its second opera house in 2005. Oslo's eighty-year project for a new opera house comes to fruition in 2008. Perhaps most remarkable is the case of Finland which, like Denmark and Norway, is a country with a population of not much more than five million. Not only has it built a large new state opera house in Helsinki, but it has grown a music education system which delivers a higher proportion of musicians – singers, conductors and composers – than any other nation in Europe. Creativity is part of the curriculum.

From the New World

When Dvořák landed in New York in 1892 at the invitation of Mrs Jeanette Thurber, his appointed task was to direct America's first National Conservatory of Music, with the intention of establishing a specifically American school of composition. He repaid the compliment the next year by writing there his Symphony No. 9 in E minor, Op. 95, and the F major String Quartet, Op. 96. Both acquired 'American' nicknames and both betray 'New World' influences in their source material, but they belong firmly within a European tradition.

So has it been with American opera. The First World War was an unprecedented opportunity for the former colony to plunder the bankrupt and exhausted homelands. While coal baron Henry Clay Frick bought up 'old master' paintings for the Collection to be housed on Upper East Side, so the Metropolitan Opera on Broadway built up its unrivalled roster of *émigré* artists led by Toscanini and Caruso, Destinn and Ruffo. Since that time New York has maintained its pre-eminence as a magnet for the world's top operatic performers. No other centre has matched its economic pull over the last hundred years.

The national school of composition has proved more elusive. Black Americans only breached the Met with Marian Anderson's début in 1955. The greatest American composer of the twentieth century was arguably George Gershwin, a white Jew who exploited a 'black' musical heritage and who wrote popular shows for Broadway. His masterpiece *Porgy and Bess* has never entered the repertory of the Met. The successful American operas of the second half of the twentieth century have subscribed to an essentially European formula, even when their subject-matter has been native. The irony is that opera in the brave new world has been consistently more conservative than in the decadent old world, not only in its creation but also in its interpretation. That is partly a function of economic dependence on private paymasters, but it is also a reflection of a taste which appreciates opera as an adornment of life rather than something integral to it.

The American contribution to opera has been, above all, in its financing, packaging and marketing. Its aggressive capitalist stance has successfully broken the hegemony of the European subsidized model. It has shown that it is not only possible to fund opera without reliance on the state, but that it may even be desirable to do so. It has harnessed marketing theory and selling techniques from the commercial sector, and applied them to shifting tickets for the opera. Forget soap opera: real opera can be sold like soap powder.

Danny Newman, at Chicago Lyric Opera, adopted the subscription or *abonnement* system of selling tickets across the season from the traditional operatic nations, but transformed it into American 'hard sell'. His seminal book *Subscribe Now!* first became the bible for marketeers in the United States, and subsequently became required reading on the other side of the Atlantic. Subscribe, join the club, book early for privileged access; these are seductive arguments. They have helped to create a culture-owning class of supporters. Only towards the end of the twentieth century did this theory begin to be challenged.

The other great American legacy has been Development, a euphemism for private-sector fundraising. The emphasis is less on corporate contributions than on the charitable giving of individuals. It is a climate which encourages freedom of choice and tax breaks to nurture those choices. The biggest beneficiaries are religion, higher education and healthcare, but the arts have become equally dependent upon it. This system ensures freedom from state control, but it naturally incurs the possibility of the patron's interference. And as with most things, where America leads, Europe follows.

II   The Global Market

The fall of the Berlin Wall in 1989 spelt the end of the protected socialist model. It was less a question of ideology than of accessibility. Once CNN television news could penetrate to Dresden and Gdansk, it was impossible any longer to pretend that a controlled economically self-sufficient nation or bloc could exist. Eastern Europe behind the 'iron curtain' was the last bastion in the operatic world, but for years before Soviet and especially satellite-country artists had been guesting in the West on 'double contracts', one with a low fee that could be lodged with the state cultural agency and another with the real fee in Western currency that would reach the private bank. This has not just been a struggle between communism and capitalism. Throughout the world traditional ties and loyalties have been undermined: to family, to company, to community, to nation. All can be bought for money.

At one end of the spectrum are found the United States and its Pacific Rim neighbours like Japan. Subventions from the state account for no more than 4 percent of the total revenue of performing arts organizations in the United States, whereas 46 percent derive from tax-deductible private contributions and 50 percent from earned income (Kushner and Pollak 2004, 5). At the other end were the wholly state-owned monopolies of the socialist countries. Many non-state owned organizations in Western Europe incline towards the latter model, with a subsidy element of around 90 percent at the Netherlands Opera in Amsterdam and 70–80 percent being common in Germany, France and Italy. Somewhere in the middle comes the United Kingdom where the average is around 50 percent, though at the Royal Opera Covent Garden the subsidy proportion declined from 50 percent in the 1960s to 30 percent by the end of the century. In southern-hemisphere countries, like Australia and South Africa, it tends to be still lower. Yet, wherever on the spectrum a company finds itself, it today belongs to a mixed economy which increasingly operates across national boundaries.

For much of the twentieth century, nationalism was the dominant political force, and every nation was able to erect barriers to protect its own system of supporting opera. Today national identity is most strongly asserted by countries emerging into independence after generations of subjugation. For many of them the Soviet bloc is being replaced by the European Union. In any case, national identity is inevitably being eroded by an internationalism brought about by the ease of communication in the age of the internet. The 'common market' is the *raison d'être* of the European Union, but it is already being supplanted by the global market. This global market is a mixed economy, within which an opera company juggles its resources between the same four sectors: public subsidy; private donations; ticket sales; and other commercial earnings. The proportions may differ widely, but the practice applies worldwide.

World class

In 1959 the Bayreuth Festival mounted a new production of Wagner's *Der fliegende Holländer*. 'For the first time since 1951 I have again *Weltklasse*,' declared its director Wieland Wagner (quoted in Wechsberg 1959, 585). The Dutchman was played by the American George London and Senta by the Austrian Leonie Rysanek, two recognized stars of the Met, and Wagner's comment was something of a reproach against the casting compromises imposed by postwar austerity during the early years of Neues Bayreuth. Today those casts seem to have inhabited a golden age, but that is another story. The phrase 'world class' has come to mean better or best class, somehow a cut above provincial levels of attainment.

It was not always so. When the rebuilt Vienna State Opera was reopened in 1955, it was with Mozart's *Don Giovanni* sung in German. Nowadays, almost any small opera company will perform that opera in what passes for Italian from an entirely non-Italian speaking cast. The original-language revolution is the most visible sign of the new internationalism. What began as a gentle trend during the 1960s accelerated to a headlong rush during the final decade of the century. The process was encouraged by the introduction in Toronto in 1983 of 'surtitles' – captioned translations projected above the stage, a device widely adopted and developed by the end of the century. A handful of opera houses have held the line on opera in the vernacular: Berlin's Komische Oper, London's English National Opera, Munich's Theater am Gaertnerplatz, the Vienna Volksoper and Opera Theater of St Louis in the United States; but they are a tiny minority. The irony is that these theatres have an international reputation greater than many of the more remote companies who have embraced the 'internationalist' solution.

During the first half of the twentieth century most singers belonged to an ensemble located in their country of birth or adoption. An elite few were able to supplement native earnings by spending several months a year in America. It was convenient that the American high season was the Fall, while the Italian seasons seldom got going much before Christmas and London's international season was in the summer. Air travel has since made it practicable for leading singers to plan guest appearances within shorter periods. During the 1960s and 1970s a loose fraternity of artists colonized the top end of the world market. Their dominance was an important factor in the move towards original-language performances.

The final decade of the century has delivered further supplies of vocal talent to the burgeoning world market. The end of restricted travel for Soviet and East European artists has been matched by the emergence of a rich new seam of talent from the Far East. Japan, Korea and China have developed an appetite for Western music and a determination to train singers and instrumentalists to excel in performing it. The worldwide talent bank, the decreasing cost of travel and the homogenization of language policies mean that a casting director's net can be spread wider than ever before. While some countries maintain protectionist policies, the movement towards mobility of labour is inexorable.

Opera as commerce

The discovery of a means to record sound on cylinders transformed the distribution of music and especially opera as early as the first decade of the century. Caruso's recording of Canio's 'Vesti la giubba' made both the tenor's international career and the gramophone's. It is cynically believed that Puccini tailored his most popular arias to fit on one side of a 10-inch '78' (Harewood 1997, 592). The advent of the long-playing record at the beginning of the 1950s made recordings of complete operas widely accessible, and many of the pioneering versions from that first LP decade remain in the catalogues as 'standards' today. The further convenience of the compact disc, and the decreasing cost of production, have led to an extraordinary expansion of the recorded repertory, both backwards in musical history and forwards to capture the most up-to-the-minute performances. As a consequence, opera planners and consumers have an unprecedented range of material at their disposal. But its very availability in aural, and increasingly in visual form, in the home has questioned the need for the communal experience in the theatre. Recording is a two-edged sword, at the same time a stimulus and a substitute.

The phenomenon of the Three Tenors televised concert at Rome's Caracalla Baths for the 1990 World Cup celebrations gave operatic music a popular profile never previously attained and from which, some would argue, it has not yet recovered. Those who deplore as 'dumbing down' such concoctions of well-worn melodies amplified to be heard in large arenas should remember that such events have their antecedents. The short recordings of the Caruso era concentrated on a fairly limited popular repertory. His successor Beniamino Gigli increasingly specialized in concerts of familiar extracts in large halls, as did his contemporary Richard Tauber in the German opera and operetta repertory. One of the most influential of all singers from the middle of the twentieth century was Mario Lanza, whose career was not in the opera house but on records and in film.

While a good deal of money has been made by the artists and promoters involved in such events, commercial profit from presenting complete operas has been rarer. The impresario Raymond Gubbay has successfully marketed opera in the arena setting of the Royal Albert Hall, but has restricted himself to the six or eight 'risk-free' standard operas. His subsequent attempt to mount a commercial season in the West End ended prematurely, when ticket sales failed to secure break-even. Even the bold venture of presenting Puccini's *La Bohème*, staged by the charismatic film director Baz Luhrmann, like a Broadway musical for eight performances a week ended after six months without having recouped its investment capital. Despite its impressive tenure and undoubted appeal to a non-traditional opera public, it failed to pull in the New Jersey audiences deemed necessary to transform it into a twelve-month-plus commercial success.

When Dr Johnson coined his famous definition of opera as 'an exotic and irrational entertainment' in the mid-eighteenth century, he allowed it no great pretensions as art. It took its place among the variety of multimedia shows vying for the public's attention, being distinguishable for its foreignness and its extravagance. Today there are rival extravaganzas which cost more to produce than opera, but which jostle with it in an ever more crowded marketplace. Opera-as-art in the non-profit sector competes with opera for commercial profit, packaged as a marketable commodity. It also competes for the public's attention with a multi-million dollar musical-theatre industry, and beyond that with the vastly better-resourced film industry with its justifiable claim to be the art of the twentieth century. After 400 years opera faces a dichotomy. Pilloried as the greediest monster among the traditional arts, it is now an under-resourced pygmy within the wider entertainment industry.

III   A Century of Change

What we characterize as 'twentieth century' can probably be confined to a rather narrower span of seventy years, encompassing its third to ninth decades. The nineteenth century, on the other hand, might be said to have lasted longer than its hundred years and to have started with the French Revolution of 1789 and concluded with the Great War of 1914–18. The creative cauldron of the 1900s and the carnage at the heart of the second decade form the resonant epitaph to a century of matchless invention and discovery and destruction. If the true twentieth century begins with the Russian Revolution, its story ends with the fall of the Berlin Wall in 1989. The final decade and the arrival of the world wide web is the prelude to the twenty-first.

Opera in the first half of this twentieth century was dominated by its creative geniuses: Strauss and Puccini, Debussy and Ravel, Schoenberg and Berg, Janáček and Bartók, Stravinsky and Shostakovich, Gershwin and Weill, and the arrival of Britten. The composers set the agenda. In the second half of the century, their inspiration was more fitful and they were increasingly sidelined. Ligeti, Messiaen, Poulenc and Zimmermann are remembered for one opera each. More prolific composers such as Birtwistle and Henze are not 'box office'. While the shift towards a 'heritage culture' is partly one of critical attitude, there is no doubt that it has been exacerbated by an absolute decline in the creativity of those who compose opera. So it has become necessary to reinvent the past.

The most influential operas from the nineteenth century were *Tristan und Isolde* and *Boris Godunov*. Initially Wagner's model of symphonic development, of melodic and tonal transition, was the more dominant. Latterly Musorgsky's more discursive structure and speech-influenced rhythms became more pervasive. Then Stravinsky consciously repudiated Wagner and adopted number structures derived from Mozart and Italian opera. The Verdi revival began in Germany in the 1920s with the reclaiming of his neglected middle-period operas. It was given further emphasis in 1951 by the Italian celebrations of the fiftieth anniversary of his death. Today all of his twenty-eight operas are performed somewhere or another. After Verdi, the opera archaeologists uncovered further layers which revealed the forgotten treasures of Rossini, Bellini and Donizetti. The golden age of Italian opera from Rossini to Puccini now forms the foundation to many opera companies' programmes, and it is being supplemented by lost trinkets from Mayr, Mercadante and Pacini.

The major addition during the last third of the twentieth century was the rebirth of the baroque. First came the realization that opera began not with Gluck's *Orfeo* but with Monteverdi's. Then the opening up of the Handel canon, begun in Germany in the 1920s and greatly abetted from the 1970s by the revolution in performance practice. The 'period instrument' movement is now the dominating force in the performance of seventeenth- and eighteenth-century music. Its softer, vibrato-less sounds enable lighter voices and fleeter delivery to provide a convincing alternative to conventional grand opera. Its popularity with new and younger audiences has been a factor in winning converts to opera in the late twentieth century, especially in countries where its practice has taken a firm hold, such as France, Belgium and Holland.

The ability of the modern impresario to programme from a much wider range of opera then hitherto – from 400 rather than 200 years – has transformed the landscape. It has spawned specialist festivals on an unprecedented scale and a subculture of student productions with an enthusiasm for excavating the unknown. The choice may never have been greater, but there is a downside. Falling in love with the past has inevitably minimized the impact of the present.

Re-interpretation

At the beginning of the twentieth century the Bayreuth Festival was dedicated to preserving the work and performance practice of its founder. Today his grandson encourages ever more extreme interpretations of the same ten operas, in order to extract their 'meaning' for the present.

The cult of the theatre director in opera began when Max Reinhardt was brought in to save the premiere in Dresden of Strauss's *Der Rosenkavalier* in 1911. His reward was the creation the following year of the first version of the same composer's *Ariadne auf Naxos* for his ensemble to open the new Kleines Haus in Stuttgart. Reinhardt's legacy was the Salzburg Festival, a high-minded ideal invented in 1920 to bring together the arts of song and poetry, music and drama, under the benign tutelage of a controlling director. Strauss embodied the struggle for this union in the characters of Flamand, Olivier and La Roche in his final opera *Capriccio*, first performed in 1942.

Five years later Walter Felsenstein founded the Komische Oper in the eastern sector of Berlin. It was a theatre in which the Director was the most powerful creative force, superior to the Music Director, the singers and the composers. Felsenstein's method of working, with its long rehearsal periods and tightly knit ensemble, became the model followed by many companies within Germany and some beyond. Everything was subservient to the dramatic idea, researched and expounded by meticulous dramaturgical expertise. *Regietheater* is still the dominant influence in Germany and in many of its adjacent countries. The further away from this epicentre, the greater the scepticism, from the agnosticism of the British to the downright dismissal of it as 'Eurotrash' which is prevalent in the United States. Nonetheless, the creative power of the director and his licence to reinterpret the works of the past has been a crucial element in the survival and renewal of those works for much of the European audience.

Re-interpretation is part of the process of renewal. Monteverdi and the Florentine Camerata thought they were reinventing the amalgam of speech, song, dance and spectacle that was ancient Greek drama. Wagner believed he could recreate the spirit of Greek drama festivals on the Green Hill at Bayreuth. The difference today is that the composers have yielded this function to the directors. Not for nothing was Bayreuth's centenary production known as Chéreau's *Ring*.

Business or education?

'I'm not running an opera, I'm running a fifty million dollar business,' declared William Mason, the respected General Director of Chicago Lyric Opera, at Opera America's conference at Pittsburgh in 2004. This sentiment, so alien to the worlds of Reinhardt and Felsenstein and Wolfgang Wagner, was not disputed by Mason's fellow delegates. While most European directors would qualify such a statement, the reality is that the more successful among them are already adopting his methods: accurate budgeting, fierce control of expenditure, emphasis on generating income through fundraising and ticket sales.

Whereas late notification of grants used to mean that financial planning lagged behind artistic planning, leading to awkward disruptions when the grants were lower than anticipated, today even European companies expect to agree a Business Plan for several years in advance. It is no longer possible to assume increasing levels of fixed costs and a stable employment establishment. The key judgement is the accurate forecasting of income from all the main sources, backed up by a realistic contingency plan should that income fall short. It follows that many opera companies are seeking to reduce their traditionally high fixed costs, and to convert them to the variable costs attendant on freelance rather than full-time employees.

If public funding is decreasing in real terms, as is often the case, then the successful opera business must increase revenue from the private sector and from ticket sales. Instead of the historical focus on supply, it becomes necessary to build demand. In many places the capacity to supply exceeds known demand, so the business is highly competitive. Where demand falters, a company has to become expert in cutting back its costs, so that is may remain solvent and live to construct the next Business Plan.

This business cycle has led to a questioning of the validity of the long-established operatic institutions. A seasonal Festival or a low-budget touring company may be more flexible at adapting to changing economic conditions. A visionary Englishman, Norman Platt, founded Kent Opera in 1969 as a touring company with low overheads but high artistic aspirations. Singers and orchestra were engaged for specific repertory and were welded into an ensemble for limited periods. After twenty years, Platt retired and government funding was withdrawn. Today his model appears to have been ahead of its time.

According to the economist Peter Drucker, the sole purpose of a business is to create a customer. It is relatively easy, once the customer has been identified, to persuade him to buy again. A good first experience, followed by an efficient mailing service, will probably do the trick. It is much harder to seek out new customers from among those who have not yet chosen, for social, geographical, educational or economic reasons, to try a product. The task is simpler if a company enjoys a monopoly in its area, as many opera companies did within their communities before being undermined by late twentieth-century mobility. Today the audience has more choices to go elsewhere. Customers are only happy until they find something better.

Because of the competition, opera managers have become more nervous of taking risks. Opinion polls and audience surveys have an increased influence on choice of repertory and on the engagement of artists of known reputation. There is a tension between the perceived safe course of following the herd and the risk of striking an individual line which will seize attention by its boldness. It is a dilemma beautifully caught in Act III of John Adams's opera *Nixon in China*, with its text by Alice Goodman. Nixon realizes that he is on the brink of something extraordinary and world-changing in his meeting with Mao-Tse-Tung, but tired and lonely in his hotel on the last night of his visit he reminisces about his time in the Pacific theatre of the Second World War, when he ran a hamburger stand called 'Nick's Snack Shack'. It was the happiest time of his life. 'The smell of burgers on the grill made strong men cry . . . Done to a turn, medium-rare, rare, medium, well-done, anything you say. The Customer is King.'

Of course, listening to opera cannot be compared with the mindless consumption of hamburgers, reduced to a global battlefield for market supremacy between the equivalent of McDonald's and Burger King. Those who acquire a taste for it soon move on to sirloin steak, organic beef and even *tournedos Rossini*. There are plenty of chefs ready and willing to encourage experiment. Indeed, most opera companies subscribe to 'a mission to explain' and to lure their customers into unfamiliar tastes and territory. But during the course of the twentieth century the context has changed.

In an age when Strauss based five of his fifteen operas on ancient Greek legend, he could assume that most of his potential public had undergone a classical education. After Berg composed the five scenes of Act II of *Wozzeck* as a 'symphony' in five movements, he may have claimed that his audience should remain unaware of the musical differences between the constituent components (sonata form, fugue, largo, presto and rondo) – but he nevertheless felt justified in pointing them out in a lecture (1929). At the end of the twentieth century, most people's education does not cover these basic areas of Western cultural knowledge. The task of the opera educators is therefore massive. An inspirational teacher here, an innovative schools project there, can scarcely scratch the surface of the widespread ignorance of the fundamentals of an art-form with such deep roots in a historical culture. Unable to turn round the education system, it has to find new entry points. One is through participation in creating musical theatre, as a replacement for the disciplines of choral singing and learning a musical instrument. Another is to recognize that the knowledge once gleaned from books may now be accessed via the internet. Another is to treat television as an educational tool rather than a diversion, and to learn from the successful history and 'lifestyle' programmes.

Knowledge makes the consumer more demanding but also more loyal. Radio and television have greatly increased access to opera. Subtle broadcasters can make such programmes educational as well as entertaining. The introduction of titles above or alongside the stage, first to translate foreign-language texts but increasingly also to replicate vernacular texts, is credited by many as a decisive step in conveying information which popularizes opera. The worldwide acceptance of titles has changed the way that people listen to opera.

Turning points

Looking back over the century, it is possible to discern some turning points at which opera changed direction.

In creative terms no decade can rival the 1920s, which not only produced the enduring masterworks of Berg, Janáček, Puccini, Strauss and many more, but also fostered the greatest idealism and belief in opera as a life force. La Scala under Toscanini, the early Salzburg Festivals, a Berlin in which three rival opera houses were led by Bruno Walter, Erich Kleiber and Otto Klemperer. These examples were beacons for the rest of the century. Is it a coincidence that such creativity should have coexisted with a period of such political turmoil? The second turning point was the decade or so after World War Two, when opera companies were re-established on the basis of serious public subsidy as part of the welfare state. This philosophy also lasted for most of the rest of the century. Finally, the coming of the global market in the 1990s brought with it a questioning of those certainties. On the one hand, opera became available to a geographically and socially wider constituency than ever before. On the other, its importance on the map of culture was diminished.

Does opera have a future as a living culture, or has it transmuted into a branch of heritage? Can opera survive in an increasingly crowded global market? Has it changed out of recognition over the last hundred years, and can it go on changing? Musical theatre will continue in the twenty-first century. It may become more populist in search of its audience. Its practitioners will wish to harness technology as an aid to both creation and education. Traditional structures will crumble and be replaced by more flexible versions better able to weather changes in the labour market and in customers' demands. A pessimist will acknowledge that the golden age of opera died during the twentieth century. But an optimist will remember that the periods of the French and Russian Revolutions and the Cold War were also times of great creative invention. Art thrives in adversity.

19 Technology and interpretation: aspects of 'modernism'

In the course of the twentieth century, various technological advances had as radical an effect on the art of opera as the changes associated with 'modernism' had on the character of musical composition. Opera at the start of the twenty-first century has become at the same time both more popular and, in a particular but important sense, less popular. The music of the operas of the past is more familiar to the public than ever before – thanks to the invention and refinement of broadcasting and mechanical recording, both aural and visual. The words of operas are better understood by opera-goers than they have ever been, thanks to the introduction during the 1990s of surtitles or supertitles providing simultaneous versions of the text in opera-house auditoria.

Meanwhile, the taste of the public for classical music seems to have been growing ever more retrogressive. In an era when so-called 'serious' music broke away from the familiarly melodious and became far more theoretical and experimental, the popularity of new music steadily reduced and music lovers grew less and less amenable to genuine innovation, though new forms of lyrical expression in jazz and rock singing may offer qualification for this verdict. In colour, rhythm and harmony, modern orchestral music has tended to be far more adventurous, and the vocal lines of opera far more unpredictable, than ever before. Yet, contrary to the previous rule (until c. 1900) that the main attraction in operatic repertoires would be new or recently composed works, the rule now is that the public invariably prefers familiar operas – or operas disinterred from the distant past, never before part of the regular repertoire. The latter of course are mostly composed in the highly accessible language of baroque music. The revival of interest in the past which became such a vital factor in the field of commercial recording, and the concern for 'authentic' performance practice, have together compensated in part for the popular rejection of contemporary or avant-garde novelty. For the classical record-buying public, the performances of yesteryear are a constant challenge to the achievements of performers today.

Formerly, impresarios knew that commissioning and presenting new works would be the secret to the success of the seasons they mounted, which would often be the leading attraction of the local carnival preceding Lent. In 1900, the Dresden Opera was run by the brilliantly adventurous Generalmusikdirektor Ernst von Schuch, whose long reign in charge from 1872 to 1914 saw a total of 34 world premieres and five German first performances (including *Tosca*). In those 42 years, 123 new works were introduced to Dresden audiences, of which a mere 32 would be familiar now. Patrons from Dresden's well-established English-speaking community could buy a guide to the stories of all operas in the Dresden repertoire: *The Standard Operaglass*, by Charles Annesley. This was revised and reprinted almost every year from 1887 until the eve of the Second World War. The series includes encouraging critical responses to new operas (in 1897/8, for example, Goldmark's *The Cricket on the Hearth*, based on the story by Dickens). A high proportion of these novelties did not remain in the repertoire after the First World War. But a surprising number resurfaced at Wexford after 1972, when that idiosyncratic Irish festival started more consciously to present historical 'failures' – the artistic policy for which it became famous. The extremely limited facilities of Wexford's Theatre Royal, very unlike Dresden's Semper Opera, seldom enabled justice to be done to these lost works. The 'judgment of history' is unreliable.

But in the related fields of operatic production, interpretation and repertoire the modern age has been unlike any previous period in the 400 years of European operatic history. The opera public have been voting with their feet, providing clear commercial evidence (especially in seasons without subscription schemes) that contemporary operas are a taste they are reluctant to acquire. As a result, in the current era which some define or decry as postmodern, what changes from year to year in the opera repertoire commonly encountered is how the works are staged and look, and how their design context relates to and promotes the philosophical themes on which their stories throw dramatic light.

An expensive singers' market

Another central factor in operatic life at the opening of the twenty-first century is the commercial exploitation of a handful of vocal stars on a worldwide international scale made much easier by modern means of transport. The benefits (and disadvantages) of focused marketing are no different in opera than in any other industry. Enormous sums can be earned by a few artists whose particular capability and expressiveness suit recording. The level of reward otherwise in the world of opera is generally modest, though significantly higher than it was a century ago for such ancillary skills as tailoring, carpentry, wig-making and scene-shifting.

However, the disproportionate emphasis on the musical abilities of the greatest stars which is encouraged by modern communications media has a seriously distorting effect on popular taste at the 'local' level. Thanks to the increasingly sophisticated technology of the editing suite, there are now inevitably high expectations of accomplishment throughout the population, not just among metropolitan *cognoscenti* – a by-product of the universal availability of immaculately polished recordings of singers of genius, present and past, in the various entertainment media. Isn't it wonderful that those dependent on recordings and radio can have such elevated artistry on tap? Altered expectations may have dubious side effects. Live performance is not the same as a recording, of course, but even the greatest stars may be unable regularly to compete with their best edited work – and such assured high-quality interpretation is only occasionally to be encountered among the lower tiers of performers who supply the mass on which the pyramid of excellent accomplishment is necessarily based. As a result, everyday audiences may be increasingly unready to accept everyday standards. That could lead to an increase in the number of sublime performances – but equally it might just reduce the overall size of the live audience prepared to support more homespun endeavour in opera performed live. How much do those dependent on the artifice of recording appreciate the crucial wisdom of Shakespeare's encomium supplied by Theseus in *A Midsummer Night's Dream* (V.1.213): 'The best in this kind are but shadows and the worst are no worse if imagination amend them'? The reality of twentieth-century technology has long been undermining the whole imaginative 'culture of amendment' on which live performance should be able to count.

Opera as theatre

Before the invention of the phonograph there could be no doubt in the mind of the audience that opera was a theatrical art. Wagner was just as self-conscious a theatrical reformer as he was a musical revolutionary. Before the modern age the only way for people to become familiar with an opera away from the theatre was to read its score silently or to play its music on the piano – perhaps accompanying a partial vocal realization. Though many did their 'homework' this way, opera was a theatrical experience. The idea of concert performances of opera was almost unknown – though Berlioz's *Trojans*, of which the composer conducted extracts at Baden-Baden in 1859, was a rare exception. Thanks to records and recording, during the twentieth century opera escaped from the opera house and became, for many enthusiasts, a purely musical experience – something as private and domestic as reading a novel. That privatization of the operatic experience has been very significant – and thoroughly reflected in the development of operatic taste, or lack of development, in the course of the twentieth century.

Interpretation is no longer a matter of following the dramatic instructions or stage directions suitable to the era when the opera was created. The understanding of the stage as a representation of reality has given way increasingly to a recognition that the purpose of theatrical presentation is not just to tell a story but to employ the live figures and the context as an effective space to focus on the ideas with which the narrative, poetic text and music are concerned. This shift in approach is exactly comparable to the changes in artistic style and objective that can be seen in the development from early nineteenth-century representational painting, through the Impressionists and Post-Impressionists to modern art in its various forms. Interpretation in opera is however constrained by the concern among performers and interpreters involved in stage design and production for the autonomy and content of the work being performed. The popularity of the cinema from the 1920s onwards, with its triumphant ability to represent photographic reality, inevitably made even the most minute attempt at realism in the opera-house, substituting solid sets for the previously predominant painted cloths, seem by comparison like a mere design convention. The conventions of opera are not realistic. The choral singing and confessional solos encourage audiences to develop an objective understanding. Brecht's desire for telling 'alienation' in the theatre had, in fact, just the same motive as Schiller's wish to restore the chorus from ancient Greek drama to the neo-classical stage. Opera audiences need little prompting to remember that meaningfulness is the fundamental objective.

All these different factors are connected, of course. Exactly which is responsible for what evident unarguable consequences is harder to establish. One thing is not in doubt. The well of new hit operas has run dry since the death of Benjamin Britten in 1976 (his operatic swansong, *Death in Venice*, was premiered in 1973), and few would disagree that this, partly, reflects the complicated relationship between popular operatic taste and the kinds of non-melodic musical language available to ambitious and creative 'serious' composers. There is evidence of a dysfunction exacerbated by the technologies of recording and the ever-increasing mechanization of memory. Live performance no longer fades in the memory of the cultured element of the population – or indeed at all – as it inevitably did before the twentieth century, and that fact has had a large effect on taste.

Decline of the professional opera composer

The crucial question that needs to be posed in any operatic history of the twentieth century must surely be why an era of such progressive development and enhanced musical expressiveness witnessed the disappearance of both the hit opera and the professional opera composer. No twentieth-century composer was as prodigious as Donizetti (65 operas), Rossini (39) and Verdi (28); among the more prolific in modern times were Britten and Richard Strauss (15), Henze (14), Zandonai (13), Puccini (12), Janáček (9), Prokofiev and Schreker (8). The change was gradual, no doubt, but after 1976 it was beyond denial. Is the art of opera therefore doomed to vanish as a result? Is the new obsession with reinterpretation and re-evaluation of operas from the past a sign of decadence or just another stage in the history of 'reception'? Is song unsullied by mechanical amplification no longer a language and a resource in so-called 'classical' or 'serious' music for those refined and sometimes challenging composers from whom the ranks of opera makers have always sprung?

The fact that opera audiences supplied with surtitles are in no doubt about the text they are supposed to be hearing has a number of consequences. Composers have never in the past been able to assume that all the text they were setting would be audible. The variable acoustics of different opera-houses have meant that even when a composer had taken pains to adjust the scoring of the instrumental accompaniment to assist singers' audibility, the text would still not readily be heard in all parts of the house.

Surtitles can translate operas that are being performed in a foreign language, and sometimes even provide a written-out version of text being sung in the audience's vernacular. The balance between the elements that make up a satisfying operatic experience is consequently altered, with results as yet unmeasurable. In the past not being so accurately supplied with the text did make for a special kind of audience responsiveness to the overall effect an opera could achieve. So one result of surtitles is to constrain the audience's licence to imagine and be inspired – drawing on other communicative factors of the operatic and theatrical manifestation coming to them from the stage. Surtitles are a potent new technology and may be a dangerously two-edged sword. They compensate for the declining ability of ageing audiences to listen to and hear the words being sung. They make up for the regrettable difficulty singers face – frequently required to perform in a language whose nuances they do not understand properly and whose sound patterns they have had to learn parrot-fashion – in getting the sung text to communicate as language should. In Handel's London the opera-house auditorium was candle-lit throughout the performance. English word-books of Italian libretti were on sale to help the public cope with the language barrier. The facility of simultaneous translation therefore satisfies a not unprecedented audience desire, hitherto technologically impossible to fulfil, to understand perfectly the experience being witnessed. Naturally surtitles are overwhelmingly popular, though they may lower the theatrical temperature, and they certainly do alter the way audiences listen to the text being sung – with meaning filtered through a written medium that inevitably lacks the subjective expressive qualification supplied by a subtle, sensitive singer-actor.

Original-language performance

Another likely result may be greater internationalization of opera as a live theatrical experience, and confirmation of the primacy of original-language performances. This is already observable in Germany and Italy, where large native repertoires of opera existed for centuries and some companies until the last decade of the twentieth century generally performed most of their repertoire in translation. In April 2004, the Leipzig Opera gave Jonathan Dove's *Flight* its first production sung in German. But the French-Swiss Intendant of the newly built and much smaller 800-seat Erfurt Opera (opened in September 2003 at a cost of 60 million Euros), nearby in Thuringia, launched a new policy of performing always in the original language using surtitles – a major change for what was formerly the German Democratic Republic, where Walter Felsenstein's commitment to prominent theatrical values at the Berlin Komische Oper had always set a powerful example. For language-cultures or nations which have not already created a native operatic repertoire, the availability of surtitles is likely to make it much harder for the art of opera to be naturalized and incorporated into the native repertoire as Shakespeare in the eighteenth century was accepted and recognized in Germany because contemporary translation into German had made him a part of German literature and theatre. Considering the role played by the Reformation and vernacular Bible in European culture, the promotion and almost universal acceptance of the principle that opera is best performed in the composer's original language seems both ironical and perhaps in need of robust questioning.

The existence of Lilian Baylis's London opera company committed to performance in English, first at the Old Vic and then at Sadler's Wells Theatre, without doubt helped to sustain a climate in England favourable to English-language opera, without which Britten's genius might not have been so easily able to flower. Baylis was following a path already well-trodden by the Carl Rosa company. The ecology on which new opera depends is complex. The idea that operas are composed in one language and should not ideally be displaced from that language into another runs counter to the clearly expressed preference over the centuries of many great opera composers of the past (Mozart and Verdi, for instance). It undermines an understanding of opera as a collaborative theatrical art-form demanding in performance various creative compromises. Surtitles reinforce the impression created by opera on CD, DVD and video, that opera should be idealized as a museum art-form, something to be appreciated and worshipped rather than adapted and used.

A pantheon of geniuses

In 1800 the idea of an international operatic repertoire containing a pantheon of masterpieces was just starting to emerge. By 1900, Mozart, Verdi and Wagner were universally recognized as the presiding deities of a mature art-form to which a limited roster of composers based in five distinct European language-cultures had contributed what appeared indestructible classics. Bizet's *Carmen* was one of the most outstandingly popular works. Puccini's *Bohème* was just entering the firmament. A century later, in 2000, little had changed in the established operatic pantheon. The popularity of Puccini is inextinguishable. His operas still define basic popular taste a century after their creation. That ironical and significant indicator says much about the history of the art-form. As a generator of modern repertoire masterpieces, Puccini has been joined by perhaps four other composers capable of making a substantial impact: Strauss, Janáček, Britten and Prokofiev. In terms of audience rating and commercial viability Puccini reigns supreme, as he has done ever since 1926 when he died leaving *Turandot* unfinished. The twentieth century saw many opera composers submit themselves for public approval, like Turandot's suitors, but none displaced the achievement of Puccini – however regrettable if not disgraceful that fact has appeared to some academics and progressive impresarios. Joseph Kerman's dismissal of *Tosca* in his seminal *Opera as Drama* (1956, 13–16) was later echoed in Gerard Mortier's refusal to programme a single work by Puccini during his twenty consecutive years at the Théâtre de la Monnaie in Brussels and then at the Salzburg Festival.

The contemporary composer is free to write anything, since there is no common 'serious' musical language. Yet freedom can be a burden. Those composers who have been drawn to opera or music theatre lately have had to find for themselves a personal but appropriate lyrical language – not an easy task considering the limited contemporary market for songs or song-cycles. Song is the fundamental tool of opera, because the song or aria conveys in a unique way both the intimacy and the interiorness that are paradoxically the special core of operatic theatricality. Human song is the emotional arrow that reaches each member of the operatic audience – conveying an implacable truth of feeling. The aria supplies the equivalent in communicated intimacy to the cinematic close-up. Britten notably wrote many songs, as well as operas. Stravinsky, too, often composed for the voice, though he wrote few conventional operatic works. Both possessed a strikingly distinctive yet completely different lyrical voice. To be effective as a composer of opera requires an ability to create an effective single musical line. Line drawing is not a discipline in which every successful modern painter can excel. Lyrical specialization is equally something particular that requires a certain ear and a desire, qualities that are not necessarily relevant assets for the contemporary composer writing for instrumental ensemble or keyboard. As the common lyrical language of earlier times grew more and more distant and faint, many new operas have simply not registered in the memory as an experience of song: Richard Rodney Bennett and Stephen Oliver, for example, each had a flair for light music (night-club songs and theatre incidental music that recollected the accessible popular-song language of thirty years earlier), but each suffered significant lyrical inhibition when tackling 'serious' work. Yet, if the last quarter of the twentieth century was the least fertile period of successful operatic composition in operatic history, that does not mean all is over for the art-form. Opera has always had far more failures than successes in the ranks of newly composed works. The potential of music theatre has always been problematic.

Meanwhile, many new operas have continued to be written. The twentieth century was rich in singleton masterpieces of which Bernd Alois Zimmermann's *Die Soldaten* (1960) is a prime example, and the development of the art-form in terms of musical language and new subject-matter has been as intriguing as the observable switch in production style from more or less dutiful naturalism to a kind of morally loaded surrealism. Instead of pursuing basic narrative, many opera productions nowadays are led by a governing concept. However, the circumstances of composition have changed radically, and this change in the industry of opera-making has come about at widely different times in each of those few language-cultures that formerly were the operatic factories of the world. Though Janáček was properly recognized in his native Czechoslovakia only in his old age, it was some decades after his death before he became truly popular in, for example, Britain and Belgium.

(In the Brussels Opera, Mortier placed Janáček's name in the redecorated auditorium alongside those of Mozart and Wagner when the house was totally refurbished in 1985–6.) Britten's status and achievement began to be accepted in Germany very soon after his works achieved widespread recognition and popularity in Britain in the 1960s. But he was not properly acknowledged in France until another quarter of a century had passed. Henze is prolific but has scarcely become a popular operatic composer even within the German-language opera world with its enviable total of more than eighty opera companies. The most obvious reason for that is probably Henze's difficulty creating memorable melodic material that can be attached to the individual character.

It is not that the public cannot respond to the idiosyncratic but wonderfully expressive song-language of Berg's *Wozzeck* and *Lulu*, or of Schoenberg's *Moses und Aron*. Critics in the 1950s and 1960s, when serial composition was seen as the best way forwards, often attacked the melodious and highly accessible musical languages of Strauss and Prokofiev – though both coexisted with Berg and Schoenberg in the esteem of professionals quite happily until around 1950. The issues of memorability and singability were both consciously confronted by Prokofiev, as part of his attempt to perform a creative duty to his native Russia. Later in the 1950s, by contrast, Stravinsky consciously adopted dodecaphonic techniques in place of his previous neo-classicism. Would *The Rake's Progress* have been possible at all, if Stravinsky had changed his language earlier? Pastiche was not artistically respectable in the twentieth century. Yet progress, or at least advancing, often depends on being able to retrace steps. There are kinds of melodiousness that affect the public and kinds that do not – and melody is not all, as the composer/lyricist Stephen Sondheim has suggested, a matter of familiarity with the specific notes. In an interview with the author in London in 1973, Sondheim explained about Leonard Bernstein's songs in *West Side Story*, which he claimed were originally considered untuneful, and for which he wrote the lyrics: 'the movie came out [in 1961], and the movie company wanting to protect their investment put many thousands of dollars into the promotion. Soon as the public started to hear the songs more than once, lo and behold they could suddenly whistle them ... Tunes are a matter of hearing, of familiarity. You can whistle or hum anything if you hear it enough times. That's all.'

Perhaps precisely because of the melodic handicap with which the modernist and avant-garde movements fettered the language of lyricism, there was a premium on operatic originality and creative responsibility and a readiness to accept that the operatic form could pursue different objectives and function in different ways. The popularity of the youthful

Shostakovich's remarkable *Lady Macbeth of Mtsensk* (1934) was highly unusual and was proved by the 200 performances to cheering Soviet audiences during the two years after its premiere before Stalin banned it. In the 1920s and 1930s a popular market for new opera still existed in those language-cultures where opera had been pioneered – Germany and Italy. Britten's achievement in creating a repertoire of masterpieces for an English culture barely used to opera as a popular form was remarkable. The English-speaking world entered the opera business at almost the last moment when it was possible to do so – when the language of song was still available, and when in Britain and the USA there was an audience for new work. Both in dramatic structure and in subject matter some twentieth-century operas broke away from traditional models, and tackled unprecedented subjects. But critics of course mostly shared the taste of the public they served, rejecting avant-garde modernism. Unsurprisingly, the appetite of impresarios and companies for newly composed work and risky financial novelty declined rapidly after the 1950s. In the final quarter of the century John Adams's *Nixon in China* was almost the only opera that looked likely to enter the popular repertoire – a status confirmed by the decision of English National Opera to re-open the refurbished Coliseum with it in February 2004. The musical languages of Britten and Janáček were still considered challenging and inaccessible in the 1980s by ordinary opera-goers. Yet both Schoenberg and Berg in the 1920s and 1930s had shown that expressive melody need not be vocally graceful in a traditional sense. Right through the twentieth century operas were being successfully premiered that had distinctive individuality and achieved some recognition – from Debussy's *Pelléas et Mélisande* (1902) onwards. *Wozzeck* was rapidly recognized as original, confident and economical, both musically and dramatically, yet its composer famously declared (Berg 1927) that it should not to be regarded as setting a new path for operatic composers.

The question of modernist musical language dominated the business of new opera until the onset of minimalism, which at least restored a recognizable and variable melodic option for composers, though not quite the old techniques of conscious tuneful variation that characterized classical music until the advent of strict serialism. The problem for opera composers has always been to adapt their personal musical language to the definition of individual character through specific arias. At all stages of operatic history it has been true that characterization has depended on the confessional role of the aria. An insufficiently graspable melodic language is not a good tool for developing characterization. The respective musical palettes of Berio, Ligeti, Nono and Dallapiccola have found various beautiful solutions to the problem. But Britten and Tippett (and a few others) in the 1950s and 1960s were increasingly isolated because of their commitment to melody. What a character in opera can and should sing, and what a character in spoken drama can and should say, are similar creative issues. Recognition of precisely who the role *is* on the stage has always depended on a linear musical language that can underpin and qualify text adaptably and on the composer's skill at moulding memorable musical statements with the capacity to be conversationally variable. But thereafter the modernist agenda associated with Darmstadt and Donaueschingen helped create and sustain an anti-melodic conformism: diatonic methods were seen as totally outdated, and many opera composers felt obliged to try and be 'modern' – in other words, dodecaphonic. When he was composing his opera *Clarissa* in August 1974, Robin Holloway wrote (in a letter to the author) of 'the *prohibitions* of my musical education ... those implied by a particular climate – whose nature I indicated by quoting the widely-held (at that time) dismissal of Berg as "12-note Puccini" ... The "modern" (that is, the current state of music, the consensus, the orthodoxy) forms, the modern modes, don't allow enough to be expressed.' When *Clarissa* (which Holloway wrote uncommissioned, so passionate was he about the subject) was premiered in 1990 at English National Opera, the problem with lyrical projection to which he was referring here was crystallized in the difficulty he had finding a suitably melodic and singable manifestation for Loveless's dubious romantic seductiveness.

Popular interest in new opera continued to wane throughout the twentieth century – though in the USA the end of the century saw a sea change in support for new work, reflecting the New World's sense of identification with modern endeavour. After 1950 no new professional opera composers entered the market, no bankable names turning out a succession of popular and recognized achievements. In previous centuries there always were a few composers with the gifts of melody and theatrical timing who successfully took up operatic composition. Today there is no obvious Donizetti, though perhaps Dove has shown signs of a potentially prolific lyrical language. Philip Glass's operas are singable and depend on ghosts of diatonicism, but they create atmosphere more than memorable or characterful arias. Since the death in 1981 of American composer Samuel Barber, with his unforgettable contributions to the corpus of poetic English art-song, no composer in any language-culture seems to have made a mark as being able to compose expressive and genuinely singable songs in music that could be taken seriously – in other words in material that was not merely a reproduction of the style of tunes from the past. André Previn's opera *A Streetcar Named Desire* (1998) suffers from an overwhelming sense that it is the musical equivalent of reproduction furniture – it feels fake.

New themes and contemporary problems

The emphasis in nineteenth-century opera plots on romantic tragedy as it affected various levels of society was developed thematically in two main directions in the twentieth century. Britten in most of his operas, for example, touched delicately on the hitherto unmentionable topic of homosexuality – though the issue was seldom overtly raised. Janáček's operas shared a concern with women's position in society. And once the real seriousness of *opera seria* had been recognized, and baroque operas generally were being taken seriously on their own terms rather than disparaged for not being as modern or cinematic as Puccini's operas or some nineteenth-century works, it was possible to see how obsessive the theme of the nature of power and the inability of the powerful to rule the heart was to the eighteenth century. Thus, while Puccini reigned supreme, an alternative history was at the same time increasingly honoured thanks to the early-music movement – and to the effect of authentic musical performance on the modern popularity of great, historically significant figures like Lully, Rameau, Handel, Hasse and Jommelli.

The new radically different attitude towards past performance practice tempered any temporary triumph of serialism after 1950. There had been scholarly historical research for a century, of course. The obsession of opera before 1900 with new work was not shared by the Roman Church, for instance, whose musical policies ensured Palestrina never vanished from the current repertoire in the way Bach did, until revived by Mendelssohn. Chrysander's Händel-Gesellschaft edition of Handel's operas (1868–85) preceded by many decades the performances staged at Göttingen and Halle in the 1920s. But it was the arrival of Monteverdi's *L'incoronazione di Poppea* at Aix-en-Provence, Glyndebourne and La Scala, Milan, in the 1960s that really set the seal on the process of opening up the long-abandoned seam of old operatic works which has turned out to contain many treasures, including some indubitable masterpieces. This could have increased the sense of opera as being stuck with a 'museum' repertoire, but instead the rediscovered old works invited and merited theatrical treatment as if they were new and 'contemporary' – partly because their music and text, not always fully preserved or defined, is of unstable provenance. These are works history really forgot. Older operatic forms have often proved especially well suited to non-naturalistic and surrealistic stagings – which seem to release their theatrical quality even more convincingly. Theatre history is cyclical. Monteverdi is closer to Shakespeare and Ben Jonson and certainly a long way from the well-made play of the early twentieth century. The relocation, updating and trans-portation of mythical and classical material into contemporary garb which became commonplace in opera staging after 1976 were not unprecedented. Costumes in the theatre before the nineteenth century's concern for historical reality became paramount were usually contemporary, though outlandish or classical characters or clowns (especially the stock and beloved figures of *commedia dell'arte*) were dressed in a way that indicated their nature or role, as well as their different and foreign origin. A 1709 print shows the Ghost of Hamlet's father in medieval armour, but the prince himself in a periwig. David Garrick's mid-eighteenth-century performances of Shakespearean tragedy used contemporary dress, with perhaps a stronger realistic intent than would have concerned actors in Shakespeare's day. Like modern painters and sculptors, modern composers have been drawn to ethnic examples – writing music whose rhythm and dissonance initially seemed to relate to alien models.

Unpredictable benefits of deconstruction

Early attempts to revive Handel's operas treated their staging as if they were unsatisfactory attempts at *verismo*. Only when daring live productions played conceptual postmodern jokes with the material could Handel's and Monteverdi's innate theatricality be fully recognized in design contexts unembarrassed by their non-naturalistic emphasis on 'confessional' material. Hence the giant toy dinosaurs in Richard Jones's and Nigel Lowery's hit Munich 1994 production of *Giulio Cesare in Egitto* (see Figure 19.1). Arias in the *opera seria* need a backdrop, not a narrative moment: they are just as effective at energizing the drama as the business of a through-composed operatic scene. Aspects of operatic interpretation affected by 'modernist' changes include singing styles (*Sprechstimme*), scenery (cubism and constructivism) and acting (the Stanislavsky 'method' with its emphasis on truthful psychological naturalism, and the cinema with its rejection of emphatic overstatement often previously common in theatrical performance). 'Modernism' has imposed tough responsibilities on the creators of the genuinely new in the world of opera.

Naturally the appetite of opera audiences had to be titillated in new ways once the decline in successful and popular newly composed operas became overwhelmingly evident. In fact, new operas have always been a gamble, though new performers have often quite rapidly become bankable assets for impresarios. The Age of the Director is how the last quarter of the twentieth century has been defined by most commentators – whether they were deploring or praising the fact – and the rise of directors has certainly enabled a significant section of the opera public to

Figure 19.1 Handel's *Giulio Cesare in Egitto*, directed by Richard Jones and designed by Nigel Lowery (Bayerische Staatsoper, 1994). Photo: Anne Kirkbach, reproduced by permission of Wilfried Hösl.

appreciate being provided with novelty in a number of ways. Operas subject to 'interventionist' stagings have revealed depths and shadows not always recognized earlier. The encounter with Handel's operas and oratorios in the theatre was strikingly popular and successful in the 1980s and 1990s, progressing into an inventive, irreverent, even farcical theatricality that endorsed the genius of the works in brand-new ways. Stagings like Nicholas Hytner's and David Fielding's *Xerxes* at English National Opera (1985) were based fundamentally on the revaluation of how Handel's operas actually function in dramatic context. The newly extended operatic repertoire at the end of the twentieth century embraced operas generally ignored for centuries from before the age of Gluck and Mozart, new but old, as well as defamiliarized new productions of never-fading popular works, old but new. This reflected the emphasis opera companies typically were now placing on reinterpretative staging and conceptual revaluation, together with the value of defamiliarization as an interpretative discipline.

It is a significant coincidence that the year in which Britten died also saw the unveiling of Patrice Chéreau's centenary production of Wagner's *Ring* at Bayreuth, designed by Richard Peduzzi and Jacques Schmidt. This was conducted by the leading guru and intellectual of the musical avant-garde in Europe, Pierre Boulez, who only a few years earlier had called for opera houses everywhere to be blown up in an orgy of revolutionary fervour (though Boulez would not have wanted the Bayreuth Festspielhaus, where he in 1965 conducted Wieland Wagner's influential 1951 staging of *Parsifal*, to go up in flames). Chéreau's radical and, at the time, ferociously controversial deconstruction of Wagner's Tetralogy along Shavian-cum-Marxist lines ushered in a period in which opera staging was considered by many to be the most interesting and rewarding factor in the whole operatic experience.

Concern for meaningful representation of operas in the theatre has gone beyond the basic desire for convincing naturalism and dramatic truthfulness associated with the Vienna Opera reforms of Gustav Mahler and Alfred Roller. Anton Webern described Roller's *Tristan und Isolde* in his (unpublished) diary on 21 February 1903:

> The orange-yellow of Isolde's tent creates a lightness which contrasts wonderfully with the bright blue light shining on the sea in the distance. The second act decor is fascinating. A warm summer night, very dark blue, lit by the moon, breathes its magic onto your face. Violet shadows slip over the terrace and the house walls. The stone parapets of the terrace are entwined with superb flowers which surround the bench where the lovers are to sit ... The whole setting of the last act is full of endless sadness and despair. Under the great knotted limetree the hero lies suffering. The ground slopes, with the castle gate lower down at the back. Scattered stones and the debris of crumbling walls lie about.
>
> (Moldenhauer archives, Spokane, Washington, DC)

Roller's point, as elaborated in the almanac *Thespis: Das Theaterbuch* (1930), was that 'The stage does not provide a "picture"; it provides spaces, appropriate to the playwright's work and to the actors' words and gestures ...' Earlier, in an article entitled 'Bühnenreform' (1909), he wrote:

> Production is, after all, the art of presentation, never an end in itself ... 'Do you favour stylization or illusion?' one is continually asked, 'three-dimensional sets or backdrops?' – just as at table one is asked, 'Would you like white wine or red?' ... Each work of art carries within itself the principles of its production. – Rules and methods established today can be stood on their head by a poet who comes along and creates a work tomorrow. Should he be prevented? In Shakespeare they speak the scenery. Genius can look after itself.   (Sutcliffe 1996, 429)

The Sezession architect and designer Adolf Loos, as he reminisced in his diary-memoirs (1931/2), found the opening act of the famous Mahler–Roller *Tristan* so lavishly detailed and obtrusively familiar that he could not bear to stay for the rest, conscious that 'The carpet is Rudniker

(Prague). I've used them too. For the entrance hall. All those cushions look nice.'

Defining the limits of naturalism

In modern times, stage representation has developed in broadly two directions, towards abstracted purification on the one hand or surreal intensification on the other. Neither displaced the desire to give opera as much theatrical credibility and lifelike potency as possible: very necessarily, since opera is in itself such an essentially unreal and non-naturalistic form of theatre where what is sung is the most important and effective element. During the first decades of the century, the conviction was crystallized by the writings and limited practice of Adolphe Appia and Edward Gordon Craig that the focus of any theatrical and operatic experience would be strengthened if the trappings of naturalism were replaced by epic architectural set-designs combining platform-like monumental spaces with expressive, carefully coloured and shaded lighting. Appia only had the chance to apply his theories in Milan and Basel in the 1920s. Doing without the overt imitation of naturalistic designs can emphasize the human relationships – enhancing the focus on the individual character's singing of arias and duets which is already apparent in opera. Experimenters in Moscow (both before and after the Communist Revolution) and elsewhere demonstrated both the benefits and the disadvantages of non-realism to those few pioneers who were interested. After staging *Tristan und Isolde* at the Mariinsky, Meyerhold wrote: 'The better the acting, the more naive the very convention of opera appears; the situation of people behaving in a lifelike manner on the stage and then suddenly breaking into song is bound to seem absurd' (1910). Max Reinhardt's devotion to theatrical realism was not about imitating life in a cinematic way but seeming truthful and convincing and imaginatively diverting – in other words mobilizing the 'magic' of the theatre. Stanislavski and Nemirovich-Danchenko took little notice of Appia at the Moscow Art Theatre or at the Bolshoi's opera studio.

An engine of innovation in Germany

Otto Klemperer's innovative but not very popular Berlin regime at the Kroll Opera achieved some telling collaborations with avant-garde artists as designers. If the scene was structural in layout rather than representational, that would concentrate the audience's attention and avoid the distraction of inessential detail. Ewald Dülberg designed a set for Wagner's *Der fliegende Holländer* with platforms and ramps, rather than anything very shipshape, and Jürgen Fehling was a theatre director making his debut in opera, and no Wagnerian. Paul Schwers, critic of the *Allgemeine Musikzeitung*, wrote on 25 January 1929: 'The Dutchman, naturally beardless, looks like a Bolshevist agitator, Senta like a fanatical … Communist harridan, Erik … a pimp. Daland's crew resemble port vagabonds of recent times, the wretched spinning chamber a workshop in a women's prison.' The staging was 'a total destruction of Wagner's work, a basic falsification of his creative intentions.' László Moholy-Nagy, a month later, offered geometrical constructivist sets for *The Tales of Hoffmann* that were intended to 'create space out of light and shadow … an elaborate pattern of shapes' (1929, 219). Ernst Bloch loved the identification of Hoffmann's eerie, ghostly world with machinery (*Der Querschnitt*, March 1929).

The greatest demonstration of the benefits of non-naturalism came in the 1950s with Wieland and Wolfgang Wagner's 'New Bayreuth' productions of their grandfather's operas. A noble simplicity swept away many of what seemed undesirable Nazi associations. But once opera stories were freed from the mundane needs of narrative realism, and their philosophical themes were more nakedly exposed, it was only a short step to deconstruction – combined with a playful, surrealistic and sometimes satirical exploration of the ideas within operas. Opera productions associated with the new generation of directors from the 1970s onwards recognized how variations in location and period, and other kinds of subtextual association, could radically change the design environment and deepen the complexity of the theatrical process of interpretation.

Attempts to trace a coherent line of development in twentieth-century operatic staging – notably in the *New Grove Dictionary of Opera* (Sadie 1992) – have comparatively little to go on. Of course the history of opera and theatre design is well illustrated. What is harder to establish from the early decades of the century, before visual recording became more commonplace, is evidence of change, and the nature of the differences, in the acting of the best operatic performers. The drawing of conclusions is thus rather an artificial game which ignores how few experiments that were written about were either carried off successfully or imitated widely. However, changes in theatrical style that became commonplace during the last quarter of the twentieth century, and not only in Wagner or at Bayreuth, were not unprecedented. Theories about 'illusionism', 'naturalism', 'symbolism' and 'expressionism' tend to ignore the common practice, which was overwhelmingly conservative. Photographs and critical response demonstrate this. Thanks to the power of operatic music, especially when its narrative context was tragic, a desire for emotional truth and narrative realism usually went along with a sense of epic dignity. Directors like Visconti, Strehler and Felsenstein pursued good acting and psychological realism on the opera stage and saw the benefit of a degree of pictorialism. Although Dali, De Chirico and Picasso designed ballet sets, the surrealism of Magritte was not an influence on stage sets in opera until the 1980s and 1990s.

The decline in the quantity of successful new work emphasized the sense that opera was a finite resource – involving a pantheon of significant masterpieces. A necessary repertoire for the student and enthusiast was already recognized and largely established at the end of the nineteenth century. It has been further developed since the Second World War, with substantial representation from before the time of Gluck and a good number of twentieth-century works. This material was well served in the last twenty-five years of the century by a great number of 'interventionist' productions, re-interpreting and re-evaluating.

Chéreau's *Ring* at Bayreuth in 1976 was in many ways a romantic approach – though not in the nineteenth-century sense. It preserved and emphasized the heroic status of Siegfried in a glamorous way. It did not update the story in a precise fashion to any particular era, but in its costumes and sets it referred the audience to the period of the work's first performance (this being a celebration of the centenary of that event) and to subsequent decades when conflicting theories about economic power lay behind major wars and politics generally. In *Das Rheingold* and *Die Walküre*, Wotan wore a frock coat. In *Götterdämmerung*, Siegfried wore a dinner suit. As a follower of Strehler, Chéreau took pains to achieve an unforgettable metaphysical atmosphere for the *Todesverkundigung* scene with ominously dim lighting. Partly because of Wagner's status as a theatrical revolutionary, and because of the attention paid to the 'New Bayreuth' ethos after the war, different productions of *The Ring* at the time of the centenary and afterwards provided a broad spectrum of the ways that operatic staging was changing. It would be absurd to define an opera production merely in terms of the unusual costumes it contained. But productions of *The Ring* by Ruth Berghaus designed by Axel Manthey in Frankfurt (1985–7), by Herbert Wernicke in Brussels (1991) and by Richard Jones in London (1994–5) concurred in visualizing Siegfried for his scenes with Mime in shorts or lederhosen, then had him smartening up into a suit of sorts for *Götterdämmerung*. Jones's Wotan (as created by Nigel Lowery, perhaps the most unusual and visually accomplished of postwar British stage designers) was a sort of lollipop man, carrying a road sign instead of a spear (as if he were providing oversight and safe passage for 'schoolchildren' crossing the road). Directors such as Christoph Marthaler and Jossi Wieler were inclined at the end of the century to relocate every opera they staged in a present-day office environment or on a contemporary housing estate. The tyranny of the single set was theatrically frustrating sometimes – though it may have made sense financially. It was a fact of operatic life at a time of declining subsidies that it would be cheaper to fit out a whole chorus in contemporary clothes than in newly made period costumes. Peter Sellars usually put his opera productions in some often telling contemporary American context, though he did not help *The Rake's Progress* by setting it in a modern-day American penitentiary (1996). Jonathan Miller's *Rigoletto* at English National Opera (1983) was transposed to New York's Little Italy and became a tale of a lecherous but charming mafia boss.

Recycling the design tradition

Freedom to choose an environment entirely different in period and in location from that conceived originally by the composer and librettist is not such a break with tradition. If Verdi could move *Un ballo in maschera* from Stockholm to New England in order to satisfy the censors, it is hard to see what fault he would find with Miller's mafia spin on *Rigoletto*. For designers, directors, conductors and dramaturgs, variation in where and when the story is being unfolded is much less significant than the opportunities for revealing focus and unusual theatrical dynamics provided by the permitted or tolerated new approaches to interpretation. Different is by no means always better, but defamiliarization can often be a fertile way of shining new shafts of light into the heart of a familiar work. Familiar is after all only a comparative term. New operas in the twentieth century have not so often needed reinterpretation. Yet even a work like *Peter Grimes* proved to hold far more ambiguity than might have been suspected when staged by Willy Decker at the Monnaie in Brussels in 1994 (see Sutcliffe 1996, 406–12). The purpose of opera and of operatic interpretation in the theatre is to make the audience inhabit the material in a new way and think freshly about what the music and drama mean. The choices that interpreters may now make without constraint are also liberating for those trying to compose new operas with serious subjects and staying power. Opera has in a way much greater freedom in its staging precisely because it is not primarily a realistic or straightforwardly narrative form. In a sense, in opera, every production is a footnote to the musical definition of a community of characters engaged in mutual confession. The issue of how much sense a production makes partly depends on the readiness of the audience to lend imaginative consent to what is on offer.

An obsessive respect for the works of the past may have created a more debilitated operatic world. But it is hard to see audiences doing without the repertoire of masterpieces on which they now feed, even if a new era of creativity and fresh operatic composition ensues. A past that belongs to Handel, Mozart, Puccini, Rossini, Tchaikovsky, Verdi and Wagner – not to mention such modern masters as Adams, Adès, Barber, Barry, Bartók, Birtwistle, Bliss, Blitzstein, Britten, Busoni, Copland, Dallapiccola, Maxwell Davies, Dessau, Dukas, Enescu, Fall, de Falla, Fauré, Floyd, Gerhard, Gershwin, Goehr, Hindemith, Holst, Kalman, Knussen, Křenek, Korngold, Lehár, Martinů, Messiaen, Milhaud, Osborne, Poulenc, Ravel, Respighi, Rota, Schreker, Thomson, Tippett, Turnage, Walton, Weill, Weir, Wolf-Ferrari and Zemlinsky (to name just a few) – is unlikely to be displaced by future novelty.

Works cited

Abbate, Carolyn, 1981. '*Tristan* in the composition of *Pelléas*', *19th-Century Music* 5, 117–41

    1991. *Unsung Voices: Opera and Musical Narrative in the Nineteenth Century*, Princeton: Princeton University Press

    1992. 'Analysis', in Sadie, *New Grove Opera*, volume 1, 116–20

Adams, John and Andrew Porter, 1988. '"Nixon in China": John Adams in Conversation', *Tempo* 167, 25–30

Adlington, Robert, 1998. Review of the NMC recording of Birtwistle's *The Mask of Orpheus*, *Tempo* 204, 43

    2000. *The Music of Harrison Birtwistle*, Cambridge: Cambridge University Press

Adorno, Theodor W., 1929. 'The Opera *Wozzeck*', in *Essays on Music*, trans. Susan H. Gillespie, Berkeley and Los Angeles: University of California Press, 2002, 619–26

    1950. 'Kurt Weill – Musiker des epischen Theaters', *Frankfurter Rundschau* (15 April)

    1968. *Alban Berg: Der Meister des kleinsten Übergangs*, Vienna: Elisabeth Lafitte

    1973: *The Philosophy of Modern Music*, trans. Anne G. Mitchell and Wesley V. Blomster, London: Sheed and Ward

    1978a. *Philosophie der neuen Musik*, Frankfurt am Main: Suhrkamp Taschenbuch

    1978b. *Gesammelte Schriften*, volume 16, Frankfurt am Main: Suhrkamp

    1981. *In Search of Wagner*, trans. Rodney Livingstone, London: NLB

Adorno, Theodor and Hanns Eisler, 1994 [1947]. *Composing for the Films*, with a new introduction by Graham McCann, London: Athlone Press

Annesley, Charles, 1898. *The Standard Operaglass*, Dresden: Sampson, Low, Master and Co. Ltd and Carl Tittmann

Appia, Adolphe, 1982. *Staging Wagnerian Drama*, trans. with an introduction by Peter Loeffler, Basel, Boston and Stuttgart: Burkhäuser

    1983. *Oeuvres complètes*, ed. Marie L. Bablet-Hahn, four volumes, Lausanne: L'Age d'homme

Aronson, Arnold, 2000. *American Avant-Garde Theatre: A History*, London and New York: Routledge

Artaud, Antonin, 1958. *The Theatre and Its Double*, trans. Mary Caroline Richards, New York: Pantheon

Ashby, Arved, 2002. 'Reading Berg', *Music Analysis* 21/3, 383–415

Attinello, Paul, 2002. 'Imploding the system: Kagel and the deconstruction of modernism', in Lochhead and Auner, *Postmodern Music*, 263–85

Auner, Joseph, 1989. 'Schoenberg's Aesthetic Transformations and the Evolution of Form in *Die glückliche Hand*', *Journal of the Arnold Schoenberg Institute* 12/2, 103–28

    1996. 'In Schoenberg's Workshop: Aggregates and Referential Collections in *Die glückliche Hand*', *Music Theory Spectrum* 18/1, 77–105

    1997. ' "Heart and Brain in Music": The Genesis of Schoenberg's *Die glückliche Hand*', in Brand and Hailey, *Constructive Dissonance*, 112–30

1999. 'The Second Viennese School as a Historical Concept', in Simms, *Schoenberg, Berg, and Webern*, 1–36

Ayrey, Craig, 1996. 'Introduction: Different Trains', in Ayrey and Everist, *Analytical Strategies*, 1–32

Ayrey, Craig and Mark Everist (eds), 1996. *Analytical Strategies and Musical Interpretation*, Cambridge: Cambridge University Press

Bahr, Hermann, 1890. *Zur Kritik der Moderne*, Zurich

1891. *Die Überwindung des Naturalismus (Zur Kritik der Moderne 2)*, Dresden: Pierson

Bailey, Kathryn (ed.), 2001. *Derrick Puffett on Music*, Aldershot: Ashgate

Balakian, Anna (ed.), 1982. *The Symbolist Movement in the Literature of European Languages*, Budapest: Akadémiai Kiadó

Balázs, Béla, 1910. *A Kékszakállú herceg vára* ('Duke Bluebeard's Castle'), first printed in *Szinjáték* ('Stageplay'), 13 June

Banes, Sally, 1993. *Greenwich Village 1963: Avant-Garde Performance and the Effervescent Body*, Durham, N. C. and London: Duke University Press

Banfield, Stephen (ed.), 1995. *The Blackwell History of Music in Britain. Volume 6: The Twentieth Century*, Oxford: Blackwell

Baragwanath, Nicholas, 1999. 'Alban Berg, Richard Wagner, and Leitmotivs of Symmetry', *19th-Century Music* 23/1, 62–83

Barnes, Jennifer, 2003. *Television Opera: The Fall of Opera Commissioned for Television*, Woodbridge: The Boydell Press

Baumann, Dorothea (ed.), 1982. *Musiktheater. Zum Schaffen von Schweizer Komponisten des 20. Jahrhunderts*, Bonstetten: Theaterkultur-Verlag

Beaumont, Antony, 2000. *Zemlinsky*, London: Faber and Faber

Beckerman, Michael (ed.), 2003. *Janáček and His World*, Princeton: Princeton University Press

Beckerman, Michael and Jim Samson, 1993. 'Eastern Europe, 1918–45', in Morgan, *Modern Times*, 128–41

Beckles Willson, Rachel, 2003. '"Behold! The long-awaited new Hungarian opera has been born!" Discourses of denial and Petrovics' *C'est la guerre*', *Central Europe* 1/2 (November), 133–45

Benjamin, Walter, 1968. *Illuminations*, New York: Harcourt, Brace and World

Berg, Alban, 1927. 'A word about *Wozzeck*', *Modern Music* 5/1 (November–December), 22–4; reprinted in Jarman, *Wozzeck*, 152–3

1929. 'A Lecture on "Wozzeck"', in Redlich, *Alban Berg*, 261–85, and Jarman, *Wozzeck*, 154–70

Bermbach, Udo (ed.), 2000. *Oper im 20. Jahrhundert. Entwicklungstendenzen und Komponisten*, Stuttgart: Metzler

Bertoni, Franco, Franco Quadri and Robert Stearns, 1998. *Robert Wilson*, New York: Rizzoli

Biner, Pierre, 1972. *The Living Theatre*, New York: Horizon Press.

Blyth, Alan, 1981. *Remembering Britten*, London: Hutchinson

Boretz, Benjamin and Edward T. Cone (eds), 1968. *Perspectives on Schoenberg and Stravinsky*, Westport, Conn.: Greenwood, 1983 reprint

Boughton, Rutland and Reginald Buckley, 1911. *Music-Drama of the Future: Uther and Igraine, Choral Drama*, London: William Reeves

Boulez, Pierre, 1977. *Wille und Zufall. Gespräche mit Célestin Deliège und Hans Mayer*, Stuttgart and Zurich: Belser Verlag

Brand, Juliane and Christopher Hailey (eds), 1997. *Constructive Dissonance: Arnold Schoenberg and the Transformations of Contemporary Culture*, Berkeley and Los Angeles: University of California Press

Breton, André, 1999. *Break of Day*, trans. Mark Polizzotti and Mary Ann Caws, Lincoln, Neb. and London: University of Nebraska Press

Brett, Philip (ed.), 1983. *Benjamin Britten: Peter Grimes*, Cambridge: Cambridge University Press

Brinkmann, Reinhold, 1992. 'The Lyric as Paradigm: Poetry and the Foundation of Arnold Schoenberg's New Music', in Reschke and Pollack, *German Literature and Music*, 95–129

    1997. 'Schoenberg the Contemporary: A View From Behind', in Brand and Hailey, *Constructive Dissonance*, 196–219

Britten, Benjamin, 1944. 'Conversation with Benjamin Britten', *Tempo* 6 (February), 4–5

Brown, Julie, 1994. 'Schoenberg's Early Wagnerisms: Atonality and the Redemption of Ahasuerus', *Cambridge Opera Journal* 6/1, 51–80

Busoni, Ferruccio, 1920. 'Junge Klassizität (An Paul Bekker)', *Frankfurter Zeitung* 7, February

    1956. *Wesen und Einheit der Musik*. ed. Joachim Herrmann, Berlin: Hesse

    1983. *Von der Macht der Töne. Ausgewählte Schriften*, ed. Siegfried Bimberg, Leipzig: Reclam

    1987. *Ferruccio Busoni: Selected Letters*, trans. and ed. Antony Beaumont, London: Faber and Faber

    1999. *Briefe an Henri, Katharina und Egon Petri*, ed. Martina Weindel, Wilhelmshaven: Florian Noetzel

Butler, Christopher, 1994. *Early Modernism: Literature, Music and Painting in Europe 1900–1916*, Oxford: Oxford University Press

Caldwell, John Thornton, 1995. *Televisuality: Style, Crisis, and Authority in American Television*, Brunswick, N. J.: Rutgers University Press

Carner, Mosco, 1983. *Alban Berg: The Man and the Work*, second edition, London: Duckworth

    1992. *Puccini: A Critical Biography*, third edition, London: Duckworth

Carner, Mosco and Rudolf Klein, 1992. 'Vienna. 1830–1945', in Sadie, *New Grove Opera*, volume 4, 995–1000

Carpenter, Humphrey, 1992. *Benjamin Britten: A Biography*, London: Faber and Faber

Casella, Alfredo, 1919. 'Dissonanze . . .', *Ars nova* 3/3, 2

    1921. 'Il risveglio musicale italiano', *Il pianoforte* 11/3, cited in Pestalozza, *La Rassegna Musicale*, 593–5

    1932. 'Come e perché scrissi *La Donna serpente*', *L'Italia letteraria* (13 March), 3

    1955. *Music in My Time*, trans. Spencer Norton, Norman, Okla.: University of Oklahoma Press

Caute, David, 1994. *Joseph Losey: A Revenge on Life*, London: Faber and Faber

Chekhov, Anton, 1959. *Plays*, trans. Elizaveta Fen, Harmondsworth: Penguin

Chew, Geoffrey, 2000. 'Martinů's Three Wishes and their Fulfilment: Links between Paris and Prague in Music of the 1920s', *French Cultural Studies* 11, 367–76

　2003. 'Reinterpreting Janáček and Kamila: Dangerous Liaisons in Czech Fin-de-Siècle Music and Literature', in Beckerman, *Janáček*, 99–144

Ciarlantini, Franco (ed.), 1929. *Malipiero e le sue Sette canzoni. Scritti di Alfano [and others] ... Prefazione di G. F. Malipiero (Quaderni d'attualità 2)*, Rome and Milan: Augustea

Citron, Marcia J., 2000. *Opera on Screen*, New Haven and London: Yale University Press

Clarke, David (ed.), 1999. *Tippett Studies*, Cambridge: Cambridge University Press

Clements, Andrew, 1992. 'Music theatre', in Sadie, *New Grove Opera*, volume 8, 529–30

Clum, John M., 1999. *Something for the Boys: Musical Theater and Gay Culture*, New York: Palgrave

Collaer, Paul, 1988. *Darius Milhaud*, trans. Jane Hohfeld Galante, San Francisco: San Francisco Press

Cook, Nicholas, 1998. *Analysing Musical Multimedia*, Oxford: Clarendon Press

Cooke, Mervyn, 1993. 'Dramatic and Musical Cohesion in Britten's *A Midsummer Night's Dream*', *Music & Letters* 74/2, 246–68; abridged version in Cooke, *Companion to Britten*, 129–45

　1998. *Britten and the Far East*, Woodbridge: The Boydell Press/Britten–Pears Library

　(ed.), 1999. *The Cambridge Companion to Benjamin Britten*, Cambridge: Cambridge University Press

Cott, Jonathan, Beryl Korot and Steve Reich, 1995. 'Jonathan Cott Interviews Beryl Korot and Steve Reich on *The Cave*', *Steve Reich: The Cave*, Nonesuch 79327–2

Craft, Robert, 1972. *Stravinsky. Chronicle of a Friendship 1948–1971*, London: Victor Gollancz

　(ed.), 1982. *Stravinsky. Selected Correspondence*, volume 1, London: Faber and Faber

Cross, Charlotte M. and Russell A. Berman (eds), 2000a. *Political and Religious Ideas in the Works of Arnold Schoenberg*, New York: Garland

　(eds), 2000b. *Schoenberg and Words: The Modernist Years*, New York: Garland

Cross, Jonathan, 2000. *Harrison Birtwistle*, London: Faber and Faber

Dahlhaus, Carl, 1977. *Grundlagen der Musikgeschichte*, Cologne: Musikverlag Gerig

　1985. *Realism in Nineteenth-Century Music*, trans. Mary Whittall, Cambridge: Cambridge University Press

　1987. *Schoenberg and the New Music*, trans. Derrick Puffett and Alfred Clayton, Cambridge: Cambridge University Press

　1989. *Nineteenth-Century Music*, trans. J. Bradford Robinson, Berkeley and Los Angeles: University of California Press

　1992. 'Wagner's Musical Influence', trans. Alfred Clayton, in Müller and Wapnewski, *Wagner Handbook*, 547–62

Danuser, Hermann (ed.), 1997. *Die klassizistische Moderne in der Musik des 20. Jahrhunderts. Internationales Symposion der Paul Sacher Stiftung Basel 1996*, Winterthur: Amadeus

Daverio, John, 1993. *Nineteenth-Century Music and the German Romantic Ideology*, New York: Schirmer

Davison, Stephen, 2000. '*Von heute auf morgen*: Schoenberg as Social Critic', in Cross and Berman, *Political and Religious Ideas*, 85–110

Dean, Winton, 1999. Review-article, *Journal of the Royal Musical Association* 124/1, 127–33

Debussy, Claude, 1987 [1971]. *Monsieur Croche et autres écrits*, ed. François Lesure, revised edition, Paris: Gallimard

Deleuze, Gilles, 1983. *Nietzsche and Philosophy*, trans. Hugh Tomlinson, New York: Columbia University Press
 1994. *Difference and Repetition*, trans. Paul Patton, New York: Columbia University Press

Demény, János (ed.), 1971. *Béla Bartók Letters*, trans. Péter Balabán and István Farkas, Budapest: Corvina, and London: Faber and Faber

Dorsch, T. S. (ed.), 1965. *Classical Literary Criticism*, Harmondsworth: Penguin

Downes, Stephen, 1995. 'Themes of Duality and Transformation in Szymanowski's *King Roger*', *Music Analysis* 14/2–3, 257–91

Dukas, Paul, 1936. '*Ariane et Barbe-Bleue* (moralité à la façon de Perrault)' [1910], *Revue musicale* 17, 4–7 [in the special commemorative Dukas number, separately paginated]
 1948. *Les écrits de Paul Dukas sur la musique*, Paris: Société d'éditions françaises et internationales

Dumesnil, René, 1930. *La musique contemporaine en France*, Paris: Armand Colin
 1946. *La musique en France entre les deux guerres, 1913–1939*, Geneva: Editions du Milieu du Monde

Dussel, Konrad, 1988. *Ein neues, heroisches Theater? Nationalsozialistische Theaterpolitik und ihre Auswirkungen*, Bonn: Bouvier

Egk, Werner, 1981. *Die Zeit wartet nicht. Künstlerisches, Zeitgeschichtliches, Privates aus meinem Leben*, Munich: R. S. Schultz

Egorova, Tatiana, 1997. *Soviet Film Music: An Historical Survey*, trans. Tatiana A. Ganf and Natalia A. Egunova, Amsterdam: Harwood Academic Publishers

Ellis, Katherine, 1999. 'Wagnerism and Anti-Wagnerism in the Paris Periodical Press, 1852–1870', in Fauser and Schwartz, *Von Wagner zum Wagnérisme*, 51–83

Ellis, William Ashton (ed. and trans.), 1892–9. *Richard Wagner's Prose Works*, eight volumes, London: Kegan Paul

Engel, Carl, 1922. 'Jazz: A Musical Discussion', *Atlantic Monthly* (August), 182–9

Evans, Peter, 1989. *The Music of Benjamin Britten*, second edition, London: Dent
 1995. 'Instrumental Music I', in Banfield, *Blackwell History*, 179–277

Evidon, Richard, 1992. 'Film', in Sadie, *New Grove Opera*, volume 2, 194–200

Falck, Robert, 1992. 'Marie Pappenheim, Schoenberg, and the *Studien über Hysterie*', in Reschke and Pollack, *German Literature and Music*, 131–44

Fanning, David (ed.), 1995. *Shostakovich Studies*, Cambridge: Cambridge University Press

Fauré, Gabriel, 1930. *Opinions musicales*, Paris: Editions Rieder

Fauré-Fremiet, Philippe, 1945. 'Le genèse de Pénélope', *Revue musicale*, special number: *Le centenarie de Gabriel Fauré*, 17

Fauser, Annegret and Manuela Schwartz (eds), 1999. *Von Wagner zum Wagnérisme: Musik, Literatur, Kunst, Politik*, Leipzig: Leipziger Universitätsverlag

Favre, Georges (ed.), 1971. *Correspondance de Paul Dukas*, Paris: Durand

Fawkes, Richard, 2000. *Opera on Film*, London: Duckworth

Fay, Laurel, 1995. 'From *Lady Macbeth* to *Katerina*: Shostakovich's versions and revisions', in Fanning, *Shostakovich Studies*, 160–88

Fiechtner, Helmut, 1961. 'Die Bühnenwerke von Kurt Weill', *Österreichische Musikzeitschrift* 16, 213–17

Flinn, Caryl, 1992. *Strains of Utopia: Gender, Nostalgia, and Hollywood Film Music*, Princeton, N. J.: Princeton University Press

Ford, Andrew, 1993. *Composer to Composer: Conversations about Contemporary Music*, London: Quartet, and Sydney: Allen and Unwin

Franklin, Peter, 1985. *The Idea of Music: Schoenberg and Others*, London: Macmillan

Frigyesi, Judit, 1998. *Béla Bartók and Turn-of-the-Century Budapest*, Berkeley, Los Angeles and London: University of California Press

Frisch, Walter (ed.), 1999. *Schoenberg and His World*, Princeton: Princeton University Press

Frith, Simon, 1996. *Performing Rites: On the Value of Popular Music*, Cambridge, Mass.: Harvard University Press

Gann, Kyle, 1993. 'Inside-Out Opera', *Village Voice* (2 November)

Gara, Eugenio (ed.), 1958. *Carteggi Pucciniani*, Milan: Ricordi

Garton Ash, Timothy, 1989. *The Uses of Adversity. Essays on the Fate of Central Europe*, Cambridge: Granta

Gatti, Guido M., 1925. 'Del presente musicale in Italia', in *La musica contemporanea in Europa*, Milan: Bottega di Poesia, 18–19

Gena, Peter and Jonathan Brent (eds), 1982. *A John Cage Reader in Celebration of his 70th Birthday*, New York: C. F. Peters Corporation

Gerhard, Anselm, 1998. *The Urbanization of Opera*, trans. Mary Whittall, Chicago: Chicago University Press

Gillies, Malcolm (ed.), 1993. *The Bartók Companion*, London: Faber and Faber

Glass, Philip, 1987. *Music by Philip Glass*, New York: Harper and Row

Goebbels, Joseph, 1936. 'Der Führer und die Künste', in *Adolf Hitler. Bilder aus dem Leben des Führers*, Altona-Bahrenfeld: Cigaretten-Bilderdienst

Goldstein, Bluma, 2000. 'Schoenberg's *Moses und Aron*: A Vanishing Biblical Nation', in Cross and Berman, *Political and Religious Ideas*, 159–92

Gozenpud, A. A., 1963. *Russkiy sovetskiy operniy teatr, 1917–1941*, Leningrad: Gosudarstvennoye muzïkal'noye izdatel'stvo

Grayson, David, 1986. *The Genesis of Pelléas et Mélisande*, Ann Arbor: UMI Research Press

  1997. 'Waiting for Golaud: the concept of time in *Pelléas*', in Langham Smith, *Debussy Studies*, 26–50

Griffiths, Paul, 1994. 'The twentieth century: 1945 to the present day', in Parker, *Oxford Illustrated History of Opera*, 317–49

1995. *Modern Music and After: Directions Since 1945*, Oxford: Clarendon Press

1996. 'The Twentieth Century: To 1945', in Parker, *Oxford History of Opera*, 186–211

Groos, Arthur and Roger Parker, 1986. *Puccini: La Bohème*, Cambridge: Cambridge University Press

Grosch, Nils, 2000. 'Zum Musiktheater der Neuen Sachlichkeit', in Bermbach, *Oper im 20. Jahrhundert*, 130–54

Grun, Bernard (ed. and trans.), 1971. *Alban Berg: Letters to his Wife*, London: Faber and Faber

Hahl-Koch, Jelena (ed.), 1984. *Arnold Schoenberg–Wassily Kandinsky: Letters, Pictures and Documents*, trans. John C. Crawford, London: Faber and Faber

Hailey, Christopher, 1989. 'Between Instinct and Reflection: Berg and the Viennese Dichotomy', in Jarman, *Berg Companion*, 221–34

Haimo, Ethan, 1990. *Schoenberg's Serial Odyssey*, Oxford: Clarendon Press

Hammelmann, Hanns and Ewald Osers (trans.), 1961. *The Correspondence Between Richard Strauss and Hugo von Hofmannsthal, with an introduction by Edward Sackville-West*, London: William Collins; repr. Cambridge: Cambridge University Press, 1980

Hanslick, Eduard, 1951. *Vienna's Golden Years of Music, 1850–1900*, trans. and ed. Henry Pleasants, London: Gollancz

Harewood, The Earl of (ed.), 1997. *The New Kobbé's Opera Book*, London: Ebury Press

Harvey, Jonathan, 1999. *In Quest of Spirit*, Berkeley and Los Angeles: University of California Press

Heile, Björn, 2002. 'Collage vs. compositional control: the interdependency of modernist and postmodernist approaches in the work of Mauricio Kagel', in Lochhead and Auner, *Postmodern Music*, 287–99

Henze, Hans Werner, 1982. *Music and Politics: Collected Writings 1953–81*, London: Faber and Faber

1996. *Language, Music and Artistic Invention*, trans. Mary Whittall, Aldeburgh: Britten–Pears Library

Herbert, David (ed.), 1979. *The Operas of Benjamin Britten*, London: Hamish Hamilton

Hermand, Jost, 1979. 'Expressionism and Music', in Pickar and Webb, *Expressionism Reconsidered*, 58–73

Hinton, Stephen (ed.), 1990. *Kurt Weill: The Threepenny Opera*, Cambridge: Cambridge University Press

Hobsbawm, Eric, 1994. *The Age of Empire*, London: Abacus

Hoérée, Arthur, 1938. *Albert Roussel*, Paris: Editions Rieder

Hofmannsthal, Hugo von, 1919. *Die Salzburger Festspiele* [booklet of the talk to the *Salzburger Festspielgemeinde*], Vienna

Holloway, Robin, 1979. *Debussy and Wagner*, London: Eulenberg

Holmberg, Arthur, 1996. *The Theatre of Robert Wilson*, Cambridge and New York: Cambridge University Press

Honegger, Arthur, 1925. Interview with Roland-Manuel, *Dissonances* 2, 85–6
  1966 [1951]. *I am a Composer*, trans. Wilson O. Clough and Allan Arthur
    Willman, London: Faber and Faber
Huebner, Steven, 1993. 'Massenet and Wagner: Bridling the Influence', *Cambridge
    Opera Journal* 5/3, 223–38
Huntley, John, n.d. [1947]. *British Film Music*, London: Skelton Robinson
Hurd, Michael, 1978. 'Rutland Boughton, 1878–1960', *Musical Times* 119, 31–3
  1984. 'The Glastonbury Festivals', *Musical Times* 125, 435–7
Jackson, Russell (ed.), 2000. *The Cambridge Companion to Shakespeare on Film*,
    Cambridge: Cambridge University Press
Jackson, Tim, 2004. 'Representations of "Exile"and "Consolation" in
    Hindemith's *Mathis der Maler*', in Walton and Baldassarre, *Musik im Exil*, 141–87
Jarman, Derek, 1989. *War Requiem: The Film*, London: Faber and Faber
Jarman, Douglas, 1989a. *Alban Berg: Wozzeck*, Cambridge: Cambridge University
    Press
  (ed.), 1989b. *The Berg Companion*, London: Macmillan
  1991. *Alban Berg: Lulu*, Cambridge: Cambridge University Press
  1997. 'Secret Programmes', in Pople, *Cambridge Companion to Berg*, 167–79
Jefferson, Alan, 1985. *Richard Strauss: Der Rosenkavalier*, Cambridge: Cambridge
    University Press
Joe, Jeongwon, and Rose Theresa (eds), 2002. *Between Opera and Cinema*, New
    York and London: Routledge
John, Nicholas (ed.), 1991. *Bartók Stage Works*, London: John Calder
Jowitt, Deborah, 1997. *Meredith Monk*, Baltimore: Johns Hopkins University Press
Kabalevskiy, D. B. (ed.), 1977. *S. S. Prokof'yev i N. Ya. Myaskovsky: Perepiska*,
    Moscow: Sovetskiy kompozitor
Kahan, Sylvia, 2003. *Music's Modern Muse: A Life of Winaretta Singer, Princesse de
    Polignac*, Rochester, N. Y.: University of Rochester Press
Kalinak, Kathryn, 1992. *Settling the Score: Music and the Hollywood Film*, Madison:
    University of Wisconsin Press
Kallir, Jane, 1984. *Arnold Schoenberg's Vienna*, New York: Rizzoli
Kamuf, Peggy, 1994. 'The Replay's the Thing', in Levin, *Opera through Other Eyes*,
    79–105
Kandinsky, Wassily, 1965. *Über das Geistige in der Kunst* [1912], with an
    introduction by Max Bill, Bern: Benteli Verlag
Kandinsky, Wassily and Franz Marc, 1912. *The Blaue Reiter Almanac*, ed. Klaus
    Lankheit, New York: Da Capo, 1989 reprint of English translation
Karlin, Fred, 1994. *Listening to Movies: The Film Lover's Guide to Film Music*, New
    York: Schirmer
Kater, Michael H., 1997. *The Twisted Music: Musicians and their Music in the Third
    Reich*, New York: Oxford University Press
Kater, Michael H. and Albrecht Riethmüller (eds), 2003. *Music and Nazism. Art
    under Tyranny, 1933–1945*, Laaber: Laaber
Keathley, Elizabeth L., 2000. ' "Die Frauenfrage" in *Erwartung*: Schoenberg's
    Collaboration with Marie Pappenheim', in Cross and Berman, *Schoenberg and
    Words*, 139–77

Keller, Hans, 1994. *Essays on Music*, ed. Christopher Wintle, Cambridge and New York: Cambridge University Press

Kemp, Ian, 1984. *Tippett: The Composer and His Music*, London: Eulenberg

Kennedy, Michael, 1995. *Richard Strauss*, second edition, Oxford: Oxford University Press

    1999. *Richard Strauss. Man, Musician, Enigma*, Cambridge: Cambridge University Press

Kerman, Joseph, 1989 [1956]. *Opera as Drama*, second edition, London and Boston: Faber and Faber

Kershaw, David, 1995. 'Film and Television Music', in Banfield, *Blackwell History*, 125–44

Kienzle, Ulrike, 2000. 'Wo bleibt da der berühmte "Zeitwille"?', in Bermbach, *Oper im 20. Jahrhundert*, 75–129

Kirk, Elise K., 2001. *American Opera*, Urbana: University of Illinois Press

Kloss, Erich (ed.), 1909. *Richard Wagner an Freunde und Zeitgenossen*, second edition, Berlin and Leipzig: Schuster & Loeffler

Köhler, Franz-Heinz, 1968. *Die Struktur der Spielpläne deutschsprachiger Opernbühnen von 1896 bis 1966*, Koblenz: Verband Dt. Städtestatistiker

Kornick, Rebecca Hodell, 1991. *Recent American Opera: A Production Guide*, New York: Columbia University Press

Kostelanetz, Richard, 1994. *On Innovative Performance(s): Three Decades of Recollections on Alternative Theater*, Jefferson, N. C.: McFarland and Co.

    (ed.), 1997. *Writings on Glass: Essays, Interviews, Criticism*, New York: Schirmer.

Kramer, Lawrence, 1990. 'Culture and musical hermeneutics: the Salome complex', *Cambridge Opera Journal* 2/3, 269–94

Kroó, György, 1981. 'Data on the Genesis of *Duke Bluebeard's Castle*', *Studia Musicologica* 23, 79–123

    1993. 'Opera: *Duke Bluebeard's Castle*', in Gillies, *Bartók Companion*, 349–59

Kühn, Alfred, 1894. 'Manon Lescaut von Puccini', *Neue Zeitschrift für Musik* 61, 62–4

Kurtz, Michael, 1992. *Stockhausen: A Biography*, trans. Richard Toop, London: Faber and Faber

Kushner, Roland J. and Thomas H. Pollak, 2004. *The Finances and Operations of Non-profit Performing Arts Organizations in 2001 and 2002*, Washington, D. C.: Performing Arts Research Coalition

Labelle, Nicole, 2001. 'Roussel, Albert', in Sadie and Tyrrell, *New Grove*, volume 21, 806–10

Labroca, Mario, 1934. 'Vita e musica nell'Italia nuova', *La Rassegna musicale* 7/1, cited in Pestalozza, *La Rassegna musicale*, 233–7

Laloy, Louis, 1906. 'Musique et danses cambodgiennes', *Le Mercure musical*, 15 August, 98–112

    1912. *La musique chinoise*, Paris: Henri Laurens

Lamb, Andrew, 2000. *150 Years of Popular Musical Theatre*, New Haven: Yale University Press

Landowski, Marcel, 1966. [Catalogue of Works], Paris: Salabert

Langham Smith, Richard, 1992a. 'Bruneau, Alfred', in Sadie, *New Grove Opera*, volume 1, 619–21

1992b. 'Paris. 1870–1902', in Sadie, *New Grove Opera*, volume 3, 873–9

(ed.), 1997. *Debussy Studies*, Cambridge: Cambridge University Press

2000. 'Ravel's Operatic Spectacles', in Mawer, *Companion to Ravel*, 188–210

Leach, Robert, 1989. *Vsevolod Meyerhold*, Cambridge: Cambridge University Press

Leafstedt, Carl S., 1999. *Inside Bluebeard's Castle: Music and Drama in Béla Bartók's Opera*, New York and London: Oxford University Press

Leicester, H. Marshall, Jr, 1994. 'Discourse and the film text: four readings of *Carmen*', *Cambridge Opera Journal* 6/3, 245–82

Leoncavallo, Ruggero, n.d. *Appunti vari delle* [sic] *autobiografici di R. Leoncavallo* ('Autobiographical notes and observations by R. Leoncavallo'), typescript, copy in the Fondo Ruggero Leoncavallo, Locarno: Biblioteca Cantonale

Lesure, François, 1980. *Claude Debussy: Iconographie*, Geneva: Editions Minkoff

1991. 'La longue attente de *Pelléas* (1895–1899)', *Cahiers Debussy* 15, 3–12

(ed.), 1993. *Claude Debussy, Correspondance 1884–1918*, Paris: Hermann

2003. *Claude Debussy: Biographie critique, suivie du Catalogue de l'oeuvre*, Paris: Fayard

Lesure, François and Roger Nichols (eds), 1987. *Debussy Letters*, trans. Roger Nichols, London and Boston: Faber and Faber

Levin, David J. (ed.), 1994. *Opera through Other Eyes*, Stanford, Calif.: Stanford University Press

Lewin, David, 1968. '*Moses und Aron*: Some General Remarks, and Analytic Notes for Act I, Scene 1', in Boretz and Cone, *Perspectives on Schoenberg and Stravinsky*, 61–77

Lieberson, Jonathan, 1988. 'Nixon in Brooklyn', *New York Review of Books* (21 January), 35

Ligeti, György, 1983. *György Ligeti in Conversation*, London: Eulenberg

Lindenberger, Herbert, 1984. *Opera: The Extravagant Art*, Ithaca and London: Cornell University Press

Lochhead, Judy, 1997. 'Lulu's Feminine Performance', in Pople, *Companion to Berg*, 227–44

Lochhead, Judy and Joseph Auner (eds), 2002. *Postmodern Music/Postmodern Thought*, New York: Routledge

Lockspeiser, Edward, 1978. *Debussy: His Life and Mind*, two volumes, Cambridge: Cambridge University Press

London, Kurt, 1936. *Film Music: A Summary of the Characteristic Features of its History, Aesthetics, Technique; and Possible Developments*, trans. Eric S. Bensinger, foreword by Constant Lambert, London: Faber and Faber

Loos, Adolf, 1931/2. *Ins Leere Gesprochen 1897–1900: Plus Trotzdem 1900–1930*, Innsbruck: Brennerverlag

Loppert, Max, 1993. 'An Introduction to *Atlas*', *Atlas: An Opera in Three Parts*, ECM 78118-21491-2

Macek, Petr (ed.), 1993. *Colloquium Bohuslav Martinů. His Pupils, Friends and Contemporaries. Brno, 1990*, Brno: Masarykova Universita

Maconie, Robin, 1990. *The Works of Karlheinz Stockhausen*, second edition, Oxford: Clarendon Press

Maeterlinck, Maurice, 1892. *Pelléas et Mélisande*, Brussels: Lacomblez

1901. *Théâtre*, three volumes, Brussels: Lacomblez; *Ariane et Barbe-Bleue* (1899) appears in volume 3

Magee, Bryan, 2000. *Wagner and Philosophy*, London: Allen Lane

Malcolm, Noel, 1990. *Georges Enescu: His Life and Music*, London: Toccata Press

Malipiero, Gian Francesco, 1913. 'Del dramma musicale italiano e dei suoi pregiudizi', *Musica* 7/23 (8 June), 1

Mann, Erika (ed.), 1983. *Wagner und unsere Zeit*, Frankfurt am Main: Fischer Taschenbuch Verlag

Marks, Martin Miller, 1997. *Music and the Silent Film: Contexts and Case Studies, 1895–1924*, New York and Oxford: Oxford University Press

Marranca, Bonnie, 1992. 'Meredith Monk's Atlas of Sound: New Opera and the American Performance Tradition', *Performing Arts Journal* 40 (January)

Marsh, Robert C., 1992. 'Chicago', in Sadie, *New Grove Opera*, volume 1, 840–42

Mawer, Deborah (ed.), 2000. *The Cambridge Companion to Ravel*, Cambridge: Cambridge University Press

McCracken, Alison, 1999. '"God's Gift to Us Girls": Crooning, Gender, and the Re-creation of American Popular Song, 1928–1933', *American Music* 17, 365–95

McGuinness, Patrick, 2000. *Maurice Maeterlinck and the Making of Modern Theatre*, Oxford: Oxford University Press

McKellar, Shannon, 1999. 'Music, Image and Ideology in Britten's *Owen Wingrave*: Conflict in a Fissured Text', *Music & Letters* 80/3, 390–410

McLuhan, Marshall, 1964. *Understanding Media: The Extensions of Man*, New York: McGraw-Hill

Mellers, Wilfrid, 1984. 'Turning the Screw', in Palmer, *Britten Companion*, 144–52
    1999. 'Tippett at the Millennium: A Personal Memoir', in Clarke, *Tippett Studies*, 186–99

Mendelson, Edward (ed.), 1993. *W. H. Auden and Chester Kallman: Libretti and Other Dramatic Writings 1939–1973*, London: Faber and Faber

Merman, Ethel, 1955. *Don't Call Me Madam*, London: W. H. Allen

Messiaen, Olivier, 1935. Unpublished letter to Paul Dukas, January 1935, enthusing about the performance of *Ariane et Barbe-Bleue* at the Paris Opéra
    1936. 'Ariane et Barbe-Bleue de Paul Dukas', *Revue musicale* 17, 79–86 [in the special commemorative Dukas number, separately paginated]
    1938. 'Billet Parisien: Un spectacle Darius Milhaud', *Syrinx* (March), 25–6

Messing, Scott, 1988. *Neoclassicism in Music: From the Genesis of the Concept Through the Schoenberg/Stravinsky Polemic*, Ann Arbor: UMI Research Press

Meyer, Martin, 1983. *The Met – One Hundred Years of Grand Opera*, London: Thames & Hudson

Meyerhold, Vsevolod, 1910. Article based on a November 1909 lecture, *Yezhegodnik Imperatorskikh teatrov* 5 (St Petersburg); reprinted in Meyerhold's *O Teatre* (1913), 56–62

Mila, Massimo, 1947–8. 'Situation de l'opéra en Italie', *Polyphonie 1:* 'Le théâtre musical', 105–112

Mitchell, Donald and Philip Reed (eds), 1991. *Letters from a Life: Selected Diaries and Letters of Benjamin Britten 1913–1976*, volume 1: 1923–39; volume 2: 1939–45, London: Faber and Faber

Moholy-Nagy, László, 1929. *Von Material zu Architektur*, Munich: Albert Langen

Monk, Meredith, 1993. 'Process Notes', *Atlas: An Opera in Three Parts*, ECM 78118-21491-2.

Monk, Meredith and Ken Smith, 2002. 'Singing the Unsayable: Meredith Monk in Conversation with Ken Smith', *Gramophone* (November), 28.

Mordden, Ethan, 1978. *Opera in the Twentieth Century: Sacred, Profane, Godot*, New York: Oxford University Press
    1997. *Make Believe: The Broadway Musical in the 1920s*, New York: Oxford University Press

Morgan, Robert P. (ed.), 1993. *Modern Times. From World War I to the Present*, London: Macmillan

Morrison, Simon, 2002. *Russian Opera and the Symbolist Movement*, Berkeley, Los Angeles and London: University of California Press

Müller, Ulrich and Peter Wapnewski (eds), 1992. *Wagner Handbook*, trans. and ed. John Deathridge, Cambridge, Mass., and London: Harvard University Press

Nattiez, Jean-Jacques, 1993. *Wagner Androgyne: A Study in Interpretation*, trans. Stewart Spencer, Princeton: Princeton University Press

Neef, Sigrid and Hermann, 1992. *Deutsche Oper im 20. Jahrhundert. DDR 1949–1989*, Berlin: P. Lang

Nichols, Roger, 1987. *Ravel Remembered*, London: Faber and Faber
    1996. *Conversations with Madeleine Milhaud*, London: Faber and Faber

Nichols, Roger and Richard Langham Smith, 1989. *Claude Debussy: Pelléas et Mélisande*, Cambridge: Cambridge University Press

Nyman, Michael, 1986. Introductory note to *The Man Who Mistook His Wife for a Hat: A Chamber Opera by Michael Nyman*, New York: Columbia Masterworks
    1999. *Experimental Music: Cage and Beyond*, second edition, Cambridge: Cambridge University Press

Orenstein, Arbie, 1975. *Ravel: Man and Musician*, New York: Columbia University Press
    1990. *A Ravel Reader: Correspondence, Articles, Interviews*, New York: Columbia University Press

Osmond-Smith, David, 1991. *Berio*, Oxford: Oxford University Press
    1992. 'Sciarrino, Salvatore', in Sadie, *New Grove Opera*, volume 4, 268–9

Otten, Willen Jan and Elmer Schönberger, 1978. 'Louis Andriessen's *Matthew Passion and Orpheus*', *Key Notes* 7, 22–34

Page, Tim [n.d.]. 'Making of the Representative for Planet 8', *Grove Dictionary of Opera* (*Grove Online*)

Pahissa, Jaime, 1954. *Manuel de Falla: His Life and Works*, London: Museum Press

Palmer, Christopher (ed.), 1984. *The Britten Companion*, London: Faber and Faber
    1990. *The Composer in Hollywood*, London and New York: Marion Boyars

Parker, Roger (ed.), 1994. *The Oxford Illustrated History of Opera*, Oxford: Oxford University Press
    (ed.), 1996. *The Oxford History of Opera*, Oxford: Oxford University Press

Parrott, E. O. (ed.), 1989. *How to be Tremendously Tuned in to Opera*, Harmondsworth: Viking/Penguin

Payne, Anthony, 1963. 'Dramatic use of tonality in *Peter Grimes*', *Tempo* 66–7, 22–6

2001. 'Delius, Frederick', in Sadie and Tyrrell, *New Grove*, volume 7, 161–9

Pečman, Rudolf (ed.), 1967. *Bohuslav Martinů's Bühnenschaffen* [Proceedings of the International Music Festival in Brno, 1966], Prague: Czech Music Information Centre

Perle, George, 1985. *The Operas of Alban Berg, volume 2: Lulu*, Berkeley and Los Angeles: University of California Press

Perrault, Charles, 1697. *Histoires, ou Contes du temps passé, avec des moralitez*, Paris: Claude Barbin

Perrin, Glyn, 1981. 'Mauricio Kagel: filmed music/composed film', *Contact* 23 (Winter), 10–15

Pestalozza, Luigi (ed.), 1966. *La Rassegna musicale*, Milan: Feltrinelli

Pickar, Gertrud B. and Karl E. Webb (eds.), 1979. *Expressionism Reconsidered: Relationships and Affinities* (Houston German Studies 1), Munich: Fink

Pizzetti, Ildebrando, 1945. 'La musica e il dramma' [1932], in *Musica e dramma*, Rome: Edizioni della Bussola, 53–4

Pople, Anthony (ed.), 1997a. *The Cambridge Companion to Berg*, Cambridge: Cambridge University Press

1997b. 'The Musical Language of *Wozzeck*', in Pople, *Companion to Berg*, 145–64

Priest, Deborah, 1999. *Louis Laloy (1874–1944) on Debussy, Ravel and Stravinsky*, Aldershot: Ashgate

Pritchett, James, 1993. *The Music of John Cage*, Cambridge: Cambridge University Press

Puffett, Derrick, 1989. 'Berg and German Opera', in Jarman, *Berg Companion*, 197–219

2001. 'Tippett and the Retreat from Mythology', in Bailey, *Derrick Puffett*, 138–58

Redlich, H. F., 1957. *Alban Berg: The Man and his Music*, London: John Calder

Reich, Steve, 2002. *Writings on Music, 1965–2000*, Oxford and New York: Oxford University Press

Reich, Steve and Jonathan Cott, 1985. 'Steve Reich in Conversation with Jonathan Cott', *Steve Reich: The Desert Music*, Nonesuch 79101–2

Reich, Steve and Beryl Korot, 2003. 'A Theater of Ideas: Steve Reich and Beryl Korot on *Three Tales*', *Steve Reich/Beryl Korot: Three Tales*, Nonesuch 79662–2

Reschke, Claus and Howard Pollack (eds), 1992. *German Literature and Music 1890–1989: An Aesthetic Fusion* (Houston German Studies 8), Munich: Fink

Revill, David, 1992. *The Roaring Silence – John Cage: A Life*, New York: Arcade Publishing

Rich, Alan, 2000. *An American Voice: Houston Grand Opera Celebrates Twenty-Five World Premieres*, Houston: Houston Grand Opera

Riethmüller, Albrecht, 2003. 'Stefan Zweig and the Fall of the Reich Music Chamber President, Richard Strauss', in Kater and Riethmüller, *Music and Nazism*, 269–91

Ringer, Alexander L., 1980. 'Schoenberg, Weill, and Epic Theater', *Journal of the Arnold Schoenberg Institute* 4/2, 77–98

Roberts, Julian, 1988. *German Philosophy: An Introduction*, Cambridge: Polity

Rogers, Holly, 2004. 'Fitzcarraldo's Search for Aguirre: Music and Text in the Amazonian Films of Werner Herzog', *Journal of the Royal Musical Association* 129/1, 77–99

Roller, Alfred, 1909. 'Bühnenreform? ['Stage Reform?']', *Der Merker* 1/5 (10 December), 193–7; reproduced, in an English translation by Meredith Oakes, in Sutcliffe, *Believing in Opera*, 427–31

  1930. *Thespis: Das Theaterbuch*, ed. Roessler, Berlin: Bühnenvolksbundverlag

Rosselli, John, 1991. 'Italy: The Decline of a Tradition', in Samson, *Late Romantic Era*, 126–50

Rupprecht, Philip, 2001. *Britten's Musical Language*, Cambridge: Cambridge University Press

Rushton, Julian, 1981. *Wolfgang Amadeus Mozart: Don Giovanni*, Cambridge: Cambridge University Press

Rye, Matthew, 1995. 'Music and drama', in Banfield, *Blackwell History*, 343–401

Sabaneev, Leonid, 1935. *Music for the Films: A Handbook for Composers and Conductors*, trans. S. W. Pring, London: Sir Isaac Pitman and Sons Ltd

Sachs, Harvey, 1978. *Toscanini*, London: Weidenfeld and Nicolson

Sadie, Stanley (ed.), 1992. *The New Grove Dictionary of Opera*, four volumes, London: Macmillan

Sadie, Stanley and John Tyrrell (eds), 2001. *The New Grove Dictionary of Music and Musicians*, second edition, 29 volumes, London: Macmillan

Salzman, Eric, 1988. *Twentieth-Century Music: An Introduction*, third edition, New Jersey: Prentice-Hall

Samson, Jim (ed.), 1991. *The Late Romantic Era: From the Mid-19th Century to World War I*, London: Macmillan

Scheer, Edward (ed.), 2004. *Antonin Artaud: A Critical Reader*, New York: Routledge

Schloezer, Boris de, 1923. 'La musique', *La revue contemporaine* (1 February), 245–8

Schmidgall, Gary, 1990. *Shakespeare and Opera*, New York and Oxford: Oxford University Press

Schmidt, Carl B., 1995. *The Music of Francis Poulenc: A Catalogue*, Oxford: Clarendon Press

Schmitt, Natalie Crohn, 1982. 'John Cage, nature and theater', in Gena and Brent, *Cage Reader*, 17–37

Schmitz, Eugen, 1939. 'Oper im Aufbau', *Zeitschrift für Musik* 106, 380–82

Schoenberg, Arnold, 1912. 'The Relationship to the Text', in *Style and Idea*, 141–5

  1926. 'Opinion or Insight', in *Style and Idea*, 258–64

  1928a. 'Für Franz Schreker', *Musikblätter des Anbruch* 10, 81–3

  1928b. 'Breslau Lecture on *Die glückliche Hand*', in Hahl-Koch, *Schoenberg–Kandinsky*, 102–7

  c.1930. 'New Music: My Music', in *Style and Idea*, 99–106

  1931. 'Linear Counterpoint', in *Style and Idea*, 289–95

  1937. 'How One Becomes Lonely', in *Style and Idea*, 30–53

  1941. 'Composition With Twelve Tones (1)', in *Style and Idea*, 214–45

  1946. 'Heart and Brain in Music', in *Style and Idea*, 53–76

1949. 'My Evolution', in *Style and Idea*, 79–92

1964. *Arnold Schoenberg Letters*, ed. Erwin Stein, translated by Eithne Wilkins and Ernst Kaiser, London: Faber and Faber

1975. *Style and Idea: Selected Writings of Arnold Schoenberg*, ed. Leonard Stein, translated by Leo Black, London: Faber and Faber

Schöpflin, György, 2004. *Dilemmas of Identity*, London: Hurst

Schreiber, Ulrich, 2000. *Opernführer für Fortgeschrittene*. Die Geschichte des Musiktheaters. Vol. 3: *Das 20. Jahrhundert I. Von Verdi und Wagner bis zum Faschismus*, Kassel

Schubert, Giselher, 2003. 'The Aesthetic Premises of a Nazi Conception of Music', in Kater and Riethmüller, *Music and Nazism*, 64–73

Schuh, Willi (ed.), 1957. *Richard Strauss, Stefan Zweig: Briefwechsel*, Frankfurt: S. Fischer

1982. *Richard Strauss: A Chronicle of the Early Years*, trans. Mary Whittall, Cambridge: Cambridge University Press

Schwarz, K. Robert, 1993. 'From Antiquity to the Future: *The Cave* Brings Music Theater into the 21st Century', *The Cave, Conceived and Developed by Steve Reich and Beryl Korot*, London: Boosey & Hawkes.

1996. *Minimalists*, London: Phaidon

Schwinger, Wolfgang, 1989. *Penderecki. His Life and Work*, trans. William Mann, Mainz: Schott

Sheppard, W. Anthony, 2001. *Revealing Masks: Exotic Influence and Ritualized Performance in Modernist Music Theater*, Berkeley: University of California Press

Shyer, Laurence, 1989. *Robert Wilson and His Collaborators*, New York: Theatre Communications Group

Silvester, Christopher (ed.), 1998. *The Penguin Book of Hollywood*, Harmondsworth: Viking

Simms, Bryan R., 1997. 'Whose Idea Was *Erwartung*?', in Brand and Hailey, *Constructive Dissonance*, 100–11

1999. *Schoenberg, Berg, and Webern: A Companion to the Second Viennese School*, Westport, Conn.: Greenwood

2000. *The Atonal Music of Arnold Schoenberg 1908–1923*, New York: Oxford University Press

Spotts, Frederic, 1994. *Bayreuth: A History of the Wagner Festival*, New Haven and London: Yale University Press

Spratt, Geoffrey K., 1987. *The Music of Arthur Honegger*, Cork: Cork University Press

Stein, Jack M., 1960. *Richard Wagner & the Synthesis of the Arts*, Detroit: Wayne University

Stenzl, Jürg, 1990. *Von Giacomo Puccini zu Luigi Nono. Italienische Musik 1922–1952: Faschismus – Resistenza – Republik*, Buren: Frits Knuf

Stok, Danusia (ed.), 1993. *Kieślowski on Kieślowski*, London: Faber and Faber

Stravinsky, Igor, 1936. *An Autobiography*, New York: Simon and Schuster

Stravinsky, Igor and Robert Craft, 1960. *Memories and Commentaries*, London: Faber and Faber

1962a. *Conversations with Igor Stravinsky*, London: Faber and Faber

1962b. *Expositions and Developments*, London: Faber and Faber

1966. *Themes and Episodes*, London: Faber and Faber

1968 [1963]. *Dialogues and a Diary*, New York: Doubleday; London: Faber and Faber

Stravinsky, Vera and Robert Craft, 1978. *Stravinsky in Pictures and Documents*, London: Hutchinson

Street, Alan, 2000. ' "The Ear of the Other": Style and Identity in Schoenberg's Eight Songs, Op. 6', in Cross and Berman, *Schoenberg and Words*, 103–37

Sutcliffe, Tom, 1996. *Believing in Opera*, London: Faber and Faber

Szmolyan, Walter, 1971. 'Die Geburtsstätte der Zwölftontechnik', *Österreichische Musikzeitschrift* 26/3, 113–26

Tambling, Jeremy, 1987. *Opera, Ideology and Film*, Manchester: Manchester University Press

1994. *A Night in at the Opera: Media Representations of Opera*, London: John Libby

1996. *Opera and the Culture of Fascism*, Oxford: Clarendon Press

Taruskin, Richard, 1976. 'Molchanov's "The Dawns Are Quiet Here" ', *Musical Quarterly* 62/1, 190–98

1992a. 'Moscow', in Sadie, *New Grove Opera*, volume 3, 476–9

1992b. 'St Petersburg', in Sadie, *New Grove Opera*, volume 4, 129–35

1993. 'Back to Whom? Neoclassicism as Ideology', *19th-Century Music* 16/3, 286–302

1997. *Defining Russia Musically*, Princeton: Princeton University Press

Tenschert, Richard (ed.), 1955. *Richard Strauss und Joseph Gregor: Briefwechsel 1934–1949*, Salzburg: Otto Müller

Tippett, Michael, 1974. *Moving into Aquarius*, St Albans: Paladin

1980. *Music of the Angels*, London: Eulenberg

Toch, Ernst, 1937. Interview quoted in 'The Cinema Wields the Baton', *New York Times* (11 April)

Toop, Richard, 1974. 'Social critic in music', *Music and Musicians* 22/9 (May), 36–8

Torrefranca, Fausto, 1912. *Giacomo Puccini e l'opera internazionale*, Turin: Bocca

Tyrrell, John, 1988. *Czech Opera*, Cambridge: Cambridge University Press

1992. *Janáček's Operas: A Documentary Account*, London: Faber and Faber

Urtubey, Pola Suarez, 1968. 'Ginastera's "Bomarzo" ', *Tempo* 84, 14–21

Valdo-Barbey, 1926. 'Projet de mise en scène pour *Pelléas*', *Revue musical* 8 (1926), 136–42

Vaughan Williams, Ralph and Gustav Holst, 1959. *Heirs and Rebels: Letters Written to Each Other and Occasional Writings on Music*, ed. Ursula Vaughan Williams and Imogen Holst, London: Oxford University Press

Vogt, Matthias Theodor, 1990. 'Listening as a Letter of Uriah: A note on Berio's *Un re in ascolto* (1984) on the occasion of the opera's first performance in London (9 February 1989)', trans. Stewart Spencer, *Cambridge Opera Journal* 2/2, 173–85

Wagner, Cosima, 1980. *Das zweite Leben: Briefe und Aufzeichnungen, 1883–1930*, ed. Dietrich Mack, Munich and Zurich: Piper

Wagner, Richard, 1911/1914. *Sämtliche Schriften und Dichtungen*, Volks-Ausgabe, 16 volumes, Leipzig: Breitkopf und Härtel

1984. *Oper und Drama*, ed. Klaus Kropfinger, *Universal-Bibliothek* 8207, Stuttgart: Philipp Reclam Jun.

Walker, John (ed.), 2001. *Halliwell's Film and Video Guide 2002*, London: Harper Collins, seventeenth edition

Walter, Michael, 2000. *Hitler in der Oper. Deutsches Musikleben 1919–1945*, Stuttgart: Metzler

Walton, Chris, 1994. *Othmar Schoeck: Eine Biographie*, Frankfurt am Main: Atlantis

Walton, Chris and Antonio Baldassarre (eds), 2004. *Musik im Exil: Die Schweiz und das Ausland*, Berne: Peter Lang

Waterhouse, John C. G., 2001a. 'Dallapiccola, Luigi', in Sadie, *New Grove*, volume 6, 853–9

  2001b. 'Malipiero, Gian Francesco', in Sadie, *New Grove*, volume 15, 697–704

Webern, Anton von, 1912. 'Schoenberg's Music', trans. Barbara Z. Schoenberg, in Frisch, *Schoenberg and His World*, 210–30

Wechsberg, Joseph, 1959. 'Bayreuth', *Opera* 10/9, 582–5

Weill, Kurt, 2000. *Musik und musikalisches Theater. Gesammelte Schriften*. ed. Stephen Hinton, Jürgen Schebera and Elmar Juchem, Mainz: Schott

Weimann, Gabriel and Conrad Winn, 1994. *The Theatre of Terror: Mass Media and International Terrorism*, New York: Longman

Weiss, Peg, 1977. 'Kandinsky: Symbolist Poetics and Theater in Munich', *Pantheon* 35/3, 209–18

  1979. *Kandinsky in Munich: The Formative Jugendstil Years*, Princeton: Princeton University Press

White, Eric Walter, 1979. *Stravinsky: The Composer and His Works*, second edition, London: Faber and Faber

  1983. *A History of English Opera*, London: Faber and Faber

Whittall, Arnold, 1990 [1982]. *The Music of Britten and Tippett: Studies in Themes and Techniques*, second edition, Cambridge: Cambridge University Press

  1991. 'Germany: Cross-Currents and Contradictions', in Samson, *Late Romantic Era*, 340–61

  1998. Review of the NMC recording of Birtwistle's *The Mask of Orpheus*, *Musical Times* 139, 55–8

  1999. ' "Is there a choice at all?": *King Priam* and motives for analysis', in Clarke, *Tippett Studies*, 55–77

Willett, John (ed. and trans.), 1964. *Brecht on Theatre: The Development of an Aesthetic*, New York: Hill and Wand

  1970. *Expressionism*, London: Weidenfeld and Nicolson

Wingfield, Paul (ed.), 1999. *Janáček Studies*, Cambridge: Cambridge University Press

Wolff, Larry, 1994. *Inventing Eastern Europe. The Map of Civilization on the Mind of the Enlightenment*, Stanford: Stanford University Press

Wörner, Karl H., 1970. 'Schönbergs "Erwartung" und das Ariadne-Thema', in *Die Musik in der Geistesgeschichte: Studien zur Situation der Jahre um 1910*, Bonn: Bouvier, 91–117

  1973. *Stockhausen: Life and Work*, London: Faber and Faber

Zweig, Stefan, 1943. *The World of Yesterday: An Autobiography*, London: Cassell

General index

Abbate, Carolyn 282
Adam, Fra Salimbene de 36
Adami, Giuseppe 36
Adamo, Mark 204
Adams, John 55, 204, 246, 260–4, 289–90,
    318, 330
Adès, Thomas 228
Adlington, Robert 218, 219
Adorno, Theodor 20, 80, 86, 90, 95, 105, 114,
    122, 163, 231, 248, 269, 281
Aeschylus 22, 52, 163
Albeniz, Isaac 127
Aldeburgh Festival 213, 218
Alfano, Franco 34, 139
alienation technique: *see Verfremdungseffekt*
Anderson, Laurie 207
Anderson, Marian 310
Andriessen, Louis 233, 234–5
    Matthew Passion 234
    Orpheus 234
Angerer, Paul 285
Annesley, Charles 322
Ansermet, Ernest 80
Antheil, George 202–3
'anti-opera' 182–6, 195, 241, 255, 257
Antoine, André 81
Apollinaire, Guillaume 113, 141
Appia, Adolphe 22, 62, 336
Aquila, Serafino dall' 41
Aragon, Louis 250
Argento, Dominick 204, 207
Aristotle 226
Arnold, Malcolm 285
Artaud, Antonin 246, 251, 255
Ashby, Arved 96
Astaire, Adele 296, 299
Astaire, Fred 296
Astruc, Gabriel 125
Auden, W. H. 14, 51, 52, 58, 120, 216
audiences 6, 147, 156, 270, 321
Auner, Josef 92, 103

Babbitt, Milton
    Fabulous Voyage 233

Bach, Johann Sebastian 105
Bachelet, Alfred 137
Baden-Baden 133
Bahr, Herrmann 150
Baird, Tadeusz 176
Balázs, Béla 67–8, 271
ballad opera 107
Baragwanath, Nicholas 102
Barbaja, Domenico 308
Barber, Samuel 57, 206, 331
Barlach, Ernst 159
Barry, Gerald 285
Bartók, Béla 67–72, 74, 168
    The Wooden Prince 68
Baudelaire, Charles 62, 64
Baylis, Lilian 326
Bayreuth 14, 18, 21, 49, 61–2, 63, 125, 140, 212,
    312, 316, 335, 337, 338
Bazin, André 271
Beaumarchais, Pierre-Augustin
    Caron de 134
    Nozze di Figaro, Le 134
Beck, Julian 244
Beckett, Samuel 144
    Krapp's Last Tape 144
    Play 245
Beeson, Jack 204, 206
Beethoven, Ludwig van 87, 96
    Eroica Symphony 178
Beineix, Jean-Jacques 282
Bekker, Paul 109
Bel Geddes, Norman 202
Belcari, Feo 42
Bellini, Vincenzo 27–8, 107
Benco, Silvio 33–4
Benda, Georg 90
Benelli, Sem 35, 36
Benjamin, Arthur 285
Benjamin, Walter 184, 246, 259
Bennett, Richard Rodney 328
Bennett, Robert Russell 297
Benois, Alexandre 129, 181
Benvenuti, Giacomo 42
Berberian, Cathy 225

Index of operas

Page numbers in italics refer to illustrations